# THE DEVELOPING IMMIGRATION AND ASYLUM POLICIES OF THE EUROPEAN UNION

# The Developing Immigration and Asylum Policies of the European Union

## Adopted Conventions, Resolutions, Recommendations, Decisions and Conclusions

Compilation and Commentary

ELSPETH GUILD

Introduction

JAN NIESSEN

KLUWER LAW INTERNATIONAL
THE HAGUE / LONDON / BOSTON

A C.I.P. Catalogue record for this book is available from the Library of Congress.

ISBN 90-411-0254-X

Published by Kluwer Law International,
P.O. Box 85889, 2508 CN The Hague, The Netherlands.

Sold and distributed in the U.S.A. and Canada
by Kluwer Law International,
675 Massachusetts Avenue, Cambridge, MA 02139, U.S.A.

In all other countries, sold and distributed
by Kluwer Law International,
P.O. Box 85889, 2508 CN The Hague, The Netherlands.

Layout and camera-ready copy:
Anne-Marie Krens, Oegstgeest, The Netherlands

*Printed on acid-free paper*



Printed in the Netherlands

# TABLE OF CONTENTS

*ANNEX*

# CONVENTIONS, RESOLUTIONS, CONCLUSIONS AND RECOMMENDATIONS CATEGORY INDEX

# PRESIDENCY INDEX

| *Member State* | *Period* | *Meeting* | *Date* |
|---|---|---|---|
| Ireland | 1/90 | Dublin | 15.06.90 |
| Italy | 2/90 | | |
| Luxembourg | 1/91 | Luxembourg | 06.06.91 |
| Netherlands | 2/91 | Maastricht | Dec. 91 |
| Portugal | 1/92 | Lisbon | 11.12.92 |
| UK | 2/92 | London | 30.11.92 |
| Denmark | 1/93 | Copenhagen | 01.06.93 |
| Belgium | 2/93 | Brussels | 30.11.93 |
| Greece | 1/94 | Luxembourg | 20.06.94 |
| Germany | 2/94 | Brussels JHA-Council | 30.11.94 |
| France | 1/95 | | 20.06.95 |
| Spain | 2/95 | | |

| *Measures* | *Document number* |
|---|---|
| Dublin Convention | 1 |
| | |
| Palma Document | Annex |
| Work Programme | Annex |
| | |
| (1) Manifestly unfounded<br>(2) Host third countries<br>(3) No serious riks of persecution<br>(4) Establishing CIREA<br>(5) Establishing CIREFI<br>(6) Practices on expulsion<br>(7) Transit for expulsion | 2<br>3<br>4<br>5<br>6<br>7<br>8 |
| (1) Family reunification<br>(2) Expulsion of illegals<br>(3) People displaced in Yugoslavia | 9<br>10<br>11 |
| | |
| employment | 12 |
| (1) School pupils<br>(2) Study purposes<br>(3) Self-employed persons<br>(4) CIREFI<br>(5) Standard travel document<br>(6) Readmission agreement | 13<br>14<br>15<br>16<br>17<br>18 |
| Minimum guarantees for asylum procedures | 19 |
| | |

# ACKNOWLEDGEMENTS

The authors wish to thank the following individuals and organisations who assisted with this work. For comments on an earlier draft of the introduction, its author is grateful to Annette Bosscher, Antonio Cruz, Lori Lindburg and Kees Groenendijk. Invaluable sources of information were Tony Bunyan of Statewatch, Don Flynn of the Joint Council for the Welfare of Immigrants, Peter Bartram of Bartram & Company, Amnesty International's European Project (in particular, for their excellent work on the asylum resolutions), the Dutch Standing Committee of Experts (for their study on the standard readmission agreement), the Churches' Commission for Migrants in Europe, the daily Agence Europe, and the monthly Migration News Sheet. Appreciation is also extended to Christian Drews for working hard to get all the documents in order, Antonio Cruz (again), for his assistance in locating documents, and Claudia Wrobels. Finally, the authors are indebted to Julie Cator and Leslie Kemp for proof-reading the text.

# PART I

# Introduction

# THE EUROPEAN UNION'S MIGRATION AND ASYLUM POLICIES

International migration has been on the agenda of the European institutions since the early years of the European Community and the European Union. At the time of the creation of the European Community, migration for employment was considered beneficial for all parties concerned and therefore encouraged. This situation has changed gradually, as member states of the European Union currently aim to control movements of migrants and asylum-seekers. This has not been the only change. As important are the changes in the way policies in these areas are designed.[1]

The making of European policies is a long and complicated process and, traditionally, two distinctive methods have been used, namely, the active involvement of all Community institutions (Community approach), or direct consultations between the Community's member states (intergovernmental approach). A new method was introduced by establishing co-operation between member states, in association with the European Commission, in the fields of foreign affairs (1987), security (1993) and justice and home affairs (1993). This new approach is a mixture of the two other approaches with a predominant intergovernmental element (the pillar approach).[2]

---

1 In this essay, the term "European Community" is used to refer to the European Economic Community, one of the three European Communities established by the Treaties of Paris (1951) and Rome (1957). The Treaty on European Union (1991) changed the name of the European Economic Community to European Community and therefore, this is the term used throughout this article. The term "European Union" is used to refer to the Union as established by the Treaty on European Union (TEU). In 1993, the Council of the European Communities adopted the name of the Council of the European Union and the Commission of the European Communities was renamed the European Commission.

2 A great number of academic and other publications discuss how and which political philosophies are underlying the construction of the European Community and Union. See, for example, Charles Zorgbibe, Histoire de la construction européenne (Paris, 1993). For the development of Community law, for example, T.C. Hartley, The foundations of European Community law (Oxford, 1988 - second and reprinted edition of 1991) and R.H. Lauwaars en C.W.A. Timmermans, Europees gemeenschapsrecht in kort bestek (Groningen, 1991 - tweede herziene druk).

European policy-making in the migration field is certainly not less time-consuming and complicated than in other fields. This applies to policies directed at intra-Community and extra-Community migration, and to migration for employment and political reasons. It is also true for two other aspects of migration: namely, the movement and admission of migrants and refugees, and their integration into receiving societies. The Community approach is used to facilitate free movement of EC-citizens within the Community and to promote equal treatment of these persons. The inter-governmental approach is employed to deal with immigration from outside the Community and asylum. These matters are currently dealt with within the framework of co-operation on justice and home affairs (third pillar).

Just as free movement and equal treatment were of crucial importance for the development of the European Community, so common policies on immigration and asylum are indispensable for the deepening of the European Union. This essay attempts, against the backdrop of the developing overall goals of the European Communities and the European Union, to summarise the outcome of European policy-making in these fields. As such, it chronicles the achievements reached through each of the three policy-making approaches, and the variant roles European institutions have played in each.[3]

The first two chapters summarise the results of the *Community approach,* used to promote the free movement and equal treatment of EC-citizens (chapter I), and immigration and non-discrimination of so-called third-country nationals (chapter II). Community action to promote free movement and equal treatment dates back to the late fifties, and had made considerable progress by the time the internal market was launched in the mid-eighties. As for immigration and anti-discrimination policies, far less was achieved because of the limited powers granted to the Community to act on these matters. The last ten years have witnessed the expansion of free movement rights, proposals to abolish internal border controls, and recommendations for the establishment of Community policies on immigration and asylum.

---

3 Its main emphasis is on the Commission and the Council and, to a lesser extent, the European Court of Justice and the European Parliament.

During the eighties, immigration, asylum, integration and racial discrimination began to rank high on political agendas at both the national and European levels. Chapter III examines the long-standing conflict, which became more visible during the eighties, over whether to deal with these issues at the European level: by Community action or through intergovernmental co-operation.

Having decided in favour of the latter, member states established a co-operative mechanism for dealing with immigration and asylum matters. Chapter IV gives an overview of the achievements of this *intergovernmental approach* between the years 1985 and 1993. Chapter V describes the various options discussed during the intergovernmental conferences of 1990-1991 for European action on these issues. These led to the adoption of the Treaty on European Union in 1991, which marked the end of the intergovernmental approach and the beginning of a new approach to immigration and asylum: the *pillar approach*. Chapter VI summarises the achievements of the pillar strategy thus far,[4] and the views of the Council of Ministers and the European Commission on the functioning of this approach. Chapter VII concludes with some final observations.

## I FREE MOVEMENT AND EQUAL TREATMENT

The Treaty establishing the European Community (EC-Treaty) provides a firm basis for Community action on migration for employment between the member states. However, the term "migration" is not used, but rather "freedom of movement for persons", as one of the four freedoms to be established alongside freedom of movement for services, capital and goods. The promotion of free movement of persons belongs to the range of instruments being used to achieve the goals of the Community, namely harmonious development of economic activities, balanced expansion,

4 Until August 1995.

increased stability, accelerated elevation of the standard of living and closer relations between member states.[5]

*Free movement*

Articles 48-51 of the EC-Treaty provide for free movement for workers within the Community. These persons possess the right to look for and accept offers of employment in a member state other than their own and, upon taking up gainful activity, to acquire the right to reside in that member state. Articles 52-58 relate to freedom of establishment for self-employed persons, and articles 59-66 correspond to the freedom to provide services.

Community Regulations and Directives, adopted primarily between 1958 and 1972, have elaborated these Treaty provisions in the fields of residence rights, family reunification and access to the labour market. These rights were restricted to workers who are nationals of member states. They are entitled to a residence permit of five years, with the possibility of extension for another five-year period. Those who have been employed in a member state other than their own can remain there after they have reached pensionable age or if they suffer from permanent incapacity. Matters such as administrative provisions regulating the right of entry and residence, restrictions on free movement on grounds of public policy, public security or public health have been harmonised by Community law. Community law also grants residence rights to family members of nationals of member states, irrespective of their nationality.[6]

---

5 Article 2 of the EEC-Treaty. The EEC-Treaty was amended by the Single European Act (1986) and the Treaty on European Union (1991). As noted earlier, the latter changed the name of the EEC-Treaty to the EC-Treaty. References are only made to those articles in the EEC-Treaty that differ from articles in the EC-Treaty.

6 For the texts of the relevant Regulations and Directives, see J-C Séché, Freedom of movement in the Community. Entry and residence (Luxembourg, Office for Official Publications of the European Communities, 1988). For an historical overview, see J. Werquin, Vingt ans de libre circulation des travailleurs dans la Communauté. In: Europe Sociale 1/1989 (Brussels, Commission of the European Communities, 1989) and Henri de Lary, La libre circulation des personnes dans la Communauté économique européenne (Paris, 1992).

*Equal treatment*

Free movement includes the abolition of any discrimination based on nationality towards workers of the member states as regards employment, remuneration and other conditions of work and employment, as well as the granting of social and fiscal advantages. A series of legislative and other measures adopted by the Community, most notably since 1970, guarantees all workers who are nationals of a member state and their dependents – irrespective of their place of employment and residence – equality of treatment in working and housing conditions and entitlement to social security benefits.

Article 118 of the EC Treaty gives the European Commission the task of harmonising the social policies of the member states, in particular, matters related to employment, labour law and working conditions, basic and advanced vocational training, social security, prevention of occupational accidents and diseases, occupational hygiene, and the right of association and collective bargaining. Article 6 forbids any discrimination on grounds of nationality with respect to the application of the Treaty. In other words, legislative and other measures taken by the member states apply equally to all workers who possess the nationality of a member state, irrespective of their place of employment and residence.[7]

The Commission undertook many efforts to eliminate restrictions on the employment of nationals, working in certain public sectors in a member state other than their own, such as commercial providers of services (public transport, distribution of gas and electricity), operational services in the public health institutions, in education and scientific research.[8] Many

---

7 Commission of the European Communities, Internal market: Current status 1 July 1994. Community social policy (Brussels, 1994).

8 L'ouverture des functions publiques nationales aux ressortissants communautaires: bilan et perspectives. Document de travail présenté par M. Padraig Flynn, Membre de la Commission. Quatrième Conférence des Ministres des Etats membres de l'Union européenne chargés de la Function Publique (Nancy, 16 et 17 février 1995).

initiatives were also taken to provide for the mutual recognition of diplomas.[9]

As far as political rights are concerned, no Community measures were adopted until 1994, despite numerous recommendations made to that effect by the European Commission and European Parliament.[10] With the introduction of European citizenship by the Treaty on European Union, nationals of member states have the right to vote and stand as candidates in both municipal and European elections. The Commission's proposal for a Directive on voting rights in European elections was adopted in 1993, and in 1994, a Directive on voting rights in local elections was adopted.[11]

### *The Community approach*

The enactment and implementation of Community legislation must correspond to procedures established by the EC-Treaty. The European Commission has the sole right of initiative to propose legislation and monitors its application. The Council of Ministers takes the final decision on the

9 Among the measures taken were two Directives establishing two general systems of mutual recognition of diplomas and vocational education. See OJ L 19 of 24.01.89 and OJ L 209 of 24.07.92.

10 Commission of the European Communities, Voting rights in local elections for Community nationals residing in a member state other than their own. Report from the Commission to the European Parliament transmitted to the Council for information (Brussels, 1986 COM (86) 487 Final) and Proposal for a Council Directive on voting rights for Community nationals in local elections in their member state of residence (Brussels, 1988 COM (88) 371 final). A few member states have granted municipal voting rights to foreigners, irrespective of their country of origin.

11 Directive 93/109 on European elections (O J L 329 of 30.12.1993) and Directive 94/80 on municipal elections (O J L 368 of 31.12.1994). The adopted Directive on municipal elections allows for two derogations. Member states in which nationals of other member states exceed 20 percent of the population may require a minimum period of residence by such persons before allowing them to exercise their voting rights. The other derogation concerns only Belgium, and deals with the situation of a few municipalities in which the number of nationals of other member states exceeds 20 percent. These EU citizens must have resided there for more than six years before they can vote in municipal elections.

proposals of the Commission. Its work is prepared by the Committee of Permanent Representatives of the Member States in Brussels (COREPER). Until the entering into force of the Single European Act in 1987, unanimity was required for the adoption of legislation in the field of free movement, and the European Parliament needed only to be consulted (article 6 SEA). After 1987, and until the entering into force of the Treaty on European Union, decisions on legislative proposals of the Commission were taken by the Council on the basis of a qualified majority and in co-operation with the European Parliament. These changes made it easier for the Council to take decisions and increased the involvement of the Parliament. However, the Parliament was not given full powers to initiate and oversee the implementation of Community legislation. This democratic deficit notwithstanding, a wider public is aware of which measures are being prepared because of the consultation of and co-operation with the Parliament.

The Court of Justice of the European Communities ensures the uniform interpretation of Community law. The Court has played a decisive role in the development of a progressive interpretation of free movement. It has defined more clearly, for example, the grounds for expulsion of nationals of other member states. In such instances, there must be "a genuine and sufficiently serious threat to the requirements of public policy affecting one of the fundamental interests of society".[12] It has also determined that nationals of other member states can only be excluded from taking up employment in the public sector when it involves participation in the exercise of public power and responsibility for safeguarding the general interests of the state.[13]

### *Increasing importance*

The results of Community action in the fields of free movement and equal treatment are impressive. They have become relevant for an increasing number of people through the successive enlargements of the Community and through the expansion of free movement rights to categories other than workers.

---

12 Bouchereau (1977) ECR 1999.

13 See note 9.

Initially, free movement affected only workers, self-employed persons and service providers from the six founding members of the Community (Belgium, France, Germany, Italy, Luxembourg and the Netherlands). Free movement rights were enshrined in Community law before additional states joined the Community. The accession of new member states was premised on their acceptance of the "acquis communautaire", that is, the whole of Treaty provisions, legislation based thereupon, treaties concluded by the Community with third-countries and rulings of the Court of Justice. The Community enlargement to include Denmark, the United Kingdom and Ireland (in 1973) and traditional sending countries Greece (1981), and Spain and Portugal (1985), expanded the area of free movement considerably and increased the number of persons entitled to this right. After the unification of Germany (1990) and the most recent enlargement of the Community with Austria, Finland and Sweden (1995), the population of the fifteen member states numbers around 344 million people. Four percent of these persons are not nationals of the country in which they live, and one-third, or less than five million, are nationals of a member state.[14]

Since January 1994, economically-active nationals of states belonging to the European Economic Area are entitled to free movement. The European Economic Area includes all the member states of the European Union and Iceland, Liechtenstein and Norway.[15]

In the early nineties, the right of residence was extended to categories other than workers, including students, pensioners and other non-active persons, provided that they would not be dependent on the receiving state for their income and possessed adequate health insurance.[16]

---

14 Eurostat, Rapid reports. Population and social conditions, 1994 - 7.

15 Originally, all member states of the European Free Trade Association were to be included in the EEA. Austria, Finland and Sweden became full members of the Union in 1995. Switzerland, after a referendum in 1993, decided not to join the EEA. Liechtenstein joined the EEA in May 1995.

16 Directive on the general right of residence (OJ L 180/26, 1990), Directive on pensioners (OJ L 180/28, 1990) and Directive on Students (OJ L 93/96, 1990). The latter was slightly revised in 1993, after a Court ruling following a complaint lodged by the European Parliament (Parliament v Council 'students' (1992) ECR I-4193).

These impressive results cannot hide the fact that, quite often, they came about only after the reconciliation of conflicting interests between member states or between social partners (employers organisations and trade unions) at the national and Community levels. Free movement was either feared or welcomed. It was widely held that free movement, as well as enlargement of the Community, would set in motion migratory movements. This has not, however, been the case. Free movement has facilitated intra-Community migration for employment, and enlargement has often been accompanied or preceded by a decrease of migration from new to old member states or by return migration from old to new member states.

## II THIRD-COUNTRY NATIONALS AND NON-DISCRIMINATION

Immigration from outside the Community has always been considered to be primarily a matter for the individual member states. Therefore, there has been no development of a common policy on immigration and asylum, and for a long time, the need for it was not felt. The EC-Treaty does not give European institutions a clear mandate to enact legislation on matters related to immigration, asylum and the integration of non-EC nationals.[17] Nevertheless, a limited mandate has been developed to promote equality of treatment of the approximately ten million third-country nationals, through implementation of the Association and Co-operation Agreements between the Community and third-countries.

### *Significant differences*

Generally speaking, nationals from non-member states do not possess rights of residence or access to the labour market, except in cases where one is the spouse of an EC-national, or is a national of a European Economic Area

---

17 See, for example, the comments made by the Ministers responsible for immigration in their report to the European Council meeting in Maastricht in December 1991 (SN 4038/91 WGI 930). See also, Kay Hailbronner, Visa regulations and third-country-nationals in EC law. In: Common Market Law Review 31 (1994).

member state.[18] National laws dictate rules for admission and residence for these third-country nationals. Such persons do not have the right of free movement, nor even the right of visa-free travel within the Community.[19] Turks or Moroccans, for instance, legally residing in one member state, are prohibited from taking up gainful activity, or from travelling without a visa to another member state. Refugees legally residing in a member state are also excluded from free movement, but are to be granted special favour when they take up employment, establish themselves as self-employed persons or provide services.[20]

Significant differences exist among the immigration policies of member states which, to a great extent, reflect their different socio-economic development and foreign labour needs. In addition, former colonial powers, such as Portugal, Spain, France, the United Kingdom and the Netherlands, had (or still have) special obligations to citizens of their former colonies in terms of admission, residence and acquisition of nationality. Countries such as Finland, Germany and Greece grant, under certain conditions, residence rights to so-called ethnic Finns, Germans and Greeks, respectively. These persons are living in and have acquired the citizenship of another country, but frequently maintain cultural attachments to their countries of sometimes distant origin. Many may wish and are entitled to return to that country in the future. All of these differences add to the difficulties in designing and implementing common policies on entry and residence.

The situation is rather different with regard to the promotion of equal treatment. The social position of workers from third-countries is primarily regulated by national law and by bi-lateral agreements between receiving and sending countries. However, by implementing Community social policies, it will in many situations be impossible to make a distinction

18 Under the EC Association Agreement with Turkey, a Turkish worker may acquire a right of residence. A national of a Central European state with which the EC has concluded an Association Agreement has a right to set up a business in an EC-member state, by which that person acquires a right of residence.

19 Since 1995, third-country nationals have the right to travel freely in seven of the nine Schengen countries (discussed below).

20 The 1964 Declaration concerning refugees (OJ L 1225 of 22.5.64) and the 1985 Statement concerning refugees (OJ C 210 of 21.8.85).

between nationals of member states and third-country nationals. There are, for example, Directives concerning health and safety in the workplace which, for obvious reasons, do not distinguish between the two groups. The Directives on equal opportunities concerning equality between men and women apply to all workers, and not only to workers who are EC nationals.

### *European agreements*

In addition, the European Community concluded association and co-operation agreements with third-countries which often included clauses regarding migrant workers. The Association Agreement with Turkey and the Co-operation Agreements with the Mahgreb countries contain anti-discrimination clauses, which state that member states shall not discriminate on grounds of nationality between nationals of these countries and of member states with regard to working conditions, renumeration and social security. The Association Agreements with Poland, Hungary and the Czech and Slovak Republics contain similar clauses, making non-discrimination measures subject to the conditions and modalities applicable in each member state. Furthermore, Annex VI to the IVth Lomé Convention, concluded between the Community and 70 African, Caribbean and Pacific States (ACP), states that each member state shall accord to legally-employed ACP workers in their territory treatment free from discrimination based on nationality, with regard to working conditions, pay and social security benefits linked to employment.

For the European Commission, these Agreements are important steps towards the equal treatment of non-EC and EC-workers. In its 1985 Guidelines for a Community policy on migration, it writes that: "An initial step in the gradual extension of Community treatment to workers from other countries will be achieved by the implementation of co-operation and association agreements concluded between the Community and certain countries".[21] The Court of Justice ruled that provisions of the official Decisions taken by the Association Council, which are based upon the Association Agreement

---

21 Commission of the European Communities, Guidelines for a Community policy on migration. Communication transmitted to the Council on 7 march 1985 (COM (85) 48 final).

between the Community and Turkey, are binding upon member states if the Decisions are clear and precise. A similar judgement was delivered on the direct effect of the co-operation agreements.[22] In other words, these international treaties and Association Council Decisions are part of the legal order of the Community, thus entitling the Commission and the Court to monitor their application and ensure their uniform interpretation. The treaties also establish rights for the individuals concerned.[23]

### *Integration*

At the request of the Hannover European Council (June 1988), a study was commissioned on the social integration of third-country nationals for the following year. The study did not take up the question of their admission to the territory of the member states, since such matters were under examination in other contexts related to the freedom of movement for persons. The final report included a substantive account of the situation of third-country nationals living in the member states, yet contained no recommendations for improving their situation.[24] A later report, drawn up on behalf of the Commission by external experts, on the contrary, did offer several such recommendations. This included a proposal to draw up a set of basic principles on the integration of migrants, which could take a form similar to the Community Charter, and would include principles concerned with freedom of expression, freedom to come and go, non-discrimination on racial or religious grounds, equal rights for men and women, and the rights of children.[25] The Council of Ministers merely took note of the reports.

---

22 With regard to the Association Agreement with Turkey, see Demirel (1987) ECr 3719 (OJ C 12/86) and Sevince (1990) ECR I-3461. For the Co-operation Agreement with Morocco, see Kziber (1991) ECR I 199.

23 On Association and Co-operation Agreements, see Elspeth Guild, Protecting migrant's rights: application of EC-agreements with third-countries. CCME Briefing Paper no. 10 (Brussels, 1992).

24 The social integration of third-country migrants residing on a permanent and lawful basis in the member states (Brussels, 1989 SEC (89) 924 Final).

25 Policies on immigration and the social integration of migrants in the European Community (Brussels, 1990 SEC (90) 1813 final).

### *Combatting racial discrimination*

In 1986, the Council of Ministers, the Commission and the European Parliament adopted a Joint Declaration against Racism and Xenophobia. This inter-institutional Declaration condemns all forms of intolerance, hostility and use of force against persons on the basis of racial, religious, cultural, social or national differences. The three European institutions further committed themselves to "pursue the endeavour already made to protect the individuality and dignity of every member of society and to reject any form of segregation of foreigners".[26] Similarly, a May 1990 Council Resolution emphasised action to be undertaken by the individual member states.[27] It called on member states to sign and ratify existing international instruments contributing to the fight against racial discrimination, apply national laws aimed at preventing or curbing discrimination, develop systems of legal assistance, promote exchange programmes for young people and improve the education of migrant workers' children. The Commission, however, was not given substantial power to act on racial discrimination.

In 1992, the European Commission published a comparative study on anti-discrimination legislation in the member states.[28] It also consulted the social partners on the possible adoption of a code of good employment practices against racial discrimination.[29] In addition, it announced its intention to press for specific powers to combat racial discrimination, which it currently seeks to include in the next revision of the Treaty on European Union.[30]

---

26 OJ C 158 of 25.6.86.

27 OJ C 157 of 27.6.90.

28 Commission of the European Communities, Legal instruments to combat racism and xenophobia (Brussels, 1992).

29 Mary Coussey and Hans Hammelburg, A code of practice to combat racial discrimination and to promote equal opportunities at work. This report was commissioned by the European Commission and prepared by the authors for the European Human Rights Foundation (Brussels, 1994).

30 European Commission, European social policy. A way forward for the Union. A White Paper (Brussels, 1994) (COM (94) 333).

*Immigration and asylum*

In 1991, the Commission issued two communications, one on the right of asylum and the other on immigration.[31] Although the Commission believed that the two issues were interrelated, their varying treatment in specific policies, and in national and international laws, made it necessary to deal with such matters in separate communications. As far as asylum was concerned, the Commission maintained that the starting point for any measures in this area was full respect for humanitarian principles embodied in the Geneva Convention. It thus identified two points of common interest, namely, the prevention of asylum abuse, and harmonisation of the formal and substantive right of asylum. The former was considered a matter of priority, while the latter was viewed as an eventual consequence of the further deepening of the Community. It recommended that studies be undertaken on the role, structure and operation of a possible common judicial machinery. This machinery would reduce disparities between member states in the interpretation of asylum law, and would have an indirect effect on the harmonisation of administrative practices.

In its Communication on immigration, the Commission summarised four major problems confronting Community member states, specifically: the abuse of the asylum procedure, which had facilitated immigration for economic purposes; the continued need to manage the effects of steady migration pressure; control of migration flows, which in turn, was a prerequisite for the fourth area of concern; integrating legally-admitted immigrants. With regard to controlling migratory movements (including the movement of third-country nationals already legally residing in a member state), the communication referred to the work being done through the intergovernmental framework. In order to counter migratory pressures, the communication recommended the reinforcement of the association and co-operation agreements with countries of emigration. Finally, the communication identified the integration of legally residing third-country nationals as a fundamental objective for the whole of society, and suggested

31 Commission Communication to the Council and the European Parliament on immigration (SEC (91) 1855 final) and Communication from the Commission to the Council and the European Parliament on the right of asylum (SEC (91) 1857 final).

that such persons be given access to employment in other member states and be entitled to participate in Community exchange programmes for students, young workers, teachers and others.

In the 1994 Communication on immigration and asylum policies, the Commission presented again its views on these matters and listed proposals for action by the Union.[32] It identified three areas of Union action: namely, action on migration pressure, controlling migration flows, and strengthening integration policies to benefit legal migrants. By and large, this Communication was an elaborated and integrated version of the Commission's two 1991 communications on immigration and asylum. Many of its recommendations referred to the action programmes already adopted by European Councils (namely those in Edinburgh and Maastricht), and identified policy issues which were quite similar to those under discussion in the third-pillar (see chapter V).

### *External border control, visa and free travel*

In 1993, the Commission, using its new powers in accordance with article 100c (3) of the EC-Treaty, presented a proposal for a Regulation determining the third countries whose nationals must be in the possession of a visa when crossing the external borders of the member states.[33] Article 1 of this draft referred to the Annex, which contained a list of 129 countries whose nationals must have a visa in order to enter a member state. The member states were requested to adopt this proposal no later than 31 December 1994. The adoption of the Regulation by the Justice and Home Affairs Council,[34]

---

32 Commission of the European Communities, Communication from the Commission to the Council and the European Parliament on immigration and asylum policies (Brussels, February 1994, COM (94) 23 final).

33 OJ C 11/6 of 15.1.94.

34 After the entry into force of the Treaty on European Union (November 1993), the Justice and Home Affairs Council is responsible for the immigration and asylum portfolio.

however, did not occur until September 1995. By this time, the number of countries on the common visa list had been reduced to 101.[35]

The Commission also made a proposal for a "Decision, based on Article K.3 of the Treaty on European Union, establishing the Convention on the crossing of the external frontiers of the member States".[36] This was an attempt to end the deadlock on the adoption and ratification of the Convention on the crossing of the external borders, which has been prepared under the intergovernmental framework (see Chapter IV). The text of the Commission's proposal was almost identical to the text prepared in the intergovernmental framework. A significant difference is that in the Commission's proposal, the European Court of Justice is declared competent to give preliminary rulings concerning the interpretation of the Convention and in disputes concerning the Convention's implementation. At the time of writing, the proposal had not been adopted by the Council of Ministers.

In 1994, the Commission presented its proposal for a Council Regulation laying down a uniform format for visas.[37] The proposal specifies that visas issued by member states be produced in the form of a uniform sticker that will be valid throughout the Union. It outlines the sticker's necessary characteristics, required information, and protection against falsification. In 1995, the Justice and Home Affairs Council adopted this proposal.

In 1995, the Commission agreed on three proposals for Directives on the elimination of controls on persons at the internal frontiers of the European Union.[38] The first proposed Directive pertains to the elimination of controls on persons crossing internal frontiers and specifies the scope of the ban on controls and formalities at internal borders. It states that the crossing of

---

35 Press release 9977/95 (Presse 262). The requirement that such a list be decided on the basis of unanimity means that any agreement could be blocked by a single member state. After 1 January 1996, however, according to article 100c of the EC Treaty, such decisions can be taken on the basis of a qualified majority.

36 O J C 11/6 of 15.1.94.

37 Proposal for Council Regulation laying down a uniform format for visa (COM (94) 0287).

38 Press release of 12 July (IP (95)726).

internal borders may not in itself give rise to control or formalities. All persons, irrespective of nationality, are to be covered by the abolition of internal controls. The removal of controls on persons requires the adoption of accompanying measures, such as the Dublin Convention (see chapter IV) and the standard visa model. Therefore, the date for the implementation of the Directive is set at 31 December 1996, which, according to the Commission, gives member states ample time to take these measures (although it is recognised, in the explanatory memorandum, that this may be unrealistic). The second proposal for a Directive concerns the right of third-country nationals to travel within the Community. According to this proposal, legally-resident third-country nationals, or those in possession of a visa issued by a member state (i.e., tourists), shall be entitled to travel to other member states without formalities at the internal frontiers. This Directive could be adopted immediately. The third proposal is more technical and concerns the modification of certain existing Directives with a view to removing any provisions calling for the presentation of identity documents while crossing an internal border.

### *Considerable differences*

There remain considerable differences between the rights enjoyed by migrants from other member states and those from outside the Community in terms of free movement rights and social rights. With the further integration of the European Union and the creation of European citizenship, additional measures need to be taken in order to prevent the gap between the two groups from becoming wider. It would seem that only a Community approach could guarantee that such measures will be applied by every member state in an identical way, because the Commission supervises the implementation of Community law and the Court ensures its uniform interpretation.

Despite proposals to that effect on the part of the European Commission, the Community approach was not used to design common policies on immigration and asylum, except for some aspects of visa policies. Member states jealously guarded their sovereignty and, from the mid-eighties onwards, began to work together intergovernmentally on these matters.

## III THE SINGLE EUROPEAN ACT AND THE INTERNAL MARKET

During the eighties, migration and asylum began to rank high on the political agenda at the national, but also, the European levels. Although Community member states more or less realised that it was no longer possible to find national answers to the phenomenon of international migration, it was nevertheless extremely difficult to create an effective framework for European co-operation on immigration and asylum matters. There not only existed conflicting views on how this co-operation should be framed, but also on which issues would need to be tackled at the European level, and which needed to remain in the exclusive domain of the individual member states.

### *The internal market*

Also during the eighties, Community member states renewed their commitment to economic and political integration. The Fontainebleau European Council (June 1984) stressed that "with a view to the creation of a genuine economic union, the Council intends, through specific commitments, both externally and internally, to give the European economy an impetus comparable to that which it gained from the founding of the customs union in the early 1960s".[39] Moreover, the Council "considers it essential that the Community should respond to the expectations of the people of Europe by adopting measures to strengthen and promote its identity and its image for its citizens and for the rest of the world".[40] The Strasbourg European Council (December 1989) recognised that "all Community policies in the economic and social spheres contribute directly and indirectly to consolidating a common sense of belonging. This movement must be broadened and accelerated by the adoption of concrete measures which will enable European citizens to recognise in their daily lives that they belong to a single entity".[41]

Between these two Council meetings, reports and treaties were prepared, negotiated and adopted which elaborated one or several aspects of this

39 Fontainebleau European Council (Bulletin EC 6-1984).

40 Ibid.

41 Strasbourg European Council (Bulletin EC 12-1989).

ambitious programme. The most important included the Commission's White Paper on the Completion of the Internal Market (1985), the Single European Act (1986, in force since 1987) and the Community Charter of Fundamental Social Rights of Workers (1989).[42]

The ultimate goal was, in the words of the famous article 7a,[43] "an area without internal frontiers in which the free movement of goods, persons, services and capital is ensured". Physical and other barriers would have to be gradually removed and the deadline was set for 31 December 1992. This so-called 1992-operation also marked the beginning of the recognition that there were no longer national answers to the phenomenon of international migration. The removal of internal border controls for persons meant that member states would share external borders and, as a consequence, would need to develop at least common admission policies. During the years to come, it was repeatedly stressed that abolishing internal frontier controls must remain compatible with the need to combat terrorism and drug-trafficking.

The principal question was how to do this in practice: through the Community or intergovernmental approach. It would soon become clear that the views of the Commission differed from those of member states, and from some states more than others.

The Commission took the initiative in 1984, by proposing a Directive on the abolition of internal border controls. During the discussions on this proposal at the Fontainebleau European Council, it became clear that harmonisation of national asylum and immigration policies was necessary.[44]

---

42 Completing the internal market. White paper from the Commission to the European Council (Milan, 28-29 June 1985) (COM (85) 310 final). The Single European Act (Bulletin EC Supplement 2/86) and the Community Charter of the Fundamental Social Rights of Workers (Luxembourg, 1990).

43 In the Treaty on European Union, which entered into force on November 1, 1993, article 8a (of the EEC Treaty) became article 7a. Although, technically, the article was referred to as article 8a until November 1993, this essay refers to the article under its current designation as article 7a.

44 According to Klaus-Peter Nanz in his article The harmonisation of asylum and immigration legislation within the third pillar of the Union Treaty – A stocktaking. In: J. Monar and R. Morgan (eds.), The third pillar of the European

One year later, the Milan European Council (June 1985) unanimously adopted the White Paper on Completing the Internal Market. This "agenda of the 1992-operation" asked the Commission to work on co-ordinating rules of residence, entry and access to employment by third-country nationals, and on the harmonisation of asylum policies. By 1988, the Commission was to present proposals to that effect.

In addition, in July 1985, the Council of Ministers adopted a Resolution on the Commission's Guidelines for a Community policy on migration. The Council recognised: "...that it is desirable to promote co-operation and consultation between member states and the Commission as regards migration policy, including vis-a-vis third countries, and [noted] the Commission's intention of drawing up an appropriate procedure to this end".[45]

A week before the Council of Ministers adopted this Resolution, and approximately one week after the White Paper's adoption, the Commission decided to set up a prior communication and consultation procedure between member states. According to this Decision, member states would be required to give the Commission and the other member states information, in good time, on "draft measures which they intend to take with regard to third-country workers and members of their families, in areas of entry, residence and employment, as well as the realisation of equality of treatment in living and working conditions, wages and economic rights, the promotion of integration into the workforce, society and cultural life, and voluntary return of such persons to their countries of origin".[46] Furthermore, member states were to share information on draft agreements related to those matters, as well as draft co-operation agreements which they intended to negotiate, or renegotiate, with third countries, when these agreements contained related provisions. This consultation procedure was intended to facilitate information-exchanges and identification of common problems, encourage the adoption of common positions to confront such problems, ensure that measures and agreements taken by member states conformed with, and did

---

Union. Co-operation in the fields of justice and home affairs (Brussels, 1994).

45 OJ C 186 of 26.7.85

46 OJ L 217 of 19.8.85

not compromise, Community policies, and facilitate further harmonisation of national legislation on third-country nationals.

*The member states against the Commission*

Understandably, the Commission was encouraged by the favourable climate for common policies created by the goal of a single market. Although the Single European Act included no provisions for common immigration and asylum policies, the Commission had good reason to believe that member states would be as responsive to initiatives in this regard as they were with regard to overall proposals for the establishment of the internal market. However, in late 1985, the governments of Denmark, France, Germany, the Netherlands and the United Kingdom brought an action before the Court of Justice to prevent the Commission from setting up this prior communication and consultation procedure. In 1987, the Court ruled partly in favour of the Commission and partly in favour of the governments. It accepted, on the basis of the EC Treaty's article 118, the Commission's procedural power "to set up the notification and consultation machinery which is to result in the adoption of a common position on the part of the member states".[47] The Court nevertheless denied the Commission's authority to "determine the result to be achieved in that consultation and to prevent the member states from implementing drafts, agreements and measures which it might consider not to be in conformity with Community policies and actions".[48] On the other hand, the Court did not accept the five member states' view that migration policy in relation to third-countries fell entirely outside the scope of the Community's social policies. According to the Court, the promotion of integration of workers from non-member states into the workforce and society was implied by article 118, in so far as this was linked to employment. It nevertheless declared the Commission Decision void, ruling that the Commission lacked competence to extend

---

47 See Joined cases 281, 283 to 285 and 287/85 and the opinion of Mr Advocate General Mancini (1987) ECR (3230). See also Kenneth R. Simmonds, The concertation of Community migration policy. In: Common Market Law Review 25 (1988). The cases submitted by Denmark, the Netherlands and the United Kingdom were declared inadmissible on the ground that they were presented to the Court out of time.

48 Ibid, joined cases.

"...the scope of the consultation procedure to cover matters relating to the cultural integration of workers from non-member states and members of their families".[49]

From this ruling, the Commission concluded that it could carry out its Decision to set up a prior communication and consultation procedure as long as it excluded matters related to the cultural integration of third-country nationals. In 1988, the Commission took a new Decision,[50] on the basis of which a consultation procedure was initiated. There was, however, no great willingness among member states to co-operate.

Undoubtedly, the Commission had noticed the changes in the political climate. Some member states considered the 1992-operation to be a purely economic affair. They were prepared to intensify their co-operation, and even to change the procedures necessary for this in order to stimulate economic progress. In their view, such efforts were not to be accompanied by co-operation in the promotion of social integration, notwithstanding the fact that in the EC-Treaty and Community policies, economic and social progress have always been inextricably linked. The resistance against interference by European institutions on social matters was strong among various member states, as evident by the United Kingdom's refusal to sign the 1989 Community Charter on Fundamental Social Rights for Workers. This climate was no more favourable for the development of Community immigration and asylum policies.

### *The Single European Act*

The change in climate became even more clear during the Intergovernmental Conference which took place between June 1985 and February 1986.[51] This Conference led to the adoption of the Single European Act, which not only gave the 1992-operation its legal basis, but also changed the Community's decision-making procedures. On certain policy issues, including matters related to free movement, unanimity was replaced by qualified majority

---

49 Ibid.

50 OJ L 183 of 14.07.88.

51 Intergovernmental conferences are held to prepare major institutional and procedural changes to the original Treaties of Rome.

voting in the Council of Ministers, and consultation with the European Parliament was replaced by the co-operation procedure. However, unanimity was still required for those measures in the field of social security needed in order to establish freedom of movement.

By inserting article 7a into the EC-Treaty, member states made free movement of persons a Community matter and granted Community institutions the authority to promote action in this regard. Member states would have many disputes and divergent views, however, on the interpretation of this article and how to implement it, as became clear during the adoption of the Single European Act. In a political Declaration on the free movement of persons attached to the Act, member states agreed that in order to promote free movement of persons, they would co-operate, without prejudice to the powers of the Community, on matters related to the entry, movement and residence of third-country nationals. They also agreed to work together in combatting terrorism, crime, traffic in drugs and illicit trading in works of art and antiques. However, in another Declaration, they stated that such action should not "affect the right of member states to take such measures as they consider necessary for the purpose of controlling immigration from third countries, and to combat terrorism, crime, the traffic in drugs and illicit trading in works of art and antiques".[52]

This co-operation indeed took shape in various forms involving all or a limited number of member states. The Commission appears to have concluded that most member governments were not yet prepared to entrust the Community to further develop policies on free movement, let alone on immigration and asylum. Consequently, it took a pragmatic position. It began to work together with the member states as much as possible, at times reminding them (and possibly, itself) that the Community approach could be more fruitful and effective than intergovernmental co-operation.

These developments notwithstanding, the Commission was not left empty-handed in every policy field. The Single European Act gave a Treaty basis to the co-operation between the member states in the sphere of foreign policy. This co-operation – the so-called European Political Co-operation

---

52 General Declaration on articles 13 to 19 of the Single European Act.

(EPC) – began in 1969. One sub-section, entitled the Judicial Co-operation Group on Criminal Law, concerned itself with judicial co-operation in penal and civil matters, while another dealt with combatting drug trafficking and terrorism. For a long time, EPC was a purely intergovernmental affair, but the Single European Act associated the Commission fully with its proceedings.[53] The Commission may have had this development in mind when it adopted its pragmatic stance, perhaps expecting to become fully associated, in due course, with co-operation between the ministers of justice and home affairs.[54] It may have been of the opinion that its role in such matters would be enhanced once it had demonstrated its willingness to co-operate with member states.

As a matter of fact, this model was followed years later when intergovernmental co-operation on justice and home affairs was incorporated in the Treaty on European Union (Title VI TEU), after which the Commission was to be fully associated with this co-operation. This included its full association with immigration and asylum matters.

## IV THE HEYDAY OF INTERGOVERNMENTALISM (1985-1993)

From 1985 until the entry into force of the Treaty on European Union in November 1993, European Community member states worked together intergovernmentally on such matters as immigration, asylum, external and internal border controls, illegal immigration, drug trafficking, combatting crime and terrorism, etc. In 1986, the ministers responsible for immigration decided to meet at least twice a year towards the end of each Community Presidency.[55] The last meeting of this kind took place in June 1993, after which the ministers met under the new arrangements set up by the Treaty on European Union. During this period numerous working groups were

53 The European Parliament was also to be closely associated with EPC proceedings, which means that the Parliament is only being regularly informed and having its views duly considered.

54 In most member states, these ministers are responsible for immigration and asylum matters.

55 The Presidency of the European Community rotates to a different member state every six months.

created, which differed in mandate and membership. As a consequence of these developments, two parallel processes were initiated almost simultaneously during the mid-1980s: one included, eventually, nine of the twelve EC member states (the Schengen Group); the other included all twelve member states.

### *The Schengen Group*[56]

France and Germany began to work on the gradual abolition of controls on persons at Franco-German borders in 1984, after lorry drivers protested against the long queues at Europe's internal borders. For that purpose, the two countries concluded the Sarrebruck Accord (1984). The Benelux countries, which had suppressed controls on persons at their internal borders in 1960, joined the initiative, leading to the 1985 signing of the Accord concerning the Gradual Abolition of the Checks at the Common Borders (or, Schengen Accord). This accord contained principle measures to be taken for the total abolition of internal borders among the signatory states. The five countries subsequently negotiated and adopted, after the unification of Germany in 1990, the text of the Convention Applying the Schengen Accord, or what has become known as the Schengen Convention. Only member states of the European Community (and European Union) can accede to the Convention. Subsequently, Italy (1990), Spain (1991), Portugal (1991), Greece (1992) and Austria (1995) have signed the Convention.

The United Kingdom, Ireland and Denmark are the only Community member states which did not become party to the Schengen Convention. The United Kingdom simply refused to lift controls at their common borders with other Schengen countries. This made it very difficult for Ireland to join Schengen because of the common travel area that exists between that country and the United Kingdom. For similar reasons, Denmark may have opted to forego membership in the Schengen Group because it perceived it to conflict with its participation in the Nordic passport union, which allowed free travel of Nordic country nationals (Denmark, Finland, Iceland, Norway and Sweden). After the 1995 enlargement of the Union, Austria has signed the Convention

56 This part of the chapter on the intergovernmental approach will, for the sake of completeness, include the developments after 1993.

and it is expected that Sweden and Finland will do the same in the near future. Denmark has recently asked for the status of observer to the Schengen Group. It is likely that an arrangement will be worked out with Norway and Iceland, which would remove the last obstacles for Nordic member states of the European Union that wish to sign the Convention.

The European Commission has participated as an observer in Schengen's Central Negotiation Group and participates in its Executive Committee and working groups.[57] The Executive Committee, composed of ministers of the member states who are responsible for the implementation of the Convention (and if necessary, assisted by experts) prepares decisions and, once they are approved, oversees their execution. Various working groups are set up, which deal with questions such as external border controls, the abolition of internal border controls, free movement of persons, a common visa list, abolition of visa requirements for third-country nationals, asylum, police co-operation, security and the setting up of an information system among law enforcement agencies (the so-called Schengen Information System, or SIS).

Increasingly, Schengen came to be seen by its member states and the European Commission as the forerunner of the 1992-operation.[58] It is no coincidence that those countries blocking progress at the level of the twelve did not join the Schengen Group. Nevertheless, in the event that the twelve would succeed in adopting Conventions "with a view to the completion of an area without internal frontiers, the Contracting Parties (to the Schengen Convention) shall agree on the conditions under which the provisions of the present Convention are to be replaced or amended in the light of the

---

57 Antonio Cruz, Schengen, Ad-hoc Immigration Group and other intergovernmental fora in view of a Europe without internal borders. CCME Briefing Paper no. 12 (Brussels, 1993) and H. Meijers et al., Schengen, internationalisation of central chapters of the law on aliens, refugees, privacy, security and the police (Leiden, second and revised version, 1992).

58 Klaus-Peter Nanz, involved in both the Schengen Group and the working groups at the level of the twelve, speaks of Schengen as a laboratory for the larger Community. See Klaus-Peter Nanz, Das Schengerer Uebereinkommen: Personenfreizügigkeit in integrationspolitischer Perpektive. In: Integration 17. Jg, 2/94, Beilage zur Europäischen Zeitung 4/94.

corresponding provisions of such Conventions. The Contracting Parties shall, to that extent, take account of the fact that the provisions of this Convention may provide for more extensive co-operation than that resulting from the provisions of the said Conventions. Provisions which are in breach of those agreed between the member states of the European Communities shall in any case be adapted in any circumstances".[59] In other words, similar agreements concluded by the member states of the European Community will take precedence over the Schengen Convention.

Intergovernmental fora at the level of the twelve Community member states dealt with many of the same issues as the Schengen working groups, and in many cases, these fora involved the same persons. In addition, several provisions and implementing measures of the Schengen Convention were replicated, totally or partially, by working groups established under the intergovernmental co-operation. For example, those provisions of Schengen dealing with the determination of the state responsible for asylum applications are, with minor differences, included in the Dublin Convention on asylum. The proposals for the European Information System (EIS) are similarly modelled on the SIS.

### *Achievements*

It would seem thus far that the Schengen process has achieved far more than the intergovernmental co-operation mechanism of the Community member states. Schengen countries have adopted two international agreements, and have established a machinery for implementing adopted measures. These agreements would appear to have a harmonising effect on the admission, immigration and asylum policies of the Schengen countries, by eliminating internal frontier controls. In addition, a Schengen Information System (SIS) was in place by December 1994, allowing for the computerised exchange of information between Schengen states on such matters as visa and asylum applications, records on persons and objects, etc. The Convention allows for free travel of third-country nationals within the Schengen area. In 1991, the Schengen Group concluded so-called readmission agreements with

59 Article 142 of the Schengen Convention, as reproduced in H. Meijers et al (1992).

Poland, requiring Poland to take back persons who entered Schengen countries illegally from or having passed through Poland. The Group has also agreed on a list of countries whose nationals would need a visa to enter Schengen countries. This list of (presently) 126 countries, for unclear reasons, is kept secret. Furthermore, agreements were reached on a series of practical and detailed matters regarding procedures on visa and the crossing of external borders, which have been subsequently detailed in handbooks distributed among relevant authorities in Schengen member states.

These achievements notwithstanding, a number of questions cast some doubt about Schengen's success. First of all, it took quite some time before the Convention came into effect. After the instruments of ratification of the five founding members were deposited, the Convention entered into force in September 1993. However, in legal terms, the Convention could only be implemented after prerequisites to its implementation (such as effective external border controls and the functioning of the information system) were met. It thus took until 1995 to meet these conditions, and even then, the Convention became operational in only seven of the nine signatory states. Italy and Greece have been unable to meet certain requirements with regard to external border controls. Moreover, France demanded the extension of the intermediate period to the end of 1995, and decided to maintain controls at its external borders.

During the years of continual postponement of the Convention's implementation, it become clear that member states did not have enough mutual trust in each others' policies. France, for example, more than once expressed its doubts about Italy's capacity to seal off its borders against illegal entry, and repeatedly criticised the Netherlands' drug policies. Other reasons for the delay were the imperfect functioning of the SIS in its early stages, and the insufficient guarantee for the protection of personal data.[60]

60 According to article 126 of the Convention, each contracting party shall "adopt the national provisions required to achieve a level of protection of personal data at least equal to that resulting from the principles of the Council of Europe Convention of 28 January 1981 for the protection of individuals with regard to automatic processing of personal data".

In terms of judicial and democratic control of the decision-making process within Schengen, much is left to be desired.[61] In fact, the absence of control by international judicial and parliamentary institutions undermines the desired harmonisation of policy measures, and easily leads to unworkable bureaucratic solutions for certain problems by depriving them of necessary political and societal support. Co-operation of this kind could also have a negative impact on the level of protection offered to asylum-seekers and foreigners. The different conditions attached to such protection by individual countries are multiplied at the Schengen level, making it even more difficult for asylum-seekers to meet all the necessary conditions.

### *Intergovernmental co-operation by the twelve*

In October 1986, during the British Presidency, the first meeting of the ministers responsible for immigration was held in London. The ministers confirmed the commitment of the member states to the promotion of free movement of persons according to the Single European Act. They insisted that problems related to crime not deflect the Community from this objective, while acknowledging that the abolition of internal frontiers must remain compatible with efforts to combat terrorism, drug trafficking, other crime and illegal immigration.

At this meeting, the ministers created the Ad-hoc Group on Immigration, composed of their closest advisers and, in those issue areas which involved Community competence, observers from the Commission.[62] The Secretariat of the Council of Ministers was to act as the Ad-hoc Group's secretariat. The Ad-hoc Group was instructed to produce a working programme, including measures to be taken and dates for their completion, and to co-ordinate its work with all those working for the completion of the internal market by 1992. It was asked to look at the following areas of concern:

---

61 Deirdre Curtin and Herman Meijers, The principle of open government in Schengen and the European Union: Democratic retrogression? In: Common Market Law Review 32 (1995).

62 The Commission observers have played a very active role in the work of the Ad-hoc Group.

1 the improvement of checks at the external frontiers of the Community;
2 the value of internal checks;
3 the role of co-ordination and possible harmonisation of member states' visa policies in improving controls;
4 the role and effectiveness of controls at internal frontiers in the fight against terrorism, drugs, crime and illegal immigration;
5 exchange of information about the operation of spot-check systems;
6 close co-operation to avoid abuse of passports;
7 measures to achieve a common policy to eliminate asylum abuse, in consultation with the Council of Europe and the UN High Commission for Refugees;
8 examination of ways in which Community travel can be improved without adding to the terrorist threat, illegal immigration, drug trafficking and other crime.

The Ad-hoc Group on Immigration was supported by six sub-groups: admission/expulsion, visas, false documents, asylum, external borders and refugees of the former Yugoslavia. These sub-groups reported to the Ad-hoc Group, which in turn reported to the Co-ordinators Group, after its establishment in 1988 (see below).

The Rhodes European Council (December 1988) decided to set up a group composed of one senior official from each member state, which would be responsible for co-ordinating member state efforts to create an area without internal frontiers. Such efforts, it stated, should be "linked to progress in intergovernmental co-operation to combat terrorism, international crime, drug trafficking and trafficking of all kinds".[63] The so-called Co-ordinators Group – Free movement of Persons (or, Rhodes Group) was charged with unblocking the "whole complex of intergovernmental and Community work in the field of free movement of persons".[64] The Group would eventually conclude that "... differing views were held on their (i.e member states') legal and political framework, in particular, on the interpretation and scope of the relevant Treaty provisions inter alia article 7a of the EC-Treaty, and the obligations flowing therefrom, the extent to which political decisions in this

63 Quoted from the Palma Document.
64 Ibid.

field had already been taken and where the competence for taking decisions and action lay".[65]

The Co-ordinators Group drafted the so-called Palma document, named after Palma de Majorca, the site of its adoption in 1989. The document consisted of an inventory of measures to be taken concerning the free movement of persons, and included a timetable for their implementation. As such, it distinguished between essential and desirable measures concerning action at external borders, internal frontiers, and inside the territory of the Community, with respect to combatting drug trafficking and terrorism, admission to Community territory, granting of asylum and refugee status, visa policies and judicial co-operation in criminal and civil matters. The document also identified the competent fora and working groups for dealing with these matters, demonstrating its faith in intergovernmental working groups and organisations to implement the various measures.[66]

The Madrid European Council (June 1989) adopted the Palma Document. The Co-ordinators Group continued to receive reports from the various other working groups (including the Ad-hoc Group), and presented their findings on a regular basis to meetings of the ministers responsible for immigration.

*Achievements*

In the period between 1985 and 1993, co-operation between the then twelve member states was structured, and the agenda for intergovernmental co-operation was set. Conventions, recommendations and resolutions were drafted, and some of them were adopted. A common visa list was developed

---

65 Ibid.

66 Among the identified fora were the Ad-hoc Group on Immigration, the various Trevi Groups, the Mutual Assistance Group, the European Committee to Combat Drugs, the European Political Co-operation Group and the Horizontal Group. The TREVI Group was initially set up in 1976 to enhance police co-operation in combatting terrorism. Various sub-groups were created to carry out specific tasks. These tasks were gradually expanded to include other areas, such as police training, organised crime, drug trafficking and security issues related to the abolition of frontier controls. See, Antonio Cruz, ibid.

and common positions were taken at a number of international conferences.[67]

*1 Conventions*

In Dublin, in June of 1990, the immigration ministers adopted the text of the Convention on the determination of the state responsible for the examination of an application for asylum lodged in one of the member states of the European Communities. The so-called Dublin Convention designates responsibility among the member states for the examination of asylum applications made in one of the member states. It contains provisions for determining the state responsible for processing an application. The Convention aims to ensure that a person's application for asylum is processed by one of the member states, and to prevent an applicant from being sent from one member state to another for the processing of the application. It is also intended to prevent applications from being lodged in more than one member state.

Ireland and the Netherlands have still not ratified the Convention. Austria, Finland and Sweden, the three new member states of the European Union, have not yet signed the Convention. The Convention will enter into force after ratification by the initial twelve signatory states.

In June 1991, an agreement could have been reached on the text of the Convention on the crossing of the external frontiers of the European Communities, were it not for a disagreement between Spain and the United Kingdom over the status of Gibraltar. The draft Convention defines

---

67 The following is based on Summary of conclusions of the meetings of the Ministers concerned with immigration held in London (20 October 1986), Brussels (28 April 1987), Copenhagen (9 December 1987), Munich (3 June 1988), Athens (9 December 1988), Madrid (12 May 1989), Paris (15 December 1988), Dublin (15 June 1990) and Rome (7 December 1990). (SN 1131/91 (WGI 735). For the position of the Commission, see its Communication on the abolition of frontier controls (SEC (92) 877 Final). See also Tony Bunyan and Frances Weber, Intergovernmental co-operation on immigration and asylum. CCME Briefing Paper no. 19 (Brussels, 1995), H. Meijers et al, A new immigration law for Europe? The 1992 London and 1993 Copenhagen rules on immigration (Utrecht, 1993) and John Handoll, Free movement of persons in the EU (Chichester, 1994).

conditions of entry and stay in the territory of the member states for a period shorter than three months. Member states are required to define authorised crossing points and to provide surveillance of their external borders. Sanctions are to be imposed for unauthorised border crossings, for example, on air or sea carriers, and some rules are specified regarding expulsion of illegal immigrants and rejected asylum-seekers. The Convention aims to harmonise visa and admission policies. Certain provisions provide for the mutual recognition of visas and the issuing of a uniform visa on the basis of common conditions and criteria. Visas will be refused on grounds of public order, national security and international relations. Furthermore, the applicant must not be on the list of inadmissible persons. Third-country nationals no longer need a visa in order to travel from one member state to another.

The immigration ministers stressed the importance of establishing a European Information System, needed in order to apply the Convention on the crossing of the external frontiers. They felt that a Convention on the European Information System would give a legal basis to such a system. A draft text provides for a system of information-exchange among member states which would give proper authorities access to reports on persons and objects for the purpose of border checks and controls, issuing visas and residence permits, and police and customs checks. Member states sharply disagree as to whether the jurisdiction of the European Court of Justice should include ruling in cases of conflict between member states, or between member states and the Commission, and whether it should be able to issue preliminary rulings on interpretation of the Convention.

*2 Common visa list*

From 1987, the ministers responsible for immigration initiated several efforts to draw up a common list of countries whose nationals would require a visa before entering a member state. According to the ministers, harmonisation of the entry document for third-country nationals must be based on solidarity, regardless of whether a member state was having problems with a particular third country. The ministers agreed on which countries constituted the common list – namely, those which had produced a large number of asylum-seekers or illegal migrants, and those which posed a security problem.[68] The ministers also agreed in principle that a list must be drawn up of countries for which visas were not required, in particular, those countries which posed no immediate immigration or security problem to any of the member states. Nationals of these countries were not required to have visas when entering a member state. In order to draft and revise such lists, a system of regular information-exchange on political developments in third-countries, particularly in crisis areas, needed to be established between member states' diplomatic representations abroad. It was only in 1995 that the ministers of justice and home affairs reached an agreement on the list (see chapter II).

### *3 Resolutions, Recommendations and Conclusions*

During 1992 and 1993, immigration ministers discussed, and occasionally adopted – after intensive preparations by civil servants, and long deliberations in numerous meetings – a number of Resolutions, Recommendations and Conclusions. The status of these adopted texts is unclear. In some cases they entail obligations; in others, they express intentions only. Normally, they leave ample room for the individual member states to implement them according to their own preferences.

In their 1992 London meeting[69] the ministers adopted three resolutions: the Resolution on manifestly unfounded applications for asylum, the Resolution on a harmonised approach to questions concerning host third countries, and the Resolution on certain common guidelines as regards the admission of particularly vulnerable persons from the former Yugoslavia. The first Resolution requires the inclusion of the concept of manifestly unfounded asylum applications in the asylum laws of the member states. An application is defined as manifestly unfounded when there is clearly no substance to the applicant's claim to fear persecution in his/her country, when the claim is based on deliberate deception or an abuse of asylum procedures. In such cases, the proper authorities may follow an accelerated

68 This list at one point included sixty countries, and at another point, more than 120. All Central European countries were originally on this list, but some of them (namely Poland, Hungary and the Czech and Slovak Republics) were removed after political developments in these countries.

69 Press release 10518/92 (Presse 230).

asylum procedure for processing claims. The second Resolution deals with the question of whether a safe third country should be responsible for the determination of the asylum application. In cases where an applicant has left a first host country which is considered to be safe, and applies for asylum in a member state, the application may not be considered, or will be subject to the accelerated procedures above.

At the same meeting, the ministers approved the Conclusions on countries in which there is generally no serious risk of persecution and the Conclusion on people displaced by the conflict in the former Yugoslavia. The first Conclusions were meant to compliment the Resolution on manifestly unfounded applications for asylum, and introduced the concept of "safe" countries of origin. The latter is intended to assist member states in harmonising their approach to applications from countries which produce high proportions of clearly unfounded applications. Assessments still need to be made of the persecution risks in individual countries, taking into account previous numbers of refugees and recognition rates, observance of human rights, the existence of democratic institutions and prospects for dramatic changes in the future. The second Conclusion expressed the willingness of the member states to admit on a temporary basis persons from the former Yugoslavia.

Finally, the ministers adopted two Recommendations, one regarding the expulsion practices to be followed by member states, and another regarding transit for the purposes of expulsion. These two Recommendations on expulsion attempt to design common practices towards persons who have unlawfully entered a member state, and who are thus liable for expulsion on grounds of public policy or national security, or towards those whose asylum applications have been rejected. The Resolutions deal with such matters as the conclusion of re-admission agreements, the escort of persons to be expelled, and the prosecution of those who facilitate the entrance of undocumented persons, or who harbour or employ clandestine workers.

In their Copenhagen meeting (June 1993),[70] immigration ministers adopted the Resolution on the harmonisation of national policies on family

70 Press release 6712/93 (Presse 90).

reunification, the Resolution on certain common guidelines as regards the admission of particularly vulnerable groups of persons from the former Yugoslavia, and the Recommendation concerning checks on and expulsion of third-country-nationals residing or working without authorisation in a member state. The Resolution on family reunification pertains only to non-EC nationals who are lawfully-resident in a member state. It recognises the right of family reunion for spouses (but not in cases where the marriage was contracted solely, or principally, for admission to the member states), children of residents between the ages of 16-18 years, and children adopted by both residents. The second Resolution emphasised that protection and assistance to refugees should be provided, preferably in the region of origin. In addition, member states should concentrate their efforts on creating safe conditions for displaced persons and provide them with sufficient resources to enable them to remain in the region. The Recommendation on expulsion identifies checks to be undertaken to detect the presence of third-country nationals residing or working illegally in a member state, as well as abuses of family reunification procedures.

*4 Clearing houses*

In Lisbon, in 1992, immigration ministers adopted the Decision establishing a clearing house for gathering, exchanging and disseminating information, and compiling documentation on all matters related to asylum.[71] This Centre for Information, Research and Exchange on Asylum (CIREA) is intended to develop a greater informal consultation which will facilitate, through competent bodies, co-ordination and harmonisation of asylum practices and policies. CIREA will operate within the framework of the General Secretariat of the Council of the European Communities, and the Commission will be fully associated with its work. Delegates from member states are also to participate in the clearing house.

At the same meeting, the ministers called for a feasibility study on the establishment of a clearing house on the crossing of external borders and immigration. At the 1992 London meeting, immigration ministers took the decision to establish the Centre for Information, Discussion and Exchange on the Crossing of Borders and Immigration (CIREFI). CIREFI is charged with

71 Press release 7273/92 (Presse 115).

gathering, exchanging, disseminating and compiling information and documentation on, among other matters, authorised and unauthorised immigration flows, genuine, forged or falsified travel documents, control procedures, legislation and policies on immigration and legislation and practice on carriers' liability.[72]

*5 Common positions*

Many common positions on immigration and asylum issues have been taken by member states and have been presented as such at international meetings. This was the case, for example, at the Ministerial Conference on the Movement of Persons from the countries of Central and Eastern Europe (Vienna, January 1991) and, to a lesser extent, meetings organised by such fora as the Council of Europe, and Executive Committee meetings of the UNHCR.

### *Meagre results*

The proliferation of international working groups dealing with police, security, immigration and asylum has lead to numerous meetings and conferences of ministers and civil servants. The question of whether these activities have resulted in more effective and humane policies, however, is not so easy to answer. A distinction can be made between how co-operation between member states took shape, and what the actual achievements of such cooperative efforts were. The goal of creating an internal market by 1993, the real or perceived security risks stemming from the abolition of internal border controls, and the continued and possibly increasing migratory movements into the Community made it necessary and urgent to work together. One could argue that the beginnings of co-operation in the sensitive areas of internal and judicial affairs – and the creation of structures needed for such co-operation – was a success in itself.[73] One

---

72 The Ministers did not adopt the Conclusions on the organisation and development of CIREFI until November 1994.

73 This is the opinion of Wenceslas de Lobkowicz, who works for the European Commission and is actively involved in the intergovernmental co-operative process. See his article, Intergovernmental co-operation in the field of migration – from the Single European Act to Maastricht. In: J.Monar and R. Morgan (eds), The third pillar of the European Union. Co-operation in the fields of

could equally argue, however, that the member states complicated the matter considerably by creating a parallel structure to the existing structures of the European Communities. No matter how one looks at this, it is not surprising that it took some time before tangible results were achieved.

The differing views on the meaning of the EC Treaty's article 7a were so pronounced that co-operation between all twelve member states was considered to be very difficult if not impossible. Member states agreed that achieving the abolition of internal frontiers must be compatible with the need to maintain their security. Denmark, Greece, Ireland and the United Kingdom consistently put more emphasis on the security aspect than other member states. They also insisted that the abolition of frontiers as specified by article 7a did not include the removal of controls for third-country nationals. Countries such as Belgium, Germany, France, Luxembourg and the Netherlands (all belonging to the Schengen Group) did not share this view, although they set some conditions on the removal of frontiers in order to guarantee the security of member states. This included a visa requirement for nationals of countries posing security or irregular emigration problems, or of countries from which numerous fraudulent asylum applications came. Secondly, all member states would need to enter into identical international commitments with respect to asylum. Finally, re-admission agreements could be concluded between the member states if one of them deemed it to be necessary. All member states agreed that the complete abolition of internal border controls would be subject to co-operation in searching for wanted persons and improved information-exchanges, improvement of international legal assistance in criminal matters (including extradition), and alignment of narcotics and arms legislation. The Commission, in the person of Commissioner Lord Cockfield (with Jacques Delors, the architect of the 1992-operation) reminded member states of their obligations under the EC-Treaty. The Commission thus reiterated its support for lifting internal border controls for all persons, including third-country nationals, which it considered to be an integral part of establishing the internal market.[74]

---

justice and home affairs (Brussels, 1994).

74 For the position of the member states and the Commission, see Summary of conclusions of the meetings of the Ministers concerned with immigration (note 68).

The deadline for the removal of obstacles to allow for full freedom of movement has passed without the objective being achieved. More than once, the European Commission has expressed its disappointment, and has suggested that if progress is not soon achieved, it "is determined to take appropriate action within the scope of its responsibility to ensure that the goals of article 7a in the area of free movement of persons are realised".[75] By this, the Commission meant, as stated by one of its Vice-presidents, Mr Bangemann, that legal action could be taken against those member states which continued to carry out internal frontier checks on persons. In later statements, the Commission softened its tone. Commissioner D'Archirafi, who succeeded Mr Bangemann as Commissioner responsible for the internal market, stressed the need for dialogue and close co-operation between the member states and the EC institutions. It was the European Parliament that finally took legal action against the Commission, in 1994, for not effectively forcing the member states to implement article 7a.

## V THE 1990-1992 INTERGOVERNMENTAL CONFERENCES

At the Madrid European Council (June 1989), the decision was taken to convene an Intergovernmental Conference on Economic and Monetary Union, followed one year later by the decision of the Dublin European Council (April 1990) to convene a second and parallel Intergovernmental Conference on Political Union. Both Conferences opened in Rome in December 1990. The Intergovernmental Conference on Political Union was to examine, among other issues, whether and how subjects presently covered by intergovernmental co-operation, such as immigration and external border controls, could be brought into the ambit of a new treaty on political union. Both the Commission and the European Parliament expressed concerns about the lack of transparency and insufficient accountability to elected bodies under the current policy-making process.

---

75 Commission statement on the report to the European Council in Copenhagen on the implementation of article 8a of the Treaty of Rome with regard to the free movement of persons. This statement was also attached to the press release issued after the Meeting of Ministers responsible for immigration in Copenhagen (June 1993) Press release 6712/93 (Presse 90).

*Preparing for Maastricht*

With a view to contributing to the debate, the Commission issued a Communication in October 1990. As for migration-related issues, the Commission noted that "the intergovernmental method, which it supported, has failed to produce any meaningful results." The Commission suggested that this delicate issue, "which undermines relations with non-Community countries, notably in the areas of immigration and the fight against drug abuse and serious crime, should be resolved (...)".[76] The Commission pointed to two possible solutions. One involved declaring the Community institutions competent to take measures concerning free movement of third-country nationals. The other would entail the recognition of the problems raised by the lack of free movement of third-country nationals "as one of the questions of vital interest in foreign and common security policy".[77] The second solution is a clear reference to European Political Co-operation, with which the Commission is associated.

In January 1991, the Luxembourg Presidency presented proposals for policy-making on immigration and asylum, and identified four options. First, member states could continue to co-operate in this area outside the framework of the new European Union. Second, reference could be made in the EC-Treaty to co-operation in this area, leaving it to the Council to work out, in a later stage, the precise details. The third option involved the elaboration of a set of Treaty provisions, defining the fields to be covered and their related decision-making procedures. Finally, policies in this area could be fully integrated into the EC Treaty, using the Community method of policy-making. Denmark was in favour of only the first or, at best, the second option. The United Kingdom, Ireland and Greece preferred the second option. France, Germany and Portugal preferred the third option, however, France and Germany viewed this as only a short-term solution, favouring the fourth option after the next stage of institutional reform. The Netherlands,

---

76 Commission of the European Communities, Intergovernmental Conferences: Contributions by the Commission. Bulletin EC, Supplement 2/91.

77 Ibid.

Belgium, Italy and Spain supported the fourth option.[78] In other words, there were at least six countries in favour of bringing immigration and asylum under the ambit of the Community institutions.

In April 1991, the Luxembourg Presidency presented their proposals for a new treaty on European Union to the Council of Ministers and the European Parliament. A pillar structure was proposed, whereby intergovernmental pillars dealing with foreign and security affairs and internal and judicial matters, would exist alongside the European Community. The Luxembourg European Council (June 1991) agreed on treaty commitments to formalise and eventually harmonise policies on asylum, immigration and aliens by 31 December 1993. Details would have to be laid down by unanimous decision of the Council, or if necessary, through the implementation of measures to be decided by qualified majority. Under this arrangement, individual member states and the Commission would be given rights of initiative. In addition, the European Council responded positively to a German proposal requesting that the Ministers responsible for immigration draw up a report for the Maastricht Council (December 1991) which would clarify definitions and specify the preparatory work needed for harmonisation, and present proposals for transitional measures needed during the period between signature and entry into force of the EC Treaty amendments.[79]

The Dutch Presidency considerably altered the Luxembourg Presidency's proposals for a new treaty on European Union. It replaced the concept of a pillar structure with a tree structure in which policy-making in various areas would stem from the Community's institutional framework. The Dutch proposal received the support of a majority of member states, but met with insurmountable resistance from Denmark, France and the United Kingdom. The Maastricht European Council adopted a version of the treaty closer to

78 Corbett gives an account of the opinion of the various member states. See Richard Corbett, The Treaty of Maastricht, (Harlow, 1993). This book, and also Werner Weidenfeld (Hrsg), Maastricht in der Analyse. Strategien und Optionen für Europa (Gütersloh, 1994), contain an analysis and the text of the many preparatory documents for the Intergovernmental Conference on Political Union, including the Luxembourg non-paper.

79 Luxembourg European Council (EC Bull /1991).

that proposed by the Luxembourg Presidency. At Germany's request a Declaration on Asylum was attached to the Treaty, which declared that co-operation between the member states on asylum was considered as a matter of priority.

*The 1991 Work programme*

The Ministers responsible for immigration, in the meantime, prepared the report requested by Germany at the Luxembourg Council. Their final report proposed a concrete work programme on immigration and asylum, without giving an opinion as to the institutional framework within which they should be dealt. The working programme on migration and asylum policy was to be carried out between the adoption of this report and the entering into force of a new treaty on political union.[80]

One part of the programme included matters related to harmonisation of policies on admission for the purposes of family reunion and formation, work (as an employed or self-employed person), study, or humanitarian reasons. The programme specified that a common approach to the question of illegal immigration be developed, including co-operation with countries of departure and transit concerning re-admission policies. In addition, possibilities for granting rights to long-term resident third-country nationals, such as access to the labour market, were in need of examination. Also, the question of root causes of migration pressure needed to be addressed, for example, by adjusting policies in the field of development aid, foreign trade and the promotion of human rights. The strengthening of support for accommodating refugees in their country or region of origin was also mentioned.

The other part of the programme entailed implementation of the Dublin Convention, including the determination of a common interpretation of the concepts used in the Convention. The harmonisation of substantive asylum law was to include the definition of the principle of first host country and a common interpretation of the definition of a refugee according to the

---

80 Report from the Ministers responsible for immigration to the European Council meeting in Maastricht on immigration and asylum policy (SN 4038/91 WGI 930).

Geneva Convention. A clearing house would be set up to exchange information on legislation, case law, policy development and implementation by the member states, as well as information concerning asylum-seekers' countries of origin.

In a Detailed Note annexed to the Report, the ministers made a number of interesting comments. They expressed their resolve to base their common policies on the principles of social justice and human rights. Therefore, although the ministers noted that immigration policies must be restricted, a clear exception needed to be made in refugee and family reunion and formation cases. Anti-discrimination policies would also need to be expanded, and integration policies intensified. In addition, the programme emphasised that third-country nationals must be able to associate themselves with the process of creating a Citizen's Europe, and urged that obstacles be removed to gradually grant them equal rights. For example, such persons could be allowed to accept job offers in states other than the member states in which they lived. Although the ministers were aware of the fact that European policy-making lacks sufficient transparency, they maintained that the results of European-level deliberations allowed for national parliamentary scrutiny and parliamentary and public debate.[81]

The Maastricht European Council agreed on the work programme and also on an institutional framework within which the programme would be implemented. It thus adopted the Treaty on European Union, which formally established co-operation between the member states on justice and home affairs. During the years to come, the work programme did not change fundamentally, only its priorities changed under the various presidencies.

### *The Edinburgh European Council*

Between the adoption and signing of the Treaty on European Union in Maastricht (December 1991 and February 1992, respectively) and its entry into force in November 1993, lie nearly two years of heated debates in

81 This hardly reflects reality as experienced by members of the European Parliament, national parliaments, NGOs and the press, as national governments are often reluctant to share information on European policy-making on immigration and asylum matters with any of them.

national parliaments and national referenda (in three member states). During this period, intergovernmental co-operation continued much as before. The Edinburgh European Council (December 1992) noted with great satisfaction that the programme for the creation of the internal market would "in all essential respects be successfully completed by 31 December 1992".[82] Paradoxically, it also noted that the free movement of persons could not be completely assured by the first of January 1993. Much needed to be done to achieve this goal without creating dangers in public security and compromising the fight against illegal immigration. On a positive note, the Council made references to the progress achieved by the Schengen states and to Community member states' intentions to ease controls at their borders for EC-nationals.

The European Council also adopted the Declaration on principles governing external aspects of migration policy. These principles included:

1 The preservation and restoration of peace, and full respect for human rights and the rule of law, which would diminish migratory movements resulting from war and oppressive regimes.
2 The protection and assistance of displaced people in the nearest safe area to their homes.
3 The promotion of liberal trade and economic co-operation with countries of emigration, which would reduce economic motives for migration.
4 Targeting development aid and job creation, and the alleviation of poverty.
5 Efforts to combat illegal immigration.
6 The conclusion of bilateral or multilateral agreements with countries of origin or transit, to ensure that illegal immigrants were returned to their home countries.
7 The assessment of home countries' practices in readmitting their nationals after they are expelled from the territories of the member states.

82 European Council in Edinburgh. Conclusion of the Presidency. In: European Commission, The European Councils. Conclusions of the Presidency 1992-1994 (Luxembourg, 1995).

8 The increase in co-operation in responding to the particular challenge of persons fleeing from armed conflict and persecution in former Yugoslavia.

The Declaration welcomed the progress made by immigration ministers during the last few years, in particular, their adoption of Recommendations, Resolutions and Conclusions. It also recognised that uncontrolled immigration could be destabilising, while noting that the integration of legally-resident immigrants needed to be promoted, and legal measures taken, to combat racial discrimination.[83]

## VI THE TREATY ON EUROPEAN UNION AND THE THIRD PILLAR

The European Union has established the goals of promoting economic and social progress, in particular, through the creation of an area without internal frontiers, the strengthening of social and economic cohesion, and the establishment of economic and monetary union. The Union intends to assert itself on the international scene, primarily through the implementation of a common foreign and security policy. The protection of the rights and interests of the nationals of its member states will be fostered through the introduction of Union citizenship. In addition, close co-operation on justice and home affairs will be developed (article B TEU).

The European Union has three pillars: the existing European Communities (the first pillar); the already-existing, but extended, co-operation in foreign and security policies (the second pillar); and the newly established co-operation in justice and home affairs (the third pillar). The Union is served by a single institutional framework, which ensures consistency and continuity in its policies, while building upon the acquis communautaire (article C). This somewhat cryptic provision suggests that these institutions (the European Parliament, Council, Commission, Court of Justice and Court of Auditors) serve the three pillars. However, in the second and third pillar, the Commission is fully associated with the work of the Council. In matters concerning the second and third pillars, the Court of Justice has no com-

---

83 Ibid.

petence, and the European Parliament's role is weaker than it is in matters pertaining to the first pillar.

*Union citizenship*

Every person holding the nationality of a member state shall be a citizen of the Union. European citizenship, however, is not a replacement of the nationality of one of the member states, but an addition to it. Union citizenship includes the following rights (article 8 EC-Treaty):

Union citizens have the right to move and reside freely within the Union under conditions laid down by the EC-Treaty and the measures adopted to implement free movement rights. In other words, the Treaty on European Union is not extending free movement rights that have not already been accorded to member-state nationals under Community legislation. The Council of Ministers may adopt Regulations and Directives according to the assent procedure (as set out in article 189b EC-Treaty), which allows for the adoption of such legislative measures by a qualified majority, and gives the European Parliament greater influence.

Union citizens have the right to vote and stand as candidates in municipal and European elections. Measures to that effect have, in the mean time, been adopted (see Chapter I).

Consular protection will be given to Union citizens in a third country by a member state other than their own in cases where their own state is not represented in that country.

Finally, Union citizens have the right to address individually or in association with others, a petition to the European Parliament on matters within the Community's field of activity. Also, they may apply to the Ombudsman, appointed by the European Parliament.[84] These rights are granted not only to Union citizens, but to any natural or legal persons who reside, or who have their registered office, in a member state (article 138d and 138e EC-Treaty).

---

84 The European Parliament did not nominate the Ombudsman until 1995.

The Commission is required to report to the European Parliament on the application of these rights every three years.

There is no specific clause establishing a Treaty basis to combat racial discrimination, nor is there a specific provision enabling legislative action to promote equal treatment to third-country nationals. Only the annexed protocol on social policy includes a provision on Community action with regard to conditions of employment for third-country nationals legally residing in the member states.[85]

*Immigration and asylum*

The new Treaty extends the competence of the Community in the area of immigration policy to a limited degree, but also offers the possibility of bringing more elements into its competence.

According to article 100c of the amended EC-Treaty, the Council of Ministers will – on the basis of a Commission proposal, and after consultation with the European Parliament – determine the third countries whose nationals must be in possession of a visa when crossing the external borders of the member states. The Council will act on the basis of unanimity, except in cases of a sudden, threatened inflow of nationals from third countries whereby decisions can be taken by qualified majority. After 1 January 1996, these matters will be decided on the basis of a qualified majority. The Commission has used its new powers and presented proposals for a uniform format for visas and a common visa list (see Chapter II).

Article K.9 of the Treaty on European Union – the so-called bridge, or "passarelle" – offers the possibility of bringing immigration and asylum policies into the Community's competence. In a Declaration annexed to the Treaty, the harmonisation of member states' asylum policies is identified as a matter of priority. Therefore, the Council of Ministers will consider, by the end of 1993, the possibility of using the "passarelle" in gaining

85 The protocol on social policy contains an agreement on social policies between the member states, with the exception of the United Kingdom, which opted out of the agreement.

authority over asylum matters. A decision thereupon must be taken unanimously and in accordance with the constitutional requirements of the member states. The Commission prepared a report on this matter at the end of 1993, a few weeks after the Treaty on European Union entered into force (after a delay of more than a year). It sums up the advantages of a transfer of immigration and asylum matters from the third to the first pillar. For instance, decision-making processes would be more transparent, since proposals would only be made by the Commission, which makes its proposals public. The European Parliament would also be more fully involved and give its opinion. National parliaments would be involved through their surveillance of national governments during negotiations in the Council of Ministers, and in the transposition of directives into national law. Compared with the adoption of conventions and their ratification by member states, the implementation of Community legislative instruments can be more rapidly achieved. Finally, in the case of Community legislation, the European Court of Justice would guarantee a uniform interpretation. These advantages notwithstanding, the Commission was of the opinion that "the time is not yet right to propose the application of article K.9 so soon after the entry into force of the Treaty on European Union".[86] The Council of Ministers, referring to this report, decided to postpone a decision on this matter until the end of 1995, because of the belated entry into force of the Treaty.[87]

On the whole, immigration and asylum remain matters for intergovernmental co-operation. This co-operation will henceforth be carried out in the framework of officially-established Co-operation in the fields of Justice and Home Affairs (Title VI, TEU, containing article K). In order to achieve the free movement of persons, member states will regard the following areas as matters of common interest (article K1 TEU):

1 asylum policy;
2 rules governing the crossing by persons of the external borders of the EU;

---

86 Commission of the European Communities, Report to the Council on the possibility of applying Article K.9 of the Treaty on European Union to asylum policy (Brussels, November 1993 (SEC (93) 1687 Final).

87 Ibid. For the position of the Ministers, see the press release issued after the JHA Council in June 1994 Press release 7760/94 (Presse 128-G).

3 immigration policy and policy regarding nationals of third countries:
a. conditions of entry and movement by nationals of third countries on the territory of the member states,
b. conditions of residence by nationals of third countries on the territory of the member states, including family reunion and access to employment, and
c. combatting unauthorised immigration, residence and work by nationals of third countries on the territory of the member states;
4 combatting drug addiction;
5 combatting fraud on an international scale;
6 judicial co-operation on civil matters;
7 judicial co-operation on criminal matters;
8 customs co-operation; and
9 policy co-operation for the purposes of combatting terrorism, drug trafficking and other serious forms of international crime, including the exchange of information within a European Policy Office (Europol).

A few items make this intergovernmental co-operation on justice and home affairs different from co-operation on such matters in the previous period. Firstly, the list of matters of common interest must be seen as exhaustive. Other matters must be dealt with in other intergovernmental fora. Secondly, the Commission is fully associated with the work in all areas referred to in this list and, in addition, has the right of initiative on matters referred to under numbers one to six. Thirdly, one particular element of immigration policy, namely that related to visa policies, is transferred to the first pillar, and additional elements may eventually be transferred as well.

*The pillar approach*

The European Council defines the general political guidelines of the Union and gives the necessary impetus for the Union's development (article D, TEU). The Ministers of Justice and Home Affairs (JHA-Council), meeting at least two times per year, decide on proposals initiated by member states and the Commission in the first six areas of common interest, and on the initiative of any member states in the last three areas of common interest. Decisions are taken by unanimity, except on procedural matters, or when otherwise decided with the adoption of joint positions. Conventions can be adopted by a two-thirds majority (K.4 TEU).

Member states inform and consult each other in the Council of Ministers and, to that end, will establish co-operation between the relevant departments of their administration (K.3 TEU). In addition, a Co-ordinating Committee is set up consisting of senior officials. This Committee (also known as the K4 Committee), gives opinions to the Council at the Council's request or on its own initiative. It can contribute to the preparation of the Council's decisions on matters which are of common interest and which relate to the question of visas (K.4, TEU). In practice, it works in such a way that the connection between the Council and the Co-ordinating Committee is made by COREPER. Furthermore, the Co-ordination Committee (made up of its predecessor, the Group of Co-ordinators), created three Steering Committees: the Steering Group on Immigration and Asylum (the former Ad-hoc Group on Immigration), the Steering Group on Police/Custom Co-operation (the former Trevi 1975 Group, and other intergovernmental working groups), and the Steering Group on Judicial Co-operation in Civil and Criminal Matters (formerly under European Political Co-operation). The Steering Groups are supported by a series of working groups (see diagram on page 63).

The Commission is fully associated with the work of the Council, but article K.8 of the TEU – which refers to those articles in the EC Treaty that deal with the Commission's competencies and tasks – carefully omitted article 155. The latter article gives the Commission considerable powers to ensure that provisions of the Treaty and measures taken by the European institutions are applied. On the other hand, the operational expenditure of the third pillar can be charged to the budget of the Community.

The Court of Justice is not given jurisdiction to ensure the uniform interpretation of the provisions under this title of the Treaty on European Union (article 164, EC-Treaty). Only conventions adopted under article K may stipulate such a jurisdiction (K.3, TEU). The European Parliament will be regularly informed and its views will be duly taken into consideration. The Parliament may ask questions of and make recommendations to the Council, and hold a debate on the progress made in the implementation of this title of the Treaty (K.6 TEU).

This complicated structure involves numerous intergovernmental fora, while including only the Council, and to a certain extent, the Commission, among its European institutional bodies. This framework may, apart from promoting co-operation, lead to the adoption of joint positions and joint actions, and conventions which will be recommended to member states for adoption according to their respective constitutional requirements. There is no clear definition of what constitutes a joint position or action. Under international law, joint positions can be best compared with recommendations or declarations, and are not binding on the member states. The term joint action is also used in Title V of the Treaty on European Union on Common Foreign and Security Policy (the second pillar). In that context, it is stated that "joint actions shall commit the member states in the positions they adopt and in the conduct of their activity" (article J.3). Such words are entirely lacking in Title VI, on Co-operation on Justice and Home Affairs (the third pillar). Given the carefully-constructed three-pillar structure of the Union, it seems unlikely that joint action under the third pillar entails the same meaning as it does under the second.[88] In other words, it is unclear whether joint actions are legally or politically binding upon member states.

It is interesting to note that no mention is made in the Treaty on European Union of the possibility of adopting Resolutions, Recommendations, Decisions and Conclusions. In other words, such methods were not given a formal Treaty basis. One explanation for this could be that member states intended to end such practices. However, as time has indicated, this was not their intention, and such decision-making persists even in the absence of a Treaty basis.

### *The Justice and Home Affairs Councils*

The first meeting of the Ministers of Justice and Home Affairs took place in Brussels in November 1993, and was devoted, in great part, to questions related to the Union's new organisational structures and the future work programme. During the first two years of its operation, the Council adopted

---

88 See Peter-Christian Mueller-Graff, The legal bases of the third pillar and its position in the framework of the Union Treaty. In: Monar and Morgan (eds), The third pillar of the European Union. Cooperation in the fields of Justice and Home Affairs (Brugge, 1994) and Roland Bieber, Links between the "Third Pillar" (Title IV) and the European Community (Title II) of the Treaty on European Union. In: idem.

two joint actions, two conventions, and some fifty resolutions, recommendations, statements, conclusions and reports. Not all of these concerned immigration and asylum, but matters such as customs, extradition, police collaboration (Europol), drug trafficking, organised crime, etc.[89] The European Commission played an active role in this new framework of intergovernmental co-operation.

*1 Joint actions*

The only joint action in the immigration and asylum fields adopted by the Council pertained to travel facilities for students from third countries residing in a member state.[90] The action allows these pupils visa-free travel throughout the Union. One could argue, however, as the European Commission has, that this matter falls within the competence of the Community (according to article 100c, EC-Treaty).

*2 Conventions*

The Council has not proposed any conventions concerning immigration and asylum to the member states. A draft text for the Convention establishing a European Information System (EIS) has been discussed several times, without agreement on a final decision. The EIS, based on the Schengen Information System, aims to provide member states with computerised access to information on persons and objects for purposes of border controls, the issuing of visas and residence permits, etc. The draft Convention specifies which information is to be included, how data can be protected, and who has access to it, etc. Member states are divided on the question of the jurisdiction of the European Court of Justice. Some member states are entirely opposed to the Court's competence (in particular, the United Kingdom), whereas others are strongly in favour of it (including Belgium, Greece, Germany, Ireland, Luxembourg and the Netherlands).

---

89 For a list of the adopted measures, see Commission of the European Communities, Report on the operation of the Treaty on European Union (SEC (95) 731 final), also published as Commission report for the Reflection Group (Brussels, 1995). For the adopted measures on immigration and asylum, see part II of this book.

90 OJ L 327 of 19.12.1994.

The Dublin Convention has still not entered into force. In addition, the discussions on the Convention on the crossing of the external frontiers were resumed at the initiative of the European Commission, which presented a proposal for a decision on the establishment of the new Convention based on the former draft (see chapter II).

The text of this new convention – the Convention on controls on persons crossing external frontiers – is almost identical to the External Frontier Crossing Convention. No decision was taken by the Council of Ministers on these proposals. The dispute between Spain and the United Kingdom over Gibraltar, which has impeded adoption of the initial Convention, still persists. To this has been added divergent views on the role of the European Court.

On a related matter, the ministers are still waiting to discuss the result of a feasibility study on the European Automated Finger-print Recognition System (EURODAC). This system will enable member states to exchange and compare finger prints of asylum-seekers in order to detect whether such individuals have applied for asylum in more than one country.

*3 Resolutions*

Three Resolutions were adopted by the JHA Council: on the admission of third country nationals to the member states for employment (June 1994); self-employment (November 1994); and study purposes (November 1994).[91] The first resolution aims to regulate temporary migration for employment purposes. The second deals with the admission of persons who will undertake independent economic activity, or who will add to the host country's economy through investment, innovation, job creation and technology transfer. The third sets out the conditions under which students shall be admitted, such as proof of financial means to support study and maintenance, a firm offer of admission to a recognised higher education institution, and ensured departure after studies are complete.

91 Press release 7760/94 (Presse 128-G) and Press release 11321/94 (Presse 252-G).

In June 1995, the JHA Council[92] also adopted a Resolution on minimum guarantees for asylum procedures. The Resolution contains provisions on asylum-seekers' rights during their application examination, as well as appeal and review procedures. It also outlines the procedures for handling of manifestly unfounded asylum applications. An article is included which states that there should be no *de facto* or *de jure* grounds for granting refugee status to an asylum applicant who is a national of another member state. A particularly rapid or simplified procedure will be applied to the application for asylum lodged by a Union citizen in a member state.

The JHA Council also reached agreement on a Resolution on burden-sharing with regard to the admission and residence of displaced persons on a temporary basis in June of 1995. The Resolution is intended to address situations which may require harmonised action in order to facilitate member states' assistance to displaced persons during, or in anticipation of, mass influxes into the region. Some situations may require prompt action, in which case the Council's procedures for urgent action will apply. The Resolution discusses solidarity between member states, taking into account each state's contribution to the prevention or resolution of crises and "all economic, social and political factors which may affect the capacity of a member state to admit an increased number of displaced persons under satisfactory conditions".[93] After years of discussions, the ministers had not become any more precise on this issue.

Ministers failed to reach agreement on a draft Resolution on the harmonised application of the definition of refugees in accordance with article 1a of the Geneva Convention.

In addition, Ministers prepared a Resolution on the reinforcement of security of the external borders, but were unable to reach a final resolution on the text.

---

92 Press release 8133/95 (Presse 194).

93 The text of the Resolution can be found in the press release issued after the meeting of the Justice and Home Affairs Council (June 1995) Press release 8133/95 (Presse 194).

*4 Recommendations and conclusions*

In November 1993, the JHA Council adopted a Recommendation on combatting trade in human beings for the purpose of prostitution, which among other things called for international co-operation and information-exchanges between law enforcement agencies, information campaigns in diplomatic and consular circles, and between border control authorities.[94]

The JHA Council agreed on a Recommendation concerning the adoption of a standard travel document for the expulsion of third country nationals in November 1994. At the same meeting, they adopted a Recommendation which provided a sample document of a bilateral readmission agreement between an EU member state and a third country.

Finally, various Conclusions deal with such issues as combatting racism and xenophobia, the application of article K.9 (TEU) to asylum policy, the establishment of CIREA and CIREFI, relations with third countries, etc.

*Combatting racial discrimination*

Due to outbreaks of racial violence in many member states during the early nineties, combatting racism and xenophobia ranked high on the agenda of the various European institutions. For its part, the JHA Council prepared a report in 1994 on racism and xenophobia, which included a number of specific proposals. The report recommended that member states use a multiagency approach involving schools, social services, police, etc, in addressing issues of racism and xenophobia. In order to raise awareness of such matters, the report recommended training for the various enforcement agencies. Furthermore, it suggested that member states explore measures to improve data collection and publication of racist and xenophobic acts. Finally, it emphasised the need for cross-border co-operation in confronting racism and xenophobia. A draft report on racism, prepared by the K.4 Committee one year later, essentially reiterated these recommendations.[95]

---

94 Justice and Home Affairs Council Brussels, 29 and 30 November 1993. Press release 10550/93 (Presse 209).

95 Projet de rapport du Comité K.4 au Conseil Justice et Affaires intérieures sur racisme et xénophobie (Bruxelles, le 4 novembre 1994 - 10595/94).

In the meantime, the Corfu European Council (June 1994), at the initiative of President Mitterrand and Chancellor Kohl, set up a Consultative Commission. This Commission was charged with presenting proposals on combatting racism in the areas of education and training, information and media, and police and justice. The Cannes European Council (June 1995) took note of the report, which called for the granting of European citizenship and free movement to third-country nationals after five years of legal residence, as well as the extension of Community competence to act on the elimination of all forms of discrimination based on race, ethnic origin or religion. The Consultative Commission was asked to extend its work in order to study the feasibility of a European Monitoring Centre on Racism and Xenophobia. The monitoring of racism was apparently deemed to be of greater importance than the adoption of the Consultative Commission's proposals, which had specifically outlined action needed to be taken at the Union level.[96]

*The 1996 Intergovernmental Conference*

In 1996, an intergovernmental conference (IGC) will be convened which will review the Treaty on European Union and examine those provisions of the Treaty in need of revision, bearing in mind the objectives of the Union (article N TEU). The Corfu European Council (June 1994) established a Reflection Group to prepare for this conference. The Group consists of representatives of the Ministers of Foreign Affairs and the President of the European Commission. Two representatives of the European Parliament participate in the work of the Group, which also exchanges views with the other institutions and organs of the European Union. These institutions were invited to prepare reports on the functioning of the Treaty on European Union before the work of the Reflection Group began. The Group is currently examining and elaborating ideas "relating to the provisions of the Treaty on European Union for which a revision is foreseen and other possible

96 Activities of the Consultative Commission on racism and xenophobia. Final report. (Brussels, 23 May 1995 - 6906/1/95). Cannes European Council (26 and 27 June 1995) Presidency Conclusions (SN 211/1/95).

improvements in a spirit of democracy and openness, on the basis of the evaluation of the functioning of the Treaty as set out in the reports".[97]

The Council and the Commission published their reports before the work of the Reflection Group began.[98] Interestingly, these reports have much in common in their assessment on the functioning of the third pillar. Both reports come to the conclusion that extremely limited use has been made of the new instruments provided for in article K.3 of the TEU. The reports offer as possible explanation the continuing differences of opinion on the nature and legal effects of such instruments. The Commission's report, however, goes further in its discussion of the slow process entailed in the adoption and implementation of conventions, particularly as there are no established, binding deadlines. It also points to the fact that most decisions must be taken unanimously, which has proved to be "a major source of paralysis".[99] Finally, there is no provision for monitoring the implementation of adopted measures.

Both reports note that the cumbersome Union structure, which currently consists of five levels (see diagram on page 63), clearly needs to be re-evaluated. The parallel functioning of the first and third pillar has further complicated decision-making within the Union. Not only do both pillars deal with aspects of free movement, but the line between the two pillars is not always clear. In addition, free movement is tied to security, considered primarily as a matter for national governments.

---

97 Corfu European Council (press edition). See further, Simon Hix, The 1996 intergovernmental conference and the future of the third pillar. CCME Briefing Paper no. 20 (Brussels, 1995).

98 Draft report of the Council on the functioning of the Treaty on European Union (Brussels, 1995 - 5082/95). European Commission, Intergovernmental Conference 1996. Commission report for the Reflection Group, (Luxembourg, 1995). The Court of Justice of the European Communities also published its report on the IGC 1996, see Report of the Court of Justice on certain aspects of the application of the treaty on European Union – Contribution of the Court of First Instance for the purposes of the 1996 Intergovernmental Conference (Proceedings no 15/95 – Luxembourg, 1995). For the report of the European Parliament, see Simon Hix, op.cit.

99 European Commission, Intergovernmental Conference 1996. Commission report for the Reflection Group (Luxembourg, 1995).

Furthermore, no use has been made of the Treaty's clauses for exercising qualified majority voting, nor for transferring certain matters to the first pillar. Similarly, the Community has not been charged for any activity undertaken in the framework of the third pillar. It is not within the scope of the Commission and Council reports to outline possible solutions to these problems. The reports are, rather, ideas for discussion within the Reflection Group. In addition to addressing the overall matters of the Union's structure and decision-making procedures, the Reflection Group may well present proposals as to how to improve immigration and asylum policy-making at the European level.

## VII SOME FINAL OBSERVATIONS

The European Union's efforts to design common policies in the fields of migration, asylum and integration are without vision or direction. Moreover, the way in which policies are being shaped lack transparency and efficiency, and suffer from insufficient parliamentary and judicial control.

Migration is an integral part of Europe's history and is of vital importance for the societies and persons concerned. The protection of refugees and migrants is cherished in Europe's religious and humanistic traditions. It is thus unfortunate and regrettable that migration and asylum have become strongly linked with such issues as law enforcement and combatting crime. Without solid evidence, it is taken for granted that the lifting of internal border controls-and the subsequent need for the development of common complementary measures at external borders-will have a negative effect on the security of EU member states. Consequently, the development of migration and asylum policies depend on the success of measures to ensure member states' security. Furthermore, when the safety of the state is perceived to be at stake, respect for human rights and the democratic decision-making process come under pressure. This is what is currently transpiring in Europe, threatening to undermine some of the fundamental values of liberal democracies.

There is a clear need to manage or regulate migratory movements in order to protect the rights and interests of both migrants and the members of receiving societies. Continuous consultations at the European level that include all European institutions could lead to an assessment of the present and future needs of immigrants, and to an agreement on how to share responsibilities for the protection of refugees.[100] This could mean that, for the time being, no new immigrants are admitted for the purpose of employment. It could also mean that, in addition to proportionate reception of refugees between member states, other forms of refugee protection are developed. Moreover, polices to address the root causes of forced migration would likely ease the inclination of governments to take restrictive measures and, at the same time, offer them the opportunity to live up to humanitarian obligations worldwide.[101]

The interdependence of the member states of the European Union in social, economic and political realms necessitates a common approach to immigration, asylum and integration matters. Unfortunately, the debates on these issues have become increasingly re-nationalised. Whereas citizens of the member states are called upon to think and act European, and to elect a European Parliament, governments at the same time continually convey the message that their voices can only count in national political arenas. Consequently, no common vision on immigration, asylum and integration is being developed.

If business proceeds as usual, there will be only a limited group of people inside and outside of national governments and European institutions who will be aware of what is going on. But even those who are involved in the decision-making at the European level will have difficulties in formulating an overview of events. This is due in part to the fact that many of the officials involved in these deliberations are composed of civil servants from member states, and even then, frequently come from different departments. In addition, the relationship between the Steering Groups and COREPER is not clear. Furthermore, although the Commission is fully associated with the proceedings of the co-operation on Justice and Home Affairs, it cannot participate in all working group meetings (and those of Schengen), simply because it does not possess the available staff.

---

100 For proposals to that effect, see Jan Niessen, The making of European immigration polices. CCME Briefing Paper no. 15 (Brussels, 1994).

101 See Jan Niessen and Roger Zegers de Beijl, International migration, economic development and human rights. CCME Briefing Paper no. 18 (Brussels, 1994).

Given the fact that there is no common vision, civil servants are deprived of clear direction. Consequently, measures adopted tend to originate from the lowest common denominator, which is usually restrictive. To complicate matters, the status of adopted instruments are unclear under international law. In addition, the instruments as described by the Treaty on European Union are not frequently used. Among the available devices that are not specified by the treaty, there exists a clear hierarchy. A Resolution is stronger than a Recommendation, which is itself stronger than a Conclusion. The mechanism employed likewise seems to have implications for the body chosen to work on a particular subject matter. It often happens that before an issue is dealt with, it bounces back and forth between steering groups and working groups.

Finally, the obscure mixture of supranationalism and international co-operation creates a democratic deficit, which will only increase if intensified European co-operation is not matched with adequate judicial and democratic control at the same level. In most member states of the Union, immigration and asylum are sensitive issues which often result in polarised debates. In such a climate, policy discussions and decisions on the protection of refugees and the integration of migrants can only profit from open and frank discussions at all levels.

Working structures in the fields of justice and home affairs

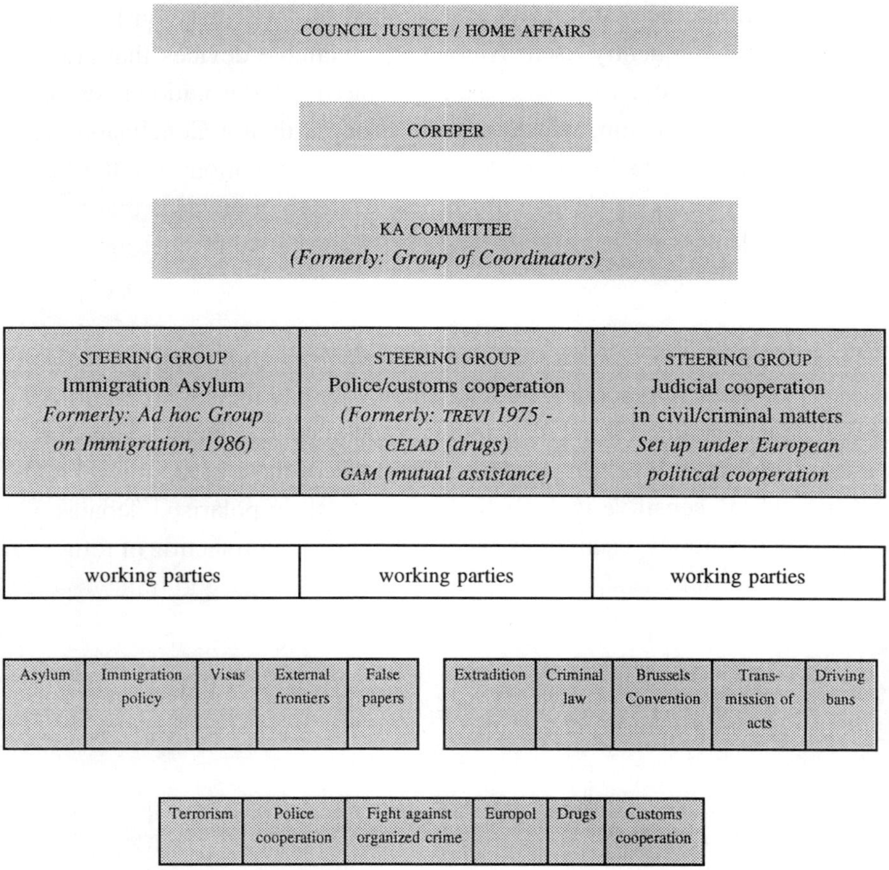


Source: European Commission

# PART II

# Compilation and Commentary

# 1 DUBLIN CONVENTION and Measures for its Implementation

A Convention determining the State responsible for examining applications for asylum lodged in one of the Member States of the European Communities, ("Dublin Convention").

B Declarations in the minutes of the Conference of Immigration Ministers of the Member States of the European Communities (Dublin, 15 June 1990).

C Standard form for determining the State responsible for examining an application for asylum.

D Implementation of the Dublin Convention.

E Calculation of periods of time in the framework of the Dublin Convention.

F Conclusions on the transfer of asylum applications under the provisions of the Dublin Convention.

# A

# Convention determining the State responsible for examining applications for asylum lodged in one of the Member States of the European Communities

Dublin, 15 June 1990

His Majesty The King of the Belgians, Her Majesty The Queen of Denmark, The President of the Federal Republic of Germany, The President of the Hellenic Republic, His Majesty The King of Spain, The President of the French Republic, The President of Ireland, The President of the Italian Republic, His Royal Highness The Grand Duke of Luxembourg, Her Majesty The Queen of the Netherlands, The President of the Portuguese Republic, Her Majesty The Queen of the United Kingdom of Great Britain and Northern Ireland,

Having regard to the objective, fixed by the European Council meeting in Strasbourg on 8 and 9 December 1989, of the harmonization of their asylum policies;

Determined, in keeping with their common humanitarian tradition, to guarantee adequate protection to refugees in accordance with the terms of the Geneva Convention of 28 July 1951,[1] and the New York Protocol of 31 January 1967[2] relating to the Status of Refugees, hereinafter referred to as the "Geneva Convention" and the "New York Protocol" respectively.

Considering the joint objective of an area without internal frontiers in which the free movement of persons shall, in particular, be ensured, in accordance with the provisions of the Treaty establishing the European Economic Community,[3] as amended by the Single European Act.[4]

---

1 Treaty Series No. 39 (1954), Cmnd. 9171.
2 Treaty Series No. 15 (1969), Cmnd. 3370.
3 Treaty Series No. 47 (1988), Cmnd. 455.
4 Treaty Series No. 31 (1988), Cmnd. 372.

Aware of the need, in pursuit of this objective, to take measures to avoid any situations arising, with the result that applicants for asylum are left in doubt for too long as regards the likely outcome of their applications and concerned to provide all applicants for asylum with a guarantee that their applications will be examined by one of the Member States and to ensure that applicants for asylum are not referred successively from one Member State to another without any of these States acknowledging itself to be competent to examine the application for asylum;

Desiring to continue the dialogue with the United Nations High Commissioner for Refugees in order to achieve the above objectives;

Determined to cooperate closely in the application of this Convention through various means, including exchanges of information,

Have decided to conclude this Convention and to this end have designated as their Plenipotentiaries [names omitted].

Who, having exchanged their Full Powers, found in good and due form, Have agreed as follows:

*Article 1*

1. For the purposes of this Convention:

   (a) Alien means: any person other than a national of a Member State;

   (b) Application for asylum means: a request whereby an alien seeks from a Member State protection under the Geneva Convention by claiming refugee status within the meaning of Article 1 of the Geneva Convention, as amended by the New York Protocol;

   (c) Applicant for asylum means: an alien who has made an application for asylum in respect of which a final decision has not yet been taken;

(d) Examination of an application for asylum means: all the measures for examination, decisions or rulings given by the competent authorities on an application for asylum, except for procedures to determine the State responsible for examining the application for asylum pursuant to this Convention;

(e) Residence permit means: any authorization issued by the authorities of a Member State authorizing an alien to stay in its territory, with the exception of visas and "stay permits" issued during examination of an application for a residence permit or for asylum;

(f) Entry visa means: authorization or decision by a Member State to enable an alien to enter its territory, subject to other entry conditions being fulfilled;

(g) Transit visa means: authorization or decision by a Member State to enable an alien to transit through its territory or pass through the transit zone of a port or airport, subject to the other transit conditions being fulfilled.

2. The nature of the visa shall be assessed in the light of the definitions set out in paragraph 1, points (f) and (g).

*Article 2*

The Member States reaffirm their obligations under the Geneva Convention, as amended by the New York Protocol, with no geographic restriction of the scope of these instruments, and their commitment to cooperating with the services of the United Nations High Commissioner for Refugees in applying these instruments.

*Article 3*

1. Member States undertake to examine the application of any alien who applies at the border or in their territory to any one of them for asylum.

2. That application shall be examined by a single Member State, which shall be determined in accordance with the criteria defined in this Convention. The criteria set out in Articles 4 to 8 shall apply in the order in which they appear.

3. That application shall be examined by that State in accordance with its national laws and its international obligations.

4. Each Member State shall have the right to examine an application for asylum submitted to it by an alien, even if such examination is not its responsibility under the criteria defined in this Convention, provided that the applicant for asylum agrees thereto.

   The Member State responsible under the above criteria is then relieved of its obligations, which are transferred to the Member State which expressed the wish to examine the application.

   The latter State shall inform the Member State responsible under the said criteria if the application has been referred to it.

5. Any Member State shall retain the right, pursuant to its national laws, to send an applicant for asylum to a third State, in compliance with the provisions of the Geneva Convention, as amended by the New York Protocol.

6. The process of determining the Member State responsible for examining the application for asylum under this Convention shall start as soon as an application for asylum is first lodged with a Member State.

7. An applicant for asylum who is present in another Member State and there lodges an application for asylum after withdrawing his or her application during the process of determining the State responsible shall be taken back, under the conditions laid down in Article 13, by the Member State with which that application for asylum was lodged, with a view to completing the process of determining the State responsible for examining the application for asylum.

This obligation shall cease to apply if the applicant for asylum has since left the territory of the Member States for a period of at least three months or has obtained from a Member State a residence permit valid for more than three months.

*Article 4*

Where the applicant for asylum has a member of his family who has been recognized as having refugee status within the meaning of the Geneva Convention, as amended by the New York Protocol, in a Member State and is legally resident there, that State shall be responsible for examining the application, provided that the persons concerned so desire.

The family member in question may not be other than the spouse of the applicant for asylum or his or her unmarried child who is a minor of under eighteen years, or his or her father or mother where the applicant for asylum is himself or herself an unmarried child who is a minor of under eighteen years.

*Article 5*

1. Where the applicant for asylum is in possession of a valid residence permit, the Member State which issued the permit shall be responsible for examining the application for asylum.

2. Where the applicant for asylum is in possession of a valid visa, the Member State which issued the visa shall be responsible for examining the application for asylum, except in the following situations:

   (a) if the visa was issued on the written authorization of another Member State, that State shall be responsible for examining the application for asylum. Where a Member State first consults the central authority of another Member State, inter alia for security reasons, the agreement of the latter shall not constitute written authorization within the meaning of this provision.

(b) where the applicant for asylum is in possession of a transit visa and lodges his application in another Member State in which he is not subject to a visa requirement, that State shall be responsible for examining the application for asylum.

(c) Where the applicant for asylum is in possession of a transit visa and lodges his application in the State which issued him or her with the visa and which has received written confirmation from the diplomatic or consular authorities of the Member State of destination that the alien for whom the visa requirement was waived fulfilled the conditions for entry into that State, the latter shall be responsible for examining the application for asylum.

3. Where the applicant for asylum is in possession of more than one valid residence permit or visa issued by different Member States, the responsibility for examining the application for asylum shall be assumed by the Member States in the following order:

(a) the State which issued the residence permit conferring the right to the longest period of residency or, where the periods of validity of all the permits are identical, the State which issued the residence permit having the latest expiry date;

(b) the State which issued the visa having the latest expiry date where the various visas are of the same type;

(c) where visas are of different kinds, the State which issued the visa having the longest period of validity, or where the periods of validity are identical, the State which issued the visa having the latest expiry date. This provision shall not apply where the applicant is in possession of one or more transit visas, issued on presentation of an entry visa for another Member State. In that case, that Member State shall be responsible.

4. Where the applicant for asylum is in possession only of one or more residence permits which have expired less than two years previously or one or more visas which have expired less than six months previously and enabled him or her actually to enter the territory of a Member State,

the provisions of paragraphs 1, 2 and 3 of this Article shall apply for such time as the alien has not left the territory of the Member States.

Where the applicant for asylum is in possession of one or more residence permits which have expired more than two years previously or one or more visas which have expired more than six months previously and enabled him or her to enter the territory of a Member State and where an alien has not left Community territory, the Member State in which the application is lodged shall be responsible.

*Article 6*

When it can be proved that an applicant for asylum has irregularly crossed the border into a Member State by land, sea or air, having come from a non-Member State of the European Communities, the Member State thus entered shall be responsible for examining the application for asylum.

That State shall cease to be responsible, however, if it is proved that the applicant has been living in the Member State where the application for asylum was made at least six months before making his application for asylum. In that case it is the latter Member State which is responsible for examining the application for asylum.

*Article 7*

1. The responsibility for examining an application for asylum shall be incumbent upon the Member State responsible for controlling the entry of the alien into the territory of the Member States, except where, after legally entering a Member State in which the need for him or her to have a visa is waived, the alien lodges his or her application for asylum in another Member State in which the need for him or her to have a visa for entry into the territory is also waived. In this case, the latter State shall be responsible for examining the application for asylum.

2. Pending the entry into force of an agreement between Member States on arrangements for crossing external borders, the Member State which authorizes transit without a visa through the transit zone of its airports

shall not be regarded as responsible for control on entry, in respect of travellers who do not leave the transit zone.

3. Where the application for asylum is made in transit in an airport of a Member State, that State shall be responsible for examination.

*Article 8*

Where no Member State responsible for examining the application for asylum can be designated on the basis of the other criteria listed in this Convention, the first Member State with which the application for asylum is lodged shall be responsible for examining it.

*Article 9*

Any Member State, even when it is not responsible under the criteria laid out in this Convention, may, for humanitarian reasons, based in particular on family or cultural grounds, examine an application for asylum at the request of another Member State, provided that the applicant so desires.

If the Member State thus approached accedes to the request, responsibility for examining the application shall be transferred to it.

*Article 10*

1. The Member State responsible for examining an application for asylum according to the criteria set out in this Convention shall be obliged to:

   (a) Take charge under the conditions laid down in Article 11 of an applicant who has lodged an application for asylum in a different Member State.

   (b) Complete the examination of the application for asylum.

   (c) Readmit or take back under the conditions laid down in Article 13 an applicant whose application is under examination and who is irregularly in another Member State.

(d) Take back, under the conditions laid down in Article 13, an applicant who has withdrawn the application under examination and lodged an application in another Member State.

(e) Take back, under the conditions laid down in Article 13, an alien whose application it has rejected and who is illegally in another Member State.

2. If a Member State issues to the applicant a residence permit valid for more than three months, the obligations specified in paragraph 1, points (a) to (e) shall be transferred to that Member State.

3. The obligations specified in paragraph 1, points (a) to (d) shall cease to apply if the alien concerned has left the territory of the Member States for a period of at least three months.

4. The obligations specified in paragraph 1, points (d) and (e) shall cease to apply if the State responsible for examining the application for asylum, following the withdrawal or rejection of the application, takes and enforces the necessary measures for the alien to return to his country of origin or to another country which he may lawfully enter.

*Article 11*

1. If a Member State with which an application for asylum has been lodged considers that another Member State is responsible for examining the application, it may, as quickly as possible and in any case within the six months following the date on which the application was lodged, call upon the other Member State to take charge of the applicant.

   If the request that charge be taken is not made within the six-month time limit, responsibility for examining the application for asylum shall rest with the State in which the application was lodged.

2. The request that charge be taken shall contain indications enabling the authorities of that other State to ascertain whether it is responsible on the basis of the criteria laid down in this Convention.

3. The State responsible in accordance with those criteria shall be determined on the basis of the situation obtaining when the applicant for asylum first lodged his application with a Member State.

4. The Member State shall pronounce judgment on the request within three months of receipt of the claim. Failure to act within that period shall be tantamount to accepting the claim.

5. Transfer of the applicant for asylum from the Member State where the application was lodged to the Member State responsible must take place not later than one month after acceptance of the request to take charge or one month after the conclusion of any proceedings initiated by the alien challenging the transfer decision if the proceedings are suspensory.

6. Measures taken under Article 18 may subsequently determine the details of the process by which applicants shall be taken in charge.

*Article 12*

Where an application for asylum is lodged with the competent authorities of a Member State by an applicant who is on the territory of another Member State, the determination of the Member State responsible for examining the application for asylum shall be made by the Member State on whose territory the applicant is. The latter Member State shall be informed without delay by the Member State which received the application and shall then, for the purpose of applying this Convention, be regarded as the Member State with which the application for asylum was lodged.

*Article 13*

1. An applicant for asylum shall be taken back in the cases provided for in Article 3(7) and in Article 10 as follows:

   (a) the request for the applicant to be taken back must provide indications enabling the State with which the request is lodged to ascertain that it is responsible in accordance with Article 3(7) and with Article 10;

(b) the State called upon to take back the applicant shall give an answer to the request within eight days of the matter being referred to it. Should it acknowledge responsibility, it shall then take back the applicant for asylum as quickly as possible and at the latest one month after it agrees to do so.

2. Measures taken under Article 18 may at a later date set out the details of the procedure for taking the applicant back.

*Article 14*

1. Member States shall conduct mutual exchanges with regard to:

   – national legislative or regulatory measures or practices applicable in the field of asylum;

   – statistical data on monthly arrivals of applicants for asylum, and their breakdown by nationality. Such information shall be forwarded quarterly through the General Secretariat of the Council of the European Communities, which shall see that it is circulated to the Member States and the Commission of the European Communities and to the United Nations High Commissioner for Refugees.

2. The Member States may conduct mutual exchanges with regard to:

   – general information on new trends in applications for asylum;

   – general information on the situation in the countries of origin or of provenance of applicants for asylum.

3. If the Member State providing the information referred to in paragraph 2 wants it to be kept confidential, the other Member States shall comply with this wish.

*Article 15*

1. Each Member State shall communicate to any Member State that so requests such information on individual cases as is necessary for:

- determining the Member State which is responsible for examining the application for asylum;
- examining the application for asylum;
- implementing any obligation arising under this Convention.

2. This information may only cover:

- personal details of the applicant, and, where appropriate, the members of his family (full name – where appropriate, former name, nicknames or pseudonyms, nationality – present and former, date and place of birth);
- identity and travel papers (references, validity, date of issue, issuing authority, place of issue, etc.);
- other information necessary for establishing the identity of the applicant;
- places of residence and routes travelled;
- residence permits or visas issued by a Member State;
- the place where the application was lodged;
- the date any previous application for asylum was lodged, the date the present application was lodged, the stage reached in the proceedings and the decision taken, if any.

3. Furthermore, one Member State may request another Member State to let it know on what grounds the applicant for asylum bases his or her application and, where applicable, the grounds for any decisions taken concerning the applicant. It is for the Member State from which the information is requested to decide whether or not to impart it. In any event, communication of the information requested shall be subject to the approval of the applicant for asylum.

4. This exchange of information shall be effected at the request of a Member State and may only take place between authorities the designation of which by each Member State has been communicated to the Committee provided for under Article 18.

5. The information exchanged may only be used for the purposes set out in paragraph 1. In each Member State such information may only be communicated to the authorities and courts and tribunals entrusted with:

   – determining the Member State which is responsible for examining the application for asylum;

   – examining the application for asylum;

   – implementing any obligation arising under this Convention.

6. The Member State that forwards the information shall ensure that it is accurate and up-to-date.

   If it appears that this Member State has supplied information which is inaccurate or which should not have been forwarded, the recipient Member State, shall be immediately informed thereof. They shall be obliged to correct such information or to have it erased.

7. An applicant for asylum shall have the right to receive, on request, the information exchanged concerning him or her, for such time as it remains available.

   If he or she establishes that such information is inaccurate or should not have been forwarded, he or she shall have the right to have it corrected or erased. This right shall be exercised in accordance with the conditions laid down in paragraph 6.

8. In each Member State concerned, the forwarding and receipt of exchanged information shall be recorded.

9. Such information shall be kept for a period not exceeding that necessary for the ends for which it was exchanged. The need to keep it shall be examined at the appropriate moment by the Member State concerned.

10. In any event, the information thus communicated shall enjoy at least the same protection as is given to similar information in the Member State which receives it.

11. If data are not processed automatically but are handled in some other form, every Member State shall take the appropriate measures to ensure compliance with this Article by means of effective controls. If a Member State has a monitoring body of the type mentioned in paragraph 12, it may assign the control task to it.

12. If one or more Member State wish to computerize all or part of the information mentioned in paragraphs 2 and 3, such computerization is only possible if the countries concerned have adopted laws applicable to such processing which implement the principles of the Strasbourg Convention of 28 February 1981[5] for the Protection of Individuals, with regard to Automatic Processing of Personal Data and if they have entrusted an appropriate national body with the independent monitoring of the processing and use of data forwarded pursuant to this Convention.

*Article 16*

1. Any Member State may submit to the Committee referred to in Article 18 proposals for revision of this Convention in order to eliminate difficulties in the application thereof.

2. If it proves necessary to revise or amend this Convention pursuant to the achievement of the objectives set out in Article 8a of the Treaty establishing the European Economic Community, such achievement being linked in particular to the establishment of a harmonized asylum and a common visa policy, the Member State holding the Presidency

---

5 Treaty Series 86 (1990), Cmnd 1329.

of the Council of the European Communities shall organize a meeting of the Committee referred to in Article 18.

3. Any revision of this Convention or amendment hereto shall be adopted by the Committee referred to in Article 18. They shall enter into force in accordance with the provisions of Article 22.

*Article 17*

1. If a Member State experiences major difficulties as a result of a substantial change in the circumstances obtaining on conclusion of this Convention, the State in question may bring the matter before the Committee referred to in Article 18 so that the latter may put to the Member States measures to deal with the situation or adopt such revisions or amendments to this Convention as appear necessary, which shall enter into force as provided for in Article 16(3).

2. If, after six months, the situation mentioned in paragraph 1 still obtains, the Committee, acting in accordance with Article 18(2), may authorize the Member State affected by that change to suspend temporarily the application of the provisions of this Convention, without such suspension being allowed to impede the achievement of the objectives mentioned in Article 8a of the Treaty establishing the European Economic Community or contravene other international obligations of the Member States.

3. During the period of suspension, the Committee shall continue its discussions with a view to revising the provisions of this Convention, unless it has already reached an agreement.

*Article 18*

1. A Committee shall be set up comprising one representative of the Government of each Member State.

   The Committee shall be chaired by the Member State holding the Presidency of the Council of the European Communities.

The Commission of the European Communities may participate in the discussions of the Committee and the working parties referred to in paragraph 4.

2. The Committee shall examine, at the request of one or more Member States, any question of a general nature concerning the application or interpretation of this Convention.

   The Committee shall determine the measures referred to in Article 11(6) and Article 13(2) and shall give the authorization referred to in Article 17(2).

   The Committee shall adopt decisions revising or amending the Convention pursuant to Articles 16 and 17.

3. The Committee shall take its decisions unanimously, except where it is acting pursuant to Article 17(2), in which case it shall take its decisions by a majority of two-thirds of the votes of its members.

4. The Committee shall determine its rules of procedure and may set up working parties. The Secretariat of the Committee and of the working parties shall be provided by the General Secretariat of the Council of the European Communities.

*Article 19*

As regards the Kingdom of Denmark, the provisions of this Convention shall not apply to the Faroe Islands nor to Greenland unless a declaration to the contrary is made by the Kingdom of Denmark. Such a declaration may be made at any time by a communication to the Government of Ireland which shall inform the Governments of the other Member States thereof.

As regards the French Republic, the provisions of this Convention shall apply only to the European territory of the French Republic.

As regards the Kingdom of the Netherlands, the provisions of the Convention shall apply only to the territory of the Kingdom of the Netherlands in Europe.

As regards the United Kingdom the provisions of this Convention shall apply only to the United Kingdom of Great Britain and Northern Ireland. They shall not apply to the European territories for whose external relations the United Kingdom is responsible unless a declaration to the contrary is made by the United Kingdom. Such a declaration may be made at any time by a communication to the Government of Ireland, which shall inform the Governments of the other Member States thereof.

*Article 20*

This Convention shall not be the subject of any reservations.

*Article 21*

1. This Convention shall be open for the accession of any State which becomes a Member of the European Communities. The instruments of accession will be deposited with the Government of Ireland.

2. It shall enter into force in respect of any State which accedes thereto on the first day of the third month following the deposit of its instrument of accession.

*Article 22*

1. This Convention shall be subject to ratification, acceptance or approval. The instruments of ratification, acceptance or approval shall be deposited with the Government of Ireland.

2. The Government of Ireland shall notify the Governments of the other Member States of the deposit of the instruments of ratification, acceptance or approval.

3. This Convention shall enter into force on the first day of the third month following the deposit of the instrument of ratification, acceptance or approval by the last signatory State to take this step.

The State with which the instruments of ratification, acceptance or approval are deposited shall notify the Member States of the date of entry into force of this Convention.[6]

6 UK: Cm 1623 September 1991. European Communities no 40 (1991).

*B*

# Declarations in the minutes of the Conference of Immigration Ministers of the Member States of the European Communities (Dublin, 15 June 1990)

The Ministers took note of the text in the Draft Convention determining the State responsible for examining applications for asylum lodged in one of the Member States of the European Communities.

The Ministers noted:

– the eleven Members States were in a position to sign the Convention;

– a statement by the Danish Minister to the effect that his country was unable to sign the Convention for the time being, and that he intended to continue in his attempts to ensure that Denmark would also be in a position to sign the Convention.

The Ministers of the eleven other Member States decided, therefore, to proceed with the signing of the Convention, on the understanding that if Denmark had not signed the Convention by 7 December 1990 the majority would then sign a convention to which the countries concerned would be the contracting parties.

The Ministers agreed to enter the following declarations in the Conference minutes:

1. The parties hereby declare that in order to ensure that applicants for asylum are given adequate guarantees they will keep open the option of extending the co-operation provided for in this Convention to other States by allowing them to subscribe, by means of appropriate instruments, to commitments identical to those laid down in this Convention.

2. The Member States take the view that it is not necessary to supplement Article 15(6) of the Convention by providing that only data which have been applied for in a permitted manner and in good faith may be com-

municated because they consider this goes without saying and that therefore no provisions to cover the point are needed.

3. The Member States agree to submit an annual report to the Committee on the checks they carry out on the appropriate use of the information referred to in Article 15.

4. The Member States note that other possibilities provided for under international law are not excluded should it prove impossible to reach an agreement with regard to the revision of the Convention pursuant to the provisions of Article 17(2).

5. The Member States consider that where this Convention is suspended at the initiative of one of them, in accordance with Article 17, the Convention shall continue to apply as between the other Member States.

6. The Member States consider that the draft Convention on the crossing of the external borders of the Member States of the European Communities is closely linked to other instruments necessary for the realization of Article 8a of the Treaty establishing the European Economic Community, and, in particular, to the Convention determining the State responsible for examining applications for asylum lodged in one of the Member States of the European Communities. The Member States underline the need to intensify the work on the abovementioned draft with a view to finishing work before the end of 1990. The entry into force of the Convention on the crossing of the external borders of Member States should be brought about as soon as possible after the Convention on asylum comes into force.

7. The Federal Republic of Germany declares that the German Democratic Republic is not a foreign country in relation to the Federal Republic of Germany.

   With reference to the Declaration by the Government of the Federal Republic of Germany on the definition of the expression "German national" annexed to the Treaty establishing the European Economic Community of 25 March 1957, the Federal Republic of Germany would point out that this Convention is not applicable to Germans within the meaning of the abovementioned Declaration.

8. The Netherlands is acting on the principle that, as this is a matter concerning all twelve countries, the approval procedure will not commence in the capitals until Denmark has also signed the Convention. In any event, the Netherlands will not start this procedure until Denmark has signed.

9. The Netherlands declares that, as regards the definition of the concept of "application for asylum", the use of the term "seeks from a Member State protection" means that the person involved is an alien who when submitting an application for asylum, claims refugee status and in that capacity requests permission to stay in the Member State in question.

10. The Kingdom of Spain declares that if, in accordance with the provisions of Article 19 of the Convention, the United Kingdom should decide to extend the applicability of the Convention to Gibraltar, such application will be without prejudice to the position of Spain in the dispute with the United Kingdom concerning sovereignty over the isthmus.

The original of these minutes, as signed by the Conference President and Secretary, will be deposited, along with the Convention, with the Irish Government.

A copy of these minutes will be sent to the signatory States.

*C*

# Standard form for determining the state responsible for examining an application for asylum

PHOTO

PERSONAL PARTICULARS

1. Family name ____________
   Maiden name ____________

2. Other names ____________

3. Does the applicant use/has he/she used other names? ☐ Yes ☐ No

   What are/were they? ____________

4. Date of birth ____________

5. Place of birth ____________
   District/region ____________
   Country ____________

6. Nationality (ies) (indicate all)
   (a) current ____________
   (b) previous ____________
   (c) none/stateless ____________

7. Sex ☐ Male ☐ Female

8. Name of father ____________________

9. Name of mother ____________________

10. Marital status ☐ Single ☐ Married
☐ Widowed ☐ Divorced

11. Current address ____________________
____________________

12. Last address in home country/country of origin ____________________

13. *Spouse*: family name, maiden name, other names, sex, date of birth, place of birth, place of residence (If the spouse is seeking asylum, a separate form should be completed)

____________________________________________

14. *Children*: family name, other names, sex, date and place of birth, place of residence (indicate all children; a separate form should be completed for children over 16 years of age if asylum is sought)

(a) ____________________________________________
(b) ____________________________________________
(c) ____________________________________________
(d) ____________________________________________
(e) ____________________________________________

15. *Place and date of the application for asylum in the country of residence* ____________________
____________________

IDENTITY PAPERS

16. National passport ☐ Yes ☐ No
Number ____________________
Issued on ____________________
By ____________________
Valid until ____________________

17. Document replacing passport ☐ Yes ☐ No
    - Number ____________
    - Issued on ____________
    - By ____________
    - Valid until ____________

18. Other document ☐ Yes ☐ No
    - Number ____________
    - Issued on ____________
    - By ____________
    - Valid until ____________

19. In the absence of documents: ☐ Departed without documents
    ☐ Lost ☐ Stolen

    (specify whether they may have contained a valid visa or residence permit and, if so, indicate the issuing authority and date of issue as well as the period of validity)

    when, where? ____________

    ☐ Other reasons
    which? ____________

RESIDENCE DOCUMENTS/VISAS

20. Does the asylum applicant possess a residence document/visa for the country of residence?

    ☐ Yes ☐ No
    ☐ Residence permit
    ☐ Visa
    ☐ Transit visa

    - Type ____________
    - Issued on ____________
    - By ____________
    - Valid until ____________

| | |
|---|---|
| 21. Does the asylum applicant possess a residence document/visa for another EEC Member State? | ☐ Yes ☐ No |
| Which State? | __________ |
| | ☐ Residence Permit<br>☐ Visa<br>☐ Transit visa |
| Type | __________ |
| Issued on | __________ |
| By | __________ |
| Valid until | __________ |
| 22. Does the asylum applicant possess a residence document/visa for a non-member country? | ☐ Yes ☐ No |
| Which country? | __________ |
| Type | ☐ Residence ☐ Visa<br>☐ Transit visa |
| Issued on | __________ |
| By | __________ |
| Valid until | __________ |

TRAVEL ROUTES

| | |
|---|---|
| 23. Departure from home country/country of origin on | __________ |
| by | ☐ Public transport (what form?)<br>__________<br>☐ Own vehicle<br>☐ Other means (how?)<br>__________ |

| | |
|---|---|
| 24. Entry in country of residence on | ____________________ |
| by | ☐ Public transport (what form?) |
| | ____________________ |
| | ☐ Own vehicle |
| | ☐ Other means (how?) |
| | ____________________ |
| Border post | ____________________ |
| Avoided border controls at | ____________________ |
| 25. Did the asylum applicant enter via another Member State? | |
| Which was the first Member State entered? | ____________________ |
| | ____________________ |
| by | ☐ Public transport (what form?) |
| | ____________________ |
| | ☐ Own vehicle |
| | ☐ Other means (how?) |
| | ____________________ |
| Border post | ____________________ |
| Avoided border controls at | ____________________ |
| 26. Travel route from point of departure from home country/country of origin to point of entry into country of residence | ____________________<br>____________________<br>____________________<br>____________________ |

INTERIM RESIDENCE IN OTHER COUNTRIES

| | |
|---|---|
| 27. Residence in another country after leaving home country/country of origin | ☐ Yes ☐ No |
| from – to | ________________ |
| in | ________________ |
| Residence was | ☐ Authorized<br>☐ Unauthorized |
| Period of validity of permit | ________________ |
| Purpose of residence | ________________ |
| Address in non-member country | ________________<br><br>________________ |
| Accommodation in | ☐ Hotel/boarding house<br>☐ Dwelling<br>☐ Camp<br>☐ Other (Where ) |
| Was the asylum applicant in danger of being expelled? | ☐ Yes ☐ No |
| To which country? | ________________ |
| Why? | ________________ |
| Reasons for continuing journey | ________________ |

PREVIOUS ASYLUM PROCEDURES

| | |
|---|---|
| 28. Has the asylum applicant ever previously applied for asylum or recognition of refugee status in the country of residence or in another country? | ☐ Yes ☐ No |

When and where? ____________________

Was any decision taken on the application? ☐ Yes ☐ Not known
☐ Yes, refused
☐ Yes, deferred
☐ Yes, accepted

When was the decision taken? ____________________

DETAILS OF PREVIOUS RESIDENCE IN THE EUROPEAN COMMUNITY

29. Has the asylum applicant ever previously resided in the country of residence or in another EEC Member State? ☐ Yes ☐ No

If so, details of periods and places of residence ____________________
____________________

PARTICULARS OF FAMILY MEMBERS LIVING IN EEC MEMBER STATES OR IN A THIRD COUNTRY

30. Relatives in:
(a) the country of residence or another EEC Member State ☐ Yes ☐ No
(b) another country which is not the country of origin ☐ Yes ☐ No

Where there are such family members, specify their names, addresses, family relationship and status (e.g. refugee, employed person, etc.) ____________________
____________________

| | |
|---|---|
| 31. Has the asylum applicant been ordered to leave the territory of the country of residence or another Member State? | ☐ Yes ☐ No |
| If so, via what places and routes is the journey to be effected? | ______________________<br>______________________<br>______________________ |
| When and by what authority was that decision taken? | ______________________<br>______________________ |

Member State providing the information:

- Ministry/Ministries competent for determining responsibility for examining the asylum application in the Member State providing the information:

- Department:

- Contact in case of need:

  Name:
  Position:
  Address:
  Telephone no:
  Fax no:

# Proof or intelligence used by the Member State providing the information

[The contents of the Annex will be specified once the inventory of the means of proof used by each Member State has been drawn up.]

# *D*

# Implementation of the Convention determining the state responsible for examining applications for asylum lodged in one of the Member States of the European Communities[7]

*(a) Lodging an application for asylum*

An application for asylum is regarded as having been lodged from the moment the authorities of the Member State concerned have something in writing to that effect: either a form submitted by the applicant or an official statement drawn up by the authorities.

In the event of a non-written application, the period between the statement of intent and the drawing up of the official statement must be as short as possible.

*(b) Reaction to a request that charge be taken of an applicant (Article 11(4))*

Any response to a request that charge be taken of an applicant with a view to staying the effect of the provision concerning the three-month deadline laid down in Article 11(4) must take the form of a written communication.

*(c) Exceeding the eight-day period (Article 13(1)(b))*

1. Article 13(1)(b) of the Convention makes it very clear that Member States are obliged to respond to the application to take back the applicant within eight days of its submission.

---

7 Lisbon, 11 and 12 June 1992.

2. In exceptional cases Member States may, within this eight-day period, give a provisional reply indicating the period within which they will give their final reply. The latter period must be as short as possible and may not in any circumstances exceed a period of one month from the date on which the provisional reply was sent.

3. If the Member State fails to react

   – within the eight-day period mentioned in paragraph 1
   – within the one-month period mentioned in paragraph 2

   it will be considered to have agreed to take back the applicant for asylum.

*(d) Measures to expel an alien*
*(Article 10(4))*

The Member State responsible for examining the application must provide proof that the alien has actually been expelled from the territory of the Twelve. These are therefore concrete acts of expulsion, involving an obligation relating to the result rather than the intention, which in effect means that in such cases the Member State must provide written proof.

*(e) Departure from the territory of the Member States*
*(second subparagraph of Article 3(7))*

Where the applicant for asylum himself produces proof that he has left the territory of the Member States for more than three months, the second Member State may examine the veracity of that information, if necessary by contacting the third country in which the applicant claims to have been living during that time.

In other cases the Member State in which the initial application was lodged has to provide proof, in particular of the date of departure and the destination of the applicant for asylum. In the context of co-operation between Member States, the Member State in which the second application was lodged is best able to give the date on which the applicant for asylum returned to that State.

*(f) Exceptions where the applicant for asylum is in possession of a visa (Article 5(2))*

Article 5(2) provides for three separate cases where the responsibility of a Member State for examining the application for asylum ceases even if the applicant for asylum is in possession of a valid visa issued by that State.

The first exception (subparagraph (a)) concerns a visa issued on the authorization of another Member State; as a general rule, exceptional cases should be proved by the Member States which invoked them.

The second exception (subparagraph (b)) arises from a situation in which an application is lodged in a State in which the applicant is not subject to a visa requirement; there will be no need to seek proof since the problem is not relevant.

The third exception (subparagraph (c)) refers to the case of an applicant for asylum who is in possession of a transit visa issued on the written authorization of the diplomatic or consular authorities of the Member State of final destination; the question of burden of proof is irrelevant here since there is prior written confirmation that the transit visa was issued.

*(g) Determination of Member State responsibility in the event of an applicant possessing several residence permits or visas (Article 5(3)(c))*

In the event of an applicant possessing several residence permits or visas issued by different Member States (in particular in the case of Article 5(3)(c)), proof for the purposes of determining the Member State responsible does not arise in that the relevant information appears in the entry document produced by the applicant for asylum.

*(h) Determining the periods of time and actual entry into a State (first and second subparagraphs of Article 5(4))*

As regards the determination of the periods of time, the date of expiry of residence permits or visas is calculated from the date on which the application for asylum is lodged.

In addition, checking the expiry date of residence permits and visas is not necessary if such information appears on the applicant for asylum's papers.

As regard proof that the individual has *actually* entered a Member State, the following situations should be distinguished:

- if an applicant for asylum has actually entered a Member State, proof can be provided through information supplied by the Member State in which the application for asylum was lodged;

- if an applicant for asylum has not left the territory of the Member States, the Member State which issued the expired residence permit or visa has to provide the information required;

- if an applicant for asylum himself supplies the information that he has left the territory of the Member States, the second Member State in which an application was lodged will check the truth of the statements.

These rules apply in respect of actual entry in both subparagraphs of paragraph 4.

*(i) Irregular crossing of the border into a Member State (Article 6)*

Proof that an applicant for asylum has irregularly crossed the border into a Member State (Article 6(1)) must be examined after the list of means of proof has been drawn up.

Proof of a Member State ceasing to be responsible when the applicant for asylum lodges his application in the Member State where he has lived for six months (second paragraph of Article 6) must be supplied in the first instance by the Member State invoking this exception in a spirit of collaboration between the Member States concerned.

If the applicant for asylum claims that he has lived in a Member State for more than six months, it is for that Member State to check the truth of those statements. The initial information to the other Member State concerned will in any case have to include statements made by the applicant for asylum which may be used subsequently as counter-indications.

*(j) Formal rules for approval by the applicant for asylum*

Approval must be given in writing.

As a general rule an applicant must give his approval when the Member State claiming responsibility for examining the application submitted a request for exchange of information.

The applicant for asylum must in any case know to what information he is giving his agreement.

The approval concerns the reasons given by the applicant for asylum and, where applicable, the reasons for the decision taken with regard to the applicant.

*(k) Notification procedures*

The system of exchange of information must also include data on notification procedures. Accordingly, notification must be given:

- as quickly as possible in writing;
- using the technical means available;
- to the Member States claiming responsibility for examining an application for asylum.

Such notification, which will avoid the possibility of two procedures being initiated simultaneously in two Member States, applies in respect of Article 3(4) and Article 12.

Where implementation of a decision determining responsibility is suspended, such suspension is notified so that the Member States are kept fully informed. It is extremely useful for the Member State where the application was lodged to be informed that an applicant for asylum is not being transferred pending a decision in his case by the second Member State.

*E*

# Calculation of periods of time in the context of the Dublin Convention

When determining the periods referred to in the Convention, Saturdays, Sundays and public holidays should be included in the calculations.

With particular reference to the periods mentioned in Article 11(4) and Article 13(1)(b):

- the period is to begin on the day following receipt of the application;

- the final day of the period is the deadline for sending the reply.

# *F*

## Conclusions on the transfer of asylum applicants under the provisions of the Dublin Convention[8]

*Introduction*

1. Articles 3(7), 4, 5, 6, 7 and 8 set down the circumstances in which responsibility for examining an asylum *application* made in one Member State (hereafter described as the "first" Member State) shall be assumed by another Member State (hereafter described as the "second" Member State).

2. Article 10(1)(a), (c), (d) and (e), Article 11(5) and Article 13(1)(b) set down obligations and timescales regarding the transfer or taking back of the *applicant* from the first to the second Member State. The term "transfer" is used below both for the case of taking charge and taking back.

3. The arrangements for transfer of the applicant are set out below.

*Notification of the applicant*

4. The first Member State will inform the applicant as soon as possible when a request is made under the provisions of Articles 11 and 13 to another Member State to take charge of or to take back an applicant and of the outcome of this request. Where responsibility is transferred to the second Member State, this notification shall inform the applicant of his liability for transfer to the second Member State under the provisions of Article 11(5) and Article 13(1)(b) and subject to any relevant national laws and procedures. Where the transfer is to be made as described in paragraph 5(a)(b) below, this notification will include information about the time and place to which the applicant should report on arrival in the second Member State.

---

8 London, 30 November and 1 December 1992.

*Transfer of the applicant*

5. When it is agreed that the applicant should be transferred to the second Member State, the first Member State will be under an obligation to ensure as far as possible that the applicant does not evade the transfer. To this effect, the first Member State will determine, in the light of the circumstances of each case, and in accordance with national laws and procedures, how transfer of the applicant should take place. This may be either:

   (a) on his own initiative, with a deadline being set;

   (b) under escort, the applicant to be accompanied by an official of the first Member State.

6. Transfer of the applicant will be considered completed when either the applicant has reported to the authorities of the second Member State specified in the notification given to him, when the transfer is under 5(a) above; or when he has been received by the competent authorities of the second Member State, when transfer is under 5(b) above.

7. When transfer is under 5(a) above, the second Member State will inform the first as soon as possible after the transfer is completed, or where the applicant has failed to report within the specified deadline.

*Deadlines for transfer*

8. Articles 11(5) and 13(1)(b) provide that transfer and taking back must be concluded within one month of the second Member State accepting responsibility for examining the asylum application. Member States will make every effort to conform with these deadlines where transfer is made under paragraph 5(b) above.

9. If a transfer has been arranged under the provisions of 5(a) above, but is not completed because of the failure of the applicant to co-operate, the second Member State may begin examination of the application on the information available to it on the expiry of the deadlines specified in Articles 11.5 and 13.1(b). If the application is refused, the second

Member State will remain liable for taking back the applicant under the provisions of Article 10(1)(e) unless the provisions of Article 10(2), (3) or (4) apply.

| *Countries* | *Date of Signature* | *Date of Ratification* |
|---|---|---|
| Belgium | 15 June 1990 | 10.08.95 |
| Denmark | 13 June 1991 | 13.06.91 |
| France | 15 June 1990 | 10.05.94 |
| Germany, Federal Republic of | 15 June 1990 | 21.09.94 |
| Greece | 15 June 1990 | 03.12.92 |
| Ireland | 15 June 1990 | |
| Italy | 15 June 1990 | 26.02.93 |
| Luxembourg | 15 June 1990 | 22.07.93 |
| Netherlands | 15 June 1990 | |
| Portugal | 15 June 1990 | 19.02.93 |
| Spain | 15 June 1990 | 10.04.95 |
| United Kingdom | 15 June 1990 | 01.07.92 |

COMMENTARY

*Status:* International convention only open to states which are members of the European Communities (Article 21).

*Entry into force:* This can only occur 3 months after deposit of all the instruments of accession (Article 22). The Convention has yet to be ratified by all Member States.

*International obligations engaged:*

(1) The Universal Declaration of Human Rights 1948
(2) The UN Convention Relating to the Status of Refugees 1951 and Protocol 1967
(3) The European Convention on Human Rights 1950
(4) European Convention for the Protection of Individuals with regard to the Automatic Processing of Personal Data 1981

(5) The Treaties of the European Communities

*Summary:*

The Convention is designed to regulate responsibility among the Member States of the European Union for the examination of asylum applications made anywhere within the territory. It contains detailed provisions for the determination of the state responsible in the following order of priority:-

(i) where a spouse or child under 18 has been recognised as a refugee under the UN Convention relating to the Status of Refugees 1951 and Protocol 1967 ("UN Convention") by one state, that state shall be responsible for the application. In respect of child applicants under 18 the presence of a parent recognised as a refugee determines responsibility;

(ii) if the applicant holds a valid residence permit, the issuing state is responsible;

(iii) if the applicant holds a valid visa, the issuing state is responsible (subject to a proviso in respect of transit visas);

(iv) if the applicant holds more than one residence permit or visa, the state which issued the longest in duration or the last to be issued is responsible;

(v) if the applicant arrived irregularly, the state through which he or she first entered the territory of the Union subject to a six month time limit;

(vi) if no other Member State can be designated, then the one where the application is made must determine it.

Consequential articles regulating the movement of the person, data exchange etc are included. Dispute resolution is by way of a committee of government representatives and only available to contracting parties.

*Comments: The Beginning of an European Union Asylum Policy*

The Dublin Convention was signed in June 1990 but has yet to be ratified by all the Member States. Although the Convention itself is open only to Member States of the European Union it is likely that parallel conventions may be entered into once the Convention itself is in force extending the scope of the system of responsibility for asylum applicants to other countries. Provision for this is made in Declaration I of the minutes of the conference at which the Convention was signed. The mechanism for such extension is by way of "appropriate" instruments containing commitments identical to those laid down in the Convention. The Declaration specifies no requirement that such states must be signatories of the UN Convention. However as the purpose is stated to be "to ensure that applicants for asylum are given adequate guarantees" this must be a minimum requirement.

*Relationship with the European Communities Treaties*

The Convention is an intergovernmental product of the Single European Act 1987 which created the objective within the European Union of an area without internal frontiers for the movement of persons.[9] The internal market was to come into full operation on 1 January 1993, article 7A EC. It has yet to do so, as has the Dublin Convention yet to come into force. The Member States realised that the creation of an internal market without internal frontiers for persons would mean that not only their own citizens but also citizens of third countries (hereinafter third country nationals) would be able to move freely without border checks across the Union.[10] One question which immediately followed was what to do about asylum applicants – the Member States foresaw the possibility of an asylum applicant refused refugee status in one EC state, who on account of the lack of internal borders, could easily arrive in another Member State and make a further asylum application. In theory, an asylum applicant could have had (at that time) 12 opportunities to have his or her asylum application considered.

---

9 The Palma Document, point B.

10 Commission Answer, 9 December 1993 OJ No C 349/2 of 9.12.94.

Additionally, problems had arisen and continued to arise in respect of asylum applicants who fail to apply for asylum in the first EC state to which they arrive but travel on to a state where they prefer to apply for asylum. Asylum applicants tend not to be particularly welcome in any EC state and this type of movement had resulted in the preferred state to which the asylum applicant applies trying to send the asylum applicant back to the previously traversed state to make the application there. The first state equally unwilling to take responsibility for the asylum applicant not infrequently bounces the applicant back to the preferred country. This problem, which has been called refugees in orbit, needed to be addressed and the context of the internal market focused the attention of the Member States on the issue.

The European Agreement on the Transfer of Responsibility for Refugees concluded in the context of the Council of Europe[11] was not adequate for the purposes of a frontier free Europe. First, the difficult question of the status of a person claiming to be a refugee but not yet recognised as such is not addressed in the Agreement.[12] Secondly, the Agreement presupposes that the relevant states can easily identify the date of admission of the refugee to the territory for the purposes of the Agreement.[13]

The Dublin Convention was the first serious attempt of the Member States to coordinate asylum policy within the European Union and the choice of the instrument was decisive. The Member States have subsequently tended to avoid the use of the convention format for further work they have done in respect of coordinating immigration and asylum policy.[14] It is unclear why this is the case, though the delays involved in securing ratification of conventions may be an important factor. Additionally, conflict between Member States regarding dispute resolution mechanisms has hindered

11 European Agreement on Transfer of Responsibility for Refugees 1980.

12 Article 1, European Agreement on Transfer of Responsibility for Refugees 1980.

13 Article 3 ibid.

14 The draft Convention on the crossing of the external borders of Member States, the European Extradition Convention and the Europol Convention are exceptions to the rule.

conclusion of two other conventions currently under consideration.[15] While some states recognise the need to give competence to the European Court of Justice to resolve disputes relating to conventions which are intrinsically tied to the Union other states are adamantly opposed to any increase of jurisdiction of that Court.

This question, however, does not arise in respect of the Dublin Convention as it contains no provision relating to the Court of Justice but rather includes an administrative dispute resolution mechanism. Notwithstanding regular statements of intent to ratify the Convention made at every Council summit following signature, five years later this process still has not been completed.

It is indeed curious that the Convention has been drafted by reference to the European Communities treaties but distinct from the Community structures. Although the dispute resolution mechanism, a Committee, is to be chaired by the Presidency of the European Council, the European Commission may participate in its discussions and the Secretariat of the Committee and the working parties are to be provided by the General Secretariat of the Council, there is no clear demarcation of the Convention's relationship with the Community. This lack of clarity may result from a lack of consensus on how best to coordinate immigration and asylum policy in the Union. Some states challenged the competence of the European Community over immigration policy in what they consider to be unjustified interference in matters of their national sovereignty when called upon to advise the Commission on legislative changes in the field in 1985.[16] From this challenge it was very clear that a number of the larger Member States did not wish at that time to coordinate their activities in the field within the context of Community law. Nonetheless, considering the nature of the internal market it is difficult to see how the movement of asylum applicants could or can be regulated outside the scheme of Community law.

---

15 The draft Convention on the crossing of the external borders of Member States has still not been signed. The Europol Convention has now been signed subject to a 12 month delay to sort out conflict between the Members States on whether jurisdiction to the European Court of Justice should be allowed.

16 *Germany, France, Netherlands Denmark and UK v Commission* [1987] ECR 3203.

The Treaty on European Union, by Title VI, Cooperation in the Fields of Justice and Home Affairs, has given some legitimacy to the process of coordination of immigration and asylum policy bringing what was previously intergovernmental activity with no legal basis whatsoever into the framework of the European Union though outside the control of the Court of Justice and effective participation of the Parliament. Whether this is resulting in actual progress is unclear.

*Relationship with the UN Convention*

The UN Convention defines a refugee as a person who, owing to a well-founded fear of being persecuted for reasons of race, religion, nationality, membership of a particular social group or political opinion, is outside the country of his or her nationality and is unable or, owing to such fear, unwilling to avail him or herself of the protection of that country, or who, not having a nationality and being outside the country of his or her former habitual residence, and is unable or, owing to such fear unwilling to return to it.[17]

The UN Convention itself provides no guidance on determination procedures for the purposes of recognising a person as refugee. However, the UNHCR Handbook on Procedures produced at the request of the Executive Committee of the High Commissioner's programme[18] provides guidance under General Principles. The Handbook states that a person is a refugee within the meaning of the Convention as soon as he or she fulfils the criteria of the definition. This would necessarily occur prior to the time at which his or her refugee status is formally determined. Recognition of refugee status does not therefore make a person a refugee but declares him to be one. He or she does not become a refugee because of recognition but is recognised because he or she is a refugee.[19]

17 Article 1A UN Convention.

18 UNHCR Handbook on Procedures and Criteria for Determining Refugee Status, Geneva 1988.

19 UNHCR Handbook paragraph 28.

The declaratory nature of recognition of refugee status under the UN Convention means that all asylum applicants must be protected as refugees until such time as they are recognised or refused recognition.

The underlying principle of the Dublin Convention – to provide a framework within which Member States can ensure that an asylum applicant gets only one opportunity to have an asylum application considered – presumes that the same asylum application made in any Member State will result in the same outcome. It further presupposes that the application of the underlying obligation not to return a refugee to the country where he or she fears persecution as contained in the UN Convention[20] gives rise to similar forms of protection across the Union. Neither of these presumptions were true at the time the Dublin Convention was signed and it is still not the case. However, the adoption of a Resolution on minimum guarantees for asylum procedures in March 1995 is, at least, a critical first step in this direction.[21]

| ASYLUM APPLICATIONS BY CITIZENSHIP: TURKEY | | | | |
|---|---|---|---|---|
| | *Belgium* | *Germany* | *France* | *UK* |
| 1991 | 1083 | 23877 | 9915 | 2111 |
| 1992 | 838 | 28327 | 1770 | 5635 |
| RECOGNITION RATE AS REFUGEES BY CITIZENSHIP: TURKEY | | | | |
| | *Belgium* | *Germany* | *France* | *UK* |
| 1991 | 9 | 1669 | 2243 | 90 |
| 1992 | 31 | 1351 | 1391 | 460 |

*Source: Migration Statistics 1994, EUROSTAT*

As guardians of the UN Convention the fundamental concern of the Office of the UN Commissioner for Refugees (UNHCR) is to ensure that refugees receive protection. As signatory states to the UN Convention the Member States are obliged to cooperate with the UNHCR.[22]

20 Article 33 UN Convention relating to the status of Refugees.

21 See document 18 infra.

22 Article 35 UN Convention.

"Since sovereign States have the primary responsibility for respecting and ensuring the fundamental rights of everyone within their territory and subject to their jurisdiction,[23] effective protection of refugees requires action by the Government of the country of asylum on their behalf. UNHCR's role in providing *international* protection consequently, and above all, involves ensuring that Governments take the necessary action to protect all refugees within their territory, as well as persons seeking admission at their borders who may be refugees. The fulfilment of the High Commissioner's international protection function requires the active cooperation and support of the Government concerned, and the support of the other countries of the international community".[24]

The current High Commissioner is deeply concerned about developments in Europe and their impact on refugees. She recently wrote:-

"Now the political and strategic value of granting asylum seems to have diminished while the financial costs have rocketed. Western Europe has experienced much more than a decade of slow and uneven growth, punctuated by intermittent recession. Unemployment has continue to grow even in periods of modest recovery. Foreigners and racial minorities have been made scapegoats for the hard times, with refugees and asylum-seekers sometimes singled out for racist attack."

"Deeply troubled governments have resolved to get a grip on immigration and asylum systems that are perceived to be out of control. In so doing they have implemented a number of measures designed to deter or deflect the entry of illegal immigrants."

"Regrettably, many of the measures have an impact on the admission of refugees as well as illegal immigrants. There are no built-in mechanisms for distinguishing between the two, and few safeguards have yet been es-

---

23 Article 2(1) International Covenant on Civil and Political Rights 1966.

24 Note on International Protection to the UN General Assembly, UNHCR, 7 September 1994.

tablished to make sure that people who are in need of protection can slip through the newly erected barriers to entry".[25]

This concern of the High Commissioner regarding the commitment of European states to the protection system of the Convention does not appear misplaced. The European Commissioner responsible for asylum issues, Mrs A Gradin recently stated:

"The efforts to create a system to combat illegal migration between Member States must be pursued with much more imagination. Trafficking in people is economically rewarding, just as the trafficking in drugs. The economic potential in this area is in fact enormous. This is particularly true for the trafficking of women. If prosecutors do not take this phenomenon more seriously, we are heading for a new slave market. Cooperation with governments in sending and transit countries must be strengthened and much better targeted."

"Another prerequisite in the development of a system which would entail a higher degree of solidarity between European States is cases of mass arrivals of asylum-seekers. The Dublin Convention is a necessary but rather modest beginning. The boat exodus from Albania, the mass arrivals of the Bosnians and the ticking migration bombs in the East and in the South tell us that pressures indeed will be growing".[26]

In view of the clear signals of the European Commissioner's speech, the UN High Commissioner is well justified to have concerns about the commitment in Europe to protection of persons fleeing persecution. First, Mrs Gradin ignores the fact that the traffic in people to Europe has become profitable because of the obstacles to access which the European governments have put in place as referred to by the UN High Commissioner. This is leaving aside the legal nicety of differentiating between traffickers to which Mrs Gradin refers pejoratively and Europe's commercial airlines whose business is the movement of persons in and out of Europe.

---

25 Refugees and Asylum-seekers: A Challenge to European Immigration Policy, Sadako Ogata in Towards a European Immigration Policy, October 1993.

26 Speech by Mrs Anita Gradin, at the European Forum "Justice and Home Affairs in the European Union" Bonn, 11 May 1995.

Secondly, it must inevitably be the case that those persons whose very lives and physical integrity are at risk by persecution from their governments or forces their government does not or cannot control are the exact same persons with the highest incentive and need of traffickers, the only persons who offer the hope of getting them out of danger in their own countries and through the increasingly impenetrable walls of Europe.

Thirdly, the feared creation of a new slave market in Europe is the result of the inadequacy of the immigration and asylum policies of the European states to provide protection and security to people who fear worse treatment if returned to their home state. It would seem logical that, unless people are afraid of even worse treatment in their country of origin, they will not submit to slavery conditions in Europe as the only alternative to returning to their country of origin.

Fourthly, the juxtaposition of the spectre of mass arrivals of persons fearing persecution to the need for strengthening exclusionary measures highlights exactly the fear of the UN High Commissioner that the European states no longer place a high value on granting asylum. In other words, keeping people at risk of persecution in their own state out of Europe may be easier than protecting them from persecution by admitting them to Europe.

The fact that asylum applicants do not necessarily seek asylum in proportionate numbers to the resident population of each Member State is not the fault of asylum applicants. However, the principle of the Dublin Convention that in the absence of certain countervailing factors such as the presence of close family members recognised as refugees in one state, the state responsible for allowing the asylum applicant into the internal market should determine the asylum application, would appear to be designed to push the obligation of determination on to states bordering third countries and those with large international air and sea ports. The Dublin system began as a logical development of the internal market. The difficulty is that what might have been a solution providing some security to asylum applicants in an integrated Europe is now being used to move asylum-seekers out of the Union altogether.[27]

---

27 See commentary on Documents 2, 3 and 4 infra.

*Consequences of the Dublin System for Neighbouring Countries*

Article 3(5) of the Convention provides that any Member State retains the right pursuant to its national laws, to send an applicant for asylum to a third state, subject to compliance with the UN Convention. This means that the undertaking of article 3(1) of the Member States to examine the application of any alien who applies for asylum at the border or in their territory is qualified. The examination may be limited to the issue of whether there is a third country outside the Union which can be held responsible for a substantive consideration of the application.

This conclusion as regards the relationship between article 3 (1) and (5) is reinforced by article 1(b) and (d) of the Resolution on a harmonised approach to questions concerning host third countries[28] which states that the principle of returning an asylum applicant to a third country for consideration of his or her asylum application is to be applied to all asylum applicants (article 1(b)). Further, only if the asylum applicant cannot in practice be sent to a host third country shall the provisions of the Dublin Convention apply (article 1(d)). This position is strengthened in article 1(b) of the Resolution on manifestly unfounded applications for asylum.[29] Here the Member States have specified "without prejudice to the Dublin Convention, all applications for asylum may not be subject to a determination by a Member State of refugee status under the terms of the Geneva Convention on the Status of Refugees when it falls within the provisions of the Resolution on host third countries ..." (article 1(b)).

Accordingly the Member States have through the Resolutions adopted after the signing of the Dublin Convention actively pursued and developed what may be termed a third country policy on asylum applications. The purpose of this policy would appear to be to reduce the administrative burden of determining asylum applications and the attendant costs of caring for asylum applicants during the process by moving applicants as quickly as possible from the territory of the Union to some other third state.

---

28 Document 3 infra.
29 Document 2 infra.

These costs are not inconsiderable. It has been estimated that in 1992 OECD countries incurred costs of US$6 billion in social assistance and processing costs for non-valid asylum cases.[30] However in the same year between 30-40% of asylum applicants were accepted either as refugees or on humanitarian grounds even though they did not, in the opinion of the determining state fully meet the UN Convention definition.[31] With such costs at stake, the consequence of moving this burden to third states, mainly on the Union's borders is likely to have two results: –

(1) a reduction in the level of protection for asylum-seekers as the resources available in third states will inevitably be more limited (the only bordering countries of the Union which have comparable resources to the EU are Norway and Switzerland);

(2) the risk of undermining the concerted efforts of the Union and other international bodies to enshrine human rights protection in all policies of third states. If the EU states with their wealth, administrative and legal resources are unwilling to protect asylum applicants how much less so will be, for instance, the Central and Eastern European Countries which are only beginning to develop human rights' infrastructures. This problem was highlighted in the Commission's most recent communication on Immigration and Asylum 1994.[32]

The Dublin system has now resulted in a specimen readmission agreement adopted by the EC ministers and designed specifically for this situation.[33] The complexity of readmission agreements already adopted is astonishing. In five years a web of agreements across Central and Eastern Europe has developed which could result in an asylum applicant being in orbit for months while he or she is bounced from country to country in accordance with these agreements.[34] The fate of persons who are so passed back across

---

30 Responses to Western Europe's Immigration Crisis, N Hopkinson, Wilton Park Paper 14, March 1994 p.4.

31 Responses to Western Europe's Immigration Crisis, ibid.

32 Commission Communication to the Council and the European Parliament on Immigration and Asylum February 1994; COM(94)23.

33 Document 17 infra.

34 France Terre d'Asile chart in ECRE Report of Biannual General Meeting 1992.

a chain of responsibility is uncertain. The European Council on Refugees and Exiles (ECRE) is currently undertaking a study to find out what is happening in practice. However, it may be that in fact these agreements are, in the end, of limited value and that increasing numbers of asylum applicants arrive with no knowledge of what countries they have passed through (for instance when travelling overland in the back of vehicles) or apply for asylum with no papers evidencing the nature of their arrival in the state.

*Data Protection*

In view of the sensitivity of information regarding asylum applicants and the fact that any leak of information regarding their identity to the country where they fear persecution may result in the persecution of family members left behind, data protection provisions in the Convention are most noticeable by their weakness. Provision is made for extensive information on individuals to be passed from one state to another including the grounds on which a person has applied for asylum.[35]

In particular, on request, Member States are *obliged* to communicate:-

(i) personal details of the applicant and family members which includes full names and any former names, nicknames or pseudonyms, present and former nationality and date and place of birth;

(ii) identity and travel papers including references, validity, date of issue, issuing authority, place of issue;

(iii) other information necessary for establishing the identity of the applicant. No guidance is given on what this could include;

(iv) place where the application was lodged;

(v) residence permits or visas issued by a Member State (but not of any other state);

---

35 Article 15.

(vi) place where the application was lodged;

(vii) date of any previous asylum application lodged, date of present application and the stage in the proceedings and decision taken, if any.

However, a Member State is *permitted* to transmit other information in accordance with the Convention, specifically, the grounds of the application and if applicable the grounds of any decision reached. This information may only be transmitted with the consent of the applicant.[36]

The Convention states that the exchange must take place between designated authorities but places no limit on the authorities which may be designated. Information exchanged may only be communicated to authorities, including courts and tribunals, entrusted with determining the state responsible for examining the application, examining the application and implementing obligations arising under the Convention. However, this list covers almost anyone coming into contact with the asylum applicant including, potentially, airline staff who may be implementing obligations under the Convention.

No limit is placed on the length of time data may be kept ("a period not exceeding that necessary for the ends for which it was exchanged") nor does the sending state retain any control over the future use of the data. Although the asylum applicant has a right to receive, on request, the information exchanged concerning him or her as long as it remains available,[37] it is no specific state's responsibility to ensure that the applicant knows of the right or is provided with the information. Although the person has a right to have information corrected or erased if he or she can establish that it is inaccurate or should not have been forwarded, there is no specific mechanism regulating how this is to occur or which state is responsible.

Information is to receive the same protection as is given to similar information in the receiving state.[38] So, where information is passed from a state with highly developed data protection legislation to one with little such

36 Article 15(4).
37 Article 15(7).
38 Article 15(10).

legislation, the lesser protection applies. Whether this would be in conformity with national data protection legislation is a matter of speculation. Whether and under what circumstances such data might be recorded in one of the new data systems designed to establish exclusion lists for the Union remains unknown.[39]

In a Declaration to the minutes of the Conference which adopted the Convention, the Member States declared that "it is not necessary to supplement Article 15(6) of the Convention by providing that only data which have been applied for in a permitted manner and in good faith may be communicated because they consider this goes without saying and that therefore no provisions to cover the point are needed".[40] However they agreed to submit an annual report of the Committee established under the Convention on the checks which they carry out on the appropriate use of the information referred to in Article 15.

The minimum requirements in respect of automatically processed data already accepted by the Member States are contained in the Convention of Data Protection concluded under the auspices of the Council of Europe.[41]

The issue of compliance with the Convention on Data Protection is side stepped in Article 15(12) of the Dublin Convention. By virtue of this provision only where a Member State wishes to computerise information it either must or may communicate is it subject to a requirement to comply with the principles of the Convention on Data Protection. There is no obligation to comply with the Convention itself or indeed to ratify the Convention. However the Member State is obliged to entrust an appropriate national body with the independent monitoring of the processing and use of data forwarded under the Dublin Convention. There is no mechanism to regulate the obligation to transmit data with the requirement, in cases of computerisation, to respect the principles of the Convention on Data Protection.

---

39 for instance the Schengen Information System and the European Information System.

40 Declaration 15 June 1990 supra.

41 European Convention for the Protection of individuals with regard to the Processing of Personal Data 1981.

The "common core" data protection principles provide that personal data shall be:

- obtained and processed fairly and lawfully;
- stored for specified and legitimate purposes and not used in a way incompatible with those purposes;
- adequate, relevant and not excessive in relation to the purposes for which they are stored;
- accurate and, where necessary, kept up to date;
- preserved in a form which permits identification of the data subject for no longer than is required for the purpose for which those data are stored.

"Sensitive" personal data (data revealing racial origins, political opinions or religious or other beliefs, as well as personal data concerning health or sexual life, or criminal convictions) must be subject to special safeguards. Appropriate measures must be taken to ensure that personal data is protected against accidental or unauthorised destruction or accidental loss as well as against unauthorised access, alteration or dissemination.

Everyone has the right to know of the existence of databases containing personal data and the right:

- to obtain confirmation whether data on him or her are contained in any such database;
- to be given a copy of such data on request;
- to be able to challenge the data and to obtain rectification or erasure of the data if appropriate; and
- to have a remedy against any refusal to grant these rights.

The Convention on Data Protection forms part of the system of protection of private life under Article 8 European Convention on Human Rights (ECHR). However, the exclusion of any reference to the European Convention on Human Rights means it is unclear the extent to which its protection may by extension apply to the Dublin Convention.

Although the Convention on Data Protection applies specifically to automatically processed data the principle of protection designed to give effect to Article 8 ECHR should apply to all data whether automatically processed or not. The UK government understands that in Belgium, Denmark, France, Germany, the Netherlands and Portugal the legislation applies to manual files as well as to computer files, either as a general rule or in some specific circumstances. It is also understood that in Belgium, Denmark, France, Germany, Italy, Portugal and Spain the data subject's consent is required in relation to the use of either all data or of sensitive data.

"In the context of Community law, the European Court of Justice has consistently held that fundamental rights are an integral part of the general principles of law the observance of which the Court ensures, in accordance with constitutional traditions common to the Member States, and the international treaties on which the Member States have collaborated or of which they are signatories".[42]

In view of the formulation by the European Court of Justice of its obligation to ensure respect for human rights in the field of application of Community law it is likely that due regard would be given to the requirements of the Convention on Data Protection if not independently then as a clarification of the right to protection of private life contained in Article 8 ECHR.

The current state of ratification of the Convention on Data Protection is as follows:–

42 *Hoechst v Commission* [1989] ECR.

Convention for the protection of individuals with regard to automatic processing of personal data 1981

| *Member States* | *date of signature* | *date of ratification or accession* | *date of entry into force* | *R : reservation D : declarations T : territorial* |
|---|---|---|---|---|
| Austria | 28/01/81 | 30/03/88 | 01/07/88 | D |
| Belgium | 07/05/82 | 28/05/93 | 01/09/93 | D |
| Denmark | 28/01/81 | 23/10/89 | 01/02/90 | D/T |
| Finland | 10/04/91 | 02/12/91 | 01/04/92 | D |
| France | 28/01/81 | 24/03/83 | 01/10/85 | D |
| Germany | 28/01/81 | 19/06/85 | 01/10/85 | D |
| Greece | 17/02/83 | 25/04/90 | 01/08/90 | D |
| Ireland | 18/12/86 | 10/02/88 | 01/06/88 | D |
| Italy | 02/02/83 | 24/08/93 | 01/12/93 | D |
| Luxembourg | 28/01/81 | 02/09/93 | 01/01/94 | D |
| Netherlands | 20/01/88 | 31/01/84 | 01/10/85 | D |
| Portugal | 14/05/81 | 29/09/82 | 01/10/85 | D/T |
| Spain | 28/01/82 | 26/08/87 | 01/12/87 | |
| Sweden | 28/01/81 | | | |
| UK | 14/05/81 | | | |

However, as the European Court of Justice has no competence over the interpretation of the Dublin Convention it remains unclear how the applicant may obtain redress in a manner uniform across the Member States and consistence with Community law. The full consequences of this lack of competence are considered in greater depth below.

In those Member States where international agreements have direct force of law and take precedence over national provisions, the mandatory obligation of Article 15 of the Dublin Convention to provide information about an asylum applicant to another state would prevail over national data protection legislation. If the receiving state has not ratified the Convention on Data Protection and has a lower standard of national protection then the asylum applicant may indeed be at risk.

Further, where the sending Member State has implemented the Convention on Data Protection, the mandatory nature of Article 15 of the Dublin Convention may result in a conflict between international obligations where the state requesting the data has inadequate legislation.

For the applicant, this means that protection in respect of sensitive data about him or her which may be disseminated arises from national law in the state where he or she applies for asylum and possibly, after the exhaustion of all domestic remedies, protection could be sought from the European Court of Human Rights.

The problematic nature of data protection under the Dublin Convention is exacerbated by the corresponding provision in the specimen readmission agreement.[43] At Article 8 of the specimen agreement, the wording of the data transmission obligation differs from that of the Dublin Convention. Here it states that insofar as personal data have to be communicated in order to implement the agreement, such information may concern only the following:-

(1) the particulars of the person to be transferred and, where necessary, of the members of the person's family (surname, given name, any previous names, nicknames or pseudonyms, aliases, data and place of birth, sex, current and any previous nationality);

(2) passport, identity card and other identity or travel documents and laissez-passer (number, period of validity, date of issue, issuing authority place of issue etc);

(3) other details needed to identify the persons to be transferred;

(4) stopping places and itineraries;

(5) residence permits or visas issued by one of the contracting parties;

(6) where the applicant is in transit to yet another destination, the place where the asylum application was submitted, the date of submission of any previous asylum application, the date of submission of the present

43 Document 18 infra.

asylum application, the present stage of the procedure and the content of any decision taken.

A comparison with the Dublin Convention is as follows:–

| NO | DUBLIN CONVENTION | READMISSION AGREEMENT |
|---|---|---|
| 1 | Obligation:-<br>Each Member State shall communicate to any Member State that so requests... | Insofar as personal data have to be communicated in order to implement this agreement... |
| 2 | Data:-<br>(a) Personal details of the applicant, and, where appropriate, the members of his family (full name - where appropriate, former name, nick names or pseudonyms, nationality present and former date and place of birth) | The particulars of the person to be transferred and, where necessary, of the members of the person's family (surname, given name, any previous names, nicknames or pseudonyms, aliases, date and place of birth, sex, current and any previous nationality) |
| | (b) Identity and travel papers (references, validity, date of issue, issuing authority, place of issue etc) | Passport, identity card and other identity and travel documents and laissez-passer (number, period of validity, date of issue, issuing authority, place of issue etc) |
| | (c) Other information necessary for establishing the identity of the applicant | Other details needed to identify the persons to be transferred |
| | (d) places of residence and routes travelled | stopping places and itineraries |
| | (e) Residence permits or visas issued by a Member State | Residence permits or visas issued by one of the Contracting parties |

| NO | DUBLIN CONVENTION | READMISSION AGREEMENT |
|---|---|---|
| | (f) Place where the application was lodged; date any previous application for asylum was lodged; the date the present application was lodged, the stage reached in the proceedings and the decision taken, if any | [in transit cases] the place where the asylum application was submitted and the date of submission of any previous asylum application; the date of submission of the present asylum application; the present stage of the procedure and the content of any decision taken |
| | (g) Reference (restricted) to Convention on Data Protection; no reference to European Convention on Human Rights | No reference to any data protection convention but reference to European Convention on Human Rights |

A comparison of the obligations on data exchange in the two documents reveals that although they are broadly similar they differ in wording and in the nature of the obligation. Whereas there is a clear obligation under the Dublin Convention to supply information on request and no control to ensure its use is within the ambit of the request, under the specimen readmission agreement the obligation is worded in terms of implementation of the agreement. Therefore a party could refuse to provide information requested if it established that the information was not necessary to the implementation of the agreement. In the specimen readmission agreement none of the protection measures contained in the Dublin Convention, such as access for the applicant to information exist.

Further, under the Dublin Convention there is no protection to ensure that information provided in accordance with Article 15 will not be transmitted on, for instance, under a readmission agreement. Although Article 15(5) provides the information exchanged may be used for one of three purposes:–

(i) determining the Member State responsible
(ii) examining the application; or
(iii) implementing any obligation arising under the Convention

the definition of examining an applicant in Article 1(1)(d) includes all the measures for examination, decisions or ruling given by the competent authorities. However from Article 3(1) and (5) it appears that an examination may include one limited to determining a third state to which the applicant may be sent.

*The European Convention on Human Rights – Protection from Torture; Family life and Effective Remedies*

The Dublin Convention makes no reference to the European Convention on Human Rights 1951 though the Member States' obligations under the ECHR are directly engaged. These obligations apply in respect of all persons within the jurisdiction of the Member States.[44] All Member States have ratified the Convention. Three fundamental obligations under the ECHR are involved:-

(i) The right to protection from torture, inhuman and degrading treatment or punishment, including return to a country where this is likely to occur (Article 3 ECHR):

The European Court of Human Rights has held that this obligation extends to the return of a person to a country where he or she is likely to suffer torture, inhuman or degrading treatment or punishment.[45]

Unlike the UN Convention, the obligation is not limited to those circumstances where the person either fears persecution within the meaning of the UN Convention or the fear is based on the UN Convention grounds of race, religion, nationality, membership of a social group or political opinion. According to some commentators, increasingly, Member States are accepting asylum applicants on grounds related to the European Convention on Human Rights rather than the UN Convention.[46] This means the Article 3 ECHR protection is more widely granted than recognition as a refugee. The exclusion of this protection from the Dublin Convention is odd in such circumstances.

---

44 Article 1 ECHR.

45 *Soering v UK* [1989] Ser A 162.

46 Responses to Western Europe's Immigration Crisis, N Hopkinson, Wilton Park Paper 84 March 1994.

Article 1 of the Dublin Convention defines an application for asylum as "a request whereby an alien seeks from a Member State protection under the Geneva Convention by claiming refugee status within the meaning of Article 1 of the Geneva Convention as amended by the New York Protocol". Accordingly it does not apply to Member States' obligations arising from an application for protection under Article 3 ECHR.

(ii) The right to family life: – Article 8 ECHR requires the respect for private and family life. No interference by a public authority is justified unless within the exceptions contained in the Article itself. The limitation on transfer of responsibility for consideration of an application on family grounds to those circumstances where a spouse or child under 18 is recognised as a refugee under the UN Convention in the other Member State does not necessarily satisfy this requirement.

First, this means that where a close family member has been allowed to stay in another Member State on the basis of Article 3 ECHR there is no obligation to transfer responsibility so that the family can be reunited. Where people flee civil war and ethnic cleansing they may be unable to travel together or even to the same country. However each family member will be required to apply for and have his or her application considered in the Member State through which he or she first passed unless one of them wins the "asylum lottery" and is recognised as a refugee. As there is no provision for cross-recognition of refugee status among the Member States let alone cross-recognition of humanitarian status under Article 3 ECHR not only may the family be divided during the determination procedure but at the end of it there is no certainty of family reunion. In many Member States the substantive processing of asylum applications takes at least six months and not infrequently can stretch to six years. There is no provision even for visits on humanitarian grounds to another state until the application has been determined.

Secondly, the category of family members is so restricted that it only covers the minimum recommendation of the UN Handbook.[47] The Handbook recommends that the principle of family unity in practice be extended to aged parents, and other dependents if they are living in the same household. For the purposes of Article 8 ECHR no specific limitation on the definition of the family applies. It is a matter of fact whether family life exists and deserves protection. However the European Court of Human Rights has held that family life entitled to protection under the Convention cannot be qualified by an obligation to cohabit,[48] nor is it limited to children under 18.[49]

(iii) Right to an effective remedy: Article 13 ECHR. In the determination of the rights contained in the Convention all persons are entitled to an effective remedy. Therefore in so far as the Dublin Convention contains no provision relating to remedies for applicants (and in respect of data transmission, this obligation also applies to protection of the person's private life), it is problematic.

For example, where an asylum applicant is to be transferred from a state where there are effective remedies in respect of the application to one where the remedies are not effective, perhaps because they do not exist, or have no suspensive effect which prevents return to the country of persecution while the remedy is being pursued or because they are so inaccessible financially or judicially as to be ineffective, the obligation under Article 13 ECHR is engaged.

It is an inadequate response to suggest that there is no need to build into a convention as specific as the Dublin Convention human rights guarantees as any person aggrieved may seek redress from the European Court of Human Rights. In the context of European Community, the European Court of Justice has held that the European Convention on Human Rights has a particular significance within

47 Handbook on procedures and criteria for determining Refugee Status, UNHCR 1988 para 185.

48 *Berrehab v Netherlands* [1988] Ser. A No. 138.

49 *Djeroud v France* [1991] Ser. A No 191-B; j*Mustaquim v Belgium* [1991] Ser A. No 193.

Community law. Measures incompatible with respect for human rights which have been recognised and guaranteed shall not be permitted in Community law.[50] Accordingly it would be most irregular if supporting instruments to Community law such as the Dublin Convention were not bound by the same high standard of human rights protection.

*The Right to Apply to Asylum – Universal Declaration of Human Rights*

Article 14 of the Universal Declaration on Human Rights provides that everyone has the right to seek and to enjoy in other countries asylum from persecution. This right to seek asylum does not imply necessarily the right to receive it, that is a matter for the sovereign state to which the request has been addressed. However it does imply that the request will be properly and thoroughly considered. Further, in accordance with Article 10 of the Declaration, everyone is entitled to full equality and to a fair and public hearing by an independent and impartial tribunal in the determination of his or her rights and obligations.

The right to seek asylum may therefore be a right to which the obligation of a fair and public hearing applies. The right to seek asylum must necessarily engage the state to which the application is made. In order for the right to have meaning it presupposes respect by the state. In other words, the obligation to provide a thorough and proper consideration and a fair and public hearing must attach to the state where the application is submitted.

If, for the purposes of the Declaration, the European Union wishes to be treated as the equivalent of a single state so that the obligations contained in the Articles 14 and 10 apply to the whole territory then this should have been made clear in the Dublin Convention. Instead Article 3(3) of the Convention states that the application shall be examined by [the state] in accordance with its national laws and its international obligations. As the Universal Declaration is an international obligation of all the Member States as well as a commitment by those states to the international community and

50 *ERT* [1991] ECR I-2925.

therefore not susceptible to unilateral variation it is difficult to see how the Member States can fulfil both obligations simultaneously.

Under the Dublin Convention an asylum applicant who has submitted an application in one state, may after living in that state for six months (or possibly more depending on the length of the Dublin Convention procedures) find he or she is about to be removed to another state without a substantive determination of the application. The lack of a guarantee in the Dublin Convention to a fair and public hearing means that under the system of transfer of the responsibility the sending state cannot be confident that its obligations are fully assumed by the receiving state.

*Procedural Guarantees and Judicial Control*

While the Dublin Convention regulates in fairly minute detail the fate of individuals, it makes no provision for judicial protection of the individual. The interpretation of the Convention vis-a-vis individuals is left to national courts (in the event that under national constitutional arrangements such courts have jurisdiction), and as regards the parties, to the Committee established under the Convention (article 18) comprised of a representative of each state. The Committee is competent to examine, at the request of one or more Member States, any question of a general nature concerning the application or interpretation of the Convention.

The individual has no guarantee of access to a dispute resolution mechanism. However the individual has the greatest incentive and concern to ensure that his or her expectation of protection in accordance with the UN Convention is observed. In a number of Member States, international agreements do not, by virtue of ratification alone, become part of domestic law (eg UK, Germany) . In others they can (eg Netherlands, France). No steps are required to transform the Convention into domestic law in those states where it does not have such status. Indeed, already alternative national implementing legislation has been adopted in some states such as the UK. Therefore the asylum applicant seeking to challenge his or her transfer to another state in accordance with the Dublin Convention assuming that a national court has jurisdiction may not be able to rely on the wording of the Convention itself as this may or may not be part of national law in the sending or receiving state.

The inadequacy of procedural safeguards for the individual under the Dublin Convention is particularly striking in comparison with international agreements on extradition where the movement of alleged criminals is at stake. In extradition matters the rule of speciality applies whereby a person may only be extradited to face charges which were the subject of the extradition order. Re-extradition to a third-state is prohibited in Europe without the consent of the first state.[51]

Even in the field of extradition where the Member States have recently agreed a new convention to apply among themselves to simplify extradition procedures, the guarantees for the individual are enormous in comparison with those of the Dublin Convention.[52] The simplified procedure is subject to the person's consent to its application which consent can only be given before a competent judicial authority of the requested state.[53]

Further, in the new extradition convention, should the surrender of the person to the requesting state not take place within 20 days of the date on which the extradition decision was notified under the convention's rules, the person shall be released from custody.[54] In comparison with an asylum applicant, whose only offence has been to seek protection from persecution in his or her country of origin, the alleged criminal under extradition proceedings has substantially better protection in the law.

From the asylum perspective, if comparable provisions applied, then the applicant could only be returned lawfully to another state with his or her consent, and a guarantee that the asylum application would be considered in accordance with the UN Convention together with the procedural guarantees of Article 13 ECHR to an effective remedy. Further, the consent of the original sending state would be required before the applicant could be removed to a third state. Before such further consent could be given the

51 Article 15 European Convention on Extradition 1957.

52 Convention on simplified extradition procedure between the Member States of the European Union, 10 March 1995, OJ C 78/1 of 30.3.95.

53 Articles 6 and 7, Convention on simplified extradition procedure between the Member States of the European Union.

54 Article 11 Convention on simplified extradition procedure between the Member States of the European Union.

original state would need to be satisfied the third state would comply with all the obligations and safeguards of the first and second states. There is no such protection for asylum applicants under the Dublin Convention.

However this problem is not limited to the individual who finds him or herself between two states. Article 12 provides that the state in which the application for asylum has been made shall determine which state is responsible for the examination of the application. If it appears the person has travelled through a number of Member States it is for the state where the application is made to choose to which state to return the applicant. In view of the enthusiasm exhibited by most Member States to any increase in numbers of asylum applicants, it is very difficult to see how this can work effectively in practice. The lack of a proper interpretative mechanism is an invitation for the Convention to result in great suspicion on the part of a state receiving a demand that it receive an asylum applicant currently in another Member State on the basis of the Convention. How is the state to satisfy itself that the sending state has made a proper consideration of the relevant evidence as to which state to seek to burden?

The only dispute resolution mechanism is a Committee of representatives of the contracting parties (Article 18). It must resolve questions of a general nature concerning the application or interpretation of the Convention (Article 18(2)). It must decide by unanimity except in respect of suspension of the Convention under Article 17(2). The chair of the Committee revolves every six months with the presidency of the European Union. This is a very weak dispute resolution mechanism. It is certainly of no assistance to an aggrieved individual who has no access to it in any event.

With such a quasi legal dispute mechanism it is difficult to see how the recital that the Member States are determined in keeping with their humanitarian traditions to guarantee adequate protection to refugees in accordance with the UN Convention can be honoured. The Member States recently agreed a Resolution on minimum guarantees for the asylum procedure.[55] However, this Resolution does not resolve many issues of judicial control of asylum determination systems. Further, without a supra

55 See document 19.

national judicial mechanism it seems inevitable that national interpretation of the Convention obligations will vary.

Indeed, upon UK ratification of the Dublin Convention a member of Parliament asked the relevant minister what steps had been taken to ensure that there were effective judicial remedies with suspensive effect in all Member States for asylum applicants who might be returned from one Member State to another under the Convention. The minister answered:-

"None. Those are matters which are the responsibility of individual Member States according to their national laws and procedures...".[56]

56 Hansard, 15 July 1992 written answer 331 and 332.

# 2 RESOLUTION on manifestly unfounded applications for asylum[57]

MINISTERS OF THE Member States OF THE EUROPEAN COMMUNITIES responsible for Immigration, meeting in London on 30 November and 1 December 1992, agreed:

HAVING REGARD to the objective, fixed by the European Council meeting in Strasbourg in December 1989, of the harmonization of their asylum policies and the work programme agreed at the meeting at Maastricht in December 1991;

DETERMINED, in keeping with their common humanitarian tradition, to guarantee adequate protection to refugees in accordance with the terms of the Geneva Convention of 28 July 1951, as amended by the New York Protocol of 31 January 1967, relating to the Status of Refugees;

NOTING that Member States may, in accordance with national legislation, allow the exceptional stay of aliens for other compelling reasons outside the terms of the 1951 Geneva Convention;

REAFFIRMING their commitment to the Dublin Convention of 15 June 1990, which guarantees that all asylum applicants at the border or on the territory of a Member State will have their claim for asylum examined and sets out rules for determining which Member State will be responsible for that examination;

AWARE that a rising number of applicants for asylum in the Member States are not in genuine need of protection within the Member States within the

57 SN 4822/92 WGI 1282 AS 146.

terms of the Geneva Convention, and concerned that such manifestly unfounded applications overload asylum determination procedures, delay the recognition of refugees in genuine need of protection and jeopardize the integrity of the institution of asylum;

INSPIRED by Conclusion No. 30 of the Executive Committee of the United Nations High Commissioner for Refugees;

CONVINCED that their asylum policies should give no encouragement to the misuse of asylum procedures;

MAKE THE FOLLOWING RESOLUTION:

*Manifestly unfounded applications*

1. (a) An application for asylum shall be regarded as manifestly unfounded because it clearly raises no substantive issue under the Geneva Convention and New York Protocol for one of the following reasons:

   - there is clearly no substance to the applicant's claim to fear persecution in his own country (paragraphs 6 to 8); or
   - the claim is based on deliberate deception or is an abuse of asylum procedures (paragraphs 9 and 10).

   (b) Furthermore, without prejudice to the Dublin Convention, an application for asylum may not be subject to determination by a Member State of refugee status under the terms of the Geneva Convention on the Status of Refugees when it falls within the provisions of the Resolution on host third countries adopted by Immigration Ministers meeting in London on 30 November and 1 December 1992.

2. Member States may include within an accelerated procedure (where it exists or is introduced), which need not include full examination at every level of the procedure, those applications which fall within the terms of paragraph 1, although an application need not be included within such procedures if there are national policies providing for its acceptance on

other grounds. Members States may also operate admissibility procedures under which applications may be rejected very quickly on objective grounds.

3. Member States will aim to reach initial decisions on applications which fall within the terms of paragraph 1 as soon as possible and at the latest within one month and to complete any appeal or review procedures as soon as possible. Appeal or review procedures may be more simplified than those generally available in the case of other rejected asylum applications.

4. A decision to refuse an asylum application which falls within the terms of paragraph 1 will be taken by a competent authority at the appropriate level fully qualified in asylum or refugee matters. Amongst other procedural guarantees the applicant should be given the opportunity for a personal interview with a qualified official empowered under national law before any final decision is taken.

5. Without prejudice to the provisions of the Dublin Convention, where an application is refused under the terms of paragraph 1 the Member State concerned will ensure that the applicant leaves Community territory, unless he is given permission to enter or remain on other grounds.

*No substance to claim to fear persecution*

6. Member States may consider under the provisions of paragraph 2 above all applications the terms of which raise no question of refugee status within the terms of the Geneva Convention. This may be because:

   (a) the grounds of the application are outside the scope of the Geneva Convention: the applicant does not invoke fear of persecution based on his belonging to a race, a religion, a nationality, a social group, or on his political opinions, but reasons such as the search for a job or better living conditions;

   (b) the application is totally lacking in substance: the applicant provides no indication that he would be exposed to fear of persecution or his story contains no circumstantial or personal details;

(c) the application is manifestly lacking in any credibility: his story is inconsistent, contradictory or fundamentally improbable.

7. Member States may consider under the provisions of paragraph 2 above an application for asylum from claimed persecution which is clearly limited to a specific geographical area where effective protection is readily available for that individual in another part of his own country to which it would be reasonable to expect him to go, in accordance with Article 33.1 of the Geneva Convention. When necessary, the Member States will consult each other in the appropriate framework, taking account of information received from UNHCR, on situations which might allow, subject to an individual examination, the application of this paragraph.

8. It is open to an individual Member State to decide in accordance with the conclusions of Immigration Ministers of 1 December 1992 that a country is one in which there is in general terms no serious risk of persecution. In deciding whether a country is one in which there is no serious risk of persecution, the Member States will take into account the elements which are set out in the aforementioned conclusions of Ministers. Member States have the goal to reach common assessment of certain countries that are of particular interest in this context. The Member State will nevertheless consider the individual claims of all applicants from such countries and any specific indications presented by the applicant which might outweigh a general presumption. In the absence of such indications, the application may be considered under the provisions of paragraph 2 above.

*Deliberate deception or abuse of asylum procedures*

9. Member States may consider under the provisions of paragraph 2 above all applications which are clearly based on deliberate deceit or are an abuse of asylum procedures. Member States may consider under accelerated procedures all cases in which the applicant has, without reasonable explanation:

(a) based his application on a false identity or on forged or counterfeit documents which he has maintained are genuine when questioned about them;

(b) deliberately made false representations about his claim, either orally or in writing, after applying for asylum;

(c) in bad faith destroyed, damaged or disposed of any passport, other document or ticket relevant to his claim, either in order to establish a false identity for the purpose of his asylum application or to make the consideration of his application more difficult;

(d) deliberately failed to reveal that he has previously lodged an application in one or more countries, particularly when false identities are used;

(e) having had ample earlier opportunity to submit an asylum application submitted the application in order to forestall an impending expulsion measure;

(f) flagrantly failed to comply with substantive obligations imposed by national rules relating to asylum procedures;

(g) submitted an application in one of the Member States, having had his application previously rejected in another country following an examination comprising adequate procedural guarantees and in accordance with the Geneva Convention on the Status of Refugees. To this effect, contacts between Member States and third countries would, when necessary, be made through UNHCR.

Member States will consult in the appropriate framework when it seems that new situations occur which may justify the implementation of accelerated procedures to them.

10. The factors listed in paragraph 9 are clear indications of bad faith and justify consideration of a case under the procedures described in paragraph 2 above in the absence of a satisfactory explanation for the applicant's behaviour. But they cannot in themselves outweigh a

well-founded fear of persecution under Article 1 of the Geneva Convention and none of them carries any greater weight than any other.

*Other cases to which accelerated procedures may apply*

11. This Resolution does not affect national provisions of Member States for considering under accelerated procedures, where they exist, other cases where an urgent resolution of the claim is necessary, if it is established that the applicant has committed a serious offence in the territory of the Member States, if a case manifestly falls within the situations mentioned in Article 1.F of the 1951 Geneva Convention, or for serious reasons of public security, even where the cases are not manifestly unfounded in accordance with paragraph 1.

*Further action*

12. Ministers agreed to seek to ensure that their national laws are adapted, if need be, to incorporate the principles of this Resolution as soon as possible, at the latest by 1 January 1995. Member States will from time to time, in cooperation with the Commission and in consultation with UNHCR, review the operation of these procedures and consider whether any additional measures are necessary.

*Commentary*

*Status:* Resolution adopted by Ministers of the EC Member States outside the ambit of the European Communities Treaties.

*Entry into force:* The Ministers undertook to ensure that national legislation would be adopted to reflect the Resolution's principles as soon as possible and at the latest by 1 January 1995 (Article 12).

*International obligations engaged:*

(1) Universal Declaration of Human Rights 1948
(2) UN Convention relating to the Status of Refugees 1951 and Protocol 1967

(3) UN Convention against Torture and other Cruel, Inhuman or Degrading Treatment or Punishment 1984
(4) European Convention on Human Rights 1950
(5) European Communities Treaties
(6) The Dublin Convention 1990

*Summary:*

The Resolution seeks to harmonise law and practice in the Member States relating to the rapid rejection of asylum applications in certain categories as defined by it. The preamble contains a commitment to adequate protection for refugees under the UN Convention; acknowledges that persons may need protection though not coming within the terms of the UN Convention; takes note of the "rising number of asylum applicants not in genuine need of protection" and determines that asylum procedures should give no encouragement to abuse.

Member States *must* introduce into their asylum laws the concept of a manifestly unfounded application. They *may* introduce accelerated procedures for applications alleged to be manifestly unfounded or "operate admissibility procedures under which applications may be rejected very quickly on objective grounds". Member States must reach initial decisions on applications deemed to be manifestly unfounded within one month of application and appeal or review procedures may be abridged. The only procedural guarantee is that the applicant *should* be given the opportunity of a personal interview with a qualified official before a final decision is taken.

There are two grounds on which an application may be determined manifestly unfounded:

(i) There is clearly no substance to the applicant's claim to fear persecution in his or her own country.

This category includes: anyone whose fear of persecution is not based on a Convention ground; there is no indication that the person will be exposed to a fear of persecution; the applicant's story is inconsistent, contradictory *or* fundamentally improbable and therefore lacks credibility; the applicant could seek effective protection in another part of his or her own country and it would be reasonable to expect the applicant to go there; the country is one fulfilling the criteria of the Conclusions on countries in which there is generally no serious risk of persecution.[58]

(ii) The claim is based on deliberate deception *or* is an abuse of asylum procedures.

An application may fall into this category where an applicant: maintains that false documents or a false identity are genuine and bases the application upon them; deliberately makes false representations about the claim after applying; in bad faith destroys, damages or disposes of any passport, other document or ticket either to establish a false identity for the asylum application or to hinder the consideration of the application; deliberately conceals that an asylum application has been made in another country; makes an application to forestall an impending expulsion measure when there were earlier opportunities to make the application; flagrantly fails to comply with substantive obligations relating to the asylum procedures; where an application made in another country has been rejected after an examination "comprising adequate procedural guarantees" and in accordance with the UN Convention.

Where there is an allegation of deliberate deception or abuse of asylum procedures, none of the factors can outweigh a well-founded fear of persecution for a Convention reason.

*Comments: The Concept of a Crisis*

According to the preamble of the Resolution, its objective, as fixed by the European Council meeting in Strasbourg 1989 is the harmonisation of asylum policies among the Member States. The Member States confirm their commitment to guaranteeing adequate protection to refugees within the terms of the UN Convention, and re-affirm their commitment under the Dublin Convention. The Resolution is stated to be inspired by Conclusion number 30 of the Executive Committee of UNHCR.

---

58 Document 4 infra

However, an asylum application may not be the subject to determination by a Member State of refugee status if it falls within the provisions of the Resolution or host third countries.[59] The consequences of this prohibition will be considered in commentary on document 3 infra.

Although the preamble notes that there are compelling reasons outside the UN Convention for allowing persons to remain no specific reference is made to the Member States obligations under Article 3 of the European Convention on Human Rights which prohibits return of a person to a country where he fears torture or inhuman or degrading treatment.[60] No reference is made to Article 3 of the UN Convention against Torture[61] which similarly prohibits the return of a person to a country where he or she may suffer torture.

The rationale for the Resolution may, in fact, be found in recital 6 which spells out in terms the fears of the Member States that their asylum determination procedures are becoming overloaded with applications which are ultimately unsuccessful.

In order to address this concern the Member States agreed in the Resolution to implement screening procedures designed to identify at an early stage applications which, because they are not expected to succeed, are subject to more limited procedural guarantees. Any agreement which has these particular objectives must find satisfactory solutions to two problems:

(i) The definitions applied to exclude persons from the full determination procedure must be sufficiently precise and clear so that the chance of error is limited as far as possible.

---

59 Document 3 infra

60 *Soering v UK* [1989] Ser. A 162

61 UN Convention against Torture and other Cruel, Inhuman or Degrading Treatment or Punishment 1984

(ii) As error is an inevitable part of any administrative system which involves substantial numbers of persons adequate procedural safeguards must be included.[62]

What is at stake in this Resolution is one of the most basic principles contained in virtually all international human rights instruments, the protection of the individual from torture, inhuman or degrading treatment or punishment.[63]

In view of the determination expressed by the Member States to guarantee adequate protection to refugees in accordance with the UN Convention and in particular the fact that the Resolution was inspired by Conclusion number 30 of the Executive Committee of UNHCR, the Resolution it may be useful to examine it against those obligations.

Conclusion 30 of the Executive Committee of UNHCR (1983) is entitled the Problem of Manifestly Unfounded or Abusive Applications for Refugee Status or Asylum. The Conclusion was endorsed by the Executive Committee of the High Commissioner's programme upon the recommendation of the sub-committee of the whole on international protection of refugees. This includes some of the Member States. Accordingly, Conclusion number 30 may be an expression of the political will of at least some of the Member States in 1983.

According to sub-paragraph (d) of the Conclusion, the Executive Committee considered "that national procedures for the determination of refugee status may usefully include special provision for dealing in an expeditious manner with applications which are considered to be so obviously without foundation and not to merit full examination at every level of the procedure. Such applications may be termed either 'clearly abusive' or 'manifestly unfounded' and are to be defined as those which are clearly fraudulent or not related

62 Amnesty International, Europe: Harmonization of Asylum policy. Accelerated procedures for "manifestly unfounded" asylum claims and the "safe country" concept (November 1992).

63 See Article 3 Universal Declaration of Human Rights, Article 7 ICCPR, UN Convention against Torture and other Cruel, Inhuman or Degrading Treatment or Punishment, Article 3 ECHR etc.

to the criteria for the granting of refugee status laid down in the 1951 United Nations Convention relating to the Status of Refugees nor to any other criteria justifying the grant of asylum."

Accordingly it is against this threshold which the Resolution must be tested. This threshold was approved by the Executive Committee itself and therefore constitutes the sanctioned interpretation of the UN Convention.

The Conclusion permits asylum applications to be termed as manifestly unfounded in two circumstances:

(i) Those which are clearly fraudulent;

(ii) Those not related to the criteria for the granting of refugee status in accordance with the UN Convention or any other criteria justifying the grant of asylum.

It should first be noted that in the Resolution no reference is made to "any other criteria justifying the grant of asylum". Article 1(a) states that an application shall be regarded as manifestly unfounded "because it clearly raises no substantive issue" under the UN Convention alone. To the extent that the Resolution fails to provide for "any other criteria justifying the grant of asylum" which must be taken as a reference to obligations under other international instruments it fails the comparison test with the UN Conclusion.

*Clearly Fraudulent Applications*

In the Resolution, articles 9 and 10 contain the specific provisions relating to this head which in the Resolution is defined as "deliberate deception or abuse of asylum procedures". The question which arises here is whether the criteria and definition of articles 9 and 10 satisfy the high standard of "clearly fraudulent" applications as referred to in the UN Conclusion.

Article 9(a) provides that where an applicant has, without reasonable explanation, based his application on false identity or on forged or counterfeit documents which he has maintained are genuine when questioned about them the application will fall within this category. There is no limitation as to the circumstances in which the asylum applicant has maintained the documents are genuine, for instance, at the border when the applicant is still in sight of officials from the country where he fears persecution or, when he or she has not yet had an opportunity to make an asylum application and is questioned about identity by officials on the street.

Article 9(b) provides that an application shall be determined as manifestly unfounded where the applicant has, without reasonable explanation, deliberately made false representations about his claim, either orally or in writing, after applying for asylum. This is not limited to false representations about the claim in the context of the consideration of the asylum application. Accordingly, false representations about the claim in order to obtain housing or in attempting to seek a visa from a third state could trigger this ground.

Article 9(c) provides that the application shall be considered manifestly unfounded if, without reasonable explanation, the applicant has, in bad faith destroyed, damaged or disposed of any passports, other document or ticket relevant to his claim, either in order to establish a false identity for the purpose of his asylum application or to make the consideration of his application more difficult.

It is not difficult to imagine circumstances where an asylum applicant faced with being returned to another Member State where he or she knows no-one and has no family from a State where he or she has managed to arrive and has family whose asylum applications are currently under consideration would be tempted to conceal details of his or her route. This could then be classified as destruction of documents in order to make the consideration of the application more difficult and render the person liable to a manifestly unfounded determination. However it would in no way reflect on the genuineness or otherwise of the substance of the application though the act of destruction of documents could be interpreted as in bad faith as its purpose would be to prevent the Member State removing the applicant to another state.

Article 9(e) provides for a manifestly unfounded determination where the person having had ample earlier opportunity to submit an asylum application, submitted the application in order to forestall an impending expulsion measure. This requires a subjective determination "ample earlier opportunity" and intentionality on the part of the applicant as to the purpose of the application.

Under the UN Convention Article 33, the obligation of states to protect asylum applicants from persecution by permitting them to remain in the state arises most specifically at the point of expulsion or return.[64] Accordingly, the fact that an application has been made in order to forestall an impending expulsion measure is exactly the situation where the Member State's obligations under Article 33 of the UN Convention are fully engaged. This is particularly so where the person has been lawfully in the state in some other capacity, for example, student or visitor. Article 31 of the UN Convention provides that Member States shall not impose penalties on refugees on account of their illegal entry or presence provided they present themselves without delay to the authorities and show good cause for their illegal entry or presence. However the requirement to apply for asylum at an early stage is only placed on persons illegally on the territory not on persons in other situations. In view of what may be a rapidly evolving situation in the country where the person fears persecution it would clearly create greater administrative confusion and over-burdening if persons who come to the Member States as students or visitors are required immediately to apply for asylum even though they may not yet be sure that the situation in their country of origin will not improve over the period of their studies or visit to such an extent that they might be able to return before the end of their stay. It is difficult to see how such a requirement comes within the ambit of "clearly fraudulent" of UN Conclusion 30.

Article 9(f) provides that an application may be deemed manifestly unfounded if the applicant has flagrantly failed to comply with substantive obligations imposed by national rules relating to asylum procedures. This requires a subjective determination of "flagrant" and a categorisation of "substantive obligations" imposed by national rules. In view of the increasing complexity of asylum determination procedures involving lengthy and detailed forms to be completed and overlapping time limits, coupled with the fact that many asylum applicants will have little or no grasp of the language of their host country, it is very difficult to see how this requirement meets the threshold of "clearly fraudulent" of UN Conclusion 30.

64 Article 33 UN Convention

Article 9(g) states that an application shall be manifestly unfounded if the asylum applicant has submitted an application in one of the Member States, having had an application previously rejected in another country following an examination comprising adequate procedural guarantees. No time limit or qualification is made to this ground. Accordingly, the asylum applicant has no protection against a manifestly unfounded determination even though the circumstances in the country of origin have changed since the application was rejected elsewhere. Again it is difficult to see how this comes within the "clearly fraudulent" criteria of UN Conclusion 30.

Article 10 introduces a subjective element in that the factors listed in Article 9 are clear indications of bad faith in the absence of a satisfactory explanation for the applicant's behaviour. The Article goes on to state that the factors cannot outweigh a well founded fear of persecution under Article 1 of the UN Convention but gives no guidance on how there is to be a comparison without a full determination of the application. Further, it is stated that no one factor carries greater weight than any other. Accordingly, a deliberately made false representation about the claim to the authorities determining it carries no greater weight than the failure to comply with a substantive obligation under national rules.

The wide variety of factors contained in Article 9 and the loose drafting cannot be compensated by the weak "let out" provision of Article 10.

*Not Related to the Criteria for Granting Refugee Status or any other Criteria Justifying the Granting of Asylum*

In so far as the Resolution deals with this aspect, it does so in articles 6 to 8. The first difficulty which arises in respect of the formulation of these provisions is that no reference is made to any other criteria justifying the grant of asylum. Accordingly, in the Resolution the Member States have excluded all provisions relating to other international instruments to which they are parties and which require the grant of asylum. On this ground alone the Resolution is deeply flawed in comparison with UN Conclusion 30. In the Resolution, the Member States appear to be hermetically sealing the UN Convention from their other international human rights obligations in such way as to negate the inter-connection of international instruments on human rights. This would seem to be a particularly unfortunate approach which if taken to its logical conclusion would require an asylum applicant to have the application considered in accordance with each and every international obligation relating to protection of integrity of the person consecutively. In view of the way in which the procedural rights including appeal rights are framed, presumably this would give rise to consecutive judicial remedies. This would be contrary to the intention of the Member States to speed up the decision making process.

Article 6(a) provides that an application shall be manifestly unfounded if the grounds of the application are outside the scope of the UN Convention, that is to say the applicant does not invoke a fear of persecution based on his or her membership of a race, religion, nationality, social group or his or her political opinion, but on reasons such as the search for a job or better living conditions. This formulation obviates one of the most difficult determinations in asylum law where an asylum applicant indicates that on the basis of persecution for one of the Convention grounds he or she is unable to work or unable to secure adequate living conditions which itself may constitute persecution. The classic cold war example of this was the situation of a highly qualified person in a Communist regime who because of his or her dissident views was not permitted to exercise a profession or given access to housing etc. In the past Member States have willingly granted refugee status to such persons. Accordingly, reasons such as the search for a better job or better living conditions may indeed be intricately connected with a well founded fear of persecution on a Convention ground.

Article 6(b) provides that a claim may be determined manifestly unfounded where it is totally lacking in substance: the applicant provides no indication that he would be exposed to fear of persecution or his story contains no circumstantial or personal details. It is unclear what the Member States are seeking to achieve by this formulation of words. On the one hand through other acts taken intergovernmentally[65] the Member States have sought to pool their information about countries which give rise to persecution, to place the burden of establishing a claim entirely on the applicant as regards circumstantial details when the Member States should and have been preparing themselves jointly to be in a position to make common assessments does

65 For instance the Decision establishing a Clearing House, Document 5 infra

not seem valid. Although the burden of proof lies clearly on the person claiming asylum there is nonetheless a duty of good faith on the State to assist the applicant to do so.[66]

For instance, would the assertion made in the UK in 1942 "I am a German Jew", have lacked sufficient circumstantial or personal detail according to the Resolution, to be categorised as manifestly unfounded?

Under Article 6(c) an application is to be manifestly unfounded if it is manifestly lacking in any credibility, the story is inconsistent, contradictory or fundamentally improbable. Determinations based on inconsistency are fraught with difficulty. Any story told twice contains inconsistencies. An acceptable threshold for credibility based on consistency is difficult to establish.

*Internal Flight Alternative*

At Article 7 the Member States have included as a ground for an application to be determined manifestly unfounded that effective protection is readily available for the individual in another part of his own country to which it would be reasonable to expect him to go. Provision is made for Member States to consult each other on the appropriate framework taking into account information received from UNHCR as regards the application of this principle. This concept is very difficult to apply in practice with any degree of certainty or safety. It presupposes a static situation in the country of persecution which will very often be unjustified.

The authorities of a state or non-governmental agents of persecution may choose to persecute persons on a Convention ground first in one area of the country. Whether such efforts to eliminate such persons in the area are successful or not the authorities or agents of persecution may decide to direct the persecution towards another part of the country. The internal flight option is for most refugees no option at all, merely a prolongation of the anxiety

---

66 Handbook on Procedures and Criteria for Determining Refugee Status, UNHCR, 1988, Paragraphs 195 to 202

and fear awaiting the commencement of persecution in the new area over which the same authorities have ultimate control.

The internal flight alternative will also depend to a very substantial degree on the personal circumstances of the individual fearing persecution. To include this in a manifestly unfounded determination where procedural guarantees are limited therefore permitting only a cursory consideration of these factors is open to question.

*Countries in which there is no Serious Risk of Persecution*

At the same meeting where the Ministers adopted this Resolution they also adopted a Conclusion on countries in which there is generally no risk of persecution.[67] At Article 8 of the Resolution the Member States state as a goal "to reach common assessment of certain countries that are of particular interest in this context". A consideration of the principles leading to a determination regarding a country will be considered below at the commentary on Document 4. Nonetheless the Member States do undertake in the Resolution to give consideration to individual claims of all applicants from such countries.

*Procedural Guarantees*

According to the Resolution the accelerated procedure which is to apply in respect of a determination of a manifestly unfounded application for asylum includes the following elements:

(i) Initial decisions should be reached as soon as possible and at the latest within one month.

(ii) Any appeal or review procedures are to be completed as soon as possible.

(iii) Appeal or review procedures may be more simplified than those generally available in other cases of rejected asylum applications.

---

67 Document 4 infra

(iv) The decision to refuse an asylum application must be taken by a competent authority at the appropriate level fully qualified in asylum or refugee matters.

(v) The applicant should be given an opportunity for personal interview with a qualified official empowered under national law before any final decision is made.

Accordingly, the asylum applicant may only rely on the fact that he or she ought to be given the opportunity of a personal interview with a qualified official. There is no obligation to provide any appeal or review procedure against a decision that the application is manifestly unfounded. Further, if there is such an appeal or review procedure there is no guarantee that it will have suspensive effect. This position is reinforced by the Resolution on minimum guarantees for asylum procedures[68] which at Articles 18 to 22 deals with manifestly unfounded asylum applications.

The minimum procedural guarantees set out in that Resolution are specifically stated *not* to apply to any application refused on the basis that it is manifestly unfounded in accordance with this Resolution.

*Manifestly Unfounded Applications and Host Third Countries*

Article 1(b) of the Resolution provides that "an application for asylum may not be subject to determination by a Member State of refugee status under the terms of the Geneva Convention on the status of Refugees when it falls within the provisions of the Resolution on host third countries". This is worded in a mandatory form – constituting a prohibition of a substantive consideration of the application if a host third country exists. The criteria for a host third country to be safe for an asylum applicant are considered below in commentary on document 3. However, it is interesting and indeed perplexing that this prohibition appears in this Resolution on manifestly unfounded applications.

68 Document 19 infra

The existence of a host third country is not specifically stated to be a ground for determining that an application is manifestly unfounded. However the inclusion of this provision under the heading of Article 1 "manifestly unfounded applications" implies this to be the case. Therefore, the limitations on procedural guarantees and the requirements of speed in determination appear to apply to any application revealing a host third country. This becomes particularly important when considering the Resolution on Minimum Guarantees for asylum procedures.[69]

69 Document 19 infra

# 3

# RESOLUTION on a harmonised approach to questions concerning host third countries[69]

Ministers of the Member States of the European Communities responsible for immigration, meeting in London on 30 November to 1 December 1992;

DETERMINED to achieve the objective of harmonizing asylum policies as it was defined by the Luxembourg European Council in June 1991 and clarified by the Maastricht European Council in December 1991;

TRUE to the principles of the Geneva Convention of 28 July 1951, as amended by the New York Protocol of 31 January 1967, relating to the Status of Refugees and in particular Articles 31 and 33 thereof;

CONCERNED especially at the problem of refugees and asylum seekers unlawfully leaving countries where they have already been granted protection or have had a genuine opportunity to seek such protection and CONVINCED that a concerted response should be made to it, as suggested in Conclusion No. 58 on Protection adopted by the UNHCR Executive Committee at its 40th session (1989);

CONSIDERING the Dublin Convention of 15 June 1990 determining the State Responsible for Examining Applications for Asylum Lodged in one of the Member States of the European Communities, and in particular Article 3(5) thereof, and WISHING to harmonize the principles under which they will act under this provision;

---

69 SN 4823/92 WG 1283 AS 147

ANXIOUS to ensure effective protection for asylum seekers and refugees who require it;

MAKE THE FOLLOWING RESOLUTION

*Procedure for application of the concept of host third country*

1. The Resolution on manifestly unfounded applications for asylum, adopted by Ministers meeting in London of 30 November to 1 December 1992, refers in paragraph 1(b) to the concept of host third country. The following principles should form the procedural basis for applying the concept of host third country:

   (a) The formal identification of a host third country in principle precedes the substantive examination of the application for asylum and its justification.

   (b) The principle of the host third country is to be applied to all applicants for asylum, irrespective of whether or not they may be regarded as refugees.

   (c) Thus, if there is a host third country, the application for refugee status may not be examined and the asylum applicant may be sent to that country.

   (d) If the asylum applicant cannot in practice be sent to a host third country, the provisions of the Dublin Convention will apply.

   (e) Any Member State retains the right, for humanitarian reasons, not to remove the asylum applicant to a host third country.

   Cases falling within this concept may be considered under the accelerated procedures provided for in the aforementioned Resolution.

*Substantive application: requirements and criteria for establishing whether a country is a host third country*

2. Fulfilment of all the following fundamental requirements determines a host third country and should be assessed by the Member State in each individual case:

   (a) In those third countries, the life or freedom of the asylum applicant must not be threatened, within the meaning of Article 33 of the Geneva Convention;

   (b) The asylum applicant must not be exposed to torture or inhuman or degrading treatment in the third country;

   (c) It must either be the case that the asylum applicant has already been granted protection in the third country or has had an opportunity, at the border or within the territory of the third country, to make contact with that country's authorities in order to seek their protection, before approaching the Member State in which he is applying for asylum, or that there is clear evidence of his admissibility to a third country;

   (d) The asylum applicant must be afforded effective protection in the host third country against refoulement, within the meaning of the Geneva Convention.

   If two or more countries fulfil the above conditions, the Member States may expel the asylum applicant to one of those third countries. Member States will take into account, on the basis in particular of the information available from the UNHCR, known practice in the third countries, especially with regard to the principle of non-refoulement, before considering sending asylum applicants to them.

*Dublin Convention*

3. The following principles set out the relationship between the application of the concept of the third host country, in accordance with Article 3(5) of the Dublin Convention, and the procedures under the Convention for

determining the Member State responsible for examining an asylum application:

(a) The Member State in which the application for asylum has been lodged will examine whether or not the principle of the host third country can be applied. If that State decides to apply the principle, it will set in train the procedures necessary for sending the asylum applicant to the host third country before considering whether or not to transfer responsibility for examining the application for asylum to another Member State pursuant to the Dublin Convention.

(b) A Member State may not decline responsibility for examining an application for asylum, pursuant to the Dublin Convention, by claiming that the requesting Member State should have returned the applicant to a host third country.

(c) Notwithstanding the above, the Member State responsible for examining the application will retain the right, pursuant to its national laws, to send an applicant for asylum to the host third country.

(d) The above provisions do not prejudice the application of Article 3(4) and Article 9 of the Dublin Convention by the Member State in which the application for asylum has been lodged.

*Future action*

4. Ministers agreed to seek to ensure that their national laws are adapted, if need be, and to incorporate the principles of this resolution as soon as possible, at the latest by the time of the entry into force of the Dublin Convention. Member States will from time to time, in cooperation with the Commission and in consultation with UNHCR, review the operation of these procedures and consider whether any additional measures are necessary.

*Commentary*

*Status:* Resolution adopted by Ministers of the EC Member States outside the ambit of the European Communities Treaties.

*Entry into force:* The Ministers undertook to incorporate the principles as soon as possible and at the latest by the time of entry into force of the Dublin Convention.

*International obligations engaged:*

(1) Universal Declaration of Human Rights 1948
(2) UN Convention relating to the Status of Refugees 1951 and Protocol 1967
(3) International Covenant on Civil and Political Rights 1966
(4) UN Convention against Torture and other Cruel, Inhuman or Degrading Treatment or Punishment 1984
(5) European Convention on Human Rights 1950
(6) The Dublin Convention 1990

*Summary:*

The purpose of this Resolution is to achieve harmonisation of Member States' practices in respect of the return of asylum applicants to states outside the Union with a view to their applications being considered there.

The preamble consists of five paragraphs confirming the Member States' commitment to the UN Convention but expressing concern at the problem of refugees and asylum applicants "unlawfully leaving countries where they have already been granted protection or have had a genuine opportunity to seek such protection".

Before an asylum application is considered on its substance, Member States are to consider whether a third country should be responsible for the determination of the asylum application. If there is such a country "the application for refugee status *may not* be examined". This would appear to be a prohibition on the examination of such an asylum application. However, the Resolution provides only that the applicant "*may* be sent to that country", which would not appear to be mandatory. The provisions of the Dublin Convention only apply if there is no country outside the Union to which the asylum applicant can be sent. Nonetheless a Member State may decide, for humanitarian reasons, not to remove the asylum applicant to the third country.

Any application where a third host country can be identified may be subject to accelerated procedures under the Resolution on manifestly unfounded asylum applications.[70]

A host third country *must* meet the following criteria: the life or freedom of the asylum applicant must not be threatened (Article 33 of the UN Convention); the applicant must not be exposed to torture or inhuman or degrading treatment (not defined by reference to any international obligation); the asylum applicant must already have been granted protection by the country *or* have had an opportunity to make contact with the country's authorities to seek protection *or* there is clear evidence of admissibility to the country; there must be effective protection in the third country against refoulement as defined in the UN Convention.

Assessment of a host third country is made by each Member State *individually*. Where a positive assessment is made, the application may be treated as manifestly unfounded.

*Comments: Moving Refugee Determination Procedures out of the European Union*

This Resolution is intrinsically connected with the Resolution on manifestly unfounded applications for asylum adopted at the same meeting of Ministers of the Member States responsible for immigration in London on 30th November and 1st December 1992.

It is also related to the third act, Conclusions on countries in which there is generally no serious risk of persecution, also adopted at the same time, by the interaction among which, is intended to provide a workable policy

---

70 Document 2 supra

on asylum which enables rapid determination of a substantial proportion of asylum applications.

Article 1(b) of the Resolution on manifestly unfounded applications for asylum provides that an application for asylum may not be subject to determination by a Member State where it falls within the provisions of the Resolution on host third countries. This wording would appear to be mandatory. Where the provisions of the Resolution on host third countries apply, the accelerated procedure provided for in the Resolution on manifestly unfounded applications for asylum may be used.[71] As has been considered above in commentary on that Resolution, the procedural guarantees in respect of an accelerated procedure are limited.[72]

The objective of the Resolution on host third countries would appear to be to remove, insofar as possible, the element of choice of an asylum applicant as to the country in which he or she seeks protection from persecution. In keeping with the principle of the Dublin Convention, the wish of an asylum applicant to seek protection in a country where he or she may have relatives other than those of the first degree, or in which there is a community of fellow nationals is subordinated to the policy of the Member States to require the asylum applicant to seek protection in the first country to which he or she arrives.

The Resolution on host third countries is to be applied to all applicants for asylum whether or not they may be regarded as refugees. This relieves the state in which the application is made from considering even superficially the asylum application before investigating the possibility of returning the applicant to a third country. The Resolution's principles are to be applied before the provisions of the Dublin Convention. This means that where the state in which the asylum application is made identifies a third country outside the European Union to which the person may be returned in accordance with the Resolution, action ought to be taken first to return the ap-

71 Article 2, Resolution on manifestly unfounded applications for asylum, Document 2

72 Resolution on manifestly unfounded applications for asylum Document 2

plicant there rather than to another Member State in accordance with the Dublin Convention.

However, where the State to which the asylum application has been addressed seeks to return the applicant to another Member State in accordance with the Dublin Convention the receiving State cannot refuse to accept the applicant on the ground that the provisions of the Resolution have not been applied. This would seem self-evident considering the hierarchy of validity of the acts in question. As an international convention, the Dublin Convention is subject to the Vienna Convention on the Interpretation of Conventions whereas the Resolution, while certainly a statement of policy is of uncertain legal effect.

Curiously, the Resolution seeks to place an obligation on third countries not a party to it to consider and determine asylum applications. There is no reciprocal obligation on the Member States to apply similar principles where third countries seek to return applicants for asylum to the Member States. In this regard the Resolution is a somewhat unusual document. It is somewhat irregular in international law that one state or group of states should seek to impose obligations unilaterally or through an agreement *inter se* on other states which have not participated in or accepted the obligation.

This fundamental flaw of the Resolution is glossed over in the preamble by reference to the UN Convention and in particular the responsibility of all signatory states under articles 31 and 33 not to send a refugee back to a country where he or she would suffer persecution within the terms of the Convention. However, the Resolution does not require that the host third country be a signatory to the UN Convention. Article 2 of the Resolution merely requires that the third state must not threaten the life or freedom of the asylum applicant and must afford protection against return to the country where the person fears persecution within the meaning of the UN Convention.[73]

Even where the host third state is a party to the UN Convention there is no obligation in that Convention requiring the state through which the asylum

---

73 Article 2 of the Resolution

applicant first passed to accept responsibility for the determination of the application. Accordingly the reference to the UN Convention does not satisfactorily deal with the unilateral shift of the obligation to consider an asylum application on to states which are not parties to the Resolution.

Reference is made in the preamble to the Resolution to Conclusion number 58 of the UNHCR Executive Committee. The Conclusion must be read in the light of the Final Act of the conference which adopted the UN Convention and which recommended "that governments continue to receive refugees in their territories and that they act in concert in a true spirit of international co-operation in order that these refugees may find asylum and the possibility of re-settlement".[74] Clearly the spirit of international co-operation requires agreement and negotiation between parties as regards their responsibilities.

However, UN Conclusion 58 certainly does not sanction the type of measure envisaged by this Resolution. The UN Conclusion is properly entitled Problem of Refugees and Asylum-seekers who move in an Irregular Manner from a Country in which they had already found Protection. The concern identified by the UN Conclusion results from "the destabilizing effect which irregular movements of this kind have on structured international efforts to provide appropriate solutions for refugees".[75] It is uncertain whether the blanket refusal to consider asylum applications where there exists a potential third host state and return of applicants to that state is not likely to create destabilization in third states – exactly the consequence which the UN Conclusion seeks to avoid.

Further, Conclusion No 58 only sanctions the return of refugees and asylum seekers who move irregularly: "where they have already found protection, they may be returned to that country if:–

(i) they are protected there against refoulement and

---

74 Excerpt from the Final Act of the United Nations Conference of Plenipotentiaries on the Status of Refugees and Stateless Persons

75 Conclusion No 58 (XL) Problem of Refugees and Asylum-seekers who move in an irregular manner from a country in which they had already found protection

(ii) they are admitted to remain there and to be treated in accordance with recognised basic human standards until a durable solution is found for them".[76]

Of particular note in respect of the Resolution, is the UN Conclusion's requirement that any refugee or asylum applicant must already have found protection in the country to which they are to be returned. The Resolution at article 2(c) only requires:–

"either the asylum applicant has already been granted protection in the third country or has had an opportunity at the border or within the territory of the third country, to make contact with that country's authorities in order to seek their protection before approaching the Member State in which he is applying for asylum, or that there is clear evidence of his adminisibility to a third country".[77]

This is a very different and much weaker test than that contained in UN Conclusion 58, which requires that the asylum applicant must already have *found* protection in the state before return may be contemplated.

UN Conclusion 58 was adopted at the 40th Session of the Executive Committee in 1989. It is surprising that only three years later in 1992 the Member States adopted this Resolution which is at such variance with the principles which had so recently been agreed in the context of the UN Executive Committee on which, at that time, Belgium, Denmark, France, Germany, Greece, Italy, the Netherlands and the UK were represented.

Further, third countries which are neither parties to the Resolution nor were consulted regarding its adoption could well refuse admission of asylum applicants being returned to them by the Member State relying on the Member States' obligations under Article 14 of the Universal Declaration of Human Rights 1948. Article 14(1) provides that "everyone has the right to seek and to enjoy in other countries asylum from persecution". This right is not limited to seeking asylum in the first country traversed. Nor indeed

76 Ibid para (f) (i) and (ii)
77 Article 2 Resolution

is it limited to seeking asylum in one other country. Accordingly, in conjunction with the UN Convention requiring states to provide protection from return to countries of persecution, the UN Declaration of Human Rights provides third countries with substantial grounds in international law to decline the obligation which the Member States seek to impose upon them by virtue of the Resolution. It may be that this defect in the Resolution provided some impetus for the agreement of a specimen bilateral re-admission agreement.[78]

*Criteria of Host Third Countries*

In order to qualify as a safe country to which to return an asylum applicant, the state must fulfil four requirements:

(i) The life or freedom of the asylum applicant must not be threatened within the meaning of Article 33 of the UN Convention. This article states that "no contracting state shall expel or return (refouler) a refugee in any manner whatsoever to the frontiers of territories where his life or freedom would be threatened on account of his race, religion, nationality, membership of a particular social group or political opinion". The obligation of article 33 is subject to a proviso in article 33(2) relating to national security and danger to society.

The obligation in the Resolution does not require that the host third country be a party to the UN Convention. It is only required to fulfil the obligation of article 33 of that Convention. However, it is difficult to see how any Member State could be satisfied that the full effect of article 33 of the UN Convention is complied with unless the host third country is not only a party to the Convention but the Convention is also incorporated, or at least article 33 thereof, into national law and justiciable before the domestic courts of the state.

(ii) The asylum applicant must not be exposed to torture or inhuman or degrading treatment in the third country.

---

78 Document 18 infra

No reference is made to the international obligations which give rise to this provision. However a number of sources are immediately apparent. Article 5 of the Universal Declaration of Human Rights 1948 prohibits torture or cruel, inhuman or degrading treatment or punishment. The wording of article 5 is identical to that of article 3 ECHR in respect of which the European Court of Human Rights has held the obligation extends to returning a person to a country where prohibited treatment may be suffered.[79]

The UN Convention against Torture and Other Cruel, Inhuman or Degrading Treatment or Punishment 1984 contains, at article 3, a specific requirement that no state party shall expel, return ("refouler") or extradite a person to another state where there are substantial grounds for believing that he would be in danger of being subject to torture. Article 3(2) provides that for the purpose of determining whether there are such grounds, the competent authorities shall take into account all relevant considerations including, where applicable, the existence in the state concerned of a consistent pattern of gross, flagrant or mass violations of human rights.

This is the clearest statement in international law of the obligation not to return a person to ill treatment and also how states are to determine the likelihood of such ill treatment. A further source of this obligation arises through article 7 of the International Covenant on Civil and Political Rights 1966 which is worded identically to article 3 ECHR and article 5 of the Universal Declaration. Indeed, in view of the consistency and frequency with which the obligation to protect all persons against torture, inhuman or degrading treatment or punishment arises, this may be considered a fundamental principle of international law.

The useful assistance which has been given in determining the extent of the obligation by the UN Convention against Torture and the interpretation provided by the European Court of Human Rights on article 3 ECHR are particularly valuable for the purposes of article 2

---

79 *Soering v UK* [1989] Ser A No. 161

of the Resolution. It is most unfortunate that no reference is made to these obligations or their interpretation.

(iii) The asylum applicant must already have been granted protection in a third country or have had an opportunity at the border or within the territory of the state to make contact with that country's authorities in order to seek protection; or there must be clear evidence that the asylum applicant is admissible to the third country.

This requirement appears to mix together a number of different elements which are not necessarily co-determinate. Where an asylum applicant has already been granted protection in the third state the question arises whether that protection is adequate and whether the third state is capable of continuing to provide that protection. The situation of Somali asylum applicants in Kenya is a stark example of the problems which arise in respect of this type of situation. Although Kenya provided some protection to substantial numbers of asylum applicants from Somalia when civil war broke out in 1990 in that state, by 1995 grave questions arise as to the commitment or ability of Kenya to continue to provide protection.

It is quite a different assessment whether or not an asylum applicant has had an opportunity at the border or within the territory of a third state to make contact with the country's authorities in order to seek their protection. This is a fairly subjective assessment. It requires a determination of what is an opportunity and whether that opportunity is in fact genuine or illusory. The final criteria, evidence that the asylum applicant is admissible to a third state is also far from certain. A person fearing persecution on a UN Convention ground ought to be admissible to any country which is a signatory of the UN Convention. The only certainty of admissibility of an asylum applicant to another state is a certificate from that state's authorised authorities confirming this. However, in a spirit of reciprocity, where the authorities of a Member State are seeking such a confirmation why should the state traversed not apply the same reasoning and decline to issue a certificate on the basis the applicant has now had an opportunity to apply for asylum in the Member State which is also a signatory to the UN Convention?

(iv) The asylum applicant must be afforded effective protection in the host third country against refoulement, within the meaning of the UN Convention. It is somewhat unclear how this fourth requirement differs from the first requirement as the requirement to protect refugees against refoulement is contained in Article 33 of the UN Convention. If the host third country is one where the asylum applicant fears persecution then it cannot be a safe country and the Member State where the application for asylum has been made must necessarily determine that application. If the host third country is one which will not protect the asylum applicant from return to a country where he or she fears persecution (refoulement) then it is also clearly not a safe country. Therefore there does not appear to be any substantial difference between the first and fourth requirement.

One consequence of this Resolution in conjunction with the Resolution on manifestly unfounded applications for asylum and the Conclusions on countries in which there is generally no serious risk of persecution is that asylum applicants are most likely to be returned to the country closest to that from which they are fleeing persecution. Many asylum applicants will escape the country where they fear persecution by fleeing over land or sea borders irregularly into a neighbouring state. From that neighbouring state they may then flee to a country further afield, for instance a Member State, in which they feel greater security. However flight from the region is no longer acceptable under the principles of the Member States' asylum policy. This can have serious consequences for security in the region as has been seen over 1994/1995 with the refugee crisis in Rwanda which has had destabilising consequences for neighbouring states such as Burundi and Zaire. The flight of refugees into neighbouring Zaire and Burundi has caused substantial instability in the region and it may be that the consequences of that instability have yet to be fully played out.

Further, the application of the principles contained in the Member States' Resolutions may have the effect of creating a quasi-territorial limitation on the right of asylum. The 1967 Protocol to the UN Convention lifted the previously applicable territorial limitation of that Convention to refugees resulting from the events of the Second World War. It is interesting that by 1992 the Member States which were instrumental in the creation of the UN Convention may be reverting back to the concept of territorial asylum. Unfortunately, though, the Member States' commitment to protection of persons fleeing civil war within the region has been less than adequate as can be seen by the response to the crisis in the former Yugoslavia.[80]

Some of the countries most affected by the host third country principle are, of course, those which border on the Member States. This includes the Central and Eastern European countries (CEEC) which are also the object of the most concerted efforts of the Union to promote faster development and secure democracy. However, the burden of determining asylum applications from applicants returned to these states from the Union counteracts these efforts. In a submission by the Hungarian Delegation to the Council of Europe on 13 September 1993 on the "Safe Country Principle" from the Perspective of Transit Countries, the Hungarian Government concluded that the implementation of the principle in the Union:-

"Increasing burdens on safe transit countries can contribute to instability and xenophobia in this European region and can reduce its absorbtion capacity and co-operative ability in such case[s]".[81]
As has been stated elsewhere in respect of Hungary, with a GDP five to eight times less than that of the EU Member States, Hungary (and by extension the CEEC) cannot assume burdens Western Europe claims it is incapable to carry.[82]

One month later, in November 1993 at the Fifth Conference of European Ministers responsible for migration affairs (Council of Europe) the Ministers:–

80 See Document 11 infra

81 "Safe Country Principle" from the Perspective of Transit Countries, Hungarian Delegation to CAHAR, Council of Europe 21-22 September 1993

82 Asylum Seekers and Refugees: Hungarian Delemmas Boldizsár Nagy, Acta Juridica Hungarica 1992 34 No 1-2

"Strongly express their abhorrence of racism and xenophobia and share the current concern at the growth of these evils in Europe."[83]
Notwithstanding these two events, no reconsideration of the principle of the Resolution on host third countries has been undertaken even though its implementation is feared by one affected state at least, to undermine the ability of CEEC to fight xenophobia.

83 Conclusions, Fifth Conference of European Ministers responsible for migration affairs, 18-19 November 1993 Council of Europe

# 4 CONCLUSIONS on countries in which there is generally no serious risk of persecution[84]

1. The resolution on manifestly unfounded applications for asylum (WGI 1282) includes at paragraph 1(a) a reference to the concept of countries in which there is in general terms no serious risk of persecution.

   This concept means that it is a country which can be clearly shown, in an objective and verifiable way, normally not to generate refugees or where it can be clearly shown, in an objective and verifiable way, that circumstances which might in the past have justified recourse to the 1951 Geneva Convention have ceased to exist.[85]

*Purpose*

2. The aim of developing this concept is to assist in establishing a harmonized approach to applications from countries which gave rise to a high proportion of clearly unfounded applications and to reduce pressure on asylum determination systems that are at present excessively burdened with such applications. This will help to ensure that refugees in genuine need of protection are not kept waiting unnecessarily long for their status to be recognized and to discourage misuse of asylum procedures. Member States have the goal to reaching common assessment of certain countries that are of particular interest in this context.

---

84 SN 4821/92 WGI 1281 AS 145

85 ref: Report from Immigration Ministers to the European Council meeting in Maastricht (doc WGI 930, page 38)

To this end, Member States will exchange information within an appropriate framework on any national decisions to consider particular countries as ones in which there is generally no serious risk of persecution. In making such assessments, they will use, as a minimum, the elements of assessment laid down in this document.

3. An assessment by an individual Member State of a country as one in which there is generally no serious risk of persecution should not automatically result in the refusal of all asylum applications from its nationals or their exclusion from individualized determination procedures. A Member State may choose to use such an assessment in channelling cases into accelerated procedures as described in paragraph 2 of the Resolution on manifestly unfounded applications, agreed by Immigration Ministers at their meeting on 30 November and 1 December 1992. The Member State will nevertheless consider the individual claims of all applicants from such countries and any specific indications presented by the applicant which might outweigh a general presumption.

*Elements in the assessment*

4. The following elements should be taken together in any assessment of the general risk of persecution in a particular country:

   (a) Previous numbers of refugees and recognition rates. It is necessary to look at the recognition rates for asylum applicants from the country in question who have come to Member States in recent years. Obviously, a situation may change and historically low recognition rates need not continue following (for example) a violent coup. But in the absence of any significant change in the country it is reasonable to assume that low recognition rates will continue and that the country tends not to produce refugees.

   (b) Observance of human rights. It is necessary to consider the formal obligations undertaken by a country in adhering to international human rights instruments and in its domestic law and how in practice it meets those obligations. The latter is clearly more important and adherence or non-adherence to a particular instrument cannot in itself result in consideration as a country in which there is generally no serious risk of persecution. It should be recognized that a pattern of breaches of human rights may be exclusively linked to a particular group within a country's population or to a particular area of the country.

The readiness of the country concerned to allow monitoring by NGOs of their human rights observance is also relevant in judging how seriously a country takes its human rights obligations.

(c) Democratic institutions. The existence of one or more specific institutions cannot be a sine qua non but consideration should be given to democratic processes, elections, political pluralism and freedom of expression and thought. Particular attention should be paid to the availability and effectiveness of legal avenues of protection and redress.

(d) Taking into account the above mentioned elements, an assessment must be made of the prospect for dramatic change in the immediate future. Any view formed must be reviewed over time in the light of events.

5. Assessments of the risk of persecution in individual countries should be based upon as wide a range of sources of information as possible, including advice and reports from diplomatic missions, international and non-governmental organizations and press reports. Information from UNHCR has a specific place in this framework. UNHCR forms views of the relative safety of countries of origin both for their own operational purposes and in responding to requests for advice. They have access to sources within the UN system and non-governmental organizations.

6. Member States may take into consideration other elements of assessment than those previously mentioned, which will be reviewed from time to time.

*Commentary*

*Status:* Conclusions adopted by Ministers of the EC Member States outside the ambit of the European Communities Treaties.

*Entry into force:* There is no time limit within which implementation must take place. These Conclusions are designed to compliment the Resolution on manifestly unfounded applications for asylum.

*International Obligations Engaged:*

(1) UN Convention relating to the Status of Refugees 1951 and Protocol 1967
(2) European Convention on Human Rights 1950
(3) European Communities Treaties.

*Summary:*

These Conclusions set out the elements which Member State governments must assess before a decision is reached that return to a country of origin does not present a serious risk of persecution. An assessment that a country is one in which there is generally no serious risk of persecution appears to be individual, reached by each Member State though there is a goal of common assessment. The assessment is then used as a tool to channel asylum applicants from that state into the accelerated procedures permitted under the Resolution on manifestly unfounded asylum applications.[86] The factors to be taken into consideration are:

(i) The recognition rates of asylum applicants from the country in question over the recent past;

(ii) The observance of human rights in the country of origin including the formal obligations undertaken by the country and in practice how those obligations are met. Specific attention will be paid to patterns of breaches of human rights linked to particular groups within a

86 Document 2 infra

country's population and the extent to which such a pattern of abuse is limited to a specific area of the country;

The Conclusions specifically state that the readiness of a country to allow monitoring by non-governmental organisations of their human rights observance is relevant;

(iii) The existence of democratic institutions, democratic processes, elections, political pluralism and freedom of expression and thought. Particular attention is to be paid to the availability and effectiveness of legal avenues of protection and redress;

(iv) The stability of the country.

The assessment of all of these points depends on evidence about the country and knowledge of the practices.

The conclusion that a country is safe may only give rise to a presumption that the asylum application is unfounded. This presumption may be displaced by contrary evidence. Each applicant, therefore, must be entitled to individual consideration of his or her case.

*Comments: Presumptions against Refugee Recognition*

The purpose of these Conclusions is to identify some common principles regarding practices in foreign states which can be applied universally to determine whether there is a likelihood that the state is persecuting people on its territory or not. It is designed on an exclusion basis - if the elements identified are present then that state probably does not persecute its people.

The Conclusions are clearly designed to fit a "numbers game". An assessment of a state will only be relevant where substantial numbers of people from that state apply for asylum in the Member States. Therefore the assessment of a country is a tool for the rapid refusal of asylum applications. For example if Sri Lanka is assessed as a country which meets the criteria of the Conclusions all asylum applications from Sri Lankeens can be presumed unfounded subject to the individual displacing, on the basis of his or her personal experience, that presumption.

There can be no question that such a tool would be of assistance refusing substantial numbers of asylum applications. The question is whether it is practical, workable and fair. Clearly, it is not practical to seek to make an assessment of every country in the world. Presumably decisions on which states to put under the microscope of the Conclusions will be based on the number of asylum applicants from that state who arrive in the Member State.

Equally clearly, states anxious to maintain a good reputation among the Member States may wish to avoid an assessment or if this is not possible ensure they obtain a positive assessment. This could have a long term beneficial effect on human rights observance, internationally. The question, however, is at what cost to individuals seeking protection from persecution and at what cost to the international protection system for refugees contained in the UN Convention.

The concept of a country in which there is generally no serious risk of persecution contains two distinct and separate elements:

(i) Any country which can be clearly shown, in an objective and verifiable way, normally not to generate refugees; or

(ii) A country where it can be clearly shown in an objective and verifiable way, that circumstances which might in the past have justified recourse to the UN Convention have ceased to exist.

In respect of the first limb of the concept, as the internationally accepted definition of a refugee within the terms of the UN Convention requires that the person be outside his or her country of nationality, where a country wishes a positive classification under the first limb the first step would appear to be to limit travel of its nationals outside the country. In many "refugee producing" countries restrictions on obtaining passports and foreign travel are commonplace.

The second part of the concept, in respect of circumstances which might in the past have justified recourse to the UN Convention but have now ceased to exist, this is a curious inversion of article 1C(5) of the UN Convention. According to that provision a person shall cease to be a refugee within the terms of the Convention where he or she can no longer, because the circumstances in connection with which he or she has been recognised as a refugee have ceased to exist, continue to refuse to avail him or herself of the protection of the country of his or her nationality. The inversion of article 1C(5) from the refugee as the focus to the country leaves little room for the protection of the individual as intended by the Convention.

In respect of persons who have already been recognised as refugees, the provision provides in its second indent that the paragraph does not apply to refugees coming within the UN Convention definition who are able to invoke compelling reasons arising out of previous persecution for refusing to avail themselves of the protection of the country of nationality. Therefore while complying with the UN Convention in respect of recognised refugees, a deep division is created between those not yet recognised and those already recognised. This does not appear to be the intention of the Convention according to the official interpretation of which recognition as a refugee is declaratory only.[87]

In place of a preamble, articles 2 and 3, under the heading "Purposes of the Conclusion" include not only certain elements which might normally be expected to appear in a preamble but also the consequences of the determination that a country comes within the Conclusions.

The purposes are twofold:

(1) To assist in establishing a harmonised approach to applications from countries which give rise to a high proportion of clearly unfounded applications; and

(2) to reduce pressure on asylum determination procedures "that are at present excessively burdened with [clearly unfounded] applications".

In respect of the first aim, it is implicit that the Member States approach asylum applications from the same country differently which results in substantially different recognition rates. As long as the treatment of asylum applicants from the same country varies dramatically between Member States

87 UNHCR Handbook paragraph 28

the coherence of the Dublin Convention system is susceptible to attack both politically and judicially.

| ASYLUM APPLICATIONS: SRI LANKA | | | | | |
|---|---|---|---|---|---|
| | *Denmark* | *Germany* | *France* | *Netherlands* | *UK* |
| 1991 | 280 | 5623 | 3400 | 1821 | 3763 |
| 1992 | 361 | 5303 | 3959 | 1034 | 2085 |

| RECOGNITION AS REFUGEES: SRI LANKA | | | | | |
|---|---|---|---|---|---|
| | *Denmark* | *Germany* | *France* | *Netherlands* | *UK* |
| 1991 | 109 | 114 | 4050 | 0 | 17 |
| 1992 | 104 | 1098 | 3029 | 91 | 40 |

*Source: Migration Statistics 1994,* EUROSTAT

As regards the second purpose to reduce pressure on asylum determination systems this is a somewhat different argument based on administrative expedience.

The assessment of any particular country is to be made individually by each Member State. Therefore substantial co-ordination continues to be needed if these Conclusions are to be implemented to ensure that the assessments by each Member State do not vary *inter se*. Member States are free to use assessment of countries in order to channel cases into accelerated procedure described in article 2 of the Resolution on Manifestly Unfounded Applications.[88] However the Member States have committed themselves to consider individual claims of all applicants from such countries and any specific indications presented by the applicant which might outweigh a general presumption.

88 Document 2 infra

The Conclusions then set out the elements which are to be taken into account in the assessment of any particular state. There are four:

(i) Previous numbers of refugees and recognition rates: the assumption here is that where the rate of recognition of asylum applicants from a particular country is low this is an indication that the country is one in which there is generally no serious risk of persecution. The box above on Sri Lankan recognition rates in 1991 and 1992 indicates that on this ground alone any common assessment would be exceedingly difficult.

In view of the tendency of many states to accept asylum applicants on humanitarian grounds even though they do not, in the opinion of the determining state fully meet the UN Convention definition, this basis of assessment similarly appears to be inadequate.[89]

For instance the reluctance of the Member States to recognise vulnerable persons fleeing the former Yugoslavia is evidenced in the Resolution to this effect.[90] On an assessment based on these Conclusions it would mean that, for instance, Bosnia in 1992 would be a country in which there is generally no serious risk of persecution.

| ASYLUM APPLICATIONS 1992: FORMER YUGOSLAVIA: | | | | | |
|---|---|---|---|---|---|
| *Austria* | *Denmark* | *Germany* | *France* | *Netherlands* | *UK* |
| 7410 | 9010 | 122,666 | 2354 | 5621 | 5635 |

89 Responses to Western Europe's Immigration Crisis, M. Hopkinson, Wilton Park Paper 14, March 1994, page 4
90 Document 11 infra

| REFUGEES 1992: FORMER YUGOSLAVIA | | | | | |
|---|---|---|---|---|---|
| *Austria* | *Denmark* | *Germany* | *France* | *Netherlands* | *UK* |
| 304 | 36 | 878 | 124 | 23 | Under 3 |

*Source: Migration Statistics 1994,* EUROSTAT

(ii) Observance of human rights: The Member States recognise that mere adherence to international human rights instruments does not necessarily result in the observance of human rights. The question of how human rights obligations are fulfilled in practice is a consideration to be taken into account under the Conclusions. Further, practice is stated to be more important than the question of adherence to an instrument. However, inversion of this principle is equally accepted. Adherence or non-adherence to a particular instrument cannot itself result in finding that a country is one in which there is generally no risk of persecution. From the formulation of this statement, it would appear that the fairly simple and verifiable fact that a particular state is not a party to important international human rights instrument may be disregarded on an assessment that in practice there is generally observance of human rights. Insufficient regard is had for the grave difficulty in getting a clear picture of what is actually happening in respect of human rights within a state which will almost invariably seek to hide from the international community human rights abuses.

Indeed the Member States themselves have increased the incentive for third countries, if not to improve their human rights record, at least to prevent discovery of abuses. On 9 May 1992 the Council resolved to include a human rights conditionality clause in all agreements concluded with third countries. This clause permits the repudiation of agreements, which in most cases include provision for substantial aid and commercial advantages, in the event of serious human rights abuses by the third country.

Accordingly, it might have been more felicitous in the Conclusions for this element of assessment to have been cumulative i.e. the requirement of adherence to international human rights instrument as well as implementation rather than in the alternative.

It is curious that the wording of the UN Convention against Torture and other Cruel, Inhuman or Degrading Treatment or Punishment 1984 is not reflected in the Conclusions. Article 3 of that Convention prohibits state parties from expelling, returning or extraditing a person to another state where there are substantial grounds for believing he or she would be in danger of being subjected to torture. In order to determine the risk, article 3(2) provides that the competent authorities shall taken into account all relevant considerations including the existence in the state of a consistent pattern of gross, flagrant or mass violations of human rights.

According to the Conclusions, the Member States recognise that patterns of breaches of human rights may be exclusively linked to a particular group within a country's population or to a particular area of the country. The first part of this statement is somewhat self-evident taking into consideration the definition of a refugee in the UN Convention. A refugee is a person who fears persecution as a result of being linked to a particular group (on the basis of race, religion, nationality, membership of a particular social group or political opinion). All applicants seeking recognition as a refugee as opposed to humanitarian status must prove that they would suffer persecution as a result of being linked to the particular group. It is unclear what purpose is served by this statement in the Conclusions.

Human rights abuses in a particular area of a country raises the question of the internal flight alternative referred to at article 7 of the Resolution on manifestly unfounded asylum applications and which provides a ground for including applicants in an accelerated procedure. This has already been the subject of comment above under that Resolution.

(iii) Democratic Institutions: Consideration should be given to democratic processes, elections, political pluralism and freedom of expression and thought. The Conclusions state that particular attention should be paid to the availability and effectiveness of legal avenues of protection and redress.

While democratic institutions are an important feature of western thinking as regards human rights, they are no guarantee of the protection of minorities. Indeed, within Western Europe itself over the last 100 years there are far too many examples of apparently democratic institutions legislating for the persecution of minorities. Indeed it was one such example which gave rise to the UN Convention itself.

The availability of legal avenues of protection and redress is of course particularly important. Nonetheless, it is clear from the decisions of the European Court of Human Rights that even within the highly developed human rights systems of the Member States the availability and effectiveness of legal avenues of protection and redress are not always observed.[91]

(iv) The final element to be taken into account is an assessment of the prospect for dramatic change in the immediate future. This entails a requirement to review the assessment regularly.

As can be seen from the reaction of governments criticised for human rights abuses by respected non-governmental organisations such as Amnesty International, this type of assessment can be useful in bringing pressure to bear on countries to improve their human rights records. Such independent assessments by non-governmental organisations are playing an increasingly important role in the international enforcement of human rights obligations, not only through the pressure brought to bear on criticised governments but also providing valuable information and commentary to the UN human rights mechanisms, supranational courts and national administrations and tribunals.

91 van Dijk and van Hoof, Theory and Practice of the European Convention on Human Rights 2nd Ed; Kluwer 1990 p 520 et seq.

However, criticism of human rights abuses even by the most respected of observers does not always have a desirable result. For example on 1 February 1994 the UN published the report on human rights violations in Sudan prepared by its own Special Rapporteur. On 11 February the Sudanese government launched a fatwa against the Rapporteur personally in response.

The European Union itself, in a decision taken on 9 May 1992 determined that a human rights conditionality clause must be inserted in all agreements negotiated with third countries after that date and inserted on the renegotiation of any agreements already in existence. Since 1974 the US legislature has been both debating and applying a link between human rights and most favoured country status for trading purposes. Recently and not without some controversy this linkage was abandoned by the Clinton administration as regards China. The long term consequences for respect for human rights in that state remain unclear.

In all of these initiatives, the tension between economic interests and human rights concerns has been difficult to resolve. Adding to this existing tension yet a further element, the desire of the Member States to reduce pressure on their asylum determination systems by concluding that a country is one in which there is generally no serious risk of persecution, may not be wise or in the interests of international human rights observance.

# 5 DECISION establishing the clearing house[92]

THE MINISTERS RESPONSIBLE FOR IMMIGRATION, hereinafter referred to as "The Ministers"

Whereas Article 14 of the Convention determining the State responsible for examining applications for asylum lodged in one of the Member States of the European Communities, signed in Dublin on 15 June 1990 and Luxembourg on 13 June 1991, provides for an exchange of information;

Whereas, in their report on immigration and asylum policy to the European Council meeting in Maastricht, they decided to establish a clearing house for information, discussion and exchange on asylum;

Wishing to fulfil the task entrusted to them by the European Council meeting in Maastricht, which invited them to implement, within the proposed timescale, the programme of work contained in that report;

Considering the Declaration on asylum annexed to the Treaty on European Union;

Have decided to:

- agree to the provisions set out in the Annex for the establishment of the Centre for Information, Discussion and Exchange on Asylum (clearing house);
- ask the ad hoc Group on Immigration to draw up in proper form the act which, after ratification of the Treaty on European Union, will be

---

92 Adopted 30.11.92 and 1.12.92 London, SN 2836/93 WG1 1505

submitted to the Council for approval under the procedures laid down for that purpose;

- ask the ad hoc Group on Immigration to:

- supervise the provisional operation of the clearing house, until the abovementioned act is adopted;

- carry out further studies on the definitive structures and financing of the clearing house.

A Centre for Information, Discussion and Exchange on Asylum, hereinafter referred to as the "clearing house", to operate within the framework of the General Secretariat of the Council of the European Communities, is hereby established.

The Member States shall designate to participate in the clearing house:

- their delegates, who shall in principle be the persons dealing with asylum matters in the relevant Council body;

- officials responsible in the Member States for implementing laws and regulations on asylum and more specifically experts responsible for processing asylum applications.

The Commission shall be fully associated with the work of the clearing house.

The tasks and operating methods of the clearing house shall be as follows:

*I. Powers*

The clearing house shall:

- for the time being operate provisionally within the framework of this Decision;

- act within the framework of the provisions of the act to be adopted on the basis of the Treaty on European Union as soon as possible after the latter comes into force;

- be an informal forum for exchanges of information and consultations, without any decision-making power.

*II. Objectives*

The clearing house shall gather, exchange and disseminate information and compile documentation on all matters relating to asylum.

The aim of this exchange of information shall be the development within the clearing house of greater informal consultation, itself designed to facilitate, through competent bodies, co-ordination and harmonization of asylum practice and policies.

The clearing house may draw the attention of national bodies and/or the Council to certain problems. Those bodies via the Ministers and/or the Ministers themselves may ask the clearing house to conduct studies, which may be accompanied by proposals.

*III. Gathering of Information*

The following information shall be exchanged within the clearing house:

- Member States' legislation and rules on the right of asylum;

- important policy documents (in their final form);

- important case-law and legal principles;

- statistics.

The Ministers recognize the usefulness to the clearing house of exchanges of information concerning in particular:

- the situation in the countries of origin of applicants for asylum;

- indications available as an early warning;
- routes taken by asylum seekers and the involvement of intermediaries and/or transport operators;
- reception and accommodation conditions;
- matters already harmonized.

Data stored by the Office of the United Nations High Commissioner for Refugees or by other bodies may be taken into account.

This information is to serve as a basis for documentation and discussion and is to be disseminated under the conditions described below.

*IV. Dissemination of Information*

The Ministers, national authorities participating in the work of the clearing house and the Commission shall have access to the information held by the clearing house.

The Ministers shall determine the framework and conditions for the clearing house to disseminate information to international organizations, non-governmental organizations, universities and the media in particular.

When supplying information, Member States shall state how they wish it to be classified. A Member State may oppose the dissemination of information which it has supplied.

*Commentary*

*Status:* Decision adopted by Ministers of the EC Member States outside the ambit of the European Communities Treaties but with reference to article 14 of the Dublin Convention.

*Entry into force:* Immediate – 30.11.92.

*International obligations engaged:*

(1) Dublin Convention 1990
(2) Treaty on European Union
(3) European Convention for the Protection of Individuals with regard to the Automatic Processing of Personal Data 1981

*Summary:*

This Decision provides for the establishment of a Centre for Information, Discussion, and Exchange on Asylum (CIREA) to operate within the framework of the Secretariat General of the European Council.

Permitted to participate in the clearing house are delegates of the Member States and officials responsible for implementing laws and regulations on asylum. The European Commission is stated to be fully associated with the work of CIREA.

CIREA has no power to reach decisions and is charged with gathering, exchanging and disseminating information on:–

- Member States' legislation and rules on the right of asylum;

- important policy documents (in a final form);

- important case law and legal principles;

- statistics;

- the situation in countries of origin of applicants for asylum;

- indications available as an early warning;

- routes taken by asylum seekers and the involvement of intermediaries and/or transport operators;

- reception and accommodation conditions;

– matters already harmonized.

*Comments: In Search of Information*

The preamble of this Decision makes reference to three matters: article 14 of the Dublin Convention.[93] the Report of the Ministers responsible for Immigration to the European Council Meeting in Maastricht[94] and the Declaration on Asylum annexed to the Treaty on European Union.

Article 14 of the Dublin Convention provides that the Member States shall conduct mutual exchanges with regard to national legislative or regulatory measures or practices applicable in the field of asylum; statistical data on monthly arrival of applicants for asylum and their breakdown by nationality. The article then goes on to permit, though not require, Member States to conduct mutual exchanges as regards general information on new trends in applications for asylum and general information on the situation in the countries of origin or of provenance of applicants for asylum. As regards the provision of discretionary information, the Member States are entitled to require confidentiality.

Oddly, no reference is made to the Conclusions on countries in which there is generally no serious risk of persecution, which, in order to result in any degree of harmonisation would require substantial information on recognition rates of refugees and other information to be exchanged. Indeed the Conclusions specifically provide for exchange of information in article 2 indent 2, and was adopted at the same meeting of the Council.

The Declaration on Asylum annexed to the Treaty on European Union is best known as the plea that the area of asylum be transferred to Community competence and out of Title VI, Co-operation in the Field of Justice and Home Affairs otherwise known as the Third Pillar. As the Decision to establish the clearing house is an inter-governmental decision outside Community competence it is somewhat odd that in its preamble it specifically

93 Document 1 infra
94 Annex - Work Programme 1991

refers to the declaration which would take it out of the inter-governmental framework and into Community competence.

In the Decision, the Member State agreed to establish a Centre for Information, Discussion and Exchange on Asylum (CIREA) and directed the inter-governmental group to draw up an act, which after ratification of the Treaty on European Union; would be submitted to the Council for approval. The inter-governmental group was charged with responsibility to supervise the provisional operation of the clearing house and to carry out further studies on the definitive structures and financing of the clearing house.

Pending these events, CIREA was to operate provisionally under the authority of the Decision and to provide an informal forum for exchanges of information and consultation without any decision making power. CIREA was given three objectives:

(i) To gather, exchange and disseminate information and compile documentation on all matters relating to asylum;

(ii) To develop greater informal consultation in order to facilitate co-ordination and harmonisation of asylum practice and policy;

(iii) To draw attention of national bodies and/or the Council to certain problems (unspecified).

In view of the Resolution on manifestly unfounded applications for asylum[95] and the Resolution a harmonized approach to questions concerning host third countries[96] the need for an exchange of information and co-ordination to implement the new asylum policy was manifest. Accordingly, CIREA was first charged with exchanging information on Member States' legislation and rules on the right of asylum; important policy documents in their final form; important case law, legal principles and statistics.

95 Document 2 supra
96 Document 3 supra

Thereafter, the second category of information required for exchange through CIREA is: the situation in countries of origin of applicants for asylum; indications available as an early warning; routes taken by asylum applicants and the involvement of intermediaries and/or transport operators; reception and accommodation conditions; matters already harmonized.

Notwithstanding the very substantial and successful work done by UNHCR to set up a database on asylum law and jurisprudence, the Decision only states that "account may" be taken of such information. In view of UNHCR's responsibility as guardians of the UN Convention this seems somewhat dismissive.

It would seem likely that at the time when the Decision was reached, the Member States intended that CIREA would provide a forum of exchange on the implementation of the Resolutions and, in particular, statistics on their effect on numbers of asylum applications in each of the Member States.

The wording of the Resolution on a harmonized approach to questions concerning host third countries[97] and Conclusions on countries in which there is generally no serious risk of persecution[98] provides that each Member State will reach a decision on host third countries and countries in which there is generally no serious risk of persecution individually. With each Member State reaching a separate conclusion on each third country independently and in respect of each asylum applicant clearly the Member States need a forum in which to compare data. The possibility of embarrassing variations between Member States' policies on host countries and "no risk" countries may well have been considered substantial.

However, CIREA as the creation of an intergovernmental body, had no access to the European Community budget as it had, at that time, no standing within the European Community framework.

This problem of funding was exacerbated by the apparent antagonism of the European Parliament which in a resolution on harmonization of EC

---

97 Document 3 supra
98 Document 4 supra

asylum law and asylum policy demanded that the clearing house should be given independent status from the Member States, data relating to official decisions regarding individuals should be equally accessible to the official body in question and to the person concerned or persons or bodies empowered to act for the person and that the operations of the clearing house must be monitored by the Parliament and the information gathered accessible to UNHCR and experts in the field.[99]

As the Decision provides that only the Member State delegates and officials responsible in the Member States may participate in CIREA and that the dissemination of information from CIREA should be limited to ministries and national authorities participating in its work, the chances of the European Parliament approving a budget allocation for CIREA even if absorbed into a Community framework seemed slim.

The problem was subsequently addressed in the Treaty on European Union by Article K.8(2) which permits administrative expenditure which the provisions relating to the Third Pillar entail for the Community institutions to be charged to the budget of the European Community. However the budget is still subject to the control of the European Parliament.

Insofar as the Member States may have hoped that information provided by CIREA could form a foundation for decisions regarding host countries and countries in which there is no serious risk of persecution, other issues quickly manifested themselves. In any system to which some degree of judicial control applies to decisions on asylum, it is extremely difficult to convince the judiciary that, barring questions of national security, information on which a decision is based should not be made public or at least available to the interested parties.

The principle of equality of arms in legal proceedings is entrenched in the Member States' legal systems. It is clear that in any proceedings relating to refusal of asylum there is no equality of arms if the decision reached by the state authority was and continues to be based on information which

99 European Parliament Resolution A3-0337/92 of 18 November 1992

remains hidden from the applicant and his or her representative.[100] Accordingly, the combination of budgetary constraints and national judicial accountability has limited the effectiveness of CIREA.

There is no question that a clearing house along the lines envisaged in the CIREA Decision could have a very substantial effect on asylum policy and the decisions in individual cases resulting from such a policy. Similarly, in an increasingly integrated Europe it is clear that the pooling of information on all the areas set out in the CIREA Decision is advantageous and indeed necessary. The question then remains how to create a system which will be of value to the Member States and to refugees but not liable to the shortcomings in the form of secrecy and questionable academic credibility which some consider in-built into the CIREA system.

The European Commission acting under Article K of the Treaty on European Union commissioned a feasibility study on the establishment of an observatory on migration statistics and country of origin information. It published a prefeasibility study on the possible establishment of a European Migration Observatory in 1994.[101]

A preliminary conclusion of the study is that "despite the numerous activities by governmental, non-governmental and academic institutions in the field of immigration policies, there is a definite lack of co-ordination in the European context. Not only are the initiatives taken on a decentralised basis and are the results therefore necessarily of a fragmented nature, but more importantly there is a very wide *gap between policy making bodies and researchers*. It happens very often that policy makers are not informed about the results of relevant research, whereas for researchers it is difficult to get to know what subjects policy-makers would be interested in most. This is especially true with regard to the area of root cause policies and to some extent also concerning integration policies. A possible European Migration

100 see for instance admissibility decision, European Commission of Human Right in *Chahal v UK* App. No 22414/93 of September 1994

101 Prefeasibility study on the possible establishment of a European Migration Observatory, European Commission, Luxembourg 1994

Observatory could perhaps help bridge the gap by trying to ensure the timely availability of policy relevant information".[102]

The study considered the activities of CIREA and its remit. According to the study, CIREA obtains data every trimester concerning the previous months from the participating states. It then disseminates its processed information back to the Member States, the European Commission and UNHCR. This information is then tabulated in two tables, table one on number of asylum applications lodged which would be available to all persons on request; and table two, decisions taken which would not be openly accessible as a result of requests of some states.

According to the prefeasibility study investigations, the Council Secretariat sees CIREA's immediate future in two areas:

"To play a vital part in the harmonisation of national statistical concepts and subsequently to make figures more comparable... to provide its services also with respect to the number of expulsions of unwanted aliens from the Member States".[103]

Following the detailed analysis of the prefeasibility study, four questions in particular required further clarification:

(i) How effectively are the relevant bodies (inter-governmental, academic, private and European institutions) currently fulfilling their respective mandates or aims?

It would appear from the study that the lack of co-ordination and the limited extent to which the different sectors interact in effective exchange of information makes this a real and pressing question.

(ii) Is the function of "translating research findings into concrete policy suggestions in a European context" sufficiently covered by any of the institutions?

---

102 Prefeasibility study ibid p.45
103 Prefeasibility study ibid p.40

The fact that such an aspect remains needing clarification would indicate that CIREA has not filled this gap. Indeed, considering the findings of the prefeasibility study on the actual activities of CIREA it is difficult to see how it is in any position even to participate in such an activity.

(iii) Are any other migration-related areas not covered which would be useful for Member States and the European institutions?

This is a very interesting question and in view of the establishment of two bodies under the Third Pillar, CIREA and CIREFI it is something of a surprise that the question still remains unanswered.[104]

(iv) If the answers to questions 2 and/or 3 are negative and positive respectively, what organisational specifics are required by a potential European Migration Observatory?

The study goes on to provide two analytical suggestions, one concerning the position of current migration related activities and the second concerning operational options of a potential European Migration Observatory. One of the questions which the authors of the prefeasibility study found arising most often was the question of access to information informing policy in the field. As has been identified in respect of the possible establishment of a European Migration Observatory, unless there is very clear delineation of information, both input and output which is open and if necessary policy decisions which may not be open, then the credibility of the Observatory, particularly outside the European institutions, will be in doubt. As it is put in the study "the more open the potential Observatory will be, the more credibility it will have outside the European institutions".[105]

Because of the limitations of CIREA as regards access to information which by virtue of article IV is limited to ministers, national authorities participating in the work of clearing house and the Commission (with a specific provision

104 See document 15, Conclusions on organisation and development of CIREFI infra

105 Prefeasibility study ibid p.52

for Member States to classify information to oppose dissemination) it would be difficult, even if the staff of CIREA sought to take steps in that regard, for it to obtain the active assistance and participation of the European academic world as there would be no exchange of information.

Accordingly, the problem identified by the prefeasibility study of the lack of co-ordination between academic research on countries of origin, conditions of persecution and related matters and the formulation of policy is in no way assisted by the creation of CIREA. In an answer to a Parliamentary question in the UK, in July 1993 the relevant Minister refused even to place in the Parliamentary library an analysis of the use by Member States of terms to express definite concepts of asylum statitistics referred to in a recent report of CIREA.[106] Indeed, the Minister advised that material requested regarding the principles for dissemination of information from CIREA was not public.[107]

Although the decision to establish CIREA was taken at the end of 1992, more than 18 months later in July 1993 the UK Parliament was advised that there was no specific funding for CIREA. Its activities were supported by a small number of officials in the General Secretariat of the Council of the European Communities who also have other duties and accommodation is provided within the offices of the Council.[108] As regards the funding implications for participation in CIREA the UK Parliament was advised that there were none apart from travelling and subsistence expenses, presumably of UK officials attending meetings.[109] In 1994 the UK Parliament was advised that four meetings of CIREA had been planned for that year.

---

106 Hansard, 22.7.93 Written Answers
107 Hansard, 22.7.93 Written Answers
108 Hansard, 22.7.93 Written Answers
109 Hansard, 22.7.93 Written Answers

# 6 DECISION setting up a Centre for Information, Discussion and Exchange on the Crossing of Borders and Immigration (CIREFI)[110]

1. At their meeting in Lisbon on 11 and 12 July 1992, the Ministers with responsibility for immigration called upon the ad hoc Group on Immigration to submit a feasibility study for the establishment of a Centre for Information, Discussion and Exchange (Clearing House) for their meeting in December 1992. The ad hoc Group on Immigration hereby submits to Ministers its conclusions on this matter.

2. The ad hoc Group considers that the setting up of such a centre for information concerning the crossing of borders and immigration (CIREFI) would be beneficial.

*Reasons for the establishment of CIREFI*

3. The immigration work programme endorsed by Ministers at Maastricht in December 1991 (WGI 930) encompasses a wide range of topics – admission policies, common approaches to the problems of illegal immigration, analysis of the causes of immigration pressure – on which close and detailed co-operation between Member States is called for. Successful developments in these areas will require reliable data and information flows.

4. Information on a number of issues is already made available and exchanged between Member States on an ad hoc basis as required on any particular occasion. Experience has, however, shown that the exchange and collation of information have not always been particularly effective

---

110 Adopted 30.11.92.

or rapid; questionnaires tend to be given low priority and need to be carefully drafted to elicit appropriate information. The ad hoc Group considers that there would be benefit in having a permanent mechanism for the regular exchange of information, supported, as the equivalent clearing house on asylum (CIREA) already is, by staff from the General Secretariat of the Council of the European Communities.

5. Unlike the current Sub-Groups, which under the arrangements contemplated for the implementation of the Maastricht Treaty are intended to be temporary and to be disbanded once they have fulfilled their mandate, such a body would provide a regular, permanent vehicle for the exchange of information, with a dedicated staff. Under the Maastricht Treaty arrangements this would be the primary institutional arrangement for exchange of information on an ongoing basis between Member States.

*Recommendation*

6. The ad hoc Working Group on Immigration accordingly invites Ministers responsible for immigration to endorse the establishment of such a Centre for Information, Discussion and Exchange on the crossing Borders and Immigration (CIREFI), as a forum for exchanges of information and consultations, during the first half of 1993. Ministers are also invited to endorse the following broad tasks and operating methods for the Centre.

*Functions*

7. The function of the clearing house would be to gather, exchange and disseminate information and compile documentation on matters relating to immigration and the crossing of borders, with a view to the development of greater informal consultation, close co-operation and consultation of competent bodies and increased dissemination of information to Member States. It would aid the rapid exchange of practical information between officials responsible for controls at the external borders for the purpose of combatting illegal immigration. If agreed, the clearing house will, in due course, provide a focal point under the institutional arrangements established by the Maastricht Treaty for information on matters taken under consideration in the course of implementing the work programme adopted by Ministers. It will also serve as the mechanism

for consultation and collaboration on practical matters between the relevant departments of the Member States.

8. The clearing house will not seek to duplicate or replace other arrangements which are already in place for co-operation between the Member States. In particular, it will not seek to assume the role or functions of the Rapid Consultation Centre, established following an informal Ministerial meeting held in March 1991, or to duplicate work undertaken by the Centre for Information, Discussion and Exchange on Asylum (CIREA). It may, however, work in conjunction with the Asylum Clearing House on matters which fall within the sphere of interest of both.

*Gathering of Information*

9. Information on the following matters would be exchanged within the clearing house:

   - authorised immigration flows;

   - unlawful immigration flows (country of origin, routes, means of transport);

   - unlawful immigration methods (with a view to preventing and halting attempts at unlawful immigration);

   - genuine, forged or falsified travel documents;

   - control procedures;

   - legislation bearing on immigration control procedures and information on immigration policies generally;

   - the question of rejected asylum applicants and illegal immigrants who abuse the asylum procedure, in conjunction with the clearing house on asylum (CIREA);

   - information on the expulsion of illegally present third country nationals;

- information on carriers' liability legislation and practice, including data on inadmissible passenger arrivals and routings; and

- statistics.

10. The clearing house would also have, as one of its functions, practical co-operation by experts on operational matters, including in the field of forged documents, and would supersede the existing forged documents Sub-Group as the forum for such work. Such co-operation might include the organisation and oversight of relevant training seminars.

*Access to information*

11. The clearing house would report to the ad hoc Working Group on Immigration and to its Sub-Groups (or to the successor bodies under the Union Treaty arrangements) on any matter on which its assistance was required or which it felt should be brought to notice.

12. Ministers, national authorities participating in the work of the clearing house, their officials (including officials responsible for border control) and the Commission would also have access to the information held by the clearing house.

*Constitution*

13. The clearing house would operate under the direction of the ad hoc Working Group on Immigration or its successor body. It would not itself have any decision-making powers, but could draw attention to specific problems and make proposals.

14. The Member States would designate to participate in the clearing house appropriate national experts, who might be officials responsible in the Member States for implementing laws and regulations on those matters set out above, together with other suitable individuals whose particular experience or expertise (eg, statisticians) might be beneficial.

15. The clearing house would be supported by suitably qualified staff of the General Secretariat of the Council. In all probability, and in order to avoid unnecessary bureaucracy, such staff would be those also employed in connection with the clearing house dealing with asylum matters (CIREA).

The details of the organisation of CIREFI are to be discussed by the Sub-Group "External Frontiers" on the basis of WGI 1240 and in the light of proposals submitted by the German delegation. Detailed proposals should be submitted to the ad hoc Group on Immigration as quickly as possible.

*Commentary*

*Entry into force*: The Decision to establish the clearing house was adopted on 30.11.92.

*International obligations engaged:*

1. European Convention for the Protection of individuals with regard to the automatic processing of personal data 1981.

*Summary:*

This Decision provides for establishment of a Centre for Information Concerning the Crossing of Borders and Immigration (CIREFI). As in respect of the sister centre on asylum, CIREA,[111] CIREFI is staffed from the General Secretariat of the European Council and is permanent.

The purpose of CIREFI is to provide "a regular, permanent vehicle for the exchange of information, with a dedicated staff".[112] It was intended that following the entry into force of the Treaty on European Union, CIREFI would be the primary institutional arrangement for exchange of information on an on-going basis between Member States in its field.

---

111 See Document 5 supra.

112 See Article 5.

CIREFI is to have no decision making powers[113] and is intended to share staff with CIREA. It is charged with gathering, exchanging, disseminating and compiling information and documentation on matters of immigration and crossing of borders in the following areas:

(i) Authorised immigration flows;

(ii) Unlawful immigration flows (country of origin, roots, means of transport);

(iii) Unlawful immigration methods (with a view to preventing and halting attempts at unlawful immigration);

(iv) Genuine, forged or falsified travel documents;

(v) Control procedures;

(vi) Legislation bearing on immigration control procedures and information on immigration policies generally;

(vii) The question of rejected asylum applicants and illegal immigrants who abuse the asylum procedure, in conjunction with CIREA;

(viii) Information on the expulsion of illegally present third country nationals;

(ix) Information on carriers' liability legislation and practice, including data on admissible passenger arrivals and routings; and

(x) Statistics.

*Comments: Who are Irregular Migrants?*

One of the issues which has proved problematic in achieving any progress on common action in fields of immigration and asylum has been the lack

---

113 See Article 13.

of knowledge about and concern of the Member States as to what is actually going on in other Member States. The establishment of two separate centres for information, CIREA with responsibility for asylum and CIREFI with responsibility for immigration was an early attempt to try to overcome the mistrust which, it was viewed, arose from this lack of knowledge.

*The Need for Exchange of Information*

The Decision, taken in 1992, reflects the difficulties and concerns which were becoming acute with the proposed deadline for implementation of article 7A EC and the abolition of internal borders for persons travelling within the territory of the Member States. These concerns are most clearly set out in the Palma document[114] which reflects the high political priority of concern on the movement of persons and the sense of uncertainty as regards the consequence of such free movement.

In order to achieve co-operation, a minimum level of trust and confidence needed to be fostered. The informal meetings of officials in inter-governmental fora outside the ambit of the European Community which was already occurring needed to be given some status and structure. One difficulty after the political changes in Europe in 1989 was a proliferation of inter-state groups of officials discussing and determining programmes on movement of persons with specific regard to the movements anticipated from the Central and Eastern Europe. It was increasingly apparent that the Member States needed a structured forum to resolve their position among themselves so that difference among them did not surface for the first time "in public". Further, in order to reach common positions it was clear that some exchange of information was required.

It appears from the decision that CIREFI was intended to provide a place in private where officials could exchange ideas and concerns within a structure but away from public scrutiny. The only exception to the "Member States only" rule was the admission of the Commission as an observer. However, the remit of CIREFI was drafted extremely widely. It would seem that the

114 See Annex, the Palma Document, Free Movement of Persons - a Report to the European Council by the Co-ordinators Group, June 1991.

Member States wished to provide sufficient scope for CIREFI to develop without need for a change of principles. As with any forum established without apparent funding or personnel, a wide remit and subject to a rule of secrecy, little progress can be made. Firstly the officials themselves must undertake, voluntarily, further duties in addition to their normal workloads in their Member State. Secondly, there is little discipline within a wide scope to resolve the competing interests of the different Member States as to what or how any aspect should be progressed. Thirdly, with a rule of secrecy there is no effective way to ensure that the information fed into the system is correct or that any agreement reached within its scope is applied or applied consistently. Fourthly with no public scrutiny there is no potential "embarrassment factor" for inactivity.

*The Background*

In 1985 the European Commission adopted a decision setting up a prior communication and consultation procedure on migration policies in relation to non-member countries.[115] This decision included an obligation that Member States notify the Commission, *inter alia*, of draft measures with regard both to workers who are nationals of non-member countries and to members of their families, including illegal entry, residence and employment, equality of treatment in living and working conditions, wages and economic rights, integration into the workforce, society and cultural life and their voluntary return to their countries of origin.

The aim of the measure was to secure cooperation to facilitate the mutual exchange of information and the identification of problems of common interest and, in relation to those problems, to facilitate the adoption of a common position, particularly as regards international instruments relating to migration.[116] It was also aimed at examining the possibility of Community or national measures to harmonise national legislation on foreigners.

---

115 Decision 85/381, OJ L217/22, 1985.

116 *Germany & Ors v Commission* [1987] ECR 3203.

The Member States opposed the decision strenuously and to the extent of seeking its annulment by the Court of Justice.[117] The consequence of Member State's opposition was that the Commission withdrew from the fray and left the Member States to get on with third country immigration policy on their own. It was not until the adoption of this Decision in 1992 that the Member States managed to reach agreement among themselves on a proposal not dissimilar to that the Commission had proposed in 1985. The significant difference between the two proposals is the role of the Community. In the CIREFI Decision, the Commission's role is as a mute observer. There is no question of Community harmonisation and indeed, CIREFI itself is specifically excluded from giving instructions to the Member States. At the time of its adoption, the CIREFI proposal was no more than a "free floating" Decision of a number of states among themselves with no constitutional framework. This state of affairs was changed with the introduction of Title VI of the Treaty on European Union (the Third Pillar).

It is unfortunate that the Member States chose to challenge the proposal of the Commission which at the relevant time had the resources and commitment to carry out comprehensive work on immigration control, only seven years later to decide to pursue the same investigations, this time in a forum lacking resources and an effective way to reach and maintain political consensus.

*Definitional Problems*

Migration is an extremely complex field of study full of contradictory trends, assumptions and theories.[118] Obtaining any clear picture of stocks of foreign nationals let alone flows has proven both contentious and difficult.[119] The emphasis in the Decision to establish CIREFI on unlawful immigration flows presupposes a common definition of unlawful immigration or, at the very least, some definition of unlawful immigration in each Member State and

---

117 *Germany & Ors v Commission* ibid.

118 See prefeasibility study on the possible establishment of European Migration Observatory, European Commission, Luxembourg 1994.

119 Eurostat, Migration statistics 1994.

some method of tracking flows.[120] Indeed, a starting place at the very least would be a definition of "lawful migrant", be it common or several. However, even this is lacking.

"The United Nation's definition of an international migrant (someone who declares the intention of being there/away for one year or more) often cannot be applied to stock or flow data. The definition of migration is often based on a recorded change of residence. This is notoriously difficult to define as residence may be temporary or permanent or something in between (Poulain *et al*) 1991). An individual may have more than one residence, or none."

"In some countries an immigrant is someone who intends being a resident there for more than three months (eg, Belgium, Italy); elsewhere it is six months (Netherlands) or twelve (UK, Ireland), or there may be no definition period (Germany). This makes comparison of data between countries very difficult. Even where statistical offices may attempt to influence data collection using standardised definitions such as those of the UN, the administrative needs of departments and ministries supplying the data often result in definitions which use different lengths of time. Sometimes intention to stay or leave is recorded, in other cases actual stay or time spent away is recorded historically. Only rarely is it possible to match the two types of data or to record those cases where the actual length of time spent away is the same as the previously stated intention".[121]

This problem is well exemplified in UK law. Where a person seeks to enter the UK, for instance as a visitor, and is so admitted by an immigration officer, if at the time of entry the person was contemplating certain other activities in the UK, for instance working, he or she will be, in law, an illegal entrant.[122] Even if the person does not then proceed to undertake any other activity and leaves before the end of his or her permitted period of residence he or she will have been an illegal entrant throughout the period that he or

120 Migration and Population Change in Europe, Dr J Salt, Research Paper number 19 UNIDIR, 1993.

121 Immigration and Population Change in Europe, Ibid, page 8.

122 Macdonald's Immigration Law and Practice, Macdonald and Blake Third Edition, Butterworths 1991, Chapter 16.

she was in the UK. With over 10 million persons being admitted to the UK in all capacities every year[123] and with a definition of an illegal entrant which is as subjective and potentially inclusive as that contained in UK law, it is impossible to make any estimation about flows of unlawful migration.

When the above problem of definitions is multiplied times 15 Member States the task of CIREFI is clearly formidable. In view of the definitional difficulties in the migration field, it is certainly not comprehensive nor necessarily a solution, to define down to the most specific the elements in respect of which information is being sought. When looking at a field as complex and diverse as migration stocks and flows the temptation is always, when faced with the apparent impossibility of determining what is going on in a comprehensive sense, to concentrate on administrative measures taken in the face of the unknown. In other words, rather than seeking to get to grips with concepts of migration, it may be easier to exchange information on the procedures of border officials. This is what appears to have happened with CIREFI.

*Structural Problems*

The work of CIREFI has been hampered from the outset by a number of inbuilt weaknesses:

(i)

An extremely wide ambit covering areas such as unlawful immigration flows in respect of which there is no consistency as regards definition or reliable statistics. Further, to collect statistical information as CIREFI was charged to do, would require expert statisticians in constant contact with diverse statistical authorities in the Member States which are by no means uniform, and very substantial resources to produce information of any value whatsoever.

123 Control of Immigration: Statistics United Kingdom 1993 cm 2637, Table 3.1.

EUROSTAT has now taken the lead in the collection of migration statistics both in its series, Statistics in Focus and its recent first publication on migration statistics.[124] However, even EUROSTAT with all its resources is having grave difficulties producing statistical information which is reliable. It has yet to produce any work on illegal migration.

(ii) Sources of information:

No guidance is given on how CIREFI is to gather, exchange, compile and disseminate information and documentation or whence they are to collect it. However, the assumption in the Decision appears to be that information will be obtained from the Member States in the first instance. Information for the statistics which CIREFI is to compile may be collected by various different government departments, for instance, interior ministries, labour ministries, social affairs ministries etc. Each ministry will be collecting information for its own purposes which will not necessarily co-relate with those of other ministries in the same state or with similar ministries in other Member States. Just as with statistical information, other information on control procedures, legislation bearing on immigration control procedures and information on immigration policies generally is likely to be extremely difficult to co-relate and require a substantial investment of resources if it is to result in comprehensible, let alone valuable, information.

In any event, many of the sources of information on immigration are outside the ministries. In particular, the work of academics, institutes and non-governmental organisations in compiling, obtaining and analysing information has been extremely important in all Member States to the development of knowledge on migration.[125] In order to obtain any real picture on migration these sources would need to be included.

(iii) Access to information:

According to articles 11 and 12 of the Decision only ministers, national authorities participating in the work of the clearing house, their officials

124 EUROSTAT, Migration Statistics 1994, Luxembourg.
125 Prefeasibility study ibid.

and the Commission are to have access to information held by the clearing house. This presents two difficulties in respect of the reliability of information from CIREFI. First, unless there is a two way flow of information, non-governmental experts and academics are normally unwilling to share their information. Secondly, without the co-operation of extra-ministerial sources of information the work of CIREFI must necessarily be impoverished.

Further, where information and reports are kept confidential within the ministries there is no external control on the reliability of information exchanged. The vital control mechanism, public accountability, to ensure reliability which in turn fosters co-operation is lacking from the Decision.

The seeds of discontent sown into the fabric of CIREFI on its establishment in 1992 appear to be bearing the expected fruit. In 1994 the Member States adopted Conclusions of the organisation and development of CIREFI which give some indications of its progress.[126]

126 See comments on document 16 infra.

# 7 RECOMMENDATION regarding practices followed by Member States on expulsion[127]

Ministers of the Member States of the European Communities responsible for Immigration, meeting in London on 30 November and 1 December 1992

WITH A VIEW to reflecting the best practices existing in Member States and to meeting the requirements of speed, efficiency, effectiveness and economy with regard to expulsion;

TAKING ACCOUNT of the need for effective means to identify, apprehend and expel those who are required to leave the territory of the Member States;

NOTING that this Recommendation does not affect the provisions of international Conventions currently in force on extradition;

NOTING that this Recommendation is without prejudice to Community law;

NOTING that this Recommendation does not apply to people refused entry at the border or who are identified attempting to cross the border illegally;

ADOPTED THE FOLLOWING RECOMMENDATION:–

## *I General Policy*

1. Member States will ensure that without prejudice to Community law, their policies and practice with regard to expulsion are fully consistent with their obligations under the 1951 Geneva Convention relating to the Status of Refugees and the 1967 New York Protocol. Account should

---

127 SN 4678/92 WG11266.

also be taken of other relevant international instruments, including the 1950 Convention for the Protection of Human Rights and Fundamental Freedoms.

2. Subject to the above, the general rule should be that people found:

   (i) to have entered or remained unlawfully in Member States (where their stay has not been regularised);

   (ii) to be liable to expulsion on grounds of public policy or national security; or

   (iii) to have failed definitively in an application for asylum and to have no other claim to remain,

   should be expelled, unless there are compelling reasons, normally of a humanitarian nature, for allowing them to remain. In addition, consideration should be given to the question whether, in appropriate circumstances, a person who has been working in breach of immigration/aliens or related provisions should be expelled.

3. In accordance with Article 15(2) of the draft External Frontiers Convention expulsion should be to the country of origin or to any other country to which the individual may be admitted. Where a person is being expelled on public policy or national security grounds this should not be to another Member State unless the individual has a right of residence there.

4. There should be provision for expulsion under either criminal or administrative law.

5. People being expelled should be notified in an appropriate manner of the reasons for the decision unless the interests of national security make such notification undesirable.

6. Whenever there is any doubt about a person's ability to understand the language in which an interview is being conducted, consideration should be given to the provision of an interpreter.

7. There should be a right to be represented and an appropriate means to challenge expulsion decisions.

8. Expulsion should take place as soon as possible after the decision to expel the individual has been taken.

*II Restrictions on Personal Liberty*

1. There should be power in appropriate circumstances to restrict the personal liberty of people liable to expulsion.

2. Any restriction on liberty should be limited to the period necessary to effect expulsion, including identification, the making of any necessary arrangements and the provision of tickets, travel documents and escorts.

3. Appropriate places of custody should be available, where possible providing accommodation separate from that used by prisoners.

4. People in custody with a view to expulsion should have reasonable access to legal advisers and others in accordance with the general rules relating to the place of custody.

*III Documentation*

1. Any necessary arrangements for the identification and documentation of the individual should be made at the earliest possible opportunity.

2. Insofar as legislation does not already so permit consideration should be given to the introduction of laws to allow the fingerprinting of those to be expelled, to assist identification.

3. With a view to minimising delays in obtaining necessary travel documents and/or visas, early contact should be established with the

Embassy or Consular authorities of States to which expulsion is to be effected and/or through which transit will be necessary.

4. Where a travel document is not held and cannot be arranged within a reasonable period, consideration should be given to the use of a 'one-way' document similar to that referred to in paragraph 3.38 and Appendix 8 of Annex 9 to the Chicago Convention.

*IV Re-admission Agreements*

1. Insofar as re-admission agreements do not already exist, consideration should be given to establishing them with appropriate States. Where possible, such agreements should be multilateral, but where this is not possible bilateral agreements should be considered. Consideration should be given to preparing agreements in a standard format and, in the case of multilateral agreements, these might be along the lines of that between Poland and the Schengen States, with such adaptations as appear necessary to take account of national situations and practical experience of that agreement.

2. When re-admission agreements have been concluded Member States should communicate details of them to Community partners.

3. Specific measures should be adopted bilaterally or multilaterally as required with a view to improving existing arrangements among Member States for re-admission.

*V Prosecution of Facilitators of Illegal Entrants and those who Harbour People who have Entered or Remained Unlawfully and Action against those who Employ Illegal Entrants*

1. Insofar as legislation does not already exist, Member States should consider the introduction of laws which would provide for the prosecution of people who knowingly facilitate or attempt to facilitate the entry or transit of illegal entrants, and, subject to appropriate safeguards, of those who knowingly harbour those who have entered or remained unlawfully. It will be particularly appropriate to provide for the prosecution of those who commit such acts for reward or in an organised way. It is also recommended that appropriate measures should be taken to combat the employment of those known to have entered or remained in breach of the immigration or aliens provisions or who are not authorised to work under immigration/aliens or related provisions.

2. Consideration should also be given to the question whether it would be appropriate to have power to expel people subject to immigration/aliens provisions who have been involved in the facilitation, harbouring or employment of illegal immigrants.

3. The European Convention on Mutual Assistance in Criminal Matters provides a cooperative framework between countries enabling those signatory to it to obtain and supply evidence for use in criminal proceedings, both in their own country and in others, and to facilitate the appearance of individuals from one country, in criminal proceedings to another. Insofar as national policy permits, Member States are encouraged to enter into arrangements which would enable them to assist their Community partners, for example in obtaining evidence, or service of summonses or other judicial documents on suspects or witnesses.

*VI Confiscation of Modes of Transport used by those who Facilitate Illegal Entrants*

1. Insofar as legislation does not already exist, Member States should consider the introduction of laws which would permit a court, which had convicted a person of knowingly facilitating or attempting to facilitate unlawful entry, to order that the vehicle, ship or aircraft used

should be forfeited. However, such legislation might specify limits on the exercise of the power to order confiscation, relating, for example, to the knowledge of the owners and to the size and nature of the vehicle, ship or aircraft involved.

### *VII Transit During the Course of Expulsion*

1. Where a person who is being expelled cannot be sent direct to his point of destination, arrangements for the expulsion should be in accordance with the guidelines set out in WGI 1110.

### *VIII Escorts*

In order to ensure that a person being expelled reaches the intended destination, consideration should always be given to the question whether an escort is required. Escorts may be necessary either for those who require assistance or those who are likely to resist expulsion and may be a potential danger to themselves or others. Early consultation with the carrier is recommended in cases in which an escort may be necessary.

### *IX Selection, Training and Equipment of those Involved in Expulsion*

1. All staff charged with the duty of expulsion should be appointed for the purpose and should receive appropriate training.

2. Staff should be properly trained and equipped to tackle the problems of illegal immigration and traffickers. In considering Forgery Detection Training it will be particularly appropriate to take account of the evaluation of the Pilot Course for Training Instructors from Member States.

3. Bearing in mind that costs of investigation, detention and removal can be reduced if illegal immigrants can be prevented from entering Member States, there are benefits to be gained from providing appropriate technical equipment, for example for the detection of forged and falsified documents.

4. Account should be taken of initiatives already underway in other fora on which Member States are represented.

*X Exchanges of Information*

1. With a view to combating the unlawful trafficking of illegal immigrants, Member States should arrange for appropriate exchanges of information with their Community partners, perhaps through CIREFI, if established.

2. With a view to encouraging appropriate exchanges of information the principles set out in the Appendix to this paper are commended to Member States.

3. It is acknowledged that in considering the exchange of personal information States will have to take account of relevant national Data Protection legislation. It is noted that the need for an international agreement containing an appropriate standard for data protection should be considered.

4. Subject to the need to comply with national legislation and data protection requirements, where fingerprints have been taken for the purpose of documenting a person liable to be expelled, Member States should be prepared to make them available to another Member State, if this will assist in making arrangements for expulsion and the individual does not have an acceptable travel document.

# APPENDIX

## EXCHANGES OF INFORMATION

*1. Contacts for Exchange of Information*

1.1 It is desirable to have broad exchanges of information, which might involve exchanges of operation experience. These present an opportunity for discovering the practices used by traffickers of illegal immigrants and to take action to prevent them.

1.2 In addition, there is value in having personal contacts for the exchange of information, and the value of such contacts could be increased by countries exchanging officers for training or other purposes. This is relevant not only in neighbouring countries but elsewhere also.

1.3 The Presidency proposes to circulate a questionnaire designed to supplement and up-date existing information about useful points of contact in other Member States.

*2. Exchange of Non-personal Information*

2.1 Exchange of non-personal factual information have a most important part to play in combating illegal immigration. These exchanges might be of both an informal, albeit structured nature, and of a formal nature.

2.2 The speed of exchanging information is most important.

2.3 Information should be exchanged about the routes and the methods of illegal entry that were used; about the transit points that illegal entrants and their traffickers used; about the nationalities involved; and in particular about emerging trends concerning those nationalities.

2.4 It is also important to have information about the main types of vehicle used and to consider what could be done to deter people from trying to travel illegally, for example by the use of publicity when traffickers are caught and in particular when traffickers are sentenced to imprisonment or are otherwise punished, for example by confiscation of the ship, aircraft or vehicle used.

2.5 Account should be taken of arrangements already in force, for example those which have been reached within groups such as the Schengen Group and TREVI, in order that those planning exchanges of information might benefit from the experience already gained.

*3. Exchange of personal information*

Arrangements for the exchange of information about those known or suspected of involvement in organized illegal entry may assist considerably in combating it. It is of particular importance that the information passed should be sufficient to enable the individual to be readily identified, and that it should be passed speedily to the competent authorities in other Member States.

*Commentary*

*Status:* Recommendation adopted by Ministers of the EC Member States outside the ambit of the European Communities Treaties.

*Entry into force:* There is no time limit within which implementation must take place. Similarly there is no sanction for failure to comply.

*International obligations engaged:*

(1) ILO Convention 97, 1949
(2) UN Convention relating to the Status of Refugees 1951 and Protocol 1967
(3) International Covenant on Civil and Political Rights 1966
(4) ILO Convention 143, 1975
(5) European Convention on Human Rights 1950
(6) European Communities Treaties

*Summary:*

This Recommendation sets out a framework for expulsion policy for the Member States. It is not specific in its personal scope to third country nationals however it is stated to be without prejudice to Community law and the UN Convention and provides that account should be taken of other relevant international instruments including the European Convention on Human Rights.

The principle of the Recommendation is that persons coming within three categories should generally be expelled:

(1) Those who have entered or remained unlawfully in a Member State (where their stay has not been regularised);

(2) Those who are liable to expulsion on grounds of public policy or national security; or

(3) Those who have failed definitively in an application for asylum and have no other claim to remain.

Where there are compelling reasons, normally of a humanitarian nature, such persons may be allowed to remain. Additionally, persons who have worked in breach of immigration, aliens or related provisions should be considered for expulsion.

Expulsion should be normally to the country of origin or to any other country to which the individual may be admitted. This may be another Member State except where the person is being expelled on public policy or national security grounds in which circumstances the person should not be expelled to another Member State unless the person has a right of residence there.

A choice of either criminal or administrative law for expulsion is recommended. As regards safeguards for the individual the person must be notified of the decision in an appropriate manner subject to a national security proviso and where in doubt as to the person's ability to understand the language, consideration should be given to the provision of an interpreter. There should be a right to representation and appropriate means to challenge expulsion decisions. Restrictions on personal liberty should be included in national law subject to reasonable access for legal advice.

Persons being expelled should be fingerprinted to assist identification. Readmission agreements with third countries should be considered in order to facilitate expulsion.

Member States should consider the introduction of laws which would prosecute persons knowingly facilitating or attempting to facilitate entry or transit of illegal entrants subject to appropriate safeguards. Provisions should also be brought into force for persons knowingly harbouring persons who have entered or remained unlawfully. Further, persons who have been involved in facilitating, harbouring or employment of illegal immigrants (not subject to criminal prosecution necessarily) should be liable to expulsion.

Confiscation of vehicles used by a person convicted of knowingly facilitating or attempting to facilitate unlawful entry should be considered.

Provisions are included relating to training of persons involved in expulsion and for information regarding immigration (see comments on CIREFI supra).

*Comments: Harmonising the Unknown*[128]

International law recognises the right of states to admit or refuse to admit to their territory any alien subject only to obligations arising from international human rights instruments. However, international law does not recognise the right of a state to refuse admission to or expel its own nationals.[129]

Once a state has admitted an alien to reside on the territory any attempt to expel the alien must satisfy the limitations on expulsion arising from international obligations including those protecting private and family life[130] and prohibiting collective expulsion of aliens.[131]

---

128 This commentary is based on the excellent work done on the subject by Peter Bartram and Don Flynn for the Immigration Law Practitioners' Association.

129 Article 13 UN Universal Declaration of Human Rights 1948; Article 12(4) International Covenant on Civil and Political Rights 1966 .

130 Article 12 UN Universal Declaration of Human Rights 1948 ;Article 8 European Convention on Human Rights 1950.

131 Article 4 ECHR Fourth Protocol.

Further, within the framework of Community law Article 8A EC creates citizenship of the Union. If this citizenship qualifies for protection in international law as a genuine citizenship, then the expulsion of a citizen of the Union outside the Union is prohibited.

Although the Recommendation is not limited to third country nationals, the expulsion of citizens of the Union from any one Member State is likely to be an intra Community matter and therefore not subject to the Recommendation. However, the question arises of Community engagements in respect of the expulsion of third country nationals. These engagements through agreements with third countries have given rise to residence rights for third country nationals which have direct effect in the Member States.[132]

The Member States are obliged by the good faith article of the Treaty to take all appropriate measures, whether general or particular, to ensure fulfilment of the obligations arising out of the EC Treaty or resulting from action taken by the institutions of the Community.[133] The loose personal scope of this Recommendation is not helpful as it allows confusion as to the subject matter of the Recommendation. For example, a Turkish worker in a Member State whose residence right is protected by Community law is entitled to a higher threshold of security against expulsion than a Columbian worker.[134] The failure to clarify to whom the Recommendation applies blurs this distinction and increases the possibility of error.

The European Court of Justice has held that the Community's tasks and the objectives of the Treaty would be compromised if Member States were able to enter into international commitments containing rules capable of affecting rules already adopted in areas falling outside common policies or of altering their scope.[135] In so far as the Recommendation is an international commit-

---

132 See for instance Turkey/EC Association Agreement 1963, Additional Protocol 1970 and Association Council Decision 1/80 as regards the residence right of Turkish workers confirmed by the jurisprudence of the European Court of Justice.

133 Article 5 EC.

134 Article 14 Association Council Decision 1/80.

135 Opinion 2/93 ECJ; OJ No C 109 of 19.4.93.

ment its provisions must not affect rules already adopted in areas of Community competence.

The need to protect the individual from the prospect of unjust and unfair expulsion from a territory in which he or she has established residence must be foremost in any body of law or policy which pays due regard to civil and human rights. International law recognises that state authorities have the right to protect fundamental interests of society by expelling persons who, by virtue of their nationality and residency status, might be liable to expulsion. However, international law also makes it clear that it is not appropriate to punish all breaches of laws and regulations by foreign nationals with the sanction of expulsion. There will always be a need to strike a balance between what is necessary in a democratic society and the operation of natural justice and the rights of the individual.

*General Policy on Expulsion*

Section I of the Recommendation sets out general principles for which expulsion may be justified. Member States are at the outset reminded of their obligations under international law, but this section does not, in terms, require the observance of those fundamental rights. This is notwithstanding the fact that the international obligations of the Member States must, in the hierarchy of legal measures take precedence over the Recommendation.

In as much as all Member States are signatories to the European Convention on Human Rights it would have been appropriate for the Recommendation, if not to require incorporation of the Convention itself directly into domestic law, at least to ensure that national immigration laws and practices expressly give effect to rulings of the European Court of Human Rights. This is so especially in the context of the need for protection from inhuman or degrading treatment.[136] respect for private and family life,[137] the provision of effective remedies to prevent unwarranted interference with basic

136 Article 3 ECHR.
137 Article 8 ECHR.

rights[138] and non-discrimination on the grounds of sex or ethnic origin in the exercise of these rights.[139]

For example, in the UK little attempt has been made to ensure that British laws on expulsion give full effect to the Court's judgments in cases such as *Berrehab*,[140] *Beldjoudi,*[141] *Mustaquim*[142] and *Abdulaziz.*[143] The Recommendation could have directed that people with strong family ties or long residence from infancy should, in general, *not* be expelled. Whilst recognising that expulsion may be appropriate for transgression of the criminal law, states should be urged not to expel persons lawfully resident simply because of trivial offences where expulsion would be a disproportionate response.

There are however positive aspects to the general policy. For example, Section I, article 7 provides that all persons threatened with expulsion should have "a right to be represented and an appropriate means to challenge expulsion decisions". This Recommendation should lead to the introduction in all Member States of rights of appeal before expulsion for all persons whether they are deemed to have entered the country illegally or stayed beyond their permitted period.

*Restrictions on Personal Liberty*

Recommendation provides in Section II article 2 that "any restriction on liberty should be limited to the period necessary to effect expulsion, including identification, the making of necessary arrangements and the provision of tickets, travel, documents and escorts". This should prevent the person being detained for a lengthy period until such time as the facts can be established and a decision made on whether expulsion is appropriate.

---

138 Article 13 ECHR.
139 Article 14 ECHR.
140 *Berrehab v Netherlands* ECHR [1988] Ser. A. No 138.
141 *Beldjoudi v France* ECHR [1991] Ser. A. No 234-A.
142 *Mustaquim v Belgium* ECHR [1991] Ser. A. No. 193.
143 *Abdulaziz, Cabales & Balkandali v UK* ECHR [1985] Ser. A. No 94.

To prevent abusive or unreasonable detention, it would have been helpful for the Recommendation to state in terms that detention should always be subject to regular review by a court or independent tribunal with a right to representation. Indeed, both in the context of review of detention and the means of challenging expulsion decisions themselves, provision for representation available free for those without the means to pay may be a corollary of obligations engaged under the European Convention on Human Rights.[144]

*Identity and Documentation*

Section III of the Recommendation urges Member States to provide themselves with powers to fingerprint those to be expelled "to assist identification".

The question of fingerprinting is referred to again in Section X at article 4 in the context of the exchange of information between Member States. At this point, however, the reason for fingerprinting is extended beyond that of assisting identification to "the purpose of documenting the person liable to be expelled".

Fingerprinting "to assist identification" and for "the purpose of documenting a person to be expelled" are two separate objectives. For the former purpose fingerprinting would take place in a limited number of circumstances where the authorities have reasonable grounds for believing they know the true identity of an individual and have access to a set of fingerprints which will place the matter of identification beyond dispute.

The subsequent reference to fingerprinting for the purpose of documenting a person to be deported seems to suggest a much broader power which could move in the direction of the routine fingerprinting of all persons caught up in the expulsion process, even when questions of their identity are not in dispute.

The potential for abuse of such a wide power, for instance agencies with access to this information, not to mention the position of individuals whose

---

144 *Airey v Ireland* ECHR [1981] Ser. A. 41.

details are wrongly or unlawfully recorded, may outweigh any social good which might be obtained through an increase in the marginal efficiency of immigration control bodies.

*Readmission Agreements*

The Recommendation advocates, at Section IV, that readmission agreements on the model of the Schengen states agreement with Poland be concluded between the Member States and appropriate third countries. The effect of the Schengen/Poland model would be that the third country commits itself in advance to receiving all persons whom the immigration authorities of the Member States choose to expel without consideration of the individual circumstances of each case.

The Member States have now adopted a specimen bilateral agreement on 30.11.1994. For further comment please see document 18 below.

*Prosecution of Facilitators, Harbourers and Employers of Illegal Entrants*

Although the heading refers to "illegal entrants", in the first paragraph this concept is already conflated "those who have ... remained unlawfully". This is a confusion of categories which means that two entirely different groups of people are threatened with sanctions which may not be appropriate in many situations.

The concept of illegal entry is quite separate from that of remaining in breach of the law. In the former case all aspects of the person's entry and residence are held to be unlawful; in the latter the unlawful element might involve only a minor infraction of some aspects of national immigration regulations, e.g. a delay in reporting a change of address to the authorities. It appears that the possibility of criminal prosecution should apply equally to one who renders assistance to a person who is outside the law from the start and, for example, one who offers support to a student who has breached the law by accepting a temporary part-time job to help finance her studies. It may be neither practical nor just to permit the prosecution of, for instance, the relatives of a student in prohibited employment, for, say, allowing her to reside in their family home.

Persons in breach of conditions of entry are seldom without some plea of mitigation which, whilst not always sufficient to prevent their expulsion, would certainly make it unreasonably harsh to make others who have rendered assistance by harbouring the proper subject of criminal proceedings. This is particularly so where a person offering assistance has acted in good faith.

*Confiscation of Modes of Transport of those Facilitating Illegal Entry*

The proposals set out in Section VI call for the introduction of laws which would permit the confiscation of vehicles, ships or aircraft used by persons convicted of aiding illegal entry. This could lead to the authorities and the courts imposing draconian penalties on people who, technically in breach of the law, have acted in good faith in the belief that the individual whose entry has been assisted will, after entry, be able to establish grounds for residence.

The preamble to the Recommendation provides that none of its proposals are intended to apply to people "who are identified attempting to cross the border illegally". It would appear therefore that the penalty of confiscation of means of transport will not apply to carriers who are assisting a person to present him or herself at the frontier without having the necessary documentation to qualify for entry.

This form of carrier sanction is an extension of the existing sanction applied in most Member States of carriers of inadmissible aliens by way of fines. A recent study on carriers' liabilities indicates that almost all Member States have introduced such legislation except Spain, Ireland and Luxembourg.[145] However, the introduction of such legislation has not resulted in harmonisation of national law but appears to have spawned even greater diversity than existed before:-

"Although it is evident that carrier sanctions relate not only to policies of controls of the EU external borders but also to plans for the suppression of

145 Shifting Responsibility Carriers' Liability in the Member States of the European Union, A Cruz, Pluto Press 1995 p.6.

internal borders, there has been no co-ordination whatsoever, either among the twelve Member States of the Union or the nine Member States of the Schengen Group, to approximate their respective policies and practices. Carrier sanctions have, apparently, never been considered as an issue to be taken up by any of the working groups or sub-groups set up to ensure the creation of a Schengen area without internal borders. Consequently, there was no exchange of information on the experiences of the Member States which introduced such legislation earlier. Bills to this 1effect were simply introduced and amended in accordance with the strength of opposition parties before reaching the stage of final approval".[146]

*Exchanges of Information*

At Section X there is an outline of measures allowing the exchange of information between the authorities of the Member States on matters relating to the expulsion of individuals.

According to paragraph 1.1 of the Appendix, the exchange of information will present an "opportunity for discovering practices used by traffickers of illegal immigrants and to take action to prevent them". At paragraph 1.2 there is reference to a "value in having personal contacts for the exchange of information, and the value of such contact will be increased by such countries exchanging officers for training or other purposes". What is envisaged therefore is an extensive collaboration between immigration and police authorities across Member States involving the transfer of information on the personal details of individuals, their movements and activities and the suspicions which are being entertained by the immigration control bureaucracies.

This Recommendation was adopted two and a half years before a framework of law was agreed at Union level to regulate police and immigration

---

146 Ibid p.6.

authority collaboration of this order.[147] The fundamental questions of data protection arise here, specifically:–

(1) will individuals know that a record of their activities has been created and is being exchanged across Member States?
(2) Will they be able to demand sight at least of this information?
(3) How will they be able to challenge the accuracy of its details?
(4) Will they be able to have their records struck out when the inappropriateness of detailing their activities and movements has been acknowledged, or its inaccuracy established?
(5) Will people who have unfairly suffered as a consequence of these measures have a right of redress and compensation?

Measures such as these can have detrimental consequences for citizens and others with legitimate expectations of residence in and travel to and from Member States. Adequate assurance and guaranteed legal protections in these areas are therefore necessary.[148]

*Conclusion*

The concerns of the police and immigration control authorities in an area of social policy must be carefully balanced against the recognition of individual rights and freedoms as protected in international human rights instruments. International obligations should not be seen as an "obstruction" to police and immigration authorities power. Rather they are the counterbalance which guarantee the principles of democracy and rule of law.

147 Europol Convention signed June 1995.

148 Please see also comments on data protection in the context of the Dublin Convention document 1 above.

# 8 RECOMMENDATION regarding transit for the purposes of expulsion[149]

The Ministers of the Member States of the European Communities meeting in London on 30 November and 1 December 1992 responsible for Immigration,

CONSIDERING Member States' practices with regard to transit for the purposes of expulsion;

WHEREAS those practices should be more closely aligned with a view to their harmonization;

WHEREAS the measures to be applied must meet the requirements of speed, efficiency and economy,

RECOMMEND application of the following guidelines:

I

For the purposes of this Recommendation, "transit" means the passage of a person who is not a national of a Member State through the territory or through the transit zone of a port or an airport of a Member State.

II

A Member State which has decided to expel a third-country national:

- to a third country, should as a rule do so without the alien passing through the territory of another Member State;

---

149 19579/92 IMMIG 2 Annex F to Annex II.

- to another Member State, should as a rule do so without the alien passing through the territory of a third Member State.

III

1. Where particular reasons so warrant, in particular reasons of efficiency, speed and economy, a Member State may request another Member State to authorize the entry into its territory and transit through that territory of a third-country national who is subject to expulsion.

2. Before submitting such a request, the State which has taken the expulsion measure will ascertain that in normal circumstances the continuation of the journey of the person expelled and his admission into the country of destination are assured.

3. The State to which such a request is addressed will comply with it subject to the cases detailed at VI.

IV

The State taking the expulsion measure will notify the transit State whether the person being expelled needs to be escorted.
The transit State may:

- authorize the State which has taken the expulsion measure to provide the escort itself;

- or decide to provide the escort itself;

- or decide to provide the escort in collaboration with the State which has taken the expulsion measure.

V

1. The request for transit for the purposes of expulsion should contain information relating to:

   - the identity of the alien being expelled;

- the State of final destination;
- the nature and date of the expulsion decision; the authority which took the decision;
- the evidence for believing that the alien is admissible into the country of final destination or into the second transit country;
- the travel documents or other personal documents in the possession of the person concerned;
- the identity of the body making the request;
- the conditions relating to passage through the requested State (schedule, route, means of transport, etc.);
- the need for an escort and the escort arrangements.

2. The request for transit for the purposes of expulsion should be addressed as soon as possible to the authorities responsible for expulsion in accordance with the relevant internal law of the requested State, and they should reply promptly.

3. The transit State may request information, in particular regarding the necessity of transit.

VI

Cases in which transit for the purposes of expulsion may be refused:

- where, in the case of transit overland, the alien constitutes a threat to the public order, national security and international relations of the transit State;
- where, the information referred to at V.3 is considered unsatisfactory.

VII

If, for whatever reason, the expulsion measure cannot be enforced, the State through which the transit is being carried out may return the person expelled, without formality, to the territory of the requesting State.

VIII
Responsibility for costs

Where the costs of expulsion cannot be borne by the alien or by a third person, the requesting State will take responsibility for:

– the travel costs and other expenses, including escort costs, incurred until the alien whose transit has been authorized leaves the Member State of transit;

– where applicable, the costs of return.

IX

These recommendations do not preclude closer co-operation between two or more Member States.

X

A Member State intending to conduct negotiations with another Member State or with a third country on transit for the purposes of expulsion will inform the other Member States thereof in good time.

XI

This Recommendation does not affect the provisions of the European Convention for the Protection of Human Rights and Fundamental Freedoms of 4 November 1950 or those of the Convention relating to the Status of Refugees.

It does not affect the provisions of international Conventions currently in force on extradition and extradition in transit.

It may not have the effect of substituting transit for the purposes of expulsion for extradition and transit extradition procedures.

## *ADDENDUM*

to the Recommendation regarding transit
for the purposes of expulsion
(WGI 1275)

1. With a view to meeting the requirements of efficiency, speed and economy in connection with necessary transit, a distinction may be drawn between the different measures taken by the Member States to effect expulsion by way of air, water and overland transport.

2. Expulsion by air and passage through the transit zone of an airport in connection therewith should be excluded from the scope of the provisions on requesting authorisation for entry and transit (see WGI 1275, III), so that in such cases the country of transit is merely informed.

3. Notification of transit for the purposes of expulsion by air should contain information as described in WGI 1275, V, concerning requests for transit.

4. In the case of expulsion overland or by water, requests and notifications for entry into or transit through the territory of a State are to be addressed to a central contact body indicated by the country of transit, in accordance with the recommendations contained in WGI 1275.

   In the case of expulsion by air, were transit to be refused by the transit country, this information should be transmitted to the requesting State within a period of 24 hours of the transit being notified.

5. A common list of contact bodies should be drawn up by the Member States.

   In case of expulsion by air, direct contacts should be made with the appropriate official(s) at the transit airport in question or, depending on national procedures, with any other appropriate official, provided the 24-hour rule (see point 4 above) is respected.

*Commentary*

*Status:* Recommendation adopted by Ministers of the EC Member States outside the ambit of the European Communities Treaties.

*Entry into force:* There is no time limit within which implementation must take place. Similarly there is no sanction for failure to comply.

*International obligations engaged:*

(1) Universal Declaration of Human Rights 1948
(2) UN Convention relating to the Status of Refugees 1951 and Protocol 1967
(3) UN Convention relating to the Status of Stateless Persons 1954
(4) ILO Convention 143
(5) European Communities Treaties
(6) European Convention on Human Rights 1950

*Summary:*

This Resolution is designed to regulate practices of Member States in respect of third country nationals who are being expelled from the territory of one state through the territory of another Member State before reaching the final destination. The Recommendation places an obligation on the sending stage to obtain consent from the transit state to expulsion through its territory together with an assurance from the sending state that it has ascertained "that in normal circumstances the continuation of the journey of the person expelled and his admission into the country of destination are assured".

Transit through other Member States of third country nationals who are being expelled to a further destination either inside or outside the Union, should be avoided according to the Recommendation.

*Comments: Touring Europe Without a Visa*

The expulsion of third country nationals tends to be a costly and often time consuming activity for Member States. It also gives rise to substantial concerns about human rights obligations and more than once Member States have been found in breach of their obligations to protect private and family life under Article 8 ECHR by reason of expulsion decisions.[150]

Accordingly there has always been a temptation for Member States merely to take third country nationals they wish to expel to their nearest border, albeit with another Member State; and direct the alien to leave.[151] Reference is made in the Recommendation to only two international human rights obligations, the European Convention on Human Rights and the UN Convention relating to the Status of Refugees. However specific reference is made to international conventions relating to extradition and extradition in transit. A safeguard is included at Article XI that the Recommendation "may not have the affect of substituting transit for the purposes of expulsion for extradition and transit expedition procedures".

The Recommendation makes no reference to the way in which an expulsion decision is reached or any safeguards which should apply to the legality either of the decision of expulsion which has been taken or protection for the proposed transit state as regards complicity in the expulsion of an individual contrary to international human rights obligations.

The sending state is not required to seek the authorisation of the transit state as regards the expulsion. The obligation contained in Article III is limited to "where particular reasons so warrant... a Member State *may* request another Member State to authorise entry into its territory and transit through that territory..." (emphasis provided). The non-binding nature of this provision which leaves the discretion apparently to the sending state to decide where it is appropriate actually to request authority to expel a third

150 *Berrehab v Netherlands*; *Moustaquim v Belgium*; *Djeroud v Belgium*; *Beldjoudi v France*, supra.

151 For example the so-called Roosendaal expulsion whereby aliens being expelled from Netherlands were placed on a train the next stop for which was in Belgium see Nederlands Vreemdelingenrecht 2nd ed, Kuijer & Steenbergen, NCB 1994.

country national through another Member State's territory seriously compromises the effectiveness of the Recommendation.

The Recommendation includes no definition of its personal scope. "Transit" is defined as the passage of a person who is not a national of a Member State through the territory or through the transit zone of a port or an airport of another Member State.[152] There is no definition of a third country national to whom the Recommendation applies. Therefore the possibility of conflict with European Community law is not inconsiderable. For instance, third country national family members of citizens of the Union exercising free movement rights in another Member State are fully protected to the same degree as the citizen of the Union against expulsion measures by the State.[153] Further, businesses established in one Member State which send part of their labour force to another Member State including third country national members of their labour force, to provide services are entitled to the protection of their right under Article 59 EC for the purposes of a provision of services.[154] The Court of Justice has yet to consider the businesses right to protection against expulsion of its labour force from the Member State where the services are being provided, however it seems unlikely that this protection would be less than that provided to natural persons who are citizens of the Union exercising rights under Article 59 EC.

Further, under some agreements between the Community and third countries protection of residence is assured to third country national citizens of those third countries, most notably in the context of the subsidiary legislation to the Turkey/EC Association Agreement 1963 and 1970 Protocol. Without a specific personal scope which excludes persons whose expulsion is regulated by Community law, Member States risk both a breach of their obligations under the Treaties and constitutional confusion in the Union.

Article IV makes provision for the escort of persons being expelled. Where the sending state has determined that "particular reasons so warrant" and

152 Article 1 of the Recommendation.
153 Article 1(2) Directive 64/221.
154 *Van der Elst* [1994] ECR.

has requested the transit Member State for authority to expel the person through the second state's territory and there is a need in the view of the sending Member State for an escort the transit state must decide whether to authorise the sending state to provide the escort, provide the escort itself or provide an escort in collaboration with the sending state. This again raises the question of the validity of the expulsion decision. The transit state, which has no control or right to information regarding the expulsion decision itself becomes a party to the expulsion and therefore potentially liable in international law for the consequences. The way in which expulsion is carried out may engage obligations as regards torture, inhuman or degrading treatment.[155] There have been a number of reports of persons being expelled from Member States under escort dying as a result of the treatment which they receive at the hands of the escort.[156]

*Data Protection:*

At Article V of the Recommendation the information which is to be provided by the expelling state to the transmitting state is set out. This includes:

(i) The identity of the alien being expelled;

(ii) The state of final destination;

(iii) The nature and date of the expulsion decision; The authority which took the decision;

(iv) The evidence for believing that the alien is admissible into the country of final destination or into a second transit country;

(v) The travel documents or other personal documents in the possession of the person concerned;

---

155 Article 3 ECHR; Article 5 Universal Declaration of Human Rights, 1948; Article 7 International Covenant on Civil and Political Rights 1966.

156 See for example the Joy Gardner case UK 1994 where a woman subject to a deportation order died during police and immigration officers' procedures to effect her departure.

(vi) The identity of the body making the request;

(vii) The conditions relating to passage through the requested state (schedule route, means of transport, etc);

(viii) The need for an escort and the escort arrangement.

There is no reference whatsoever to any provision of international or domestic data protection conventions, laws or norms. Further, there is no limitation on the use of the information provided nor is there any reference to any control or even the right to be informed for the person whose information is being so passed.[157]

*Detention:*

In view of the practice of a number of Member States to detain persons in respect of whom a definitive decision to expel has been made pending the execution of the order, the question of speed within which the expulsion takes place is of particular importance.

Where expulsion will involve transit through another Member State there is no time limit on the period within which the application for authorisation from the transit state must be made. There is no obligation as regards the time within which the transit state must reply to a request for authorisation. Therefore where the person is in detention he or she could be held for a very extensive period of time even where the person wishes to return to the country of origin before execution is concluded.

*Certainty:*

Nowhere in the Recommendation is there an obligation on either the expelling state or the transmitting state to verify the nationality of the person being expelled or any certainty that the person to be expelled will be admitted in the final country of destination or in a second transit country. The only reference to this aspect of expulsion is in article 5 regarding information

157 See comments on the Dublin Convention, supra.

to be given to the transit state which includes "the evidence for believing that the alien is admissible into the country of final destination or into the second transit country". The individual therefore has no certainty as to where or under what circumstances he or she may come to be in any third state. This issue is one which arises in respect of all of the measures relating to expulsion adopted by the Member States either intergovernmentally or within the ambit of the Treaty on European Union. All of these measures focus on reinforcing the right of the state in which a third country national finds him or herself to expel the person.

However, expulsion requires the active participation of at least two states, the expelling state and the receiving state. Where there is no question as regards the nationality of the person being expelled, reliance may be placed on article 13 of the Universal Declaration of Human Rights 1948 which provides at paragraph 2 that "everyone has the right... to return to his country". It is a norm of international law that states may not refuse admission to their own nationals.[158] However there is no obligation on any *other* country to admit a non-national being expelled for any purpose whatsoever from another state. The reference to a second transit country therefore creates substantial problems as regards certainty of ultimate destination.

Further the question of nationality and determining of what country, if any, a person is a national has become increasingly acute with the changing face of Europe, in particular. Persons who were nationals, for instance, of the Soviet Union may or may not have become or have an opportunity to become nationals of the successor states.

The protection in international law for stateless persons is unfortunately limited. Article 31 of the UN Convention relating to the Status of Stateless Persons 1954 only protects stateless persons lawfully on the contracting state's territory. However this necessarily raises questions of the position of a stateless person who has been lawfully on the territory of a Member State and through no fault of his or her own but rather by the refusal of the authorities to extend his or her permission to reside becomes unlawfully

158 International Migration Law, Dr R Plender, p.71.

present there. In such circumstances any subsequent decision to expel may be challengeable on the basis of the country international obligations.

Additionally, any attempt to expel a person in such circumstances either definitively to a state of which he or she may or may not be a national or by transit through one state potentially leading to a chain of transit expulsions through numerous states with no certainty as to the final destination may give rise to a breach of the obligation under Article 3 ECHR not to subject a person to torture, inhuman or degrading treatment as interpreted by the European Court of Human Rights.[159] Article VII of the Recommendation provides that if an expulsion measure cannot be enforced the transit state may return the person to be expelled without formality back to the sending state.

The result of these provisions is that the person being expelled has no certainty as to where he or she may, in the end, be left. This may be at the border with some territory of which he or she at one time had citizenship, it could be in a third state which is unable or unwilling to send the person on to any other state or back, or, after an arduous and potentially lengthy circuit of the world, back in the state which began the process. As a result of such a circuit intimate details of the person's life and existence may have been transmitted to substantial numbers of states with no guarantee as to the accuracy of the information provided or the use to which it may subsequently be put.

Finally, at Article VIII, the cost of expulsion is to be borne first by the alien or if that is not possible by a third party. In so far as this relates to migrant workers it is contrary to Article 9 of ILO Convention 143 which states:

"In case of expulsion of the worker or his family, the cost shall not be borne by them."

---

159 *Soering v The UK* [1989] Ser A 161.

# 9 RESOLUTION on the Harmonization of national policies on family reunification.[160]

At their meeting of 1 June 1993, Ministers agreed on the following resolution on harmonization of national policies on family reunification.

1. Ministers of Member States of the European Communities responsible for Immigration, meeting in Copenhagen on 1 June 1993, adopted the following Resolution on the harmonization of national policies on family reunification.

2. This question was included as a priority item in the programme for harmonization of immigration policies adopted by Immigration Ministers and endorsed by the European Council at the conclusion of the Netherlands Presidency in December 1991, and work on it has continued during both the Portuguese, United Kingdom and Danish Presidencies.

3. The question of family reunification is already to some extent governed by international Conventions to which some or all of the Member States are parties, as well as by basic provisions of their national laws. The obligations flowing from these Conventions and from basic national laws have been taken into account in the process of seeking further harmonization between the Member States, which does not affect those obligations.

4. On the other hand, there is also a need to control migration flows into the territories of the Member States. This is considered to be one of the factors for the successful integration of immigrants who are lawfully resident within the territories of Member States.

---

160 AD HOC GROUP IMMIGRATION Copenhagen, 1 June 1993 [SN 2828/1/93 WGI 1497. REV 1].

5. With these considerations in mind, Ministers resolved that the national policies of Member States in respect of family reunification for immigrants resident in their territories should be governed by the principles set out below. They agreed to have regard to these principles in any proposals for the revision of national legislation. They further agreed to seek to ensure by 1 January 1995 that their national legislation is in conformity with them. The principles are not legally binding on the Member States and do not afford a ground of action by individuals.

6. The harmonization principles are confined at this stage to family reunification in respect of persons who are not nationals of a Member State but who are lawfully resident within the territory of a Member State on a basis which affords them an expectation of permanent or long-term residence.

7. A number of Member States have different policies in respect of the family members of their own nationals, whilst others treat non-EC nationals settled in their territories on the same basis as their own nationals for the purpose of family reunification. This question is not affected by the present Resolution.

8. Policy in respect of the admission to Member States of the family members of nationals of Member States who are exercising a right of free movement of persons is governed by Community law. When the Agreement on the European Economic Area comes into force, the position of family members of nationals of EFTA States will be governed by that Agreement.

9. Member States have separate policies and practices in respect of other categories of resident non-EC nationals, i.e. those who do not have an expectation of permanent or long-term residence (notably persons who are granted permission to work in a Member State for a fixed period, and students). In some cases persons in these categories are excluded from family reunification.

   Nor does this Resolution cover family reunification in respect of persons who have been granted refugee status, for whom some Member States have more favourable policies.

The harmonization of policy in respect of the families of persons in these categories will be further examined in the course of considering admissions policies in respect of them.

PRINCIPLES GOVERNING MEMBER STATES' POLICIES ON FAMILY REUNIFICATION

*Non-Community nationals to whom the Principles relate*

1. These principles, which do not affect Community law, will be applied in respect of the family members of non-EC nationals who are lawfully resident within the territory of a Member State on a basis which affords them an expectation of permanent or long-term residence.

   Third-country nationals present in the territory of a Member State on a short-term basis (for example, students and persons admitted for employment for a fixed term) are outside the scope of these principles. The question of what constitutes an expectation of permanent or long-term residence is for determination by reference to national laws and policies.

*Family members normally entitled to enter and remain in a Member State*

2. The Member States will normally grant admission, under the conditions set out in the remainder of this Resolution, to

   - the resident's spouse (that is, a person bound to him or her in a marriage recognized by the host Member State),

   - the children, other than adopted children, of the resident and his or her spouse,

   - children adopted by both the resident and his or her spouse while they were resident together in a third country, in accordance with a decision taken by the competent administrative authority or court of that state and which is recognized and accepted by the Member State of residence, and where the adopted children have the same rights and obligations as the other children and there has been a definitive break with the family of origin.

The spouse and the children may be admitted only for the purpose of living together with the resident.

*Waiting periods*

3. Member States reserve the right to require non-EC nationals to be lawfully present in their territory for certain periods of time before family members may be reunited with them under the terms of these principles.

*Further conditions concerning spouses*

4. Member States reserve the right to determine whether a marriage was contracted solely or principally for the purpose of enabling the spouse to enter and take up residence in a Member State, and to refuse permission to enter and stay accordingly.

5. A wife and her children will not be admitted for the purpose of family reunification if the marriage is polygamous and the resident already has a wife resident in the territory of a Member State.

*Other children*

6. Member States reserve the option of admitting a child (including an adopted child) where the child is the offspring of the resident or of his/her spouse, but not of the couple involved. When determining whether or not to accept such a child, the Member State shall consider whether the resident and his/her spouse or either of them, hold parental authority, have been granted custody of the child and have the child effectively in their charge.

7. Member States reserve the possibility of admitting a child adopted by both the resident and his or her spouse while one or both were resident in a Member State provided that the child has been adopted in accordance with a decision taken by the competent administrative authority

or court of the State of origin and which is recognized and accepted by the Member State of residence, and where the adopted child has the same rights and obligations as the children referred to in paragraph 2 and there has been a definitive break with his family of origin.

*Further conditions concerning children*

8. In order to qualify for admission for the purpose of family reunification children must be below a maximum age, which the Member States agree should be between 16 and 18 years, and must not have married or have formed an independent family unit or be leading an independent life.

9. Member States will consider whether an adoption has been arranged solely or principally for the purpose of enabling the child to enter and take up residence in a Member State, and whether to refuse permission to enter and stay accordingly.

*Other family members*

10. Member States reserve the possibility of permitting the entry and stay of family members, other than those envisaged in paragraphs 2, 6 and 7 of this Resolution, for compelling reasons which justify the presence of the person concerned.

*Conditions of stay for family members admitted to the Member States*

11. An authorization to stay on the basis of family reunification may, for such a period as the Member State concerned determines, be conditional upon the continued fulfilment of the criteria for admission.

12. Within a reasonable period of time following their admission, family members, in accordance with the national legislation in each Member State, may be authorized to stay on a personal basis independently from the person whom they joined on the basis of family reunification and, if appropriate, be authorised to work.

13. The authorization to stay granted to a family member may be terminated at any time if there are grounds for presuming that it was obtained by means of fraud or forgery.

*General conditions of entry and stay*

14. A person will not normally be admitted to the territory of a Member State for the purpose of family reunification without a visa or other prior written authorization for that purpose, issued by the Member State in which the family intends to reside. The application must normally be made whilst the family member concerned is outside the territory of the Member State concerned.

    A visa or other prior written authorization will not be issued unless the applicant meets all the criteria for entry and stay in the territory of the Member State concerned as set out in these principles.

15. Family members must also, in principle, be in possession of valid travel documents which are recognized by the Member State in which the family intends to reside.

16. Member States reserve the right to make the entry and stay of family members conditional upon the availability of adequate accommodation and of sufficient resources to avoid a burden being placed on the public funds of the Member State concerned, and on the existence of sickness insurance.

17. Member States will normally refuse entry and stay to a family member if his presence would constitute a threat to national security or public policy ("ordre publique"). They reserve the right to refuse entry and stay on grounds of public health.

*Commentary*

*Status:* Resolution adopted by Ministers of the EC Member States outside the ambit of the European Communities Treaties. At paragraph 5 of the preamble it is stated that the principles set out in the Resolution are not binding on the Member States nor do they afford a ground of action by individuals.

*Entry into force:* The Ministers undertook to adapt national legislation to conform with the Resolution by 1 January 1995.

*International obligations engaged:*

(1) Universal Declaration of Human Rights 1948
(2) International Covenant on Civil and Political Rights 1966.
(3) UN Convention on the Rights of the Child 1990
(4) ILO Convention 143 concerning Migrant Workers 1975
(5) European Convention on Human Rights 1950
(6) European Social Charter 1961
(7) European Convention on the Legal Status of Migrant Workers 1977

*Summary:*

The Resolution makes the following provisions:

(i) It applies only to family members of non EC nationals who are lawfully resident in the territory of a Member State on a basis which affords them an expectation of permanent or long term residence.

(ii) Admission should normally be granted to: spouses provided the marriage is recognised by the host state, children of the resident and his or her spouse (though further limitations may be placed on admission of children of only one spouse); children adopted by both residents (in accordance with a competent administrative authority decision).

(iii) Member States may reserve the right to impose a waiting period of lawful residence before family reunification may be applied for, and to make family reunion dependent on adequate means of support, accommodation and health insurance.

(vi) *Spouses*

Member States may refuse admission to a spouse if the marriage was contracted solely or principally for the purpose of admission to the Member State. In respect of polygamous marriages only one wife and her children are to be admissible.

(v) *Children*

Member States will normally admit children of both parties to the marriage but are not required to do so. They may admit children of one party to the marriage. Regard shall be had to whether the parent in the Member State has parental authority over the child. In respect of adopted children, an adoption order of a competent administrative authority or court of the state of origin recognised in the Member State is necessary. Only children adopted when the couple were resident abroad are to be considered for admission, though Member States reserve the possibility of admitting other adopted children. Children are only admissible if they are under the age of between 16-18 depending on the preference of the Member State. They must be unmarried and not have formed an independent family or be leading an independent life.

(vi) *Other Family Members*

Other family members are only admissible where there are compelling reasons to justify their presence. This applies to children not otherwise qualifying, parents, grandparents and other relatives.

(vii) *Conditions*

Authorization to stay may be conditional upon continuing to fulfil the admission criteria. After an unspecified but "reasonable" period of time family members may be authorised to stay on an independent basis. Authorization to stay may be terminated if there are grounds for presuming it was obtained by fraud or forgery.

(viii) *General Conditions*

Family members will not normally be admitted to the territory without a visa or other prior written authorization for family reunion purposes. The application must normally be made while the family member is outside the Member State and will not be issued unless the person fulfils all the criteria of entry and stay. Family members must, in principle, have valid travel documents. Also, there is a national security or public policy proviso permitting exclusion.

There is no reference in the Resolution to procedural safeguards or rights of appeal.

*Comments: Compliance with International Commitments?*

*Existing Obligations of Member States*

The right to family life appears so consistently in human rights conventions as to qualify for consideration as a norm of international law. Among the conventions *inter alia* protecting family life to which the Member States are parties are found:

(i) The European Convention of Human Rights, Article 8, which requires states to respect the family and private life of all persons within their jurisdiction.

(ii) The European Social Charter, Article 19(6) the obligation to facilitate the reunion of the family of a foreign worker defined as *at least* the spouse and dependent children under 21 years.

(iii) The European Convention on the Legal Status of Migrant Workers, Article 12 requiring admission of spouses and unmarried, minor, dependent children subject to available housing. Signatory states may introduce a waiting period but it may not exceed 12 months.

(iv) ILO Convention 143, Article 13 requiring states to facilitate reunification of families including spouses, dependent children and parents.

(v) Universal Declaration of Human Rights Articles 12 and 16 enshrining the right protection of family life and to marry and found a family.

(vi) International Covenant on Civil and Political Rights, Article 17 protecting the individual from interference with privacy or family.

(vii) UN Convention on the Rights of the Child.

The right to family life is among the most fundamental aspects of human rights protection, the protection of which appears in similar wording in almost all international human rights instruments. It has been the subject of numerous judgments by international tribunals in consideration of its extent.

The right is most frequently expressed in two forms:

(i) The right to marry and found a family.[161]

(ii) The protection of privacy and family life from interference subject to national security and public policy provisos.[162]

The Member States are parties to most if not all of these international instruments therefore the compatibility of the Resolution with these obligations merits consideration. In those states where international treaty obligations take direct effect in the national legal order by reason of adherence to the treaty (for instance Netherlands, Belgium) national courts are obliged to test national provisions against treaty commitments. In other Member States where international treaty obligations only take effect in the national legal order if implemented by virtue of national law (for example Germany, UK) national courts may only have regard to those aspects which have been so implemented.

---

161 Article 23 ICCPR; Article 16 Universal Declaration of Human Rights; Article 12 ECHR for example.

162 Article 17 ICCPR; Article 12 Universal Declaration of Human Rights; Article 8 ECHR for example.

As has been made clear by the European Court of Justice, because of the supra national nature of the Union, in the interpretation of Community law, fundamental rights are an integral part of the general principles of law the observance of which the Court ensures, in accordance with the constitutional traditions common to the Member States and the international treaties on which the Member States have collaborated or of which they are signatories.[163] However, as the Resolution was adopted by the Member States acting intergovernmentally it remains outside the ambit of the European Court of Justice. To the extent that it may be classified as part of the *acquis intergovernmental* which has been subsumed into the Third Pillar of the Union by virtue of Title VI of the Treaty on European Union, it still remains outside the competence of the Court of Justice by virtue of article L of that Treaty which limits the Court's jurisdiction to the First Pillar, the Community.

The Resolution's personal scope includes family members of non EC nationals resident within the territory of a Member State on a basis which affords them an expectation of permanent or long term residence. Leaving aside the fact that there is no common definition among the Member States of what "an expectation of permanent or long term residence" means, the personal scope is clear. All non-EC nationals (or third country nationals) are subject to the Resolution whether they were born on the territory of the Member State or whether they arrived yesterday. Most of Europe's third country nationals who have a permanent residence status or something approaching it came to the Union's territory before 1973-5 when most EU states brought a halt to primary immigration. Therefore most people affected by this Resolution will have been residing and working in the Union for 20 years or more. Otherwise put, they came to Europe and settled before 9 of the current 15 Member States joined the then European Community. It is useful, therefore, to compare the right of these third country nationals to family life in Europe with that enjoyed by, for example a Swedish migrant moving for the first time to Germany under Community law.

---

163 *Hoechst* [1989] ECR; *ERT* [1991] ECR I-2925.

*Consistency with Community Law*

The first aspect of the Resolution to be examined is its consistency or otherwise with provisions of Community law relating to family reunion for migrant citizens of the Union with their family members whether these family members are themselves citizens of the Union or not. The Community rules apply irrespective of the nationality of the family member and irrespective of where the family member is residing. Therefore, for migrant citizens of the Union there is no obligation to go through the "eye of the needle" of national law to be united with third country national family members. As soon as the citizen exercises his or her free movement right he or she is entitled to be joined immediately by his or her qualifying third country national family members irrespective of where they are or whether they have been refused family reunion rights under the national law of the citizen's home state.

Where a citizen of the Union is exercising a free movement right under the EC Treaty to work, be self employed or provide or receive services in another Member State he or she is entitled to family reunion with the following categories of persons:

*1. Spouses*[164]

The right to family reunion with spouses is unqualified. There is no provision for Member States to examine the purpose of the marriage or to refuse admission to a spouse where the marriage is valid in the national law of the state from whence the citizen of the Union and his or her spouse have come.[165] Community law will not permit abuse of its provisions[166] but whether or to what extent this permits Member States to refuse admission to a spouse on the grounds that the marriage is a sham remains deeply contested.

The right of citizens of the Union to admission of their third country national spouses cannot be made subject to any limitation on grounds of inadequate

---

164 Regulation 1612/68 article 10(1) in respect of workers; Directive 73/148 article 1 in respect of the self employed and service providers and recipients.

165 Article 4 Regulation 68/360 .

166 *Surinder Singh* [1992] ECR I-4265.

funds or income except where the right to residence is only for the purpose of studies, retirement or where the citizen of the Union is not exercising any economic activity at all.[167] In these cases the Member State may require the citizen of the Union to prove that he or she has adequate means, which may mean income to the minimum level of the social assistance available in the state.

The right of family reunion for migrant citizens of the Union is subject to a requirement that there is sufficient housing for workers' family,[168] however, this requirement can only be assessed at the date of first admission not subsequently to admission.[169] A Commission proposal for amendment of Regulation 1612/68 recommends the removal of this requirement, which has been accepted by the Council though the proposal for amendment in its entirety has yet to be adopted.

There can be no waiting period before the right of family reunion with the spouse is exercised. Third country national spouses may be required to obtain a visa but every facility must be given to expedite the issue of the visa and no charge may be made for it.[170] The spouse is entitled to at least a five year residence permit or document and is also entitled to work. The entitlement to work and reside derives from the Treaty itself therefore the residence permit is only declaratory of that right and does not create it.[171]

If the spouses do not live together, so long as the marriage has not been dissolved, and even if the spouses intend to divorce at some time in the future, the spouse is entitled to remain and to work.[172] In the determination of the rights of migrant citizens of the Union to family reunion they are entitled to an effective remedy analogous to that of own nationals.[173]

---

167 Directive 93/96 in respect of students, Directive 90/365 for pensioners and Directive -90/366 for the economically inactive.

168 Article 10(3) Regulation 1612/68.

169 *Commission v Germany* Re: Housing Conditions [1989] ECR 1263.

170 Article 3(2) Regulation 68/360.

171 *Watson & Belmann* [1976] ECR 1185.

172 *Diatta v Land Berlin* [1986] ECR 567.

173 Articles 8 and 9 Directive 64/221.

According to the Resolution, the spouses of third country nationals resident within a Member State "on a basis which affords them an expectation of permanent or long-term residence"[174] are subject to a very different regime:

(i) The spouse may only be permitted admission for the purpose of living together with the resident and the marriage must be recognised by the host state.

(ii) Waiting periods may be imposed before family reunion may be enjoyed.

(iii) The Member State may examine the marriage to determine whether it was contracted solely or principally for the purpose of enabling the spouse to enter and take up residence in the Member State.

(iv) Authorization may be for such period as the Member State determines and conditional on the continued fulfilment of the requirements.

(v) A visa obtained abroad is normally a prerequisite.

(vi) The Member State may require proof of both adequate housing and sufficient resources so that the family will not become a burden on social assistance programmes in the host Member State and health insurance.

(vii) There is no provision for spouses to work in the Member State.

2. *Children*[175]

Migrant citizens of the Union are entitled in their host Member State to family reunion with their children of any nationality whether natural, theirs only and not of their spouse, of their spouse but not a blood relation to them or adopted. As regards children under the age of 21 the right is absolute and there is no requirement that the children are dependent on the migrant

---

174 Article 1 Resolution.

175 Article 10 Regulation 1612/68 in respect of workers; Article 1 Directive 73/148 in respect of the self employed and service providers and recipients.

citizen of the Union. Where the children are over 21 they must be dependent on the migrant citizen of the Union and/or spouse. However, dependency cannot be defined so as to exclude the child's right to claim social assistance benefits independently as soon as he or she arrives in the Member State.[176] The child may be required to obtain a visa but this must be provided free of charge and as quickly as possible. The same rules as regards housing, residence permits, cohabitation with the parent and working apply to children as to spouses.

There is no requirement that the children of any age or nationality of migrant citizens of the Union are unmarried or have not formed an independent life. Indeed, specific provision is made to *include* a right of admission of grandchildren of citizens of the Union.

Here again the difference between the regime which applies to migrant citizens of the Union and long-term or permanently resident third country nationals as regards admission of children is striking. In place of the above rules for migrant citizens of the Union, third country national residents must fulfil the following criteria according to the Resolution:

(i) Only children of both the third country national and his or her spouse are fully included.

(ii) Adopted children are only admissible where the adoption decision was taken by a competent authority of the state and is recognised in the Member State and where the adopted child has the same rights and obligations as other children and there has been a definitive break with the family of origin. Such children must have been adopted while the parents were resident abroad though the Member States reserve the option of considering other adopted children.

(iii) Children of only one party to the marriage may or may not be admissible at the discretion of the Member State but subject to consideration of whether the parent in the Member State has parental authority for the child.

---

176 *Lebon* [1987] ECR 2811.

(iv) The child must be single, not have formed an independent life and be under the age of between 16 and 18 (the Member State may chose the upper limit it wishes to apply subject to a minimum upper age limit of 16 and a maximum of 18).

The same limitations as apply to spouses of third country nationals also apply to their children as regards waiting periods, housing, support, cohabitation with parents, health insurance etc.

*3. Other Relatives*[177]

Migrant citizens of the Union are entitled to family reunion in the host Member State with all other family members in the ascending or descending line (ie parents, grandparents, grandchildren etc) of either the citizen of the Union or his or her spouse provided they are dependent on the citizen of the Union or his or her spouse. The same provisions as in respect of spouses apply to questions of residence permits and work. Dependency is determined in the same way as for children over 21.

Member States are also under a duty to facilitate the admission of other family members not specifically mentioned if those family members are dependent on the citizen of the Union or his or her spouse *or* if they lived under the same roof as the family in the country of origin.

Long-term or permanently resident third country nationals in the Member States, under the terms of the Resolution, are subject to a presumption against family reunion with any relatives other than spouses and children under the age of between 16 and 18. This presumption is only to be displaced where there are "compelling reasons" to justify the presence of other family members in the Member State.

The difference in the level of rights to family reunion is startling. There does not appear to have been any effort to eliminate discrimination against third country nationals permanently resident in the Member States in com-

---

177 Article 10(2)Regulation 1612/68 as regards other relatives of workers; Article 1 Directive 73/148 as regards other relatives of the self employed and service providers and recipients.

parison with migrant citizens of the Union. This is somewhat surprising in view of the numerous declarations by the European Council against racism and xenophobia.

This Resolution has the consequence of creating or emphasising different standards applicable to different foreigners on the territory in an area of fundamental rights protected by many international human rights instruments. For instance, a Greek national going to work in Denmark for the first time and possibly with the intention of remaining in Denmark only for a short period has the right to be accompanied by his or her spouse, children of any age if dependent, dependent parents, grandparents and grandchildren of the worker or his or her spouse irrespective of the nationality of those family members and subject to very carefully limited checks by the host Member State. However, a Turkish national who has lived and worked most of his or her life in Denmark and helped to build up the country may only be joined by his or her spouse subject to detailed and subjective checks which may offend his or her dignity and cast aspersions on the genuineness of his or her marriage, children up to the age of 16 or possibly 18 only if unmarried and dependent and the blood children of the marriage.

A further imbalance is created by the Resolution in comparison with Community provisions on family reunion. In those states where long-term or permanently resident foreigners are able under national law to naturalise as citizens of the state fairly easily they then become citizens of the Union entitled to Community free movement rights. Should they exercise those rights, they become entitled to Community family reunion rights. However, in those states where naturalisation is only available under arduous and restrictive conditions, third country nationals may not be able, ever, to avail themselves of Community family reunion rules for the simply reason that by virtue of the state to which they immigrated they cannot become citizens of the Union. Therefore a further discrimination is created in the long term expectations and aspirations of third country nationals in the Union.

*Compatibility with the European Convention on Human Rights*

As outlined above, the right to protection of private and family life from unwarranted interference by state authorities is contained in numerous international human rights instruments. However, only one has the benefit of an international court with jurisdiction to consider petitions from individuals who claim that their rights have been abused. This is, of course, the European Convention on Human Rights.

All the European Union Member States are parties to the Convention and all have accepted the jurisdiction of the European Court of Human Rights as regards individual petitions against the state. Accordingly, the terms of the Resolution will be measured against the right to respect for private and family life as expressed in the ECHR and interpreted by the European Court of Human Rights.

The right to respect for private and family life is contained in article 8 ECHR. It is subject to limitations on the basis of national security, public safety, the economic well being of the country, the prevention of disorder or crime, the protection of health or morals and the protection of the rights and freedoms of others.[178] Therefore the exceptions on the basis of which a state may seek to limit the right to respect for private and family life are substantially greater than those which apply to Community law.[179]

The ECHR is not an instrument designed or indeed drafted with immigration concerns in mind. In so far as it has implications for immigration policy this is coincidental and the result of the Convention's primary purpose of securing fundamental human rights for all persons within the jurisdiction of the High Contracting Parties.[180] Nonetheless, in fulfilling its function as regards all persons within the jurisdiction of the states, the Convention as interpreted by the Court of Human Rights provides a floor of rights for all persons in respect of family life below which no state party to the Convention should fall.

In considering the contents of the right to respect for family life the Court of Human Rights has not spelt out any particular list of family members

178 Article 8 ECHR.

179 see for instance *Bouchereau v UK* [1977] ECR 1999. The European Court of Justice has interpreted very restrictively the concept of public policy in Community law as a ground for expulsion of a citizen of the Union exercising a Treaty right as it is an exception to the principle.

180 Article 1 ECHR.

whose admission to a state is incumbent on the state. Instead the Court of Human Rights has considered the quality and reality of family life as the decisive factor.[181] However, this certainly may include spouses, children whether natural or adopted, parents, grandparents and grandchildren since such relatives "may play a considerable part in family life".[182] Where family life has not yet been exercised on the territory of the state party to the Convention the Court of Human Rights has considered it appropriate to ask whether there is an alternative possibility of family life being enjoyed in the state of origin of the foreign spouse.[183] Only if this is not a serious option, possibly because of the hardship this would cause for family members in the state signatory, will the Court of Human Rights proceed to consider whether the refusal to admit a family member to the state signatory is breach of the right.[184]

Because of the framework of the ECHR, the Court of Human Rights will examine the factual situation over the position in law.[185] In order for the Convention to protect family life it must first be established that family life has been established and is effective.[186] The failure of the Resolution to take this into account, for example as regards adopted children may give rise to difficulties. In one case, the Court of Human Rights held that it was contrary to the right to family life to expel the parent of a child even though the parent did not have parental control of the child. The right to contact between the child and the parent was sufficiently strong to outweigh the public interest in the expulsion of the parent.[187]

Further the right to respect for family life is not limited to those persons who can afford family life. Its potential limitation in the Resolution to those who are in current employment with sufficient income to support family members disregards the fact that the family member in the state may have

181 *Berrehab v Netherlands* supra.

182 *Marckx v Belgium* ECHR [1979] Ser A No 31.

183 *Abdulaziz, Cabales & Balkandali v UK* supra.

184 see for instance *Gul v Switzerland* Admissibility decision of the European Commission of Human Rights 10 October 1994, Application No 23218/94.

185 *Marckx v Belgium* [1979] Ser A.

186 *Alam & Khan v UK* (1976) 10 YB Eur Conv. HR 478 (Commission).

187 *Berrehab v Netherlands* supra.

been in employment for many years, paying taxes and on account of circumstances beyond his or her control is temporarily unemployed and in receipt of benefits to which he or she has contributed. In such a situation it is unclear whether a state would be found to have fully respected the family life of the person concerned.

The rights contained in the ECHR must be secured without discrimination on any ground such as sex, race, colour, language, religion, political or other opinion, national or social origin, association with a national minority, property, birth or other status.[188] Clearly there is discrimination inherent in the Resolution between one category of foreigners and another (citizens of another Member State and third country nationals).

*Compatibility with the European Social Charter and ILO Recommendation 151*

The European Social Charter was adopted within the framework of the Council of Europe and has been ratified by all the Member States. As regards migrant workers its provisions apply on the basis of reciprocity. Accordingly, its consequences and obligations on the Member States are of particular importance as regards Turkish workers in the Member States as Turkey is a signatory state of the Social Charter and therefore the obligations of the Charter extend to its nationals on the territory of other signatory states.[189]

It provides that family reunion shall be facilitated as far as possible for foreign workers permitted to establish themselves in the territory of another signatory state. "Family members" are defined as at least "wife and dependent children under the age of 21 years".[190] ILO Recommendation 151 provides a definition of family for the purposes of reunification with a migrant worker as including at least spouse, dependent children (with no age limit) mother and father.[191]

---

188 Article 14 ECHR.

189 Article 19 European Social Charter 1961.

190 Appendix Part II Article 19 paragraph 6 European Social Charter.

191 Article 15 ILO Recommendation 151.

The regulatory structure of the European Social Charter is by way of a reporting requirement and examination by a Committee of Experts.[192] The reports of the Committee of Experts are published. The Committee has construed the obligation to facilitate family reunion widely as reflecting the intention of the Charter. Exceptions which restrict family reunion have been narrowly interpreted.[193] Those states which have applied an age limit below 21 years for family reunion with children have consistently been criticised by the Committee for failure to comply with their obligations under the Social Charter.[194]

As regards the requirement of the Social Charter for the family members to be dependent, this has been defined by the Committee of Experts not to be limited to economic dependency but to include where relevant "all situations in which there is *de facto* or legal dependence under the relevant laws".[195] This specifically includes for instance moral and psychological dependence.

The Committee of Experts has commented in their Conclusions on the compatibility of waiting periods with the Social Charter. It has accepted that some waiting periods may be permissible under the Social Charter however they must be strictly limited in time.[196] For instance a legally imposed waiting period of three years is contrary to article 19(6) of the Social Charter.[197] Further, the exclusion from any possibility of family reunion for fixed term contract workers may also be contrary to the obligations under the Social Charter.[198] ILO Recommendation 151 specifically requires members, of which the Member States number, to take all possible measures to facilitate the reunification of families of migrant workers as rapidly as possible.[199] It further provides that where a migrant

---

192 Articles 21 - 25 European Social Charter.

193 Committee of Experts Conclusions VIII.

194 see for instance Conclusions X-2 (1988), XI-2 (1991) regarding Germany, and Conclusions XII-1 (1992) regarding the UK.

195 Conclusions VIII.

196 Conclusions II and XI-2.

197 Conclusions XI-2 regarding Germany.

198 Conclusions X-2 and XI-2 regarding Germany.

199 Article 13(1) ILO Recommendation 151.

worker who has been employed for at least one year cannot be joined by his or her family in that country the family should be entitled to visit the worker for at least the length or his or her annual holiday.[200]

The Committee of Experts has considered the duty of states under article 16 of the Social Charter to provide housing in conjunction with the obligation to facilitate family reunion.[201] It has concluded that the duty to facilitate family reunion implies an obligation to assist workers and their families to find housing, including in the public sector. This is also reflected in article 19(4)(c) which requires equal treatment with own nationals as regard accommodation.[202]

The consequences of the Member States obligations under the Social Charter for the Resolution are serious. First the implementation of an upper age limit on family reunion with children of any age below 21 will be contrary to the Member States' obligations under the Social Charter as regards Turkish workers on their territory. As Turkish workers constitutes the largest group of third country national workers in the Member States this is significant.[203]

Secondly, the failure to place an upper limit on waiting periods which complies with the Social Charter as regards family reunion indicates that the Member States obligations under the Social Charter have not been properly transposed into the Resolution. Thirdly, the apparent exclusion of fixed contract workers from the scope of the Resolution[204] does not accord with the Member States obligations under the Social Charter. Fourthly, requirements in respect of housing for migrant workers contained in the Social Charter are not reflected in the Resolution.

200 Article 17(b) ILO Recommendation 151.

201 Conclusions I, II, III, IV and VII.

202 Cholewinski, R, The Protection of the Right of Economic Migrants to Family Reunion in Europe, ICLQ (43) 1994.

203 According to Eurostat, Migration Statistics 1994, as at 1.1.1992 the largest non-national citizenship group in the European Economic Area (the European Union plus the European Free Trade Agreement States except Switzerland) was Turks at over 2,500,000 followed by Italians at about 1,500,000. All other nationalities were below these numbers.

204 Paragraph 9 of the Preamble.

*Conclusions*

All signatory states of international obligations should apply both the letter and the spirit of those duties which they have voluntarily undertaken. It is deeply unsatisfactory that states establish new policies in a field regulated by international obligations which exclude existing obligations and indeed may result in their breach.

This is of particular concern in respect of the European Social Charter where reciprocal obligations are involved. In the context of the reciprocal duties of the European Community, Member States have extended their obligations to one another beyond those contained in the Charter. However, in the context of this Resolution they have disregarded their reciprocal obligations to Turkey as regards Turkish workers in the Member States and undertaken to one another to apply rules to all workers, with no specific exception for Turkish workers, which are more restrictive than those which Turkey is obliged to provide to workers from the Member States within its territory.

In the context of the European Convention on Human Rights, it is not a salutary example for the Member States to pare down to the barest minimum the rights which they grant to third country nationals in the apparent hope that they have given just enough but not an iota more than the least required by their human rights obligations. The undertakings which are given to the international community should be given openly and honestly without deception or subterfuge – for instance in the expectation that by a careful wording of a national provision the state can avoid compliance with the spirit of the undertaking but still comply with the letter.

The rule of law is a fundamental principle of the European Union.[205] When the European Union adopts measures which fail to give effect to relevant decisions of international tribunals such as the European Court of Human Rights it is also failing to respect the rule of law.

---

205 F. Schockweiler, judge of the European Court of Justice, La Cour de Justice des Communautés Europées dépasse-t-elle les limites de ses attributions?, Journal des Tribunaux Droit Européen, 20 avril 1995.

# 10 RECOMMENDATION concerning checks on and expulsion of third country-nationals residing or working without authorization[206]

MINISTERS OF THE Member States OF THE EUROPEAN COMMUNITIES, RESPONSIBLE FOR IMMIGRATION

HAVING REGARD to the high priority given to promoting a common approach to the question of illegal immigration adopted by the ministers responsible for Immigration and by the European Council at Maastricht;

HAVING REGARD to the need to reinforce common endeavours to combat illegal immigration reiterated by the European Council at Edinburgh;

HAVING REGARD to the fact that this objective presupposes the improvement of means for checking and expelling third-country nationals who are in an irregular situation;

HAVING REGARD to the recommendation regarding practices followed by Member States on expulsion adopted by Immigration ministers in London[207] (WGI 1266);

NOTING that it is fundamental to expulsion practices that there should also be effective means of identifying and apprehending those to be expelled;

---

206 Brussels, 25 May 1993 [SN 3017/93 WGI 1516].

207 see document 6, Recommendation regarding practices followed by Member States on expulsion.

NOTING that the implementation of the measures outlined in this recommendation will need to take account of the nature and extent of illegal immigration to be combatted in particular Member States;

STRESSING that, in the light of the recommendation adopted at the Ministerial Conference held in Budapest on the implementation of measures to deal with uncontrolled migration, measures should be taken to combat the employment of those known to have entered or remained illegally or those whose immigration status does not allow them to work;

NOTING that this recommendation is without prejudice to Community law and also takes into account other relevant international instruments including the 1950 Convention for the protection of Human Rights and Fundamental Freedoms, the 1951 Geneva Convention relating to the Status of Refugees and 1967 New York Protocol;

NOTING in particular that this recommendation excludes from its scope:

- nationals of some EFTA countries who will have rights of free movement when the Agreement on the European Economic Area comes into force.[208]

- family members of nationals of Member States and of some EFTA countries entering or residing in the territories of Member States in accordance with Community law and the EEA Agreement;

NOTING that checks and controls on the residence and employment of third country nationals shall be decided upon and carried out by those authorities which are empowered to do so under national legislation,

ADOPTED THE FOLLOWING RECOMMENDATION:

1. Measures should be taken with a view to ensuring that third-country nationals do not remain beyond the period for which they have been

---

208 The EEA Agreement came into force on 1.1.993.

admitted or given permission to remain and that they do not work without authority to do so.

The general rule should be that persons not entitled to free movement in conformity with Community legislation and found:

(i) to have entered or remained unlawfully in Member States (where their stay has not been regularized);

(ii) to be liable to expulsion on grounds of public policy or national security; or

(iii) to have failed definitively in an application for asylum and to have no other claim to remain, should be expelled, unless there are compelling reasons, normally of a humanitarian nature, for allowing them to remain.

2. In addition, Member States may expel persons who have been working in breach of immigration/aliens or related provisions. In this context, under the same conditions, they may also expel those people who are subject to immigration/aliens provisions who have been involved in the facilitation, harbouring or employment of illegal immigrants.

3. Checks should, in particular, be carried out in respect of persons who are known or suspected of staying or working without authority, including persons whose request for asylum has been rejected.

   Member States shall examine the types of checks which would be most appropriate to introduce with a view to detecting third-country nationals who are residing or working illegally, including those persons whose application for asylum ha[ve] been rejected.

4. Checks should be conducted to ensure that third-country nationals are not entitled to free movement in conformity with Community legislation and who have received authorization for residence and, as the case may be, for employment for a limited period of time continue to fulfil the relevant conditions.

To this end, in appropriate circumstances Member States should consider undertaking checks, inter alia, in the following situations:

(i) persons who have received authorization for residence but not for employment;

(ii) persons who have received a residence permit, but whose work permit is of a limited nature;

(iii) persons who work without authorization after being admitted as short-term visitors or tourists.

Furthermore, to the extent that this is necessary, Member States should consider undertaking checks in view of detecting abuse, inter alia on:

(i) persons who have been authorized to be reunited with their family with a view to living together;

(ii) persons who have received a residence/work permit on the basis of their marriage to a person resident in the Member State.

5. The decision as to whether checks should be conducted depends on the circumstances in any given case. Exchanges of information between Member States on the type of checks and control procedures together with related legislation should be carried out within CIREFI.

6. Checks on persons suspected of residing or working illegally in Member States are to be carried out in conformity with national legislation and should be aimed at reinforcing common endeavours to combat illegal immigration to the Community.

*Commentary*

*Status:* Recommendation adopted by Ministers of the EC Member States outside the ambit of the European Communities Treaties. It is non-binding and makes reference to the preceding acts adopted intergovernmentally on expulsion.

*Entry into force:* No time limit is set for implementation of this Recommendation.

*International obligations engaged:*

(1) UN Convention relating to the Status of Refugees 1951 and Protocol 1967
(2) International Convention on Civil and Political Rights 1966
(3) ILO Convention 97, 1949 and 143, 1975
(4) European Convention on Human Rights 1950
(5) European Social Charter 1961

*Summary:*

This Recommendation seeks to establish some common parameters in respect of two areas:

(i) Checks which Member States should carry out on third country nationals to ensure that they are residing and/or working in accordance with such permission as they have been granted;

(ii) The circumstances in which a presumption arises to expel a third country national who as a consequence of a check appears not to be abiding by the terms of his or her admission to the state.

The presumption on expulsion applies where a third country national not entitled to free movement under Community law is found in the following circumstances:

(i) To have entered or remained unlawfully in Member States (where his or her stay has not been regularised);

(ii) Is liable to expulsion on grounds of public policy or national security;

(iii) Has failed definitively in an application for asylum and has no other claim to remain, unless there are compelling reasons, normally of a humanitarian nature, for allowing him or her to remain.

(iv) Member States are permitted to expel, though not subject to a presumption in favour of expulsion, persons who have been working in breach of immigration/aliens or related provisions and persons subject to immigration/aliens provisions who have been involved in the facilitation, harbouring or employment of illegal immigrants.

In order to implement the presumption in favour of expulsion, Member States should carry out checks in the following circumstances:

(i) On persons who are known or suspected of staying or working without authority including asylum applicants who have been rejected;

(ii) Persons who have received authorisation for residence and for employment for a limited period of time to ensure they continue to fulfil the relevant conditions;

(iii) Persons who have received authorisation of residence but not employment;

(iv) Persons admitted as short term visitors or tourists who work without authorisation;

(v) Persons who have been authorised to be reunited with their family with a view to living together, such check should be carried out "in view of detecting abuse";

(vi) Persons who receive a residence/work permit on the basis of a marriage to a person resident in the Member State. Again checks should be designed to detect abuse.

Information on types of checks and control procedures introduced in the Member States, together with related legislation should be carried out within CIREFI.[209]

209 See document 16 - Conclusions on the organisation and development of CIREFI.

*Comments: Battening Down the Hatches*

*Personal Scope*

The Recommendation specifically excludes from its scope nationals of some EFTA countries who have free movement rights in the Union (now limited to Norway, Iceland and Liechtenstein after Finland, Sweden and Austria joined the European Union on 1st January 1995) and also excludes family members of citizens of the Union and EFTA nationals who are exercising Community law rights on another Member State.

No mention is made to persons protected under agreements between the Community and third countries. Of particular importance here is the Turkey/EC Association Agreement 1963 and Additional Protocol 1970. The Association Council established under the Agreement, adopted Decision 1/80 which is currently in force. It provides not only for the security of residence and employment of Turkish nationals who have been admitted to the Member States in a stable and secure position, but it also limits the expulsion of such Turkish nationals. Article 14 of Decision 1/80 is worded in terms identical to those of Article 48(3)EC relating to the expulsion of citizens of the Union exercising Treaty free movement rights. The failure, properly to take into account binding and directly effective Community law is a disturbing and serious fault in any legislation. The European Court of Justice has already held that in the context of national legislation or practices which fail properly to incorporate Community law:

"If a provision of national law that is incompatible with a provision of the Treaty, even one directly applicable in the legal order of the Member States, is retained unchanged, that creates an ambiguous state of affairs by keeping the persons concerned in a state of uncertainty as to the possibility of relying on Community law and that maintaining such a provision in force therefore amounts to a failure by the state in question to comply with its obligations under the Treaty".[210]

---

210 *Commission v Italy* [1988] ECR 2961.

The adoption of the Recommendation with no limitation as to its personal scope so as to make it clear that it does not relate to this category of persons protected under Community law fails to comply with the transparency requirement established by the Court of Justice.

*Compatibility with the European Convention on Human Rights*

In the Recommendation regarding practices followed by Member States on expulsion[211] adopted on 30th November and 1st December 1992 the Member States set out the general policy on expulsion. In that Recommendation as also reflected in the Recommendation concerning checks on an expulsion of third country nationals residing or working without authorisation adopted in June 1993, the definition of persons in respect of whom a presumption to expel applies remains, in substance, constant. However the exception to the presumption on grounds of a humanitarian nature has now been limited to apply only to the third category of persons, those who have failed definitively in an application for asylum.

In the 1992 Resolution, this exception to the presumption on the basis of humanitarian grounds applied to all three categories identified. Accordingly, the 1993 Resolution in contradistinction to the 1992 Resolution does not provide a specific exception on humanitarian grounds to the presumption of expulsion for persons who have entered or remained unlawfully in a Member State (where their stay has not been regularised) and for persons liable to expulsion on grounds of public policy or national security.

This is a substantial change to the policy of the Member States and somewhat surprising in view of the jurisprudence of the European Court of Human Rights as regards the right to private and family life enshrined in Article 8 ECHR.[212] This jurisprudence clearly indicates that where a person has resided for a substantial period of his or her life in a state and has close family members in that state any attempt to expel the person is

211 Document 7 supra.

212 *Berrehab v Netherlands*; *Moustaquim v Belgium*; *Djeroud v Belgium*; *Beldjoudi v France*, supra.

likely to be contrary to Article 8 even if the decision on expulsion is taken on grounds of public policy.

In the most recent of these cases[213] in a partly concurring, partly dissenting Opinion, Mr H.G. Schermers of the European Commission of Human Rights stated:–

"I fully agree with the Court that there is well-established international law granting states full control over entry of aliens. I am not so sure, however, whether international law concerning the expulsion of aliens is not changing fundamentally as a result of growing concern for human rights and of a perceived need for solidarity among states in the face of increasing interstate relations. By admitting aliens to their territory states inevitably accept at least some measure of responsibility. This responsibility weighs even more heavily in the case of children educated in their territory. For any society, individuals like the present applicant are a burden. Even independent of human rights considerations, I doubt whether modern international law permits a state which has educated children of admitted aliens to expel these children when they become a burden. Shifting this burden to the state or origin of the parent is no longer so clearly acceptable under modern international law. It is at least subject to doubt whether a host country has the right to return those immigrants who prove to be unsatisfactory."

As Article 8 ECHR applies to all persons within the jurisdiction of the parties[214] the legality or otherwise of the person's residence is irrelevant to the obligation to protect family and private life. By apparently limiting the compelling reasons of a humanitarian nature to those persons in respect of whom an asylum application has been refused, the Member States have failed to take into account their obligations under Article 8 ECHR as interpreted by the European Court of Human Rights.

---

213 *Lamguindaz v UK* [1993] Ser A 258-C.
214 Article 1 ECHR.

*Widening the Net: Expulsion, "Related Provisions" and "Facilitating"*

As first appeared in the 1992 Recommendation, reference is made to the possibility of expelling a person who has been working in breach of immigration/aliens or related provisions. The earlier recommendation provided that "consideration should be given to the question whether, in appropriate circumstances, a person who has been working in breach of immigration/aliens or related provisions should be expelled".[215] In the 1993 Recommendation the wording has changed to state "Member States may expel persons who have been working in breach of immigration/aliens or related provisions".[216]

In the 1993 Recommendation a further category of persons are included among those who may be expelled "those people who are subject to immigration/aliens provisions who have been involved in the facilitation, harbouring or employment of illegal immigrants".[217] While this concept has not developed to the point of a presumption in favour of expulsion it is clearly moving in that direction. Again, unless tempered by human rights considerations it may not fulfil the Member States' obligations under the ECHR.

The possibility of expulsion on the basis of working in breach of "related provisions" to immigration or aliens laws is unsatisfactorily vague and could give rise to unfortunate results. For instance, if related provisions are considered to include minimum wage legislation or national insurance contribution legislation the migrant could be expelled on account of an employer's failure to comply with relevant legislation. In the UK, for example, where an employer has failed to make a national insurance contribution, even though it may have deducted such contribution from a third country national employee's wages, the employee may be liable to the relevant authorities for such contribution. The employee could therefore be deemed in breach of a related provision upon which, according to the

---

215 Document 7 - Recommendation regarding practices followed by Member States on expulsion, Article 2.

216 Document 12 - Recommendation concerning checks on an expulsion of third country nationals residing or working without authorisation, Article 2.

217 Recommendation Article 2.

Resolution, an expulsion decision could be based. This is, of course, an extreme example but it highlights the dangers attendant on loose and unsatisfactory wording.

The creation of the possibility of expulsion of people who are likely to be long term resident third country nationals as a result of having been "involved" in the facilitation, harbouring or employment of illegal immigrants creates a new and potentially serious obstacle to security of and equal treatment for long resident third country nationals in the Union. For example, a third country national family which employs on a casual basis a young foreign student to mind their child of an evening so they can go to the cinema could fall foul of this provision if the student was subject to a prohibition on employment.

Article 6(3) of ILO Convention 143 specifically provides that an employer who is prosecuted for employing illegally migrant workers "shall have the right to furnish proof of his good faith". Such a safeguard is not contained in the Recommendation. Further, the ILO Convention provides that administrative, civil and penal sanctions shall be applied to employers who illegally engage migrant workers. However, the presumption is that similar sanctions apply to all persons found guilty of the offence. The Recommendation provides that third country national employers shall be subject to differential treatment in that they should be sanctioned with expulsion, a penalty not possible in respect of own nationals and only in limited cases in respect of nationals of other Member States.

This provision in respect of expulsion for having been "involved" in the facilitation, harbouring or employment of illegal immigrants is not made subject even to a conviction of a relevant criminal offence by a criminal court in a Member State. It appears that the Member States are encouraged to implement in their national law such provisions based on an administrative assessment of such involvement. In view of the fact that the Recommendation makes no provision for any procedural guarantees, rights of appeal or other judicial controls over expulsion measures for the protection of the migrant this provision is of substantial concern. It is also of note that this provision does not even require that the migrant, subject to expulsion for being involved in the facilitation, harbouring or employment of illegal entrants, knew that the person involved was an illegal immigrant nor indeed is there any definition of who an illegal immigrant is. As the immigration status of any particular person in a Member State may not be entirely clear, for instance, where an application is pending or where they have changed from one status to another, such a potentially catastrophic sanction without any proper definition of the elements involved is unsatisfactory.

*Checks*

Verification on status of persons seems to be a matter of increasing concern to the Member States in the context of immigration policy. The 1993 Recommendation proposes that checks should be carried out in a number of areas:

(i) On persons who are known or suspected of staying or working without authority, including persons whose request for asylum has been rejected;

(ii) Persons not entitled to Community free movement rights but who have received authorisation for residence and, as the case may be, for employment for a limited period to ensure that they fulfil the relevant conditions.

Member States are advised to consider undertaking checks in the following further situations:

(i) Persons who have received authorisation for residence but not for employment;

(ii) Persons who have received a residence permit but whose work permit is of a limited nature;

(iii) Persons who work without authorisation after being admitted as short-term visitors or tourists.

Finally, Member States are encouraged to undertake checks in order to detect abuse in the following circumstances:

(i) Persons who have been authorised to be reunited with their family with a view to living together;

(ii) Persons who have received a residence/work permit on the basis of their marriage to a person resident in the Member State.

In respect of the first two circumstances in which checks should be carried out, the first question which arises is why, if persons are known to be staying and working without authority, regular checks are required. This suggests an implicit acceptance of a practice suspected of some Member States to refuse to issue work and residence permits but to tolerate the presence of third country nationals excluded from the legal labour market by their lack of documentation and from any social benefits by their lack of a residence permit.

In respect of persons "suspected" of staying or working without authority, on what basis does such suspicion arise? This presupposes a basis for suspecting who is and is not a third country national. French experience in respect of such identity legislation would indicate that factors such as colour, language and religion inform such assumptions.[218]

In respect of the second set of circumstances in which Member States should consider undertaking checks there is no limitation on the frequency with which checks may be undertaken. Third country nationals are entitled to dignity and respect just as nationals of the Member States. The increasing differentiation of treatment of third country nationals lawfully residing on the territory by way of reporting requirements and checks which seems to be foreseen by this provision is unlikely, in the longer term, to be conducive to good community relations. Depending on the frequency and circumstances, such checks may even constitute degrading treatment prohibited by Article 3 ECHR.

The purpose of the checks on persons who are residing lawfully for instance under limited work permits is apparently to ensure that the applicable limitations are observed. However, there is no limitation in time as to how long Member States may continue to check on third country nationals lawfully going about their business. ILO Convention 143 provides that:

---

218 See Plein Droit, La revue du GISTI, Denoncer et expulser, No 27, Juin 1995 and ILPA briefing to House of Lords, May 1995.

"On condition that he has resided legally in the territory for the purpose of employment, the migrant worker shall not be regarded as in an illegal or irregular situation by the mere fact of the loss of his employment, which shall not in itself imply the withdrawal of his authorisation of residence or, as the case may be, work permit".[219]

While only some Member States have ratified the Convention, all are members of the ILO. In considering to which international obligations the Court of Justice should have regard for the purposes of interpreting Community law, the court has held "international treaties concerning the protection of human rights on which the Member States have collaborated or to which they have acceded can also supply guidelines to which regard should be had in the context of Community law".[220] On this formulation, due regard should be had to Convention 143 as an international treaty which, at the very least, the Member States have collaborated upon and some have ratified.[221] The Member States should not be undermining the work of the ILO by their multilateral agreements covering areas to which they are already committed under the ILO Conventions. Those Member States which have ratified ILO Convention 143 are obliged in international law to implement it. The conclusion of an alternative multi-lateral arrangement such as the Recommendation cannot relieve them of their duties in international law.

In respect of the third category of checks aimed at detecting abuse in respect of family reunion and marriage, serious questions arise regarding respect for family life. As regards third country national family members of citizens of the Union exercising Treaty rights in another Member State, the Court of Justice has held that there is no obligation for spouses to remain living together under the same roof in the host Member State.[222] So long as a marriage is subsisting, the third country national is entitled to remain in the host Member State together with the citizen of the Union exercising rights there.

---

219 Article 8(1) ILO Convention 143, 1975.

220 *Wachauf* [1989] ECR 2609.

221 Italy, Portugal and Sweden have ratified the Convention.

222 *Diatta v Land Berlin* [1986] ECR 567.

If the first category of persons to be checked "in view of detecting abuse", that is to say, persons authorised to be reunited with their family to live together, is designed to catch out couples who subsequently ceased to live together, this clearly does not apply to migrant citizens of the Union and their third country national family members (who are outside the scope of the Recommendation in any event). To apply such provisions to own nationals and their third country national family members results in discrimination between one category of citizen of the Union and another category of citizens of the Union which raises questions of compatibility of such provisions with Article 8A EC.

The extent to which such jurisprudence relating to family members of citizens of the Union may be applicable to family members of Turkish workers protected under the Turkey/EC Association Agreement and subsidiary legislation is a matter the Court of Justice has yet to consider. However, under the Agreement, the contracting parties are to be guided by Articles 48, 49 and 50 EC.[223] Accordingly it is possible that the relevant jurisprudence on spouses developed in the context of Article 48 EC applies mutatis mutandis to admitted spouses of Turkish workers protected under that Agreement. This would then mean that the largest group by far of third country nationals in the European Union could not be penalised for failing to live with their spouses so long as they had been authorised in the first instance under national law to join the spouse in the Member State and a legal and valid marriage was subsisting.

*Legal Remedies*

Expulsion is an extremely drastic measure which may have devastating consequences for the individual's life and that of his or her family. The failure to include any reference to minimum legal protection or indeed even reference to international obligations regarding legal redress is a serious defect in this Recommendation.

223 Article 12, Turkey/EC Association Agreement 1963 and Additional Protocol 1970.

The issue of remedies against expulsion was addressed in the 1992 Recommendation at Article 2 (General Policy).[224] There the Member States confirmed their commitment to effective remedies to challenge of expulsion decisions; access to legal advice and representation; and where needed the services of interpreters. It is regrettable that these undertakings in respect of safeguards have not been repeated here. This is particularly the case as the Member States have seen fit to repeat some of the more onerous conditions of the 1992 Recommendation here.

Article 19 of the European Social Charter provides that migrant workers of the signatory states (which includes Turkey) are owed a duty by the host state "to secure that such workers lawfully residing within their territories are not expelled unless they endanger national security or offend against public interest or morality".[225] Further, the host state is obliged "to secure for such workers lawfully within their territories treatment not less favourable than that of their own nationals in respect of legal proceedings relating to matters referred to in this Article".[226] Accordingly, Turkish nationals, the largest group of migrant workers in the European Union, may rely on the Member States' obligations under the Social Charter when seeking a legal remedy.

Article 13 of the European Convention on Human Rights requires an effective remedy before a national authority for all persons whose rights and freedoms as contained in the ECHR are violated. Accordingly, in so far as an expulsion measure may be contrary, for instance to Article 3 ECHR[227] or Article 8 ECHR,[228] the Member States are under a duty to provide an effective remedy.

---

224 Document 7 infra.

225 Article 19(8) European Social Charter.

226 Article 19(7) European Social Charter.

227 the prohibition on torture, inhuman or degrading treatment or punishment including sending a person to a country where he or she is likely to suffer this.

228 the right to respect for private and family life subject to public policy provisos.

ILO Recommendation 151 provides at paragraph 33:

"A migrant worker who is the object of an expulsion order should have the right of appeal before an administrative or judicial instance, according to conditions laid down in national laws or regulations. This appeal should stay execution of the expulsion order subject to the duly substantiated requirements of national security or public order. The migrant worker should have the same right to legal assistance as national workers and have the possibility of being assisted by an interpreter".

The Recommendation, addressed to ILO members, which includes all the Member States, "should be applied within the framework of a coherent policy on international migration for employment".[229] The Member States activities in the Third Pillar are aimed at such a coherent policy within an international framework and therefore should incorporate the ILO Recommendation.

*Conclusions*

It is a simple fact of law that the categorisation of a non-national as lawfully or unlawfully present for the purposes of domestic law on the territory of a state is a matter within the domaine of national authorities. The only exception to this rule is the right of free movement and residence enjoyed under Community law or other directly effective bilateral agreements. Where the national authorities chose to define their immigration rules restrictively, they will undoubtedly find an increase in the numbers of persons who are to be classified as unlawfully present.

This will be the case in particular where a series of legal measures restricting access to the territory are introduced over a short period of time as has happened in almost all Member States.[230] A number of people who had previously been lawfully present or had access to the territory under certain conditions by the adoption of new regulations will become unlawfully

229 Paragraph 1 ILO Recommendation 151.

230 The EC Member States and Immigration in 1993, European Commission Luxembourg 1995.

present or their access to the territory will be governed by new rules of which they may not be aware.

Where a state, for instance, adopts a regulation specifying that in the event that a tourist "works" during a visit to the state the person becomes unlawfully present on the territory then the young visitor who child minds for her host family in gratitude for housing provided becomes unlawfully present on the territory. The more restrictive the regulations which are adopted by the state the larger the number of people who will, often inadvertently, find themselves in breach of those regulations.

This increase in numbers of persons unlawfully present itself may then prompt the authorities to take further action to prevent unlawful presence on the territory. This process rapidly becomes a malicious cycle every measure to prevent unlawful residence resulting in an apparent increase in numbers of persons unlawfully present.

It may be that the Union through its concentration on this aspect of harmonisation of immigration policy has created just such a cycle for itself.

# 11

# RESOLUTION on certain common guidelines as regards the admission of particularly vulnerable persons from the former Yugoslavia.[231]

CONCERNED at the continuing humanitarian crisis in the former Yugoslavia,

RECALLING the common position adopted by the European Community and its Member States at the Geneva Conference of 29 July 1992 organized by the United Nations High Commissioner for Refugees,

RECALLING the conclusions of the European Council meeting held on 11 and 12 December 1992 in Edinburgh,

DECLARING their support for the work carried out both within and outside the former Yugoslavia by the United Nations High Commissioner for Refugees and by other humanitarian organizations,

EMPHASISING that, in accordance with the approach of the United Nations High Commissioner for Refugees that protection and assistance should wherever possible be provided in the region of origin, they consider that displaced persons should be helped to remain in safe areas situated as close as possible to their homes, and that the efforts of the Member States should be aimed at creating safe conditions for these persons and sufficient funds for them to be able to remain in these areas,

---

231 The Ministers of the Member States of the European Communities responsible for immigration in the Member States of the European Communities, meeting in Copenhagen on 1 and 2 June 1993.

REAFFIRMING their willingness, in co-operation with the United Nations High Commissioner for Refugees, to admit, according to their possibilities, particularly vulnerable persons in order to afford them temporary protection,

HAVE ADOPTED THE FOLLOWING RESOLUTION:

1. Member States, in compliance with their national procedures and laws, will take suitable measures for the admittance, within the limits of the possibilities of each Member State, of particularly vulnerable persons from the former Yugoslavia in order to afford them temporary protection.

   These arrangements are especially intended to apply to:

   (a) persons from the former Yugoslavia who:

   - have been held in a prisoner-of-war or internment camp and cannot otherwise be saved from a threat to life or limb;

   - are injured or seriously ill and for whom medical treatment cannot be obtained locally;

   - are under a direct threat to life or limb and whose protection cannot otherwise be secured;

   - have been subjected to sexual assault, provided that there is no suitable means for assisting them in safe areas situated as close as possible to their homes;

   (b) persons from the former Yugoslavia who have come directly from combat zones within their borders and who cannot return to their homes because of the conflict and human rights abuses.

2. Member States will endeavour to administer such arrangements on the basis of the overall objective that persons from the former Yugoslavia who are admitted to the Member States and given temporary protection are to return to an area in the former Yugoslavia in which they can live in safety as soon as the conditions in that area make it possible to do so safely.

3. Each Member State will make every effort to take the measures required to enable the persons concerned to stay on its territory temporarily within the framework of the general objective referred to in point 2.

   To that end Member States will in particular ensure the implementation of principles conducive to conditions in which the persons admitted to their territory can live in dignity during their stay.

   Those principles shall include the following:

   - the persons concerned shall be entitled to stay temporarily as far as is possible until conditions are suitable for their return, unless their stay constitutes a threat to public order, national security or the international relations of the Member States;

   - arrangements must be made for access to resources which allow them to live in decent conditions. Each Member State will determine the appropriate level and the means of achieving this, whether by earnings from work, exceptional aid or social benefits; they will pay special attention to the possibilities for housing the persons admitted;

   - Member States will pay due heed to the possibilities for access to health care, each Member State determining the arrangements for setting up this benefit;

   - Member States will make every endeavour to ensure children can develop normally. To that end the host State will in particular ensure that they can attend school;

   - as far as is possible, arrangements will be made for contacts to be maintained with close relatives (spouses and children who are minors). In exceptional circumstances, in particular on humanitarian grounds, provisional permission to stay may be granted for this purpose;

– whenever possible, the persons concerned will be informed of the conditions of stay in the host country;

– as far as is possible, with the involvement of local authorities and associations, displaced persons will be encouraged to take part in the host country's cultural and social activities.

These principles will be implemented in respect both of persons whose admission has been organized directly by the Member States and of those who make their own way to national territory once they have been granted provisional leave to stay. Member States will in this regard be motivated by the traditions of respect for the rights of the individual on which the European Community is built.

*Commentary*

*Status:* Resolution adopted by Ministers of the EC Member States outside the ambit of the European Communities Treaties.

*Entry into force:* No specific time limit was set for the implementation of this resolution. It was adopted on 1 June 1993 and expresses the intention of the Member States.

*International obligations engaged:*

(1) UN Convention relating to the Status of Refugees 1951 and Protocol 1967
(2) UN Convention against Torture and other Cruel, Inhuman or Degrading Treatment or Punishment 1984
(3) European Convention on Human Rights 1950.

*Summary:*

This Resolution sets out the categories of persons from former Yugoslavia who should be given temporary protection by the Member States. These include:

1. those held in a prisoner-of-war or internment camps who cannot otherwise be saved from a threat to life or limb;

2. those injured or seriously ill and for whom medical treatment cannot be obtained locally;

3. those under a direct threat to life or limb and whose protection cannot otherwise be secured;

4. those subjected to sexual assault, provided that there is no suitable means for assisting them in safe areas situated as close as possible to their homes;

5. those who have come directly from combat zones within their borders and who cannot return to their homes because of the conflict and human rights abuse.

The Resolution only provides, as a general rule, that "as far as possible, arrangements will be made for contacts to be maintained with close relatives (spouses and children who are minors)". In principle, persons given temporary protection in a Member State cannot be joined by family members unless there are "exceptional circumstances" based on humanitarian grounds.

*Comments: Developing the concept of Temporary Protection*

This Resolution was adopted on 1st June 1993 at a time of intense international concern about ethnic cleansing in the former Yugoslavia and particularly in Bosnia Herzegovina. It remains the only act adopted under the intergovernmental process specifically in respect of the former Yugoslavia.

It provides a framework for the concept of temporary protection which was increasingly seen as an alternative to recognition of persons as refugees under the UN Convention.

However, the preamble of the Resolution makes no reference to any international human rights commitments of the Member States. Rather emphasis is given to what is termed the approach of UNHCR, that protection and assistance for displaced persons should be provided, wherever possible, in the region of origin. In particular the Member States committed themselves to the aim of creating safe conditions for these persons and sufficient funds for them to be able to remain in these areas. In the light of subsequent events this commitment does not appear to have been honoured.[232]

Certainly the policy of the Member States to keep persons in the region by the imposition of mandatory visa requirements on nationals of Bosnia has restricted their access to the Member States. The combination of a mandatory visa requirement and fines on carriers for transporting persons without the mandatory visa has, in the case of the former Yugoslavia, undoubtedly resulted in limiting dramatically the possibility of flight from the region. As there are no Member State diplomatic missions in Bosnia which issue visas, a Bosnian would have to travel to a third state to seek a visa to flee to a Member State. However, as soon as the Bosnian was in a third state the Resolution on host third countries[233] would apply and the asylum applicant would be unlikely to obtain a visa on the basis that he or she should seek protection in the state where he or she currently was.

The decision of the Member States not to recognise as refugees persons fleeing ethnic cleansing in the former Yugoslavia but only to provide a lower level of "temporary protection" exemplifies the concern voiced by UNHCR to the UN General Assembly:

"Most states concur with UNHCR that the Convention and Protocol apply to refugees from civil wars who have good reason to fear being victimized because of their religion, ethnic origin, clan or imputed political opinion. Many States also agree that persecution within the meaning of the 1951 Convention may emanate not only from the Government but also from de facto authorities or from other groups in situations where the national Government is either unwilling or unable in practice to provide the persons concerned with protection that would enable them safely to remain within, or to return to, their country. In some countries, however, the competent authorities, including administrative or judicial tribunals, have interpreted

232 In particular the lack of action by the Member States on the fall of UN declared safe havens for Bosnian Muslims of Screbrenica and Zepa in July 1995 to Bosnian Serb forces.

233 Document 3 infra.

the terms of the refugee definition – in particular the words ‘a well-founded fear of being persecuted’ – as requiring either a threat of persecution by the legal Government or the deliberate denial of protection by that Government of the individual concerned. Some authorities contend, moreover, that persons fleeing armed conflicts cannot qualify as refugees under the 1951 Convention unless they are ‘singled out’ for treatment different from that awaiting other members of their community. As a result, refugees fleeing ethnic or religious persecution by de facto authorities controlling a part of their country of origin, in the midst of a civil war in which it is effectively impossible for them to find safety elsewhere in their country, have been rejected as refugees under the Convention and protocol in certain countries”.[234]

There is no positive obligation on the Member States under the Resolution to accept any persons, vulnerable or otherwise from the former Yugoslavia. Rather, the Member States have only undertaken in this Resolution to take suitable measures for admittance in compliance with their national procedures and laws and within the limits of the possibilities of each State. Accordingly, should a State decide that it has no possibility of admitting a vulnerable person from the former Yugoslavia it would not necessarily be in breach of the Resolution.

Nonetheless it is of note that this is the only act adopted by the Member States which appears to have the purpose of facilitating admission of a class of persons to the Member States on humanitarian grounds.

*Personal Scope and the UN Convention relating to the Status of Refugees*

Five categories of person are intended to be covered by the Resolution and to be the subject of this preferential treatment. The difficulty with the categories is that they appear to have mixed persons who would certainly have a claim to asylum on the ground that they are refugees within the terms of the UN Convention with persons who may or may not have such a claim.

---

234 Note an International Protection to the UN General Assembly, UNHCR 7 September 1994.

The UN Convention definition of a refugee is: a person who owing to well-founded fear of being persecuted for reasons of race, religion, nationality, membership of a particular social group or political opinion, is outside his or her country of nationality and is unable or, owing to such fear, is unwilling to avail him or herself of the protection of that country.[235]

The categories covered by the Resolution are as follows:

(i) Persons who have been held in a prisoner of war or internment camp and cannot otherwise be saved from a threat to life or limb. Persons in this category are likely to be refugees within the UN definition as persons held in a prisoner of war and internment camp by and large are persons who have been subjected to this treatment on the basis of their race or religion (Muslims, Croatians, etc).

(ii) Persons who are injured or seriously ill and for whom medical treatment cannot be obtained locally. This category is for persons who may well not fall within the UN Convention definition and therefore may properly be the subject of a Resolution which provides lesser rights than those protected by the Convention.

(iii) Persons who are under direct threat to life or limb and whose protection cannot otherwise be procured. In the context of the former Yugoslavia such persons will probably come within the UN Convention definition on the basis of race, religion, nationality or social group.[236]

(iv) Persons who have been subject to sexual assault, provided that there are no suitable means for assisting them in safe areas situated as close as possible to their home. This category has been most unfortunately worded suggesting that the victims of sexual assault should be settled, ideally, as close to the perpetrators of those assaults as possible. The question of whether persecution on grounds of gender alone can come

---

235 Article 1A UN Convention relating to the Status of Refugees 1951 and 1967 Protocol.

236 In any event they would come within the category of persons entitled to protection by virtue of Article 3 ECHR and Article 3 of the Convention against Torture and other Cruel, Inhuman or Degrading Treatment or Punishment.

within the UN Convention definition of a refugee has been a matter of substantial discussion.[237] However, in the context of the former Yugoslavia as sexual assault is most frequently also related to persecution on the basis of race, religion or nationality, persons within this category may well come within the UN definition and be entitled to the higher standard of protection provided by that Convention.

(v) Persons from the former Yugoslavia who come directly from combat zones within their borders and who cannot return to their homes because of the conflict and human rights abuse. Again this category is very wide and may cover a person coming within in the UN Convention definition as well as other persons.

It is a matter of some concern that where there is a crossover between categories covered by the Resolution and categories of persons entitled to protection under the UN Convention, the generous rights under the UN Convention may be denied to persons who would otherwise be entitled to them.

Article 3 of the UN Convention requires the contracting states, which include all of the Member States, to apply the provisions of the Convention to refugees without discrimination as to race, religion or country of origin. Accordingly, to subject refugees from the Former Yugoslavia to disadvantageous treatment in comparison with persons recognised as refugees from other countries is contrary to the UN Convention.

Among the rights guaranteed to refugees under the UN Convention are:

(i) Most favourable treatment as regards the right to engage in wage earning employment accorded to nationals of a foreign country.

(ii) Treatment no less favourable than that accorded to aliens generally to enter into self-employment.

---

237 See, for instance, Female Asylum Seekers, A Comparative Study concerning Policy and Jurisprudence in the Netherlands, Germany, France, The United Kingdom, Dutch Refugee Council, April 1994.

(iii) No less favourable treatment than that accorded to aliens generally as regards housing.

(iv) No less favourable treatment then that accorded to aliens generally as regards public education.

(v) Equal treatment with own nationals as regards public relief and assistance.

(vi) Equal treatment with own nationals in respect of labour legislation and social security.

(vii) The right to travel documents.

Accordingly, as set out below on the duty on Member States, it is a substantial benefit to a person from the Former Yugoslavia to be recognised as a refugee in accordance with the UN Convention as only this will entitle him or her to these benefits.

*The Duty on the Member States*

The Resolution includes no obligation for Member States to assist or even to refrain from hindering access of vulnerable persons to their territory. Nonetheless, if vulnerable persons from the former Yugoslavia arrive in a Member State either organised directly by the Member States or by making their way to the national territory on their own, provided they have been granted provisional leave to stay, the principles of the Resolution will apply to them. There is no indication of what "provisional leave to stay" means or indeed whether it has any common content for all 15 Member States.

Once in the state, according to the Resolution, the Member States undertake to ensure:

(i) temporary stay until conditions are suitable for their return, subject to a public order, national security or international relations proviso. There is no indication of how the question of "conditions suitable for their return" is to be determined. However as this is a Resolution of the Member States it would seem that any decision regarding conditions suitable for return would need to be the subject of an agreement of equal weight by the Member States to this effect. In respect of the assessment as to whether there is safety to which the person can be returned, no regard appears to have been had to the wording of Article 3(2) of the UN Convention against Torture.[238]

(ii) to ensure access to resources whether by earnings from work, exceptional aid or social benefits. Special attention must also be paid to housing of such persons.

(iii) to "pay due heed to the possibility" for access to health care. This is somewhat surprising in view of the category of persons to be allowed to remain which consists of those injured or seriously ill and for whom medical treatment cannot be obtained locally. It cannot have been the intention of the Member States to admit such persons on the ground that they need health care and then refuse to provide it.

(iv) as regards children, the Member States are under a duty to ensure that they can attend school.

(v) as far as possible to arrange for contacts with close relatives, defined as spouses and minor children but not for family reunification (see section below on family reunification);

(vi) if possible, the person will be informed of the conditions of stay in the host country. It is difficult to believe, but the unavoidable meaning of this indent, that the Member States do not consider themselves under a duty to inform asylum applicants from the Former Yugoslavia of the conditions of stay in their states.

---

238 Article 3(2) provides that for the purpose of determination whether there are grounds for believing that a person would be in danger of being subjected to torture in another State, the competent authorities shall take into account all relevant consideration including, where applicable, the existence in the State concerned of a consistent pattern of gross, flagrant or massive violations of human rights.

(vii) as far as possible to participate in the host state's cultural and social activities.

The Member States have made it very clear that in the administration of these arrangements the objective is that persons from the former Yugoslavia who are admitted to the Member States and given temporary protection are to return to an area in the former Yugoslavia in which they can live in safety as soon as conditions in that area make it possible to do so. There is no limitation that they should only be returned to an area of the former Yugoslavia of which they are a national.

Notwithstanding the reference in the Resolution's preamble that it is "in accordance with the approach of the United Nations High Commissioner for Refugees" on protection and assistance and the reaffirmation of the Member States' co-operation with the UNHCR, no reference is made to Conclusion 22 of the UNHCR Executive Committee which specifically regulates circumstances such as those in the Former Yugoslavia.

Conclusion 22 of UNHCR Executive Committee relating to Protection of Asylum Seekers in Situations of Large-Scale Influx provides:

*"II. Measures of protection*

*A. Admission and non-refoulement*

1. In situations of large scale influx, asylum seekers should be admitted to the State in which they first seek refuge and if that State is unable to admit them on a durable basis, it should always admit them at least on a temporary basis and provide them with protection according to the principles set out below. They should be admitted without any discrimination as to race, religion, political opinion, nationality, country of origin or physical incapacity.

2. In all cases the fundamental principle of *non-refoulement* – including non-rejection at the frontier – must be scrupulously observed.

*B. Treatment of asylum seekers who have been temporarily admitted to a country pending arrangements for a durable solution*

1. Article 31 of the 1951 United Nations Convention relating to the Status of Refugees contains provisions regarding the treatment of refugees who have entered a country without authorisation and whose situation in that country has not yet been regularised. The standards defined in this Article do not, however, cover all aspects of the treatment of asylum seekers in large-scale influx situations.

2. It is therefore essential that asylum seekers who have been temporarily admitted pending arrangements for a durable solution should be treated in accordance with the following minimum basic human standards:

   (a) they should not be penalized or exposed to any unfavourable treatment solely on the ground that their presence in the country is considered unlawful; they should not be subject to restrictions on their movements other than those which are necessary in the interests of public health and public order;

   (b) they should enjoy the fundamental civil rights internationally recognised, in particular those set out in the Universal Declaration of Human Rights;

   (c) they should receive all necessary assistance and be provided with the basic necessities of life including food, shelter and basic sanitary and health facilities; in this respect the international community should conform with the principles of international solidarity and burden-sharing:

   (d) they should be treated as persons whose tragic plight requires special understanding and sympathy. They should not be subject to cruel, inhuman or degrading treatment;

   (e) there should be no discrimination on the grounds of race, religion, political opinion, nationality, country of origin or physical incapacity;

(f) they are to be considered as persons before the law, enjoying free access to courts of law and other competent administrative authorities;

(g) the location of asylum seekers should be determined by their safety and well-being as well as by the security needs of the receiving State. Asylum seekers should, as far as possible, be located at a reasonable distance from the frontier with their country of origin. They should not become involved in subversive activities against their country of origin or any other State;

(f) family unity should be respected;

(i) all possible assistance should be given for the tracing of relatives;

(j) adequate provision should be made for the protection of minors and unaccompanied children;

(k) the sending and receiving of mail should be allowed;

(l) material assistance from friends or relatives should be permitted;

(m) appropriate arrangements should be made, where possible, for the registration of births, deaths and marriages;

(n) they should be granted all the necessary facilities to enable then to obtain a satisfactory durable solution;

(o) they should be permitted to transfer assets which they have brought into a territory to the country where the durable solution is obtained; and

(p) all steps should be taken to facilitate voluntary repatriation."

These obligations on states apply only for the duration when the person remains an asylum applicant. As soon as he or she is recognised as a refugee then the superior rights contained in the UN Convention itself apply. The purpose of the UNHCR Conclusion is to establish a floor of rights of asylum applicants while their applications are being determined. The differences between the principles as set out in the Resolution and UNHCR Conclusions 22 are striking.

*Family Reunion*

Family reunion is not foreseen by the Resolution. Indeed, while Member States undertake to facilitate contact between close relatives, defined as spouses and children who are minors, only in exceptional circumstances, in particular on humanitarian grounds, should provisional permission to stay be granted for this purpose. It remains unclear what contact is, therefore, to be facilitated.

The limitation in respect of family life and indeed the exclusion of family reunion, even with spouses and minor children, unless exceptional circumstances exist, in particular on humanitarian grounds, may not be in conformity with the obligations of the Member States under Articles 3 and 8 ECHR. In particular, the Member States are under a duty not to return a person to a place where he or she fears torture, inhuman or degrading treatment under Article 3 ECHR.[239] Member States are also under a duty not to interfere with the private or family life of any person on the territory.[240]

Where a person cannot be returned to his or her country of origin on the basis of Article 3 then clearly not to permit, at the very least, first degree family members to join the person in the Member State where there is no other state where they can hope to enjoy family life is likely to be a breach of the European Convention on Human Rights.[241] These considerations are without prejudice to the question of whether persons covered by the Resolution are in fact refugees in accordance with the definition of the UN Convention.

239 *Soering -v- UK* [1989] Ser. A No 161.
240 Article 8 ECHR.
241 *Abdulaziz, Cabales & Balkandali -v- UK* [1985] Ser. A No. 94.

The Final Act of the conference which adopted the UN Convention declared that "the unity of the family, the natural and fundamental group of society, is an essential right of the refugee, and that such unity is constantly threatened".[242] Accordingly the conference recommended "Governments to take the necessary measures for the protection of the refugee's family, especially with a view to:

(1) Ensuring that the unity of the refugee's family is maintained particularly in cases where the head of the family has fulfilled the necessary conditions for admission to a particular country..."

The Recommendation applies to all refugees even if they have not fulfilled the necessary requirements for admission though particular emphasis is provided regarding those who do fulfil such requirements.

The Handbook on Procedures and Criteria for Determining Refugee Status produced by UNHCR to assist states in the application of the Convention[243] provides clarification on the application of the principle of family unity:

"185. As to which family members may benefit from the principle of family unity, the minimum requirement is the inclusion of the spouse and minor children. In practice, other dependents, such as aged parents of refugees, are normally considered if they are living in the same household...

186. The principle of unity of the family does not only operate where all family members become refugees at the same time. It applies equally to cases where a family unit has been temporarily disrupted through the flight of one or more of its members."

The UNHCR Executive Committee has in three notable Conclusions provided guidance on family reunion to signatory states of the UN Convention.[244] Conclusion 24 recommends:–

---

242 Final Act of the United Nationals Conference of Plenipotentiaries of the Status of Refugees and Stateless Persons paragraph B.

243 Geneva, 1988.

244 Conclusions 9 (1977), 15 (1979) and 24 (1981).

"...it is desirable that countries of asylum and countries of origin support the efforts of the High Commissioner to ensure that reunification of separated refugee families takes place with the least possible delay..." and "...in appropriate cases family reunification should be facilitated by special measures of assistance to the head of the family so that economic and housing difficulties in the country of asylum do not unduly delay the granting of permission for the entry of family members".

Conclusion 15 states as a general principle at (e) "In the interest of family reunification and for humanitarian reasons, States should facilitate the admission to their territory of at least the spouse and minor or dependant children of any person to whom *temporary refuge* or tenable asylum has been granted" (emphasis provided).

In the specific context of the war in Bosnia in March 1993 UNHCR issued a background paper stating:–

"The Office (UNHCR) believes that, on the basis of both protection principles and humanitarian considerations the possibility of family reunion should also be extended to persons benefitting from temporary protection, particularly where the need for such protection may be expected to last *for more than a few months*... The need for family reunion must be considered in the light of extreme hardship and suffering which many refugees from the former Yugoslavia have undergone" (emphasis provided).

Three months later the Member States adopted this Resolution not just ignoring but contradicting the advice and plea of UNHCR for family reunion for displaced persons from the former Yugoslavia.[245]

The failure of the Member States to include in the Resolution any provision for family reunion and indeed, specifically to exclude the possibility of family reunion for persons permitted to remain on their territory under its principles, undermines the authority of international human rights law.

245 See also Discussion Paper from Finland, Family Reunification of Refugees and Persons under Temporary Protection, CAHAR, Council of Europe, 20 September 1993.

# 12 RESOLUTION on limitations on admission of third-country nationals to the Member States for employment[246]

A. GENERAL CONSIDERATIONS ON POLICY

(i) The Council recalls that, in the report adopted by the European Council held in Maastricht in 1991, priority was given to the harmonization of policies on admission for work as an employed or self-employed person, although it was emphasized that these policies should of necessity be restrictive.

(ii) The Council acknowledges the contribution of migrant workers to the economic development of their respective host countries. At present, however, no Member State is pursuing an active immigration policy. All States have, on the contrary, curtailed the possibility of permanent legal immigration for economic, social and thus political reasons. Admission for temporary employment may therefore be considered only as a very narrow exception.

(iii) The Council recognizes that the present high levels of unemployment in the Member States increase the need to bring Community employment preference properly into practice by making full use of the EURES system to improve the transparency of the labour markets and facilitate placement within the European Community. The Council further recognizes that the provisions of the EC Treaty and the EEA Agreement enable job vacancies to be filled as far as possible by

246 Ministerial meeting on 20 June 1994 in Luxembourg: Council of Interior and Justice Ministers.

nationals of other Member States or of EFTA countries which are parties to the EEA Agreement.

(iv) The Council agreed not to regulate via this Resolution the issue of third-country nationals lawfully resident on a permanent basis in the territory of a Member State, but who have no right of admission and residence in another Member State.

It agreed to examine the matter at a later date.

(v) Member States reserve the right to allow, in accordance with their national law, the spouse and dependent children to accompany persons admitted in accordance with this Resolution.

(vi) In the light of these considerations, the Council resolves that the present restrictive measures should be continued and where necessary reinforced as regards the admission of third-country nationals for employment. To this end, the Council agrees that the national policies of Member States in respect of third-country nationals seeking admission to or permission to remain in their territories for employment should be governed by the principles set out below, which may not be relaxed by Member States in their national legislation. It agrees to have regard to these principles in any proposals for the revision of national legislation. The Member States will further endeavour to seek to ensure by 1 January 1996 that national legislation is in conformity with them. The principles are not legally binding on the Member States, and do not afford a ground for action by individual workers or employers.

B. PERSONS TO WHOM THIS RESOLUTION DOES NOT APPLY

The harmonization principles do not apply to:

- persons who have rights of free movement under Community law, i.e. nationals of Member States, nationals of EFTA countries parties to the Agreement on the European Economic Area and members of their families;

- third-country nationals who have been allowed admission for the purpose of family reunification to join nationals of a Member State or of a third country resident in the Member State concerned;

- third-country nationals whose access to employment is covered by rights stemming from agreements governed by Community law concluded with third countries;

- persons undertaking casual work in the course of youth exchange or youth mobility schemes, including "au pairs";

- persons entering Member States in order to pursue economic activities as self-employed persons or to set up and/or manage a business/ undertaking which they effectively control.

Such persons will be governed by the principles to be set out in a draft Resolution covering the self-employed;

- persons who are lawfully present in a Member State as:

- refugees under the terms of the Geneva Convention;

- applicants for asylum;

- third-country nationals admitted for asylum;

- displaced persons who are temporarily admitted;

- persons exceptionally allowed to stay on humanitarian grounds.

C. PRINCIPLES GOVERNING MEMBER STATES' POLICIES

*(i) General criteria*

- Member States will refuse entry to their territories of third-country nationals for the purpose of employment;

- Member States will consider requests for admission to their territories for the purpose of employment only where vacancies in a Member State cannot be filled by national and Community manpower or by non-Community manpower lawfully resident on a permanent basis in that Member State and already forming part of the Member State's regular labour market. In this context they will apply the procedure laid down in Part 11 of Regulation No 1612/68, as amended by Regulation No 2434/92, and in the light of Commission Decision No 93/569/EEC on the implementing of the Regulation, in particular with regard to Article 15(16);

- without prejudice to the application of the above two criteria, third-country nationals may, if necessary, be admitted on a temporary basis and for a specific duration to the territory of a Member State for the purpose of employment where:

  such an offer is made to a named worker or named employee of a service provider and is of a special nature in view of the requirement of specialist qualifications (professional qualifications, experience, etc.);

  an employer offers named workers vacancies only where the competent authorities consider, if appropriate, that the grounds adduced by the employer, including the nature of the qualifications required, are justified in view of a temporary manpower shortage on the national or Community labour market which significantly affects the operation of the undertaking or the employer himself;

  vacancies are offered to:

  seasonal workers, whose numbers are strictly controlled on admission to the territory of the Member States of the European Community and who undertake well-defined jobs, normally fulfilling a traditional need in the Community country concerned. Member States will restrict the admission of these workers to cases where there is no reason to believe that the persons concerned will seek to stay within their territory on a permanent basis;

  trainees;
  frontier workers;

the persons concerned are intra-corporate transferees being transferred temporarily by their company as key personnel.

*(ii) Procedure for admission for employment*

A third-country national will not be admitted for employment unless prior authorization has been given for him to take up employment in the territory of the Member State concerned. Such prior authorization may be in the form of a work permit issued either to the employer or to the employee.

In addition, third-county nationals must also be in possession of any necessary visa or, if the Member State concerned so requires, of a residence permit.

*(iii) Restrictions as to the scope of employment*

Initial authorization for employment will normally be restricted to employment in a specific job with a specified employer.

*(iv) Restrictions as to the period of admission for employment*

A seasonal worker will be admitted for a maximum of six months in any twelve-month period, and must remain outside the territories of the Member States for a period of at least six months before being readmitted for employment.

Trainees will be admitted for a maximum period of one year in the first instance. This period may be fixed at more than a year and extended exclusively for the time needed to obtain a professional qualification recognized by the Member State concerned in the sphere of their activity.

Other third-country nationals admitted to the territories of the Member States for employment will only be admitted for a period not exceeding four years in the first instance.

*(v) Applications to extend a stay for the purpose of employment*

A person already present in the territory of a Member State as a visitor or student will not in principle be permitted to extend his stay for the purpose of taking or seeking employment. Such persons must return to their own countries on conclusion of their visit or studies.

In principle a person admitted as a trainee or service provider or employee of a service provider will not be permitted to extend his stay in authorized employment except in order to complete the training or activity under contract for which he was admitted.

A seasonal worker will not be permitted to extend his stay for the purpose of taking employment of a different type. An extension of the period of his stay may be authorized to allow him to complete the work for which the original authorization was granted. However, the total length of his stay may not exceed six months in any twelve-month period.

Other workers may be permitted to extend their period of stay in authorized employment, but only if the criteria originally applied to the decision on whether to admit them for authorized employment continue to be met, in any event when the first extension is granted.

The Member States will examine the desirability of issuing a permanent residence permit to third-country nationals who have had restrictions on their employment lifted.

*(vi) Business visitors*

Nothing in these principles prevents a Member State from admitting as workers third-country nationals not residing in the territory of a Member State who are seeking entry in particular to:

- negotiate for the supply of goods or services;
- deliver goods or assemble machinery manufactured in a third country as part of a supply contract, provided that such persons will be dealing only with businesses in the territory of the Member State and not with

the general public and that any one visit and possibly the work permit does not exceed six months.

*(vii) Third countries with close links with a Member State*

Nothing in these principles prevents a Member State from continuing to admit third-country nationals to its territory for the purpose of employment pursuant to arrangements concluded by that Member State by the date of adoption of this Resolution for nationals of a third country with which it has especially close links.

The Member States will undertake as soon as possible to renegotiate such arrangements in accordance with the terms of this Resolution.

Where these arrangements concern the employees of a service provider, the Member States undertake to examine them in the spirit of this Resolution within a reasonable period of time not exceeding three years and to arrive at an assessment.

When carrying out this examination, account should be taken of the economic development of the States with which the Member States concluded the agreements in question.

The above provisions do not apply to arrangements covering employment of persons for instruction and vocational training purposes.

DEFINITIONS

'Trainees' means workers whose presence in the territory of a Member State is strictly limited in duration and closely connected with increasing their skills and qualifications in their chosen profession before returning to their own countries to pursue their careers;

'Seasonal workers' means workers who are resident in a third country but are employed in an activity dependent on the rhythm of the seasons in the territory of a Member State on the basis of a contract for a specified period and for specific employment;

'Frontier workers' means workers who are employed in the frontier zone of a Member State but who return each day or at least once a week to the frontier zone of a neighbouring country in which they reside and of which they are nationals;

'Intra-corporate transferee': a natural person working within a legal person, other than a non-profit making organization, established in the territory of a WTO member, and being temporarily transferred in the context of the provision of a service through commercial presence in the territory of a Member State of the Communities; the legal persons concerned must have their principal place of business in the territory of a WTO member other than the Communities and their Member States and the transfer must be to an establishment (office, branch or subsidiary) of that legal person, effectively providing like services in the territory of a Member State to which the EEC Treaty applies. In Italy, 'intra-corporate transferee' is defined as a natural person working within a legal person constituted as an SpA (joint stock company) or an Srl (capital stock company with limited liability).

*Commentary*

*Status:* Resolution adopted by the Ministers of the EC Member States outside the ambit of the European Communities Treaties.

*Entry into force:* The Ministers undertook to endeavour to seek to ensure that national legislation conforms with the Resolution by 1 January 1996.

International obligations engaged:

(1) International Covenant on Civil and Political Rights 1966
(2) ILO Convention 97, 1949
(3) ILO Convention 143, 1975
(4) European Convention on Human Rights 1950
(5) European Social Charter 1961

*Summary:*

The Resolution is divided into three sections: General Considerations of Policy; Persons to whom this Resolution does not apply; Principles Governing Member States' Policies.

The Resolution specifically states that it does *not* regulate the "issue of third-country nationals lawfully resident on a permanent basis in the territory of a Member State, but who have no right of admission and residence in another Member State". Family reunion for workers regulated by the Resolution is also outside its ambit.

Six categories of workers are excluded from the scope of the Resolution:

(i) citizens of the Union, European Economic Area and their family members;

(ii) third country nationals admitted for family reunion purposes;

(iii) third country nationals whose access to employment arises from Community Agreements with third countries (for instance Turkish nationals);

(iv) youth exchange and mobility schemes and au pairs;

(v) the self employed or effectively self employed;

(vi) refugees, asylum applicants, displaced persons, persons admitted on humanitarian grounds.

In principle admission for employment shall be the exception to the rule. Generally such admission should be permitted only where a vacancy cannot be filled by "national and Community manpower or by non-Community manpower lawfully resident on a permanent basis in that Member State."

An exception permits the admission of third country national labour on a temporary basis under the following conditions:

(i) the offer must be for a named worker and in view of specialist requirements;

(ii) the authorities consider that the employer's request is reasonable;

(iii) seasonal workers, trainees and frontier workers;

(iv) key personnel being transferred by their employer.

A third country national is not supposed to be "admitted for employment" unless there is prior authorization. The initial authorization will normally be restricted to employment in a specific job with a specific employer. These requirements only apply to initial authorization.

Seasonal workers are to be admitted for only six months out of every twelve months. Trainees may be granted one year's permission which is extendable and all other workers are to receive permits not exceeding four years in the first instance.

Students, visitors, trainees, service providers and their employees are in principle not to be permitted to stay for employment. Seasonal workers are not to be permitted to change sector. Extensions are only to be granted to a worker where the original criteria are still met.

A provision on "business visitors" suggests that workers seeking entry to negotiate the supply of goods or services or deliver goods or assemble machinery as part of a supply contract, should not be subject to the Resolution so long as the workers will be dealing only with businesses and not the general public.

Member States are requested to "examine the desirability" of issuing a permanent residence permit to third country nationals who have had restrictions on employment lifted.

*Comments: Labour Migration and Integration Policy*

This Resolution remained under consideration for a number of years before finally being adopted in 1994 under the Greek Presidency. Its title changed in the process to reflect increasing concerns of the Member States that the admission for employment of third country nationals to the Member States should be restricted as far as possible. This is, perhaps, not surprising in a period of historically high unemployment in the Member States. However, the Resolution is based on a premise which requires some further examination: that all Member States have curtailed the possibility of "permanent legal immigration for economic, social and thus political reasons; admission for temporary employment may be considered only as a very narrow exception".[247]

According to the Resolution "no Member State is pursuing an active immigration policy". Is it the case then that the Member States are pursuing a passive immigration policy? A recent study on the Temporary Employment of Migrants in Europe examining policy in nine European Union states concludes that notwithstanding official policy to restrict immigration "all these countries still are in need of foreign labour".[248]

*Temporary Labour Migration*

The fact that the Resolution was adopted at all may be considered "an implicit recognition that considerable labour migration to the Member States occurred during the last few years and will probably take place in the years ahead".[249] The classification of this movement as temporary migration in the Resolution indicates the Member States' intention not just to limit access by third country nationals to the Community labour market but, unless unavoidable, to prevent third country nationals from obtaining a permanent status and becoming integrated into the Union.

If there is one thing which "temporary" labour migration of the 1950s and 1960s has, in general, not been it is exactly that, "temporary". The startling exception to this general principle has been in those circumstances where

---

247 Section A (II) of the Resolution.

248 Groenendijk, K and Hampsink, R, Temporary Employment of Migrants in Europe, Reeks Recht and Samenleving 1995.

249 Groenendijk, K and Hampsink, R, Temporary Employment of Migrants in Europe, Reeks Recht & Samenleving, 1995 p 2.

return to a country of origin after a period of labour migration in another state has not resulted in the loss of residence rights in the host state.

A recent study on return patterns of labour migration to Germany is particularly interesting in this regard. The comparison of patterns indicates that where the state of origin is or has acceded during the period of labour migration to the European Union, migrant workers are more likely at the end of a period of residence in the host state to return to their country of origin.[250] Where the state of origin remains outside the Union and therefore return home may result in exclusion from the host state migrant workers seem less likely to take that risk.

| IMMIGRATION & RETURN: GERMANY 1960-1993 | | |
|---|---|---|
| | immigration | return |
| Italy | 3,654,181 | 3,249,698 |
| Greece | 1,196,473 | 1,003,255 |
| Turkey | 3,165,832 | 2,067,067 |

Source: Statistiches Bundesamt as reported in Ausländer in Deutschland $^{1}/_{95}$ ISSN 0177-1566.

Labour migration to Germany from Italy took place slightly earlier than migration from Greece and Turkey, which cover approximately the same time span.[251]

One conclusion which could be drawn from this information is that the more difficult states make labour migration, the longer migrant workers will remain in the state. Conversely, a relaxed regime of labour migration between states may increase the likelihood that temporary migration is genuinely temporary.

---

250 Ausländer in Deutschland ISSN 0177-1566-$^{1}/_{95}$.

251 for a fuller consideration of the German experience on labour migration see Immigration as an Economic Asset, the German Experience, ed S Spencer, IPPR 1994.

The European Union has already absorbed into its membership a number of the main source countries of labour migration of the 1950s and 1960 into Northern Europe, specifically, Greece, Spain and Portugal. Within the Union itself, the free movement of persons for economic activities is a fundamental objective and has, by and large, been achieved through the diligence of the European Commission and the rulings of the Court of Justice.[252]

The result of the achievement of full free movement within the Union for economic activities appears to be that nationals of the Member States have ceased to move in any appreciable numbers or for any substantial period of time.[253] This, of course, has much to do with economic convergence among the Member States, it would appear that nationals of the Member States would rather remain in their countries of origin for employment purposes if this is an option than to travel to another Member State in search of work. Even in states with appreciably higher levels of unemployment than the Union norm substantial labour migration is not apparent.[254]

*Demographics and Labour Migration Supply and Demand*

On the basis of current demographic trends within the Union, it does not seem likely that there will be any surge of young people joining the labour market in the foreseeable future, indeed, a number of states are currently failing to reach replacement levels in their population structure.[255] There remains the question of untapped sources of labour within the Union, specifically the unemployed, currently at approximately 10.9% of the Union labour force[256] and the incomplete participation rate of women in the labour

252 Articles 48 - 66 EC; subsidiary legislation to implement these provisions of the Treaty; for a consideration of the consequences of the rulings of the Court of Justice in developing the principle please see La Libre Circulation des Personnes dan L'Union Europeene, D Martin, Bruylant 1995.

253 Eurostat, Rapid Report, Population and Social Conditions 1994/7.

254 As at May 1995 the seasonally adjusted unemployment rate for the EU 15 was 10.9%. The highest rate is in Spain at 23% followed by Finland at 16.5%. A comparable bulge in immigration statistics from these countries is not apparent. Eurostat No 36/95 of 10 July 1995 and Statistics in Focus: Population and Social Conditions 1995/3.

255 Recent Demographic Developments in Europe, Council of Europe 1994.

256 Eurostat No 36/95 of 10 July 1995.

force.[257] As regards the extension of the age for continued participation in the labour force, while there are indications of an increase in statutory pensions ages in some states[258] the option of early retirement in accordance with private pension schemes may well off set this trend. Notwithstanding these potential variables, it does not appear likely that the Member States are about to sustain a dramatic change in the composition of the labour force.

Concerns in the Member States of a surge of labour migration from acceding states on admission of Spain and Portugal to the Union were, in general, not realised. The transitional arrangements of the accession treaties provided for a delay of free movement for workers from those states to the Union until 1 January 1993. Within a couple of years of accession, the Member States considered it appropriate to reduce that period to 1 January 1992.

The rapid change of perception in what were formerly considered countries of emigration, such as Italy, Greece, Spain and Portugal to a perception that they are countries of immigration also bears some analysis.[259] However, it is very difficult to assess the extent to which the perception of a change reflects a reality of substance. The relative lack of an "immigration" infrastructure – including legal provisions on labour migration coupled with actual implementation of those measures and centralised collection of data on labour migration – in a number of Southern European Member States at least in the past makes comparison difficult.[260]

Some assistance may be gleaned from the regularisation programmes undertaken in a number of those states, particularly Spain and Portugal before the introduction of comprehensive immigration laws. The Spanish second amnesty programme from 10 June to 10 December 1991 targeted two categories: wage earning and self-employed undocumented foreigners who

257 Eurostat Migration Statistics 1994.
258 for example the UK where the requirement to equalise state pension ages for men and women looks likely to result in an increase of pensionable age for women to 63.
259 Migration and Population Change in Europe, J Salt, UNIDIR 1993.
260 Migration and Population Change in Europe, J Salt, UNIDIR 1993.

entered Spain before 24 June 1985 and 17 May 1991. Continuous residence in the state was not a requirement for the first group.[261]

The Spanish programme resulted in approximately 133,000 requests for legalisation, the vast majority of which were accepted. A Portuguese programme which was carried out in 1993 was aimed at a similar group.[262] Such programmes only covered persons who have means of support at the relevant time, fulfilled the requirements of the regularisation programme and, presumably, foresaw for themselves and their families an extended future in the state.

In a country the size of Spain, with a population of almost 39 million in 1991[263] the number of applications for regularisation is perhaps surprisingly low. As the subject matter of the regularisation was labour migration, this may indicate that the perception of Southern Europe becoming an area of increasing labour migration while not necessarily incorrect, needs to be considered in the light of generally low numbers.

These observations on the European experience of labour migration are critical to maintaining some perspective on the phenomenon, its relative size and any estimate on the extent of so-called pressure to emigrate.

Two traditional states of labour migration to the Member States remain outside the Union – Turkey and the former Yugoslavia. Both these states have, over the past few years, given rise to the largest groups of asylum applicants in the Member States.[264] Some of the main receiving Member States for asylum applicants from these states, for instance, Germany, Netherlands, France and the UK permit asylum applicants to take employment subject to the fulfilment of certain conditions.[265] In view of the length of asylum procedures, this category in itself may be defined as a form of

261 Trends in International Migration, SOPEMI, OECD 1992 and 1993.

262 The EC Member States and Immigration in 1993, DGV, Brussels/Luxembourg 1995.

263 Migration Statistics 1994, Eusostat.

264 Eurostat, Migration Statistics 1994.

265 Temporary Employment of Migrants in Europe, supra.

temporary labour migration.[266] Indeed, it may be termed a form of temporary labour migration par excellence as the individual worker remains in a status entirely dependent on the authorities speed of processing his or her application. It is very rare for any residence rights to be acquired by the individual as a result of a period of residence and work on the territory of a Member State so long as he or she remains in the capacity of an asylum applicant. The decision to refuse the asylum application normally ends the period of residence. The employer's continuing need for the asylum applicant's labour is generally irrelevant to any appeal procedure open to the individual.

The Resolution indicates that labour migration is intended to be temporary and to give rise to permanent settlement only in exceptional circumstances. However, the temporary migration policies of the 1950s and 1960s equally were entered into on the basis that migrant workers would return to their countries of origin at the end of their period of work in the state. This was a more overt policy intention in respect of continental labour recruitment than as regards the UK.[267] Only in respect of migrant workers from what are now other Member States of the Union was this policy successful.[268] It is difficult to imagine that the Member States are unaware of this fact.

*The Purpose of the Resolution*

The Resolution is worded in exhortative language, indicating intentions but giving rise to few if any provisions in a mandatory form. This contrasts sharply with the way in which the Resolutions on asylum and, indeed, family unification have been drafted, containing obligations on Member States to bring their national legislation into line with the principles. It must, however, be remembered that none of the Resolutions apparently are intended to be legally binding or to give rise to rights as regards individuals. Therefore, it may be wondered what is the fundamental purpose of this Resolution. On the face of it, it sets out some principles which may be applied, for

266 Temporary Employment of Migrants in Europe, supra, the authors considered, in view of the importance of this source of temporary labour, to include asylum seekers in their survey.

267 Temporary Employment of Migrants in Europe, supra.

268 See supra.

instance that normally, authorisation for employment for third country nationals should take place while the third country national is outside the territory of the Member State. However, in view of the language used this is no more than a suggestion. Special exceptions exist to ensure that some Member States which use substantial numbers of third country national workers on the basis of short term contracts regulated by bilateral agreements will not be required to make any changes to these arrangements.[269]

The impression which is left is that the purpose of the Resolution is to underline the intention of the Member States that labour migration from outside the Union is temporary in nature. Therefore, while the Member States remain committed at least in word to continue integration policies for existing communities of long term labour migrants, the result of labour migration primarily in the 1950s and 1960s, there is an equal commitment, in so far as possible, to prevent any further communities of long term labour migrants from obtaining security of residence and thereby become the proper object of integration policies.

The Resolution provides that work permission should be issued by the authorities either to an employer or to an employee preferably for a specific position.[270] It is premised on the individual assessment of each application against two principal criteria:

(i) can the post be filled by national or Community labour?

(ii) admission for employment is the exception to the rule.

A preference for citizens of the Union is required by Community law, specifically regulation 1612/68 and decision 93/569 regarding its implementation. The difference in approach between Community measures on labour migration and the Resolution is interesting. Because free movement of workers is a fundamental principle of Community law[271] based on the principle of reciprocity, workers seeking to move are self selecting and

269 see part C(vii) of the Resolution which specifically saves existing arrangements though requests Member States to re-examine the provisions within three years.
270 Resolution part C(ii) to (v).
271 Article 48 EC.

entitled to move to look for work as well as to move to take up employment already offered.[272] Community provisions are based on nationality rather than skills related criteria. This provides the maximum flexibility to the labour market with the control of working conditions being the subject of separate provisions.

*The Balance of Power: the State, Employers and Employees*

The Resolution envisages labour migration limited to the defined needs of employers in the Union on a skills basis which must be determined while the proposed worker is outside the country. This creates a substantial burden on employers seeking labour to recruit outside the Union after efforts in the Union have proved unsuccessful. In terms of principles of supply and demand, this means that the demand must become so acute as to justify considerable expenditure by the employer in an extra-Union recruitment effort. Where the employer does not have the means to engage in such a recruitment effort then the demand remains unfilled.

Once such authorisation is granted, it should only be extended where the criteria originally applied to the decision on admission are still fulfilled. Therefore when an employee is authorised to come to the territory for the purpose of work, he or she may only have an extension of permission to remain if the employer concurs. The balance of power between the state, the employer and employee prevents any substantial operation of market forces. The employer may face a substantial increase in the cost of recruitment which it will no doubt wish to recoup. The employee will be unable to sell his or her labour to any other employer in the state unless he or she returns to the country of origin and the process begins again.

The Resolution makes the conditions for lawful employment for third country nationals in such sectors as services virtually non-existent. The emphasis on high skill levels as a minimum requirement for labour migration is not appropriate for this sector. However, it may not be realistic to expect that demand will be met by the Community labour market, particularly in view

---

272 *Antonissen* [1991] ECR 1-745.

of the decreasing levels of mobility in the Community labour market.[273] It may be this area of low skill and wage sectors are catered for by the exclusion from the rigours of the Resolution of "applicants for asylum; third country nationals admitted for asylum; displaced persons who are temporarily admitted; persons exceptionally allowed to stay on humanitarian grounds".[274] Such a wide variety of categories basically covering the same area indicates some intention.

A more traditional Community approach to labour migration may be less disruptive and more realistic. Already, Community agreements with third countries, specifically in Central and Eastern Europe provide for a limited form of free movement for self employed persons or persons running businesses. These provisions which, in respect of Poland have been in force since February 1994 do not appear to have lead to any substantial numbers of persons entering the Union. The extension to workers would seem to be the reasonable next step. The relaxation of limitations on labour migration on the basis of nationality through agreements between the Community and third countries on the Union's borders would provide legal sources of labour for Community businesses from countries which are considered to be the source of substantial illegal employment.[275] Public policy may be better served by a realistic approach to the demand for migrant labour and the inevitability of that demand being filled which enables those migrant workers most willing to migrate and close to the Union's borders to do so with a degree of dignity and lawfully on the basis of reciprocal agreements with their states.

If, indeed, the Member States' concerns about migrant workers are fuelled by fears of a new wave of migrant workers becoming settled in the Union, the example of Community policy on free movement would indicate the chances of this happening decrease when an accessible system for labour migration exists which is not so restrictive as to exclude the majority of those

---

273 Eurostat Migration Statistics 1994.

274 Article B of the Resolution.

275 All the examples of concern regarding illegal employment referred to in the 1993 Synthesis report of DGV, European Commission, refer to persons from Poland, the Czech Republic, Hungary and Slovakia; the EC Member States and Immigration in 1993, Brussels/Luxembourg 1995.

who wish to travel for work and enables them to return to their country of origin without losing the possibility of returning to the host state at a later date. Such a policy, however, would need to be pursued progressively to avoid disruption of the Community labour market.

# 13

# DECISION of 30 November 1994 on a JOINT ACTION adopted by the Council on the basis of Article K.3(2)(b) of the Treaty on European Union concerning travel facilities for school pupils from third countries resident in a Member State.[276]

THE COUNCIL OF THE EUROPEAN UNION,

Having regard to the Treaty on European Union and, in particular Article K.3(2)(b) thereof,

Having regard to the initiative by the Federal Republic of Germany,

Whereas pursuant to Article K.1 point 3 of the Treaty on European Union, policy regarding nationals of third countries is considered as a matter of common interest for the Member States;

Whereas this policy includes, in particular, the determination of conditions of entry and movement by nationals of third countries on the territory of Member States in accordance with Article K.1 point 3 (a);

---

276 Official Journal of the European Communities No L 327/1 (Joint actions adopted by the Council of the European Union) (95/795/JHA).

Whereas the granting of travel facilities for school pupils who are legal residents in the European Union is an expression of a policy pursued by the Member States with a view to improved integration of third country nationals.

HAS DECIDED AS FOLLOWS:

*Article 1*

1. A Member State shall not require a visa of a school pupil who is not a national of a Member State but who is legally resident in another Member State and who seeks to enter its territory either for a short stay or transit if:

   (a) in the framework of a school excursion, the school pupil is travelling as a member of a group of school pupils from a general education school;

   (b) the group is accompanied by a teacher from the school in question who is able to present a list of the schoolchildren he or she is accompanying, issued by the school in question on the common form contained in the Annex:

   – identifying the school pupils being accompanied;

   – documenting the purpose and circumstances of the intended stay or transit;

   (c) the school pupil presents a travel document valid for crossing the border in question, except in cases covered by Article 2.

2. A Member State may refuse entry of a school pupil if he or she does not fulfil the other relevant national immigration conditions.

*Article 2*

The list of pupils which must be carried on crossing the border in question as required by Article 1(1)(b) shall be recognised as a valid travel document in all Member States within the meaning of Article 1(1)(c) where:

- a current photograph is included on the list for any of the school pupils therein mentioned who are unable to identify themselves with an ID card bearing a photograph.

- the responsible authority of the Member State in question confirms residence status of the school pupil as well as his or her right to re-entry and ensures that the document is authenticated accordingly,

- the Member State in which the school pupils reside notifies other Member States that it wishes this Article to apply in respect of its own lists.

*Article 3*

Member States shall agree to take back without formalities school pupils who are resident third country nationals admitted into another Member State on the basis of this joint action.

*Article 4*

If, in exceptional cases, for urgent reasons of national security, a Member State needs to invoke the possibilities foreseen by Article K.2(2) of the Treaty on European Union, it shall be able to deviate from the provisions of Article 1 of this Decision in a way which takes into consideration the interests of the other Member States. The Member State in question shall inform the other Member States of this in an appropriate manner. These measures may be applied to the extent that, and as long as, this is absolutely necessary to achieve the objective.

*Article 5*

1. Member States shall ensure that their national laws are adapted to the extent necessary and the provisions of this joint action included in them as soon as possible, at the latest by 30 June 1995.

2. Member States shall inform the General Secretariat of the Council regarding the changes in national law undertaken for this purpose.

*Article 6*

Other cooperation in this area between individual Member States shall not be affected by this action.

*Article 7*

1. This Decision shall enter into force on the day of its publication in the Official Journal.

2. Articles 1 to 4 shall be applied on the first day of the second month after the notification required pursuant to Article 5 (2) regarding the changes made by the last Member State to complete this formality.

Done at Brussels, 30 November 1994.

# ANNEX

LIST OF TRAVELLERS for school trips within the European Union

<table>
<tr><td colspan="6">Name of School:</td></tr>
<tr><td colspan="6">Address of School:</td></tr>
<tr><td colspan="6">Purpose and length of trip:</td></tr>
<tr><td colspan="6">Name(s) of accompanying teacher(s):</td></tr>
<tr><td colspan="3">The accuracy of data given is confirmed.<br>The guardians of under-age pupils have consented to their participation in the trip in each individual case.<br><br>______________ ______________<br>Locality Date<br><br>Official stamp ______________<br>Headmaster (mistress)</td><td colspan="3">The accuracy of the data that follows on these travelling who are not nationals of a Member State of the EU is hereby confirmed. Travellers are authorised to re-enter (name of state)[1]<br><br>______________ ______________<br>Locality Date<br><br>Official stamp ______________<br>Aliens' Department</td></tr>
<tr><td>Serial Number</td><td>Surname</td><td>First Name</td><td>Place of birth</td><td>Date of birth</td><td>Nationality</td></tr>
<tr><td>1</td><td></td><td></td><td></td><td></td><td></td></tr>
<tr><td>2</td><td></td><td></td><td></td><td></td><td></td></tr>
<tr><td>3</td><td></td><td></td><td></td><td></td><td></td></tr>
<tr><td>4</td><td></td><td></td><td></td><td></td><td></td></tr>
<tr><td>5</td><td></td><td></td><td></td><td></td><td></td></tr>
<tr><td>6</td><td></td><td></td><td></td><td></td><td></td></tr>
<tr><td>7</td><td></td><td></td><td></td><td></td><td></td></tr>
<tr><td>8</td><td></td><td></td><td></td><td></td><td></td></tr>
<tr><td>9</td><td></td><td></td><td></td><td></td><td></td></tr>
<tr><td>10</td><td></td><td></td><td></td><td></td><td></td></tr>
</table>

Space for photographs (for travellers without ID documents with photograph).[277]

| | | | | |
|---|---|---|---|---|
| 1 | 2 | 3 | 4 | 5 |
| 6 | 7 | 8 | 9 | 10 |

*Commentary:*

*Status:* Uncertain. Joint Action of the Council of the European Union in accordance with Article K.1(3) of the Treaty on European Union. However, arguably the subject matter of the Joint Action could have been included in an implementing measure under Article 7A EC relating to the Internal Market.

*Entry into force:* The specimen agreement is recommended for use from 1 January 1995.

*International obligations engaged:*

(1) UN Convention relating to the Status of Refugees 1951 and Protocol 1967
(2) European Convention on Human Rights 1950

277 This part to be completed only by those Member States using this list as a travel document.

(3) Dublin Convention 1990.
(4) European Communities Treaties
(5) European Agreement on the Abolition of Visas for Refugees 1959

*Summary:*

The Joint Action is intended to abolish the need for a separate visa for third country national school pupils resident in one Member State and travelling as part of a school excursion and accompanied by a teacher for a short stay or transit through another Member State. It applies only in respect of students at "general education" schools where the state of residence confirms the legal residence of the student. There is no age limit on students nor any definition of the terms apparently used interchangeably: "school pupils" and "school children". Re-entry must be confirmed by the authorities of the state where the student resides.

In order to get the benefit of the Joint Action the teacher must have a list of pupils with photographs and fulfil various other requirements. There is a national security proviso.

*Comments: Structural Weaknesses of the Third Pillar*

This act is the first occasion on which the Member States have used their power under Title VI of the Treaty on European Union[278] to agree a Joint Action. One of the criticisms of the operation of Title VI by the Council has been the reluctance of the Member States to use any of the new forms of legislation provided to it by the Treaty.[279] This Joint Action is a notable exception to this general reluctance.

However, the Joint Action remains problematic as it is the clearest example so far of overlapping or conflicting competence between Community law (now the First Pillar under the Treaty on European Union) and Title VI, Treaty on European Union (the Third Pillar). Article 7A EC provides for

278 commonly known as the Third Pillar.
279 Draft Report of the Council on the Functioning of the Treaty on European Union, 5082/95, paragraph 75.

the establishment of a single market in which the free movement of goods, capital, services and persons is ensured. It has been a matter of some disagreement among the Member States as to the force and extent of this provision.

The Commission and a number of Member States take the view that Article 7A EC requires the dismantling of all controls at internal frontiers between Member States.[280] In answer to a European Parliamentary Question, the competent Commissioner stated:

"For the Commission and eleven Member States, Article [8a][281] of the Treaty relates to the abolition of controls at internal frontiers for all persons, regardless of nationality. For the United Kingdom, the move to dismantle controls applies only to Community nationals".[282]

If Article 7A EC means what the Commission and the majority of Member States believe it means then this Joint Action is contrary to the force and effect of that provision in that it usurps to the Third Pillar subject matter which belongs to Article 7A EC. Specifically, third country national school pupils, the subject of this Joint Action, are required to fulfil requirements of a Third Pillar Act rather than, or possibly in addition to, those of Article 7A EC.

On the adoption of the Joint Action the Commission issued a statement for the Council minutes as follows:

"The Commission fully supports the policy objective of the Decision regarding travel facilities for school children who are third country nationals residing in a Member State."

"However, given that the Decision affects freedom of movement within the Community of third country nationals lawfully residing in the Community,

280 Abolition of Border Controls, Commission Communications to the Council and to Parliament, 8 May 1992.

281 Renumbered article 7a after the coming into force of the Treaty in European Union.

282 Official Journal C349/2 of 9.12.94.

the Commission reserves its position on the legal basis selected by the Council. It hereby declares that the adoption of the Decision in no way prejudices the question of Community powers in this area."

"The Commission reserves the right to present proposals for Community legislation relating in particular to travel by third country nationals for short periods."[283]
This statement indicates the seriousness of the constitutional issue which is highlighted by the Joint Action.

*The Wider Issue*

The structure of the Union as established by the Treaty on European Union divides responsibility for different aspects of Union activity among the three 'pillars' of the Union: the first pillar, the Community as was; the second pillar on foreign and security policy and the third pillar on justice and home affairs. By virtue of article L of the Treaty on European Union the competence of the Court of Justice is excluded from activities in the second and third pillars.

Further, the role of the European Parliament as regards the activities of the third pillar is limited as follows: "The Presidency and the Commission shall inform the European Parliament of discussions in the areas covered by this Title. The Presidency shall consult the European Parliament on the principal aspects of activities in the areas referred to in this Title and shall ensure that the views of the European Parliament are duly taken into consideration. The European Parliament may ask questions of the Council or make recommendations to it. Each year, it shall hold a debate on the progress made in implementation of the areas referred to in this Title".[284]

The European Commission which has an exclusive right to propose legislation under the first pillar is limited to full association only under the Third Pillar.[285]

---

283 Commission Statement 81(94)1186.
284 Article K.6 Treaty on European Union.
285 Article K4(2) Treaty on European Union.

The exclusion of one fundamental institution of the Union (the Court of Justice) and the limitation of the role of another (the European Parliament) as regards the activities of the Third Pillar in particular creates constitutional uncertainty in the Union. The scope of the Third Pillar as set out in article K.1 includes:

(i) asylum policy;

(ii) rules governing the crossing by persons of the external borders of the Member States and the exercise of controls thereon;

(iii) immigration policy and policy regarding nationals of third countries including conditions of entry and movement by nationals of third countries on the territory of the Member States, conditions of residence by nationals of third countries on the territory of Member States, including family reunion and access to employment, combatting unauthorised immigration, residence and work by nationals of third countries on the territory of Member States.

As has been referred to above[286] access to the territory and residence[287] for some third country nationals is already regulated by Community agreements with third countries specifically with the countries of Central and Eastern Europe. The Court of Justice has on more than one occasion held that provisions of the subsidiary legislation under such agreements may have direct effect.

Further, Article 59 EC provides for Community competence as regards nationals of third countries who provide services and who are established within the Community.

Additionally, the Protocol on Social Policy annexed to the EC Treaty and ratified by all Member States except the UK provides at Article 2(3) that Community competence extends to:-

286 Document 12, comments infra.
287 Specifically through the agreement with Turkey.

"conditions of employment for third country nationals legally residing in Community territory".

Therefore competence on matters of access to, residence on the territory and movement within the European Union of third country nationals is a messy affair spread between the Community, the Community minus the UK and the Third Pillar.

*Confused Competence: Asylum Policy*

In respect of the Third Pillar on asylum policy, in so far as it involves intra Community movement, it touches on the internal market competence. In so far as asylum applicants may also be workers, competence under the Social Policy Protocol is engaged. Where asylum applicants are service providers or employed by service providers carrying out cross border services Articles 59 EC competence is involved.

As regards refugees, by a Declaration of 25 March 1964 the Member States undertook to consider favourably the entry onto their territory for the purpose of employment of refugees recognised as such in other Member States.[288] Of course, a Declaration does not extend competence. Nor, indeed, is it binding on the Member States. However, in general it should be recalled that the choice of form cannot alter the nature of the measure and it is for the Court of Justice to determine whether the content of a measure is wholly consistent with the form attributed to it.[289] Additionally, even a measure which is not binding cannot be regarded as having no legal effect.[290]

*Confused Competence: Crossing of External Borders*

As regards rules governing the crossing by persons of the external borders of the Member States, this has been accepted by the Commission, at least, as a matter outwith the EC Treaty. The Commission has proposed a Convention on the crossing of external borders under Article K3 of the Treaty on

288 OJ 1225/64 of 22.5.64.

289 *Grimaldi* [1989] ECR 4407.

290 *Grimaldi* supra.

European Union (ie within the Third Pillar) though this has yet to be accepted.[291] However, within Community competence by virtue of Article 100c EC is the right to determine the third countries whose nationals must be in possession of a visa when crossing the external borders of the Member States and the adoption of measures relating to a uniform format for visas.

This division of power creates a curious anomaly. If the decision on who must possess a visa and its format rests with the Community but the conditions for the issue of the visa rest with the Member States harmonised, if at all, through the Third Pillar, the Community power is dangerously close to lacking an essential quality of Community law – effet utile. There is no limitation in article 100c EC on the type of visa to which Community measures under that article apply. It must therefore be assumed that measures apply to all types of visas, including visas for the purpose of family reunion, work, etc. However, without any control over the conditions for the issue of a visa, the Community has no control over the consequences of a decision to include a country on the list those whose nationals require a visa to cross the external borders of the Union.

*Confused Competence: Immigration Policy*

As regards immigration policy regarding nationals of third countries to the territory of the Member States, Community competence is involved through agreements with third countries in particular where provision is made for nationals of those states to enjoy a right of residence or establishment in the Union. Such provisions appear in the Turkey/EC Association Agreement as regards a residence right[292] and the Poland/Czech/Hungarian/Slovak Association Agreements providing a right of establishment for nationals and/or legal persons from those states in the Union.[293]

---

291 Proposal for a decision, based on Article K3 of the Treaty on European Union establishing the Convention on the Crossing of the external frontiers of the Member States, 10 December 1993 COM(93) 684 final.

292 Article 41 Additional Protocol contains a standstill clause on the introduction of new restrictions on establishment by Turkish nationals in the Member States.

293 Articles 44-54 of each Agreement subject to sectoral limitations.

In respect of conditions of residence by nationals of third countries on the territory of Member States, Community competence arises directly by virtue of the Social Policy Protocol. The Court of Justice has held that in order to give effect to a right to work or renewal of a work permit, a right of residence must also be granted. These two aspects of the personal situation of a worker are closely linked, the grant of authorisation for work necessarily implies the right of residence.[294]

The Community Agreements with the Maghreb states all contain non-discrimination provisions regarding working conditions, pay and social security benefits for nationals of those states in the Member States which provisions have been held to have direct effect.[295] The Agreement of the Community with 69 states in Africa, the Pacific and Caribbean (Lomé IV) also contains at Annex VI a non-discrimination provision as regards working conditions, pay and employment linked social security for nationals of those states in the Union.[296] A tribunal in one Member State at least, has relied on the Annex in respect of social security rights of a national of one ACP state on its territory.[297] It is unclear whether a right to non-discrimination in working conditions for third country nationals lawfully on the territory of a Member State includes the right to continue to work. In the event that it does, the necessary link between the authorisation of work and the right of residence would have important consequences for the muddled issue of competence.

*The Constitutional Crisis*

The overlap between the two Pillars is a matter of very substantial concern for the legal integrity of the Union. Because the Member States chose a "non-binding", intergovernmental forum for their work in justice and home affairs, the normal controls of the Community to ensure consistency do not apply, specifically the role of the Commission to propose binding legislation, the active role of the European Parliament and the Court of Justice to provide

294 *Kus* [1992] ECR I-6781.

295 *Kziber* [1991] ECR 1-199.

296 Fourth ACP-EEC Convention signed at Lomé 15:12. 1989 OJ L229 of 17.8.91.

297 Le tribunal des Securite Social de Rennes Dossier 9300363 of 17 November 1994.

definitive interpretation applicable in all Member States. In order to protect the integrity of the Community legal order strict vigilance must be maintained to ensure no slippage from the First Pillar into the Third Pillar which inevitably would weaken the ever closer Union among the peoples of Europe, the first objective of the preamble to the EC Treaty.

Justice and home affairs are areas normally within the jurisdiction of both parliaments and courts on the national level. One argument which has been advanced for the exclusion of the participation at Union level of these two institutions is that sufficient control may be exercised at national level on their activities. In view of the difficulties which national parliaments have experienced in exercising any scrutiny role on the Third Pillar this proposition does not appear well founded.[298] As regards the role of national courts, their competence is limited to the assessment of national law and its compatibility with Community provisions but does not extend to the Third Pillar. Further, the role of the Court of Justice is, inter alia, to ensure the consistent application of Community law in all the Member States. No other body is charged with this role nor capable of executing it.

While matters within the ambit of article K of the Treaty on European Union are specifically outside the scope of the Community and EC competence they are, nonetheless, without prejudice to EC competence. Therefore their exercise must not conflict with the competence of the Community. The Court of Justice has made it clear that where a measure can be adopted within the competence of the Community it must be so adopted rather than by way of a multilateral agreement even if limited to the Member States.[299] The Court determined that the title given to a measure, for instance that it is an agreement of the Member States outside Community competence is not definitive of the status of the act. It is a matter for the Court to determine based on the contents and the circumstances of the act.[300]

Further, the Court of Justice has held that its jurisdiction extends to the case of all measures adopted by the institutions, whatever their nature or form

298 House of Lords Scrutiny of the Inter-Governmental Pillars of the European Union HL Paper 124 28th Report 1992/3.

299 *European Parliament v Council* [1993] ECR I-3685.

300 *Grimaldi* [1989] ECR 4407.

which are intended to have legal effects.[301] It is not sufficient for an act to be described as a "decision of the Member States" for it to escape the review of legality provided under the EC Treaty. It is for the Court of Justice to ascertain whether, having regard to its contents and all the circumstances under which it was adopted, the act in question is, in reality, a decision of the Council.

Clearly the status of these Third Pillar acts vis-a-vis Community competence sooner or later must come before the Court of Justice. In view of the limitations of the Third Pillar as regards European parliamentary and judicial control it is not unlikely that where an overlap occurs as in respect of this Joint Action, the Court may find exclusive competence to the First Pillar. In view of possible taint on it's prerogatives, it is somewhat surprising that the European Parliament has not challenged this Joint Action before the Court of Justice.

301 *European Parliament v Council & Commission* [1993] ECR.

# 14 RESOLUTION on the admission of third-country nationals to the territory of the Member States of the European Union for study purposes.[302]

A. GENERAL CONSIDERATIONS

1. The Council recalls that, in the report adopted by the Maastricht European Council (December 1991) from the Ministers responsible for immigration and asylum policy, priority was given to the harmonisation of rules for the admission of students from third countries. In the 1994 programme of work on Justice and Home Affairs, which the Council approved at its meeting on 29 and 30 November 1993 in Brussels, the completion of work on the admission of students was also given priority status.

2. The Council confirms that the international exchange of students and academics is desirable; it acknowledges that the education of students and the exchange of academics have positive implications for relations between the Member States and the States of origin.

3. The Council agrees that, at the end of their studies, students must in principle return to their countries of origin so that the knowledge and skills they have acquired are made available to those countries.

4. The Council considers it is important to ensure that the admission of third-country nationals to study in the Member States for a limited period, in principle does not turn into permanent immigration. Similarly,

302 Adopted, Brussels 30.11 and 1.12.94 799614/94.

the Council considers it is necessary to devise suitable systems to prevent those who are mainly seeking employment from receiving authorization to stay on as students.

5. The Council agrees not to regulate via this Resolution the issue of third-country nationals lawfully resident on a permanent basis in the territory of a Member State, but who have no right of admission and residence in another Member State.

   This does not affect the position of third country nationals who are already covered or who may, in the future, be covered by bilateral agreements between the Member States regarding the cooperation between institutions of higher education.

6. The Council agrees that Member States' national policies on the admission of third-country nationals for study purposes must be governed by the principles set out below, which may not be relaxed by Member States in their national legislation.

   The Council agrees that these principles have to be taken into account whenever any change is proposed to national legislation on the subject.

   The Member States should seek to ensure that by 1 January 1996 national law is in conformity with these principles. The principles are not legally binding on the Member Sates and do not afford a ground for legal action by the individual.

7. The Council agrees that there shall be a regular review of the transposition of this resolution and of the need for amendments to it.

8. The Member States should facilitate the admission and residence of students from third countries within the framework of special cooperation programmes, the financing of which is secured at national or Community level.

9. Application of the said principles does not prevent application of national rules on public policy, public health and safety.

B. PERSONS EXEMPT FROM THE SCOPE OF THIS RESOLUTION

The principles of harmonisation will not apply to:

- individuals who enjoy the right of freedom of movement under Community law, ie, nationals of the Member States, nationals of the EFTA States which are parties to the Agreement on the European Economic Area and members of their families;

- third-country nationals who have been admitted for the purposes of family reunification to take up residence with nationals of a Member State or third country who reside in the Member State in question.

C. PRINCIPLES BY WHICH THE POLICIES OF THE MEMBER STATES WILL BE GUIDED

*1. General Criteria*

Within the meaning of these principles, a student is a national of a third country admitted by a State or State recognised higher education institution or a comparable institution in a Member State of the European Union in order to:

- take up a course of study;

- study for a doctorate; or

- pursue academic activity following a course of higher education within the framework of further study or training, and the earning of income is not the principal aim.

It should also be noted that for the purposes of this resolution school pupils and apprentices are not included.

For the purpose of this resolution a person who participates in a course aimed at preparing for a specific course of university studies (eg providing language training) shall also be deemed to be a student.

*2. Requirements for Admission*

A national of a third country who requests admission as a student will have to prove to the competent authorities of the Member State that he/she:

- fulfils all the requirements applicable to foreigners as regards entry and stay in the territory of the Member State;
- has a firm offer of admission to a State or State-recognised higher education institution or a comparable institution appropriate to his/her studies for a course of study as a main activity and if so required by national legislation that this offer concurs with requirements made by the competent immigration authorities.

  Member States may also request proof of continuity between previous studies and studies to be undertaken in the host country;
- has the financial means required to support the cost of his/her studies and subsistence for himself/herself so that during his/her stay the student does not need to claim social assistance in the host Member State and the earning of an income is not the principal aim;
- if required by national legislation, has health cover for all risks in the host Member State.

A Member State may also require the student to satisfy the immigration authorities that he/she would return to his/her own country on completion of studies.

A Member State may permit persons to enter who are interested in preparing their application for studies in the respective State or who can demonstrate a genuine and realistic plan for undertaking a course of study. It may be permitted for the person concerned not to have to leave the country in order to obtain an extension of his/her authorization to stay.

Nationals of third countries who entered the Member States with the aim of working there in an employed or self-employed capacity shall on the basis of this resolution not be admitted in principle to engage in study as a main activity.

### 3. *Authorization to Reside*

The duration of residence is limited to the length of the course.

The length of the course is dictated by the duration of studies in the chosen subject. At the end of the course of study, or if the student abandons his/her studies, authorization to reside expires. Any change in subject will involve a change in the reason for residence which, as a rule, argues against a fresh authorization or an extension of the existing one if it does not take place within the initial phase of the studies.

Proof of authorization to reside will take the form of an entry in the student's passport or a particular personal identity card.

If the period of study is longer than one year, the authorization can initially be limited to a 1-year period; in that case it can be renewed on a yearly basis. Renewal will depend on the student's ability to prove that he/she fulfils the requirements for its original issue and that he/she has passed any tests or examinations set by the institution in which he/she is studying.

At the end of his course of study, or if the student interrupts his studies, a national of a third country will in principle have to leave the territory of the Member State; if he/she wishes to return to that country he/she will have to re-apply for authorization to re-enter.

### 4. *Employment Authorization*

In principle, a national of a third country who is studying in the territory of a Member State may not engage in gainful employment, either in a self-employed or employed capacity. Member States may allow short-term or subsidiary jobs. Such jobs must not affect the continuation of his/her studies; neither must they, in principle, represent an income vital for the subsistence of the student.

5. *Admission of Family Members*

National provisions will apply as regards the possible admission of family members and the taking-up of employment or study by the spouse.

Once the third country national has ended his/her studies, the spouse and children to whom authorization to stay was granted are also required to leave the territory of the Member State if they have no other authorization to remain.

*Commentary:*

*Status:* Resolution adopted by Council of the European Union in accordance with Title VI Treaty on European Union – Cooperation in the Fields of Justice and Home Affairs. It is not binding on the Member States nor is it intended to give rise to rights for individuals.

*Entry into force:* The Member States shall seek to adapt national legislation to conform with the Resolution by 1 January 1996.

*International obligations engaged:*

(1) ILO Convention 151, 1975
(2) European Social Charter 1961
(3) European Convention on Human Rights 1950
(4) European Communities Treaties

*Summary:*

The Resolution applies to higher education studies but not to school pupils or apprentices. Language students are included.

The personal scope of the Resolution is defined by exclusion. In other words, it applies to all persons not explicitly excluded. Article A(5) states that it is not the intention of the Council "to regulate via this Resolution the issue of third-country nationals lawfully resident on a permanent basis in the territory of a Member State, but who have no right of admission and residence in another Member State". Articles B and C(1) provide that the following persons are excluded from the scope:-

(i) nationals of the Member States and EEA states exercising Treaty rights;
(ii) the family members of persons within (i);
(iii) third country nationals admitted to a Member State for family reunion with either a national of the state or a third country national.

The Member States specifically exclude from the ambit of the Resolution third country nationals lawfully resident on a permanent basis in the Member States otherwise than for family reunification.

Students should be admitted to the territory providing they meet the following criteria:

(i) they fulfil all the requirements applicable to foreigners as regards entry and stay;
(ii) they have a firm offer of admission to a state or state-recognised higher education institution or a comparable institution and the offer concurs with the requirements made by the competent immigration authorities;
(iii) financial means to support studies and maintenance;
(iv) if required by national legislation, health insurance.

A Member State may require the student to satisfy it that he or she will return home on completion of the studies. A Member State may also permit entry to a person thinking about studying but not yet in possession of an offer of a place. However, Member States shall not permit entry as students to persons who aim to take employment or self employment.

The student should be authorised to reside for the length of the course. If he or she changes subject, a new authorization shall be required subject to a presumption against such new authorization. In principle students must not work but Member States may permit short term or subsidiary employment. The income from such jobs must not be vital to the student's subsistence. National law applies both to the admission of family members and whether or not they are permitted to take employment.

*Comments: The Risky Business of Investing in Studies*

This Resolution exemplifies some of the weaknesses of the Third Pillar decision making process which have become increasingly pronounced since the first intergovernmental act, the Dublin Convention. As Third Pillar acts seek to regulate increasingly detailed aspects of immigration policy so the structural defects become more problematic. The lack of a dedicated staff has led to surprisingly varied and inconsistent drafting between documents both in style and terminology. The lack of external parliamentary accountability of an effective nature means that the equivalent of a "Committee Stage" in Parliament is not available. This has two consequences, the unstable terminology is not corrected, and more importantly, the underlying assumptions and principles of the acts are not properly tested either on their own or in relation to the practical consequences of the act. The secrecy which surrounds the drafting and negotiation of the acts imbues the whole process with an "us (at the conference table) and them (the outsiders)" mentality which is not conducive to democratic process. The lack of an enforcement mechanism other than the good intentions of those who participated in the process, phrased in such a way as to raise questions as to whether any obligation in international law is undertaken (for example a common phrase is that the Member States "shall seek to ensure" implementation), makes unsatisfactory compromises too easy. As inconvenient provisions do not really have to be implemented there is no incentive for any delegation to play the disagreeable role of the spoil sport which refuses to compromise.

Five problem areas manifest in this Resolution as a result of the structural weakness of the process:

(i) *Overlap of competencies with the First Pillar*

This problem, most clearly demonstrated in the preceding document, the Joint Action on school pupils is problematic in this Resolution as well. The European Parliament, in its draft report on this Resolution[303] identifies three areas of overlapping competence with the First Pillar, specifically Title VIII Chapter III, Education, Vocational, Training and Youth; Title IX, Culture; and Title VIII, Common Commercial Policy.

As regards the first source of competence, Article 127(3) EC provides that the Community and the Member States shall foster co-operation with third countries and the competent international organisations in the sphere of vocational training. The European Court of Justice has held that the term "vocational training" includes any form of instruction which prepares a person for qualification in a specific profession, trade or employment, whatever the age or educational level of the pupils or students, and even if the curriculum includes some subjects of general education.[304]

This would certainly include part of the material scope of the Resolution which covers a "course of study, study for a doctorate or pursuit of academic activities following a course of higher eduction within the framework of further education or training".[305]

In respect of the second source of competence, culture, Article 128 EC requires action by the Community to encourage co-operation between the Member States for the improvement of the knowledge and dissemination of the culture and history of the European peoples. This would cover any aspect of education which falls outside the Court of Justice's interpretation of vocational training and thereby covered by Article 127(3) EC.

---

303 20th April 1995 DOC EN/PR/268/268346.
304 *Gravier* [1985] ECR 593.
305 Resolution, Article C(1).

(ii) *Personal scope of the Resolution*

By defining the personal scope of the Resolution negatively, ie, its provisions relate to all those who are not excluded, the Resolution is unsatisfactory. The excluded categories of persons from the Resolution is far too limited and potentially includes persons whose rights of residence derive from Community law. The European Parliament in its draft report[306] identifies six categories of persons who should be excluded from the scope of the Resolution but are not:

- third country nationals admitted to Member States to carry on a self-employed occupation;
- refugees within the meaning of the UN Convention;
- persons enjoying refugee status under the terms of national law;
- third country nationals legally resident in a Member State who enjoy rights under a bilateral agreement;
- third country nationals enjoying rights of admission by virtue of Association Agreements;
- third country nationals, and members of their families, who go to a Member State to carry out an occupation in an employed capacity and who are subject to the principles set out in the Resolution on limitations on admission of third country nationals to the Member States for employment adopted in June 1994.[307]

Accordingly, the personal scope of the Resolution defined by exclusion leaves substantial numbers of persons within its ambit whose rights of entry and residence in the Member States are regulated by other international or national instruments. Should these persons seek to pursue

306 20 April 1995, DOC/EN/PR/268/268346.
307 see document 12 supra.

studies, however in the Member States, it would appear that the requirements of the Resolution would apply.

(iii) *Unclear and unsatisfactory material scope*

Under the General Considerations section, the Member States agree a number of objectives. First, the Council confirms that the international exchange of students and academics is desirable and has positive implications for relations between Member States and the states of origin.[308] The concern of the Council appears to be to ensure "that the admission of third country nationals to study in the Member States for a limited period, in principle does not turn into permanent immigration".[309] However, the provisions of the Resolution are so vaguely worded, unclear in their extent and scope and lacking in coherence that the result of such a Resolution is that every Member State may legitimately continue whatever policies it currently has on foreign students with minimal, if any, need for amendment.

A striking example of this lack of harmonisation is Article 2 indent 1. Article 2 is entitled "Requirements of Admission". The first indent provides that a national of a third country who requests admission as a student will have to prove to the competent authorities of the Member State that he/she "fulfils all the requirements applicable to foreigners as regards entry and stay in the territory of the Member State". Such a provision clearly legitimates any national procedure and its continued existence and application.

The second indent provides that the student must have a firm offer of admission to a higher education institution, however, paragraph 3 permits Member States to admit persons who are interested in preparing their application for study in the State or who can demonstrate a genuine and realistic plan for undertaking a course of study. Therefore the requirement of an offer of admission is no requirement at all.

---

308 Article A(2).
309 Article A(4).

The Resolution is replete with such ambiguities. A careful analysis of the Resolution gives the impression that for all the words and phrases, in the end the only thing which is clear is that most Member States would rather like students to go back to their countries of origin after their studies.

(iv) *Insufficient regard for international obligations of the Member States*

The facilitation of education and vocational training is the subject of numerous international obligations of the Member States. Specific reference may be found in ILO Convention 151 of 1975[310] and the European Social Charter 1961.[311] There is no reference to these international obligations to facilitate and assist education or training in the Resolution.

Where the rules for regulating admission of students require virtually no consistency between the Member States it is very difficult to see how the facilitation obligation can be fulfilled with any degree of certainty whatsoever.

(v) *Remedies for the individual*

The Resolution contains no minimum procedural guarantees or appeal rights for individuals affected by it. This is unsatisfactory and under-

---

310 Paragraph 2 states: "migrant workers and members of their families lawfully within the territory of a member should enjoy effective equality of opportunity and treatment with nationals of the member concerned in respect of –
(a) access to occupational guidance and placement services;
(b) access to vocational training and employment of their choice on the basis of individual suitability for such training or employment, account being taken of qualifications acquired outside the territory of and in the country of employment."

311 Article 9 provides the right to vocational guidance and Article 10 the right to vocational training applicable to all persons on the territory.

mines the basic principle of the European Union as a Union based on the rule of law.[312]

For example, Article 3 provides that any change in the subject matter being studied by students will involve a change in the reason for residence which, as a rule, argues against fresh authorisation or an extension of the existing one if it does not take place within the initial phase of the study.

There is no indication of how a change of subject is to be defined, is a change from chemical engineering to industrial engineering a change of subject or not? Why should a change of subject involve a change in the reason for residence as the student is still studying and studies remain the purpose of his or her residence? Similarly, what is the initial phase of the studies? Is this to mean that the first two weeks of study where the student may decide that he or she loathes the course which he or she has embarked upon or does it mean that in the first few years? Not only is it for the administration of each Member State to make such judgements, but there is no mechanism whereby decisions even within one administration are necessarily subject to judicial control to ensure consistency and fairness. The argument often deployed to counter any demand for competence to the European Court of Justice over Third Pillar acts is that national courts can provide sufficient consistency as to make the European Court of Justice's involvement unnecessary. However, for this argument to be sustainable, there must be equivalent appeal rights guaranteed in the act itself. Such an appeal right would need clearly to specify that the appeal must go to the merits of the decision reached and the judicial authority must have power to consider the decision reached in the light of the Third Pillar act. Without harmonisation of safeguards for the individual against administrative abuse, the Third Pillar acts lack the essential components of Community decision making – transparency and proportionality.

312 See F. Schockweiler, judge of the Court of Justice, La Cour de Justice des Communautés Européenes dépasse-t-elle les limites de ses attributions? Journal des tribunaux Droit Européen 20 avril 1995.

For the third country national student studying in a Member State his or her family will have had to come up with very substantial funds in order to send that student to the Member State in order to study. The family will undoubtedly be investing resources in this student with the hope and intention that the student will obtain the qualification sought and benefit from increased economic opportunities as a result. This is a major financial investment by the whole family abroad and deserves adequate protection. The Member States would not expect third country nationals investing in, for instance, their stock markets, to do so without adequate protection against the risk of arbitrary action rendering valueless the investment.

In view of what is at stake, to refuse a student an extension of permission to remain in a Member State to complete a course of studies causes great hardship not only to the student but to his or her whole family. All of the money which was invested for the benefit of the Member State's economy to get the student part way through the course of study is wasted if that person cannot remain to finish. In view of the personal cost in monetary terms but also in hopes and expectation of the family it is incumbent on Member States to ensure that decisions on admission and extensions of stay for students are subject to appropriate judicial safeguards. Any attempt at harmonising rules on admission of third country national students to the Member States should include such safeguards.

# 15 RESOLUTION relating to the limitations on the admission of third-country nationals to the territory of the Member States for the purpose of pursuing activities as self-employed persons.[313]

A. GENERAL CONSIDERATIONS ON POLICY

1. The Council recalls that, in the report on immigration and asylum policy by the Ministers responsible for immigration adopted by the European Council held in Maastricht in 1991, priority was given to the harmonization of policies on admission for the purposes of pursuing self-employed occupation. In principle, these policies are restrictive. In any case existing obligations and future developments for example in GATT, GATS and OECD agreements must be taken into account.

2. The Council notes that the 1994 programme of priority work in the field of justice and home affairs, adopted by the Council at its meeting in Brussels on 29 and 30 November 1993, included, as a priority measure, a decision to conclude work in the field of the admission of self-employed persons.

3. The Council welcomes the progress achieved as a result of the signing of the final act and agreements under the Uruguay Round in Marrakesh on 15 April 1994 towards free international trade for the promotion of investment and the creation of jobs.

313 Adopted Brussels 30.11 and 1.12.94 11219/94.

4. The Council takes the view that to a certain extent the question of the admission of persons for the purposes of pursuing a salaried activity and that of the admission of self-employed persons can by treated distinctly. The admission of persons for the purpose of an independent economic activity who add value (investment, innovation, transfer of technology, job creation) to the economy of the host country is of benefit. Artists exercising an independent activity of significance may also be admitted.

5. The Council considers that third-country nationals should not be admitted to a Member State for the purposes of pursuing an independent economic activity when the latter is of no economic benefit to that State or any of its regions.

6. The Council considers it necessary to ensure that persons who are attempting to find employment in a dependent working relationship are not admitted as self-employed persons.

7. The Council also considers that it is necessary to avoid persons establishing themselves and embarking on a self-employed occupation without having the appropriate qualifications and/or financial means and to avoid their entering into a dependent working relationship.

8. The Council agrees not to address in this Resolution the question of third-country nationals legally resident on a permanent basis on the territory of a Member State although they do not have the right to admission or residence in another Member State. It agrees to examine this question at a later date.

9. The Council accordingly agrees that the principles set out below shall govern Member States' internal policies towards third-country nationals seeking admission to or permission to remain in their territories in order to engage in a self-employed occupation. The Council agrees that the principles set out below may not be relaxed by Member States in their national legislation. It agrees to have regard to these principles in any proposals for the revision of national legislation. The Member States will further endeavour to seek to ensure by 1 January 1996 that national legislation is in conformity with them. The principles are not legally

binding on Member States and do not afford a ground for action by individuals.

10. The Council agrees that there shall be a regular review of the transposition of this Resolution and of the need for amendments to it.

11. The Council also confirms that the application of these principles is no bar to the application of national rules on law and order, public health and national security.

B. PERSONS TO WHOM THIS RESOLUTION DOES NOT APPLY

The harmonization principles do not apply to :

- persons who have right of free movement under Community law, i.e nationals of Member States, nationals of EFTA countries parties to the Agreement on the European Economic Area and members of their families;

- third-country nationals who have been allowed admission for the purpose of family reunification to join nationals of a Member State or a third country resident in the Member State concerned;

- third-country nationals whose access to employment is covered by rights stemming from agreements concluded with third countries which are governed by Community law and by bilateral and multilateral Agreements, such as GATT, GATS or OECD agreements;

- third-country nationals entering the Member States in order to engage in paid employment. Such persons are covered by the principles set out in the Resolution on limitations on admissions of third-country nationals to the Member States for employment adopted by the Council on 20 and 21 June 1994;

- third-country nationals entering the Member States for study purposes. Such persons are covered by the principles to be set out in the Resolution on the admission of third-country nationals to the Member States for study purposes.

C. GENERAL PRINCIPLES

*Point 1*

(1) This Resolution only concerns individuals and does not affect the setting up of firms.

(2) "Activity as a self-employed person" means any activity carried out in a personal capacity or in the legal form of a company or firm within the meaning of the second paragraph of Article 58 of the EC Treaty without being answerable to an employer in either case.

(3) Only those associates actively involved and whose presence is necessary in pursuing the company's or firm's aims and in its management may be authorized to establish themselves in the host Member State's territory. In cases where those associates do not have a majority or substantial share holding in the company or firm Member States may reserve the right not to admit them except in the case of salaried persons when they have received authorization to work.

*Point 2*

(1) Member States may allow third-country nationals wishing to pursue activities as self-employed persons to enter their territory where it has been duly established that that activity will produce the benefits referred to in Section A(4) or corresponds to the activity referred to in the last sentence of Section A(4) as required by each Member State and that general legal provisions governing entry and residence have been complied with.

(2) The admission procedure should ensure that persons who quite obviously wish to engage in paid employment or whose partnership or directorship amounts to disguised paid employment are not admitted as self-employed persons. Without prejudice to the application of point 8(2), once admitted, the admission to activities as a self-employed person does not extend to looking for or accepting a job on the labour market.

*Point 3*

(1) Requests for admission must be submitted to the authorities of the host Member State which are competent under national law through the consular or diplomatic representation of the State or through another national competent authority designated for this purpose in the home country or the country of origin of the person seeking admission to pursue activities as a self-employed person.

(2) They must be accompanied by information which can be used to assess whether the planned activity meets the preconditions referred to under point 2, and also by documentary evidence that the activity will be carried out in accordance with the relevant national legislation.

(3) The following could for example be required for assessing the preconditions referred to under point 2 in accordance with national legislation:

- documents indicating the nature, scale and duration of the activity the person wishes to engage in;

- documents indicating the number of staff likely to be required;

- a description of the premises where the activity will be carried out, which should be appropriate for it;

- evidence of the funds available for the intended purpose.

(4) The following could for example be required for assessing compliance with legislation in force, in accordance with national legislation:

- proof that the self-employed person meets the conditions of the host Member State regarding professional qualifications and access to the occupation;

- in the case of companies or firms, the instrument of incorporation, evidence of publication or registration thereof, and the names of the directors and managerial staff and of the associates authorized to act on their behalf;

– proof such as police documentation or similar documents, showing the integrity of the person concerned.

*Point 4*

(1) Authorization to engage in a self-employed occupation will be granted in accordance with the provisions of national aliens legislation and in writing, for example in the form of a passport stamp or other document. Such authorization will be personal and non-transferable.

(2) The validity of the initial authorization may be limited in time. Upon application it may be extended for a further period and/or be of unlimited validity, if the conditions for access continue to obtain as provided for in national legislation.

*Point 5*

(1) All requests for renewal must, where so required under Member States' national legislation, be accompanied by documentary evidence that the self-employed person offers guarantees for the continued orderly pursuit of his occupation.

(2) At least at the time when any renewal application referred to under point 4(2) is submitted, a check may be made on the bona fide nature of the activity engaged in, whether it still corresponds to the activity for which authorization was given, the ability of the person concerned to support himself by the income from that activity and its continuing compliance with the preconditions referred to under point 2(1).

(3) Any further checks which Member States may make thereafter could in principle be limited.

*Point 6*

(1) Under the conditions laid down by national law, Member States may grant third-country nationals wishing to provide a service leave to enter their territory with authorization to carry out the relevant work for the performance of the service.

(2) "Service provider" means a self-employed person (residing abroad) whose services are sought by a person residing in a Member State in order to carry out, against remuneration, a specific task over a specific period.

*Point 7*

Persons already present in the territory of a Member State as students, trainees, seasonal workers, service providers, contract workers or for other reasons will not as a general rule be permitted to extend their stay for the purpose of establishing themselves as self-employed persons. Such persons must leave the country once the purpose of stay on the basis of which they were given leave to enter the country has ceased to apply.

*Point 8*

(1) In principle care must be taken to ensure that persons admitted to pursue activities as self-employed persons do not eventually enter into a paid employment relationship.

(2) Member States may allow self-employed persons who have acquired the right to long-term/permanent residence to seek where appropriate a work permit in order to obtain paid employment.

*Point 9*

The spouse and unmarried children under a maximum age, varying between 16 and 18 years depending on the Member State concerned, of a self-employed person will in principle be admitted to join that person, subject to the conditions set out in the Resolution concerning family reunification adopted by the Ministers responsible for immigration questions of the European Community on 1 June 1993.

*Point 10*

(1) Member States' arrangements enabling them to refuse admission on grounds of public security and public order shall not be affected by this Resolution.

(2) The provisions of this Resolution shall not affect Member States' provisions governing trades and professions or arrangements concerning the mutual recognition of vocational qualifications.

*Point 11*

Nothing in this Resolution prevents a Member State from reserving the right to admit, subject to its national law, third-country nationals who make very substantial investments in the commerce and industry of that Member State where there are strong economic reasons justifying exemption from those principles in this Resolution that limit the business activities in which the third-country national is engaged.

*Commentary:*

*Status:* Resolution adopted by the Council of the European Union in accordance with Title VI of the Treaty on European Union – Cooperation in the fields of Justice and Home Affairs.

*Entry into force:* The Member States shall "endeavour to seek to ensure" that national law is adopted to conform with the Resolution by 1 January 1996. The Resolution is not binding on the Member States and does not provide a basis for action by an affected individual.

*International obligations engaged:*

(1) General Agreement on Trade in Services (Annex to World Trade Agreement 1994)
(2) European Communities Treaties
(3) Turkey - EC Association Agreement 1963 and Additional Protocol 1970
(4) Europe Agreements between EC and Czech Republic, Hungary, Poland and Slovakia

*Summary:*

The Resolution acknowledges that it is subject to international agreements, particularly the GATT, GATS and OECD agreements. The GATS (General Agreement on Trade in Services) annexed to the World Trade Agreement is particularly relevant to any effort to limit the activities of self employed service providers.

The Member States confirm that "the admission of persons for the purpose of an independent economic activity who add value (investment, innovation, transfer of technology, job creation) to the economy of the host country is of benefit. Artists exercising an independent activity of significance may also be admitted."

However as a matter of principle third country nationals should not be admitted under an independent economic activity category if the activity is of no economic benefit to the state or its regions. No mention is made of cultural benefit though the personal scope includes artists.

The following persons are excluded from the personal scope of the Resolution:

- persons who have free movement rights under Community law and the European Economic Area Agreement and their family members;
- third country national family members of nationals of a Member State and such family members admitted for family reunion with third country nationals resident in the Member State;
- third country nationals with rights to employment stemming from bilateral and multilateral agreements;
- third country nationals coming for employment;
- third country national students.

Self employment is defined by reference to Article 58 EC and is intended to cover activities carried out in a personal capacity or as principal of a business.

Admission may be permitted provided the benefit to the state set out above is established and all national legal provisions have been fulfilled. Point 3 of the Resolution provides that requests must be submitted to the appropriate authorities with sufficient information so that those authorities can assess the application in accordance with the relevant national legislation. Some examples of what might be relevant to national legislation (though not necessarily so) are included.

The Resolution provides that all authorization shall be in writing and personal to the recipient. It may be time limited and if so on any renewal application the state may check how the person has been engaged. There is no bar on states making checks at other times.

Member States may also admit service providers but no guidance is given on how or for how long nor is there any reference to the right of Community employers to send third country national employees to carry out services in another Member State.[314]

Any third country national already in a Member State who wishes to remain for self employment in principle should leave the territory and apply to come back in the new capacity. Family reunion for the self employed is limited to spouses and unmarried children up to 16 or 18 at the option of the Member State.

*Comments: In Search of a Material Scope*

*Obligations, Implementation Dates and Enforcement*

Resolutions adopted under the Third Pillar are usually stated to contain principles which are not legally binding on the Member States nor afford a ground of action by individuals.[315] Nonetheless, Resolutions have implementation dates, in respect of this Resolution 1st January 1996 by which Member States "will further endeavour to seek to ensure" that national legislation is in conformity. This peculiar state of affairs may be seen as the clearest example of two competing trends within the Third Pillar as to its purpose and scope. On the one hand many of the original Member States of the European Community favour substantive harmonisation with binding rules and enforcement mechanisms.[316] On the other hand a number of newer Member States remain deeply concerned about the extent of their national sovereignty particularly in respect of the admission to and residence

314 See Court of Justice decision in *Vander Elst* [1994] ECR.

315 Article A(9).

316 See for instance the original Dutch proposal for the Treaty on European Union; also the Declaration on Asylum to the Treaty on European Union included at the insistence of the German Government.

of third country nationals in their territory. These Member States oppose binding harmonisation in favour of information exchange and wide principles setting parameters for national policy.

In order for an act to be binding it must be sufficiently clear and precise. The rule of law requires any binding measure to be accompanied by a right of action for an individual aggrieved by it. As the Member States make it clear that neither are the principles of the Resolution binding nor do they give rise to a right of action for an individual there is an implicit, at least, link between these two concepts. While this does not mean that the Member States necessarily accept that where rules do become legally binding they must be complimented by rights of appeal for individuals, it is persuasive. If harmonisation is to be achieved at a supra national level this requires uniformity in the application of binding rules across all of the states involved. This has been achieved in the First Pillar, the European Community, by way of binding interpretative power to the Court of Justice. The role of the individual's right to redress regarding a breach of Community law has been extremely important to the development of Community law. Some of the most important jurisprudence of the Court of Justice has arisen from individual's actions in national courts which has resulted in the courts using the reference procedure to clarify Community law.[317]

Of the three mechanisms by which Community law has progressed: a clear and precise obligation, a time limit for implementation and a right of action in respect of breach, the Resolution contains only one - the time limit. It is difficult to imagine how the time limit applies or indeed to what, let alone how it may be enforced.

Further, in the Resolution the Council "agrees that the principle set out below may not be relaxed by the Member States in their national legislation".[318] As the principles are not legally binding and there is no mechanism for enforcement by the parties, let alone aggrieved individuals, it is difficult to see the force of this statement.

317 Article 177 EC.
318 Article A(9).

*Looking for the Material Scope*

Notwithstanding the "no relaxation" clause, in view of the very loose drafting of the Resolution it is difficult to see how any judicial mechanism could determine whether national legislation was being relaxed or not. For example, under the heading General Considerations on Policy the Member States agree "the admission of persons for the purpose of an independent economic activity who add value (investment, innovation, transfer of technology, job creation) to the economy of the host country is of benefit. Artists exercising an independent activity of significance may also be of benefit".[319]

The Resolution goes on at article 11 to state "nothing in this Resolution prevents a Member State from reserving the right to admit, subject to its national law, third country nationals who make very substantial investments in the commerce and industry of that Member State where there are strong economic reasons justifying exemption from those principles in this Resolution that limit the business activities in which the third country national is engaged".

As there is no limitation on the business activities in which the third country national can engage so long as these constitute self-employment, it is very difficult to see what article 11 is seeking to address. As investment is specifically stated to be an activity which adds value to the economy it is difficult to understand what the specification of "very substantial investments" at article 11 means.

The Resolution appears to regulate, in addition to self-employment (the equivalent of article 52 EC) service provision (article 6 of the Resolution, but the equivalent in Community law of article 59 EC). This elision of two concepts with different scopes and purposes will undoubtedly cause difficulties in Community law by reason of the familiar problem - overlap of competence between Community law and the Resolution. The regulation of admission of third country nationals for self employment may indeed be properly within the scope of the Third Pillar. The movement at least

319 Article A(4).

within the Union of third country nationals in order to provide services in the territory of the Union is not.

Specifically, Article 59 second indent EC provides "the Council may, acting by a qualified majority on a proposal from the Commission, extend the provisions of the Chapter to nationals of a third country who provide services and who are established within the Community". Article 6 purports to regulate at least to a substantial degree the same personal and material scope of service provision by third country nationals. It will be a matter for the European Court of Justice to determine whether the Council's adoption of article 6 of this Resolution is indeed without prejudice to Community law.

A further elision of concepts was identified by Mr Klaus Heiner Lehne MEP in his report to the European Parliament of 16th March 1995.[320]

"Although the Title uses the term 'admission'", this covers two aspects: "admission to the territory of the Union" and "admission to the pursuit of activities of self-employed persons". If "admission to the territory of the Union" is meant, the text could be referring to an implementing measure pursuant to the Treaty on external frontiers which has not yet been adopted. If the other meaning is intended, it is concerned with labour market policy in the broader sense. Both of these aspects would be suitable cases for an EC directive. As the case stands, however, the two aspects have obviously been confused and the approach adopted is less than systematic.[321]

*A New Proviso*

A new term appears for the first time in this Resolution relating to a public policy exception. In previous Resolutions, the operation of a principle has been stated not to prevent the application of national rules on "public policy,

---

320 DOC EN/PR/268/268332.

321 Draft report to the European Parliament, 16th March 1995 on the Draft Council Resolution relating to the limitations on the admission of third country nationals to the territory of the Member States for the purpose of pursuing activities of self-employed persons, page 7.

public health and safety".[322] Article A(11) of this Resolution provides that the application of these principles is no bar to the operation of "national rules on law and order, public health and national security". This is the first occasion on which a public policy proviso has referred to national rules on "law and order" but has made no reference to public policy or public security. The Community wording of the proviso as contained in Article 48(3) EC is "subject to limitations, justified on grounds of public policy, public security or public health". It remains uncertain what the application of national rules on law and order means or why the Member States have chosen to deviate from the standard, though variable wording which they have used hitherto to cover this type of proviso.

Notwithstanding the new wording used A(1) at article 10(1) the Resolution reverts back to a more familiar proviso which enables Member States to refuse persons admission on grounds of "public security and public order". It is unclear what the intended scope of the provisos is or to what extend their scope is similar, complementary or divergent.

*What is self-employment?*

As regards the principle of admission for self-employment, the definition of persons who add value to the economy encompasses an extremely wide number of circumstances and indeed, it could be argued, has a scope not dissimilar to Article 52 EC. It could include, for instance, a street vendor selling bobbles which are made in the territory of the host state. This could satisfy the requirement of investment, job creation for the persons who make the bobbles on the territory or possibly innovation. The principle would also encompass a multi-billion ECU greenfield manufacturing site. Under the circumstances, it is not surprising that the Member States do not wish the Resolution to give rise to action by an individual.

The Resolution does not address the question of whether approval to pursue self-employed activities must be obtained while the person is outside the

---

322 See for instance Document 14 Resolution on Admission of Third Country Nationals to the Territory of the Member States of the European Union for Study Purposes, Article A(9).

country or inside the country.[323] The prohibition on persons already present in the territory as students, trainees, seasonal workers, service providers, contract workers or for other reasons changing their status to self employed persons is, therefore, difficult to understand.[324]

*Conclusion*

In general, this Resolution stands out as perhaps the most incoherent of the products of the intergovernmental process and the Third Pillar. It is difficult to determine why this should be the case as the admission of persons for self-employment can be tremendously important for the development of cross regional trade and economic co-operation. The encouragement of entrepreneurial activities is espoused by many Member States. The apparent lack of a legal infra-structure with appropriate and consistent definitions is surprising.

323 Point 3.
324 Point 7.

# 16 CONCLUSIONS on the organization and development of the Centre for Information, Discussion and Exchange on the crossing of frontiers and immigration (CIREFI).[325]

The Council recalls the decision taken by the Ministers responsible for immigration on 30 November/1 December 1992 to establish a Centre for Information, Discussion and Exchange on the crossing of frontiers and immigration (CIREFI) and notes that in the 1994 priority work programme in the field of justice and home affairs which it adopted in November 1993, CIREFI was requested to continue its work.

The Council emphasizes the urgent problems arising from illegal immigration and unlawful residence by nationals of third countries in the Member States and considers that only concerted action by the Member States on a basis of solidarity can stem or reduce the flow of unauthorized immigration.

The Council underlines the need for all Member States of the Union to combat criminal illegal immigration networks and make it impossible for them to arrange or assist large scale illegal immigration flows.

Given that further progress in cooperation between Member States requires improved exchanges of information and uniform situation assessments in order to improve coordination on a Union wide basis in the areas of illegal immigration and expulsion, the Council considers and decides that CIREFI should be, as a further step, progressively developed in the following way:

---

325 Adopted Brussels 30.11 and 1.12.94 10392/94.

1. CIREFI will assist the Member States in effectively studying legal immigration, preventing illegal immigration and unlawful residence, in effectively combating immigration crime, in better detecting forged documents and in improving expulsion practice.

2. CIREFI shall meet on a regular basis and shall consist of Expert Representatives of the Member States with logistical back-up from the General Secretariat of the Council.

3. Without prejudice to the other tasks included in the Ministerial decision of 30 November/1st December 1992, the specific tasks of CIREFI shall be to:

   3.1. collate, using standard forms, statistical information concerning
      a. legal immigration
      b. illegal immigration and unlawful residence
      c. facilitating of illegal immigration
      d. use of false or falsified travel documents
      e. measures taken by competent authorities, and draw up regular and occasional situation reports on this basis commenting on trends, developments and changes;

   3.2. analyze the information compiled, draw conclusions and, when appropriate, give advice;

   3.3. conduct exchanges of information on expulsion matters, particularly in respect of countries of destination, airports of departure or arrival, carriers, flight routes, fares, reservation possibilities, conditions of carriage, escort requirements and charter possibilities as well as on problems in obtaining repatriation travel documents.

CIREFI will submit an annual report on its activities, and any additional reports on request, to the Council Justice and Home Affairs.

Personal data may not be processed and, in particular, may not be communicated by or to CIREFI.

CIREFI will not be empowered to give instructions to Member States' authorities.

The activities of CIREFI will not affect closer cooperation between Member States.

4. CIREFI, in the form of the Standing Conference, will meet regularly or as circumstances require; as a general rule this should be once a month. Where possible, discussions adequately prepared in advance should be structured around a particular current item of common interest to permit an efficient exchange of information.

   The relevant bodies of the Council will determine priorities for CIREFI's ongoing work within the framework of the tasks assigned to it under paragraph 3.

   The logistical back-up at the General Secretariat of the Council will provide the Clearing House with the necessary administrative and organizational assistance and will contribute to prior and subsequent processing of agendas for CIREFI's meetings. The General Secretariat of the Council will, within its budgetary constraints, ensure provision of the staff and equipment required for the Clearing House to perform its tasks.

5. The Council also notes that during the time between meetings of the Standing Conference, the national central units of the Member States concerned will exchange information directly at a multilateral or bilateral level in cases requiring immediate action. In addition information *will* be exchanged as far as possible using standard forms or as events dictate using an agreed layout.

   Costs incurred by national central units, including the cost of communicating with other national central units, *will* be borne by the Member State concerned.

6. The Council considers that CIREFI may begin to carry out its work as defined in these conclusions from 1 January 1995.

*Commentary*

*Status:* Conclusions adopted by the European Council within the context of the Title VI of the Treaty on European Union, Cooperation in the Fields of Justice and Home Affairs.

*Entry into force:* As the decision to establish CIREFI was taken at the November/December 1992 meeting of the Ministers responsible for immigration, CIREFI at least in theory, already existed. However action within the framework of these Conclusions commenced as from 1 January 1995. Its activities are now regulated by the Conclusions.

*Summary:*

The Conclusions on the organisation and development of CIREFI are based on the identification by the Council of two major issues:

(i) Problems arising from illegal immigration and unlawful residence by nationals of third countries in the Member States;

(ii) The need to combat criminal illegal immigration networks and to make it impossible for them to arrange or assist large scale illegal immigration flows.

CIREFI's mandate according the 1994 Conclusions is limited to:

(i) Effectively studying illegal immigration;

(ii) Preventing illegal immigration and unlawful residence;

(iii) Effectively combatting immigration crime;

(v) Detecting forged documents;

(vi) Improving expulsion practice.

In order to carry out these functions the modus operandi of CIREFI has now been clarified and identified as consisting of three aspects:

(i) Collating, using standard forms, statistical information concerning the matters within its mandate and to draw up regular or occasional situation papers on the basis of statistics collated commenting on trends, developments and changes;

(ii) To analyse the information compiled, draw up conclusions and, when appropriate, give advice;

(iii) Conduct exchanges of information on expulsion matters particularly in respect of countries of destination, airports of departure or arrival, carriers, flight risk, fares, reservation possibilities, conditions of carriage, airport requirements and charter possibilities as well as on problems in obtaining repatriation travel documents.

The Conclusions specifically prohibit the communication by or to CIREFI of personal data. The Member States reiterate the position that CIREFI is not empowered to give instructions to Member State authorities nor can its activities affect closer co-operation between Member States. CIREFI according to the Conclusions is required to submit an annual report on its activities to the Council on Justice and Home Affairs.

In order to carry out its functions a standing conference is established though its membership is not specified. It is to meet once a month as a general rule or as circumstances require. The purpose of the standing conference is not made clear in the Conclusions. Logistical back-up is again to be provided by the Secretariat General of the Council with no specific budgetary allocation or provision for a budgetary allocation.

Emphasis is placed on the exchange of information between Member States and it is specifically stated that costs incurred by national central units, including the cost of communicating with other national central units, will be born by the Member State concerned.

*Comments: Who Pays the Piper?*

The decision to set up CIREFI was first adopted on 30th November 1992.[326] In June 1993 the Member States agreed a Resolution concerning checks on and expulsion of third country nationals residing or working without authorisation. In that Resolution exchanges of information between Member States on the type of checks and control procedures together with related legislation are to be carried out within CIREFI.[327] It is clear, from the preamble of the Conclusions on CIREFI that between its establishment in December 1992 and the adoption of the conclusion at the end of 1994 that the Member States have defined the role of CIREFI as assisting in the fight against illegal immigration and unlawful residence. It is this aspect of migration policy which appears to have elicited a substantial degree of approval, at least insofar as an objective, of the Member States.

At the time the decision to set up CIREFI was adopted in 1992, the ambit of its work was extremely wide.[328] This has now been refined and limited. However the fundamental problems identified in the commentary on the earlier Decision have not been resolved. Little progress has been made in reaching common definitions of "migration" let alone "legality" or "i-llegality" of immigration. Therefore the work of CIREFI remains extremely difficult as the fundamental co-ordination terms necessary to carry it out is not available.

In the Conclusions regarding its organisation and development first priority appears to be the collation, using standard forms of statistical information. In view of the difficulties relating to the collection and interpretation of statistical information and the fact that this role has been assumed to some extent by Eurostat it is unclear what added value CIREFI's involvement will bring.

The second task of CIREFI, to analyse the information compiled and to draw up conclusions depends first and foremost on the accuracy of the information

326 See Document 6 supra.

327 Document 10, supra, Article 5.

328 See Commentary on Document 6, supra.

which it is able to receive. The emphasis in Article 5 that Member States "*will*" exchange information appears to indicate that there have been problems in this regard and Member States have failed to provide one another with the information requested. The odd inclusion of provision at indent 2 of article 5 regarding the payment of costs relating to the exchange of information indicates that fundamental structural problems on basic matters relevant to CIREFI's operation have yet to be resolved.

The Committee on Civil Liberties and Internal Affairs of the European Parliament published a report on 12th April 1995 on the Conclusions regarding CIREFI.[329] The report focuses on the European Parliament's concerns regarding the legal basis of the Conclusions. In the view of the rapporteur the Conclusions are more than non-binding guidelines as they are preemptory in nature.

Further, the overlap with Article 7A EC on the internal market is of concern to the rapporteur. Insofar as the Conclusions are intended to develop CIREFI into a body which lays down policy on illegal immigration and results in "a hunting down of illegal immigrants" the rapporteur opposes the contents of the Conclusions.

Additionally, it is argued that activities which are not directly of a criminal nature should be dealt with by the European Information System and should be administered by the European Commission. The provisional assessment of the arrangements of the European Parliament's Committee on Civil Liberties and Internal Affairs is that CIREFI represents no more than a duplication of work which is already being undertaken elsewhere and consequently a waste of money.

Finally, the same shortcomings as regards accuracy and consistency of information available to CIREFI as a result of access to it being limited to ministerial departments and as set out in the commentary to Document 6 infra are relevant here as well.

---

329 European Parliament A4-0000/95, DOC EN PR/264/24934 12th April 1995.

# 17 RECOMMENDATION concerning the adoption of a standard travel document for the removal/expulsion of third country foreign nationals.[330]

THE COUNCIL OF THE EUROPEAN UNION,

Having regard to the Treaty on European Union and in particular Article K.1 3(c);

Whereas combating unauthorised immigration, residence and work by nationals of third countries on the territory of Member States is regarded as a matter of common interest;

Noting that consultation and cooperation on the execution of expulsion measures is considered a priority action in the 1994 work programme;

Acknowledging that a recent seminar on expulsion measures showed that the large majority of Member States experience difficulties in cases of third country nationals possessing no travel documents who are required to be expelled from their territory;

Desirous to improve the efficiency of executing expulsion measures;

Hereby recommends that:

– with effect from 1st January 1995 the attached standard travel document valid for a single journey shall be used as appropriate by all Member

330 Adopted Brussels 30.11 and 1.12.94 9738/94.

States of the Union in the case of third country nationals being expelled from the territory of the Union;

- the document shall be established in the language of the Member State executing the expulsion order;

- the document, where appropriate, shall be translated into both French and English.

# EU

Member State

Reg. No.
No. d'enregistrement

Doc. No.
No. doc.

---

Valid for one journey from/
Valable pour un seul voyage de

to/à

Name/Nom:
Given name/prénom:

Date of birth/
Date de naissance:

Height/Taille:

Distinguishing marks/
Signes particuliers:

*PHOTO*

Nationality/Nationalité:

---

Address in home country (if known)/
Addresse dans le pays d'origine (si connu)

Issuing authority
Autorité de delivrance

*Seal/Stamp*
*Sceau/Cachet*

Issued at
Lieu de délivrance

Issued on
Date de délivrance

Signature
Signature

---

Observations/Remarks

*Commentary*

*Status:* Recommendation of the Council of the European Union in accordance with Article K1.3(c) of the Treaty on European Union.

*Entry into force:* From 1 January 1995 the standard travel document should be used by all Member States.

*International obligations engaged:*

(1) European Convention on Human Rights 1950
(2) UN Convention relating to the Status of Stateless Persons 1954

*Summary:*

This Recommendation sets out the contents of a standard travel document to be issued by Member States to non-nationals of the Member States in order to facilitate expulsion from the territory of the Union.

*Comments:*

This simple Recommendation regarding the standard format of a document for expulsion of non-nationals presuppose an international legal framework which at the moment does not exist. The preamble to the Recommendation makes clear that the purpose of the standard travel document is to facilitate expulsion of third country nationals who possess no travel documents. The agreement of such a standard document is necessarily based on a number of suppositions:

(1) That the identity of a third country national with no travel document can be determined to a reasonable degree of certainty;

(2) That the third country national subject to the expulsion order possesses a nationality and that nationality can be determined with a reasonable degree of certainty;

(3) That the state to which the third country national is being expelled accepts the two preceding determinations by the Member State;

(4) That the state to which the person is to be expelled accepts the validity of the standard travel document.

All of these points give rise to an element of uncertainty. There is clearly no difficulty in international law for a state to issue a travel document to a person on request. It is, of course, open to a state to recognise any document which it chooses itself to issue and it may indeed be incumbent on a state so to recognise a document. Within certain limited parameters a state may also determine for its own purposes that a particular individual is its citizen or an alien.[331] However it is not open to that state to seek to impose on another state its determination as to the nationality of an individual. In international law, a state is only entitled to determine the nationality of its own citizen and even in those circumstances it is not always possible to require another state to recognise a particular national as a citizen of the state so seeking to do.[332]

"According to the practice of states, to arbitral and judicial decisions and to the opinion of writers, nationality is a legal bond having as its basis a social fact of attachment, a genuine connection of existence, interests and sentiments, together with the existence of reciprocal rights and duties. It may be said to constitute the judicial expression of the fact that the individual upon whom it is conferred, either directly by the law or as a result of an act of the authorities, is in fact more closely connected with the population of the state conferring nationality than with that of any other state. Conferred by a state, it only entitles that state to exercise protection vis-a-vis another state, if it constitutes a translation into judicial terms of the individual's connection with the state which has made him a national".[333]

As even the declaration of a state that an individual is its national is subject to limitations in international law as spelt out by the International Court of Justice, so must the assertion by one state that an individual is the national of another state without reference to that state be even more uncertain. Where the state refuses to issue a travel document specifying an individual to be

---

331 *Nottebohm Case* [1955] ICJ p.4.

332 *The Nottebohm Case* [1955] ICJ p.4.

333 *The Nottebohm Case* [1955] ICJ p.23.

its national this may be definitive of the individual's lack of connection with that state.

According to the UK Government, where difficulties are encountered obtaining travel documents for persons to be expelled, the delays are generally due to the foreign mission's need to verify the identity and nationality of the person concerned.[334]

Accordingly, the proposition that one state has the right to issue a travel document for the purpose, exclusively, of expelling an individual whom the state claims has no right to remain in its territory to another state of which the sending state alone purports the individual to be a national has little support in international law. Further, the issue of a travel document for the purposes of expulsion to a state of which the individual is not purported to be a national which document does not authorise re-admission to the issuing state is unlikely to create any obligation on the intended receiving state to accept the individual. Only on the basis of a bi-lateral or multi-lateral agreement with the receiving state could the expelling state seek to enforce such a regime.

In the event that the receiving state refuses to accept the travel document and/or the individual and expels him or her back to the sending state a question may then arise as regards Article 3 ECHR, the prohibition on torture, inhuman or degrading treatment or punishment.[335] The fact of seeking to expel a person with no reasonable prospect that the person will be admitted to another state may be capable of constituting inhuman or degrading treatment particularly if successive expulsions occur.

Further, under the UN Convention relating to the Status of Stateless Persons 1954 the term "stateless person" means a person who is not considered as a national by any state under the operation of its law.[336] Under Article 27 of that Convention, the contracting states are under a duty to issue identity papers to any stateless person in their territory who does not possess

334 Hansard, 19.10.94 Written Answers.
335 See expulsion cases ECHR.
336 Article 1 UN Convention relating to the Status of Stateless Persons 1954.

a valid travel document. This is not limited to persons who are lawfully on the territory. Nonetheless, the provisions of this Recommendation do not appear to relate to identity papers but rather to a travel document for the purpose of expulsion.

This peculiar Recommendation makes no provision in respect of stateless persons nor indeed does it acknowledge the existence of statelessness. In general it may be seen as a flanking measure for the next document to be considered, the specimen bilateral readmission agreement.

# 18 RECOMMENDATION concerning a specimen bilateral readmission agreement between a Member State of the European Union and a third country.[337]

The Council of the European Union:

Having regard to the Treaty on the European Union and in particular Article K.1 (3) concerning immigration policy and policy regarding nationals of third countries:

Recalling these policies are regarded as matters of common interest under the Treaty:

Determined to combat unauthorized immigration to the Member States of the Union:

Noting that the laying down of principles which must appear in bilateral and multilateral readmission agreements figures in the action plan in the field of Justice and Home Affairs which was approved by the Council and endorsed by the European Council in December 1993:

Recalling that these principles were approved by the Council in May 1994 and that it was agreed to devise a specimen readmission agreement on the basis of these principles at a later date:

---

337 Adopted Brussels 30.11 and 1.12.94 SN 10339/94.

Whereas the specimen readmission agreement is to be used flexibly by the Member States and that it may be adapted to the particular needs of the contracting parties:

Hereby RECOMMENDS that with effect from 1 January 1995 the specimen agreement attached should be used by the Member States of the Union as the basis for negotiation with third countries on the conclusion of readmission agreements.

Specimen

Agreement

between

the Government of

(... Member State...)

and

the Government

of (... third country...)

on

the readmission of persons residing without authorization

(Readmission Agreement)

The Government of (...Member State...)

and

the Government of (...third country...)

hereinafter referred to as the Contracting Parties, desirous of facilitating the readmission of persons staying illegally on the territory of the other Contracting Party, i.e. persons who do not, or who no longer, fulfil the conditions in force for entry or residence, and of facilitating the transit of persons in a spirit of co-operation and on the basis of reciprocity,

have agreed as follows:

ARTICLE 1

*Readmission of own nationals*

1. Each Contracting Party shall readmit at the request of the other Contracting Party and without any formality persons who do not, or who no longer, fulfil the conditions in force for entry or residence on the territory of the requesting Contracting Party provided that it is proved or may be validly assumed that they possess the nationality of the requested Contracting Party. The same shall apply to persons who have been deprived of the nationality of the requested Contracting Party since entering the territory of the requesting Contracting Party without at least having been promised naturalization by the requesting Contracting Party.

2. Upon application by the requesting Contracting Party, the requested Contracting Party shall without delay issue the persons to be readmitted with the travel documents required for the repatriation.

3. The requesting Contracting Party shall readmit such persons again under the same conditions if checks reveal that they were not in possession of the nationality of the requested Contracting Party when they departed from the territory of the requesting Contracting Party. This shall not apply if the readmission obligation is based on the fact that the requested Contracting Party deprived the person in question of its nationality after that person had entered the territory of the requesting Contracting Party without that person at least having been promised naturalization by the requesting Contracting Party.

ARTICLE 2

*Readmission in the case of third-country nationals who entered via the external frontier*

1. The Contracting Party via whose external frontier a person can be proved, or validly assumed, to have entered who does not meet, or who no longer meets the conditions in force for entry or residence on the territory of the requesting Contracting Party shall readmit the person at the request of that Contracting Party and without any formality.

2. For the purposes of this Article the external frontier shall be deemed to be the first frontier to have been crossed which is not a frontier common to the Contracting Parties.

3. The readmission obligation pursuant to paragraph 1 shall not apply in respect of a person who was in possession of a valid residence permit issued by the requesting Contracting Party when the person entered the territory of that Contracting Party or who was issued with a residence permit by that Contracting Party after entering its territory.

4. The Contracting Parties shall make every effort to give priority to deporting nationals of an adjacent State to their country of origin.

ARTICLE 3

*Readmission of nationals of third countries by the Contracting Party responsible for the entry*

1. If a person who has arrived in the territory of the requesting Contracting Party does not fulfil the conditions in force for entry or residence and if that person is in possession of a valid visa issued by the other Contracting Party or a valid residence permit issued by the requested party, that Contacting Party shall readmit the person without any formality upon application by the requesting Contracting Party.

2. If both Contracting Parties issued a visa or a residence permit, responsibility shall reside with the Contracting Party whose visa or residence permit expires last.

3. Paragraphs 1 and 2 shall not apply where a transit visa was issued.

ARTICLE 4

*Residence permits*

A residence permit pursuant to Article 2(3) and Article 3 means an authorization of any type issued by one Contracting Party, entitling the person to reside on the territory of that Contracting Party. This shall not include temporary permission to reside on the territory of one of the Contracting Parties in connection with the processing of an asylum application.

ARTICLE 5

*Time limits*

1. The requested Contracting Party shall reply to readmission requests addressed to it without delay, and in any event within a maximum of 15 days.

2. The requested Contracting Party shall take charge of persons whose readmission has been agreed to without delay, and in any event within a maximum of one month. Upon application by the requesting Contracting Party, this time limit may be extended by the time taken to deal with legal or practical obstacles.

ARTICLE 6

*Time limit after which the readmission obligation will lapse*

The application for readmission must be submitted within a maximum of one year of the Contracting Party noting the illegal entry and presence of the said national of a third country on its territory.

ARTICLE 7

*Transit*

1. Without prejudice to Article 11, the Contracting Parties shall allow third-country nationals to pass through their territory in transit if the other Contracting Party so requests and if admission to other possible States of transit and to the State of destination is assured.

2. It shall not be essential for the requested Contracting Party to issue a transit visa.

3. Notwithstanding any authorization issued, persons taken in charge for transit purposes may be returned to the other Contracting Party if circumstances within the meaning of Article 12 subsequently arise or come to light which stand in the way of a transit operation or if the onward journey or admission by the State of destination is no longer assured.

4. The Contracting Parties shall endeavour to restrict transit operations to aliens who cannot be returned to their States of origin directly.

ARTICLE 8

*Data protection*

Insofar as personal data have to be communicated in order to implement this agreement, such information may concern only the following:

(1) the particulars of the person to be transferred and, where necessary, of the members of the person's family (surname, given name, any previous names, nicknames or pseudonyms, aliases, date and place of birth, sex, current and any previous nationality):

(2) passport, identity card and other identity and travel documents and laissez-passer (number, period of validity, date of issue, issuing authority, place of issue, etc.):

(3) other details needed to identify the persons to be transferred:

(4) stopping places and itineraries:

(5) residence permits or visas issued by one of the Contracting Parties:

(6) in the cases covered by Article 7, the place where the asylum application was submitted and the date of submission of any previous asylum application, the date of submission of the present asylum application, the present stage of the procedure and the content of any decision taken.

ARTICLE 9

*Costs*

1. The costs of transporting persons taken in charge pursuant to Articles 1, 2 and 3 shall be borne by the requesting Contracting Party as far as the border of the requested party.

2. The costs of transit as far as the border of the State of destination, and, where necessary, the costs arising from return transport, shall be borne by the requesting Contracting Party in accordance with Article 7.

ARTICLE 10

*Committee of Experts*

1. The Contracting Parties shall provide each other with mutual assistance in the application and interpretation of this Agreement. To this end, they shall set up a Committee of Experts to:

   (a) monitor application of this Agreement:

   (b) submit proposals for resolving problems associated with the application of this agreement:

   (c) propose amendments and additions to this Agreement:

   (d) prepare and recommend appropriate measures for combatting illegal immigration.

2. The Contracting Parties shall reserve the right to agree to the proposals and measures or not to do so.

3. The Committee shall be composed of three representatives of each Contracting Party. The Contracting Parties shall appoint the Chairman and his deputies from among them, and shall also appoint alternate members. Additional experts may be associated with the consultations.

4. The Committee shall meet at the initiative of one of the Chairman and at least once a year.

ARTICLE 11

*Clause stipulating that international agreements/Conventions shall not be affected*

These agreements shall not affect the Contracting Parties' obligations arising from

1. the Convention of 28 July 1951 on the Status of Refugees as amended by the Protocol of 31 January 1967 on the Status of Refugees:

2. international Conventions on extradition and transit:

3. the Convention of 4 November 1950 for the Protection of Human Rights and Fundamental Freedoms:

4. international Conventions on asylum, in particular under the Dublin Convention of 15 June 1990 determining the State Responsible for Examining Applications for Asylum lodged in a Member State of the European Community:

5. international Conventions and agreements on the readmission of foreign nationals.

ARTICLE 12

*Entry into force*

This agreement shall enter into force on the first day of the second month following its signature. It shall not be applied until the date agreed upon by the Contracting Parties in an exchange of notes.

ARTICLE 13

*Suspension, termination*

1. This Agreement is concluded for an indefinite period.

2. After informing the other Contracting Party each Contracting Party may suspend this Agreement by giving notification on important grounds, in particular on the grounds of the protection of State security, public order or public health. The Contracting Parties shall notify each other of the cancellation of any such measure without delay via diplomatic channels .

3. After informing the other Contracting Party, each Contracting Party may terminate this Agreement on important grounds by giving notification.

4. The suspension or termination of this Agreement shall become effective on the first day of the month following the month in which notification was received by the other Contracting party.

*Done at ............ this .......... day of ............ 19.. in two originals, one in the ............... language and one in the ................. language, each text being equally authentic.*

| | |
|---|---|
| On behalf of the Government of (...Member State...) | On behalf of the Government of (...third country...) |

*Commentary*

*Status:* Recommendation adopted by the Council of the European Union in accordance with Article K.1(3) of the Treaty on European Union.

*Entry into force:* The specimen agreement should be used as a basis for negotiation with effect from 1 January 1995.

*International obligations engaged:*

(1) UN Convention relating to the Status of Refugees 1951 and Protocol 1967
(2) European Convention on Human Rights 1950
(3) The Dublin Convention 1990

*Summary:*

This Recommendation contains a draft bilateral readmission agreement for use after 1 January 1995 in negotiations between Member States and third countries regarding the return of both nationals and non-nationals across their borders.

It is designed for use primarily with neighbouring countries to those of the Union. The personal scope of the specimen agreement includes:

(i) nationals of a contracting state on the basis of proof of nationality or a valid assumption of nationality (article 1(1));

(ii) persons who were nationals of a contracting state but have been deprived of that nationality since entering the territory of the other contracting state;

(iii) a person who does not meet or no longer meets the requirements for entry or residence on the territory of one contracting party where the person can be proved or validly assumed to have entered across the frontier with the other contracting state;

(iv) a person who does not meet the requirements of entry or residence of one contracting party and is in possession of a valid visa or residence permit issued by the other contracting state.

The obligation on the contracting state is to readmit the person concerned. There is no obligation to take further steps except in accordance with article 2. The contracting states shall make every effort to give priority to deporting nationals of an adjacent state to their country of origin. However, contracting states shall allow transit deportation at the request of the other contracting state where admission to other possible states of transit and the state of destination is assured. Under such circumstances a transit visa is not required.

The time limits which apply to a request for readmission are drafted by reference to the requested state's obligations. The requested state must respond to a readmission request addressed to it without delay and in any event within a maximum of 15 days. It must then take charge of the person whose readmission has been agreed within one month. However, the requesting state may seek an extension of this time limit "to deal with legal or practical obstacles" (article 5(2)). A long stop of one year applies in respect of the requesting state if it takes no action for such a period after noting the illegal entry and presence of the person.

The personal data which may be communicated between the parties is limited to that set out in article 8. Although on the face if it, the specimen agreement is not specifically addressed to the expulsion of asylum applicants, specific provision is made for information regarding the date and place where an asylum application has been made to be transmitted between contracting states. However this is limited to cases where expulsion is for transit purposes only. Presumably, this is to prevent the transmission to one contracting state of information relating to the existence of an asylum application by one of its nationals in the territory of the other contracting state.

The application of the agreement is to be monitored by a Committee of Experts established under the agreement. The agreement is without prejudice to international agreements and Conventions under which the states have assumed obligations.

*Comments: Passing the Buck*

The specimen readmission agreement has 12 articles and is designed to create an obligation on a bilateral (or possibly multilateral basis) for states parties to expel persons assumed to be nationals or former nationals of the other party and any other nationals who are assumed to have entered one state after passing through the other contracting party with minimal formalities. Presumably it is designed to provide some underpinning in international law for other acts of the Member States relating to expulsion, and in particular the Resolution on a harmonised approach to questions concerning host third countries' which relates to asylum applicants.

The Recommendation regarding practices followed by Member States on expulsion[338] adopted on 30 November 1992, at Article IV encourages states to enter into such readmission agreements, preferably on a multi-lateral basis. It also proposes a standard format for such agreements.

338 See Document 7 infra.

*The Specimen Agreement and Asylum Applicants*

Although the specimen agreement is specifically without reference to international obligations including the UN Convention relating to the Status of Refugees, in the substantive provisions there is no requirement on either contracting state to give effect to the Convention. Therefore, instead of strengthening the obligations of contracting states under the Convention (if indeed they are parties) this is left outside the scope of the specimen agreement. A breach of obligations under the UN Convention by one state in respect of a person returned under the agreement would not trigger any repercussions under the agreement.

In December 1994 UNHCR issued a press release criticising the specimen readmission agreement on the following grounds:

- the agreement permits the return of asylum applicants to third countries where they are not able to seek and enjoy effective protection;
- such agreements may lead to situations of persecution and other violations of basic human rights;
- such agreements should contain a specific provision requiring the substantive consideration of asylum applications;
- they should include information regarding the ground of the removal decision (ie there is a safe third country which can consider the asylum application) to avoid summary rejection of asylum applications.

Amnesty International European Project also expressed its deep concern about the specimen readmission agreement and the lack of protection under it for asylum applicants.

The only protection which an asylum applicant has is that where he or she is being returned to the state where he or she fears persecution, transmission of information indicating that an asylum application was made in the sending state is not to be passed on. However, where a person is being returned in transit through a contracting state that information is to be provided.

While the types of information which may be passed to contracting states about the individual are specified in the agreement there is no limitation on to whom the information may be transmitted, under what circumstances or any limitation on future use of the information. Nor, indeed is there any control mechanism whereby the state providing the information may request to be notified as to what happened to the information it provided.

An earlier draft of the specimen agreement contained substantial provisions relating to these areas. However, all of this section was removed before the final draft was approved. There is no reference in the agreement to procedural requirements in respect of asylum applicants. There is no indication as to the authorities to be involved in the issue of notices or whether the minimum agreed standards under UNHCR Executive Committee Conclusion No 8 (XXVIII) must be adhered to:

"The competent official (eg immigration officer or border police officer) to whom the applicant addresses himself at the border or in the territory of a Contracting State, should have clear instructions for dealing with cases which might come within the purview of the relevant international instruments. He should be required to act in accordance with the principle of non-refoulement and to refer such cases to a higher authority".

In view of the importance of the specimen agreement to asylum procedures, it is unfortunate that it does not require both parties intending to enter into it to be parties to the UN Convention. It does provide at article 11 that obligations arising from the UN Convention remain unaffected. This is not the same as requiring both contracting parties of the specimen agreement to adhere, let alone apply, the UN Convention. Similarly in the same article reference is made to the ECHR. Again there is no requirement that both contracting parties adhere to that convention.

### *Data Protection: the Dublin Convention and the Readmission Agreement*

| no | DUBLIN CONVENTION | READMISSION AGREEMENT |
|---|---|---|
| 1. | Obligation:-<br>Each Member State shall communicate to any Member State that so requests. | Insofar as personal data have to be communicated in order to implement this agreement... |

| no | DUBLIN CONVENTION | READMISSION AGREEMENT |
|---|---|---|
| 2. | Data:-<br>(a) Personal details of the applicant, and, where appropriate, the members of his family (full name - where appropriate, former name, nick names or pseudonyms, nationality present and former date and place of birth | The particulars of the person to be transferred and, where necessary, of the members of the person's family (surname, given name, any previous names, nicknames or pseudonyms, aliases, date and place of birth, sex, current and any previous nationality) |
| | (b) Identity and travel papers (references, validity, date of issue, issuing authority, place of issue etc) | Passport, identity card and other identity and travel documents and laisse-passer (number, period of validity, date of issue, issuing authority, place of issue etc) |
| | (c) Other information necessary for establishing the identity of the applicant | Other details needed to identify the persons to be transferred |
| | (d) places of residence and routes travelled | stopping places and itineraries |
| | (e) Residence permits or visas issued by a Member State | Residence permits or visas issued by one of the Contracting parties |
| | (f) Place where the application was lodged<br><br>date any previous application for asylum was lodged, the date the present application was lodged, the stage reached in the proceedings and the decision taken, if any | [in transit cases] the place where the asylum application was submitted and the date of submission of any previous asylum application, the date of submission of the present asylum application, the present stage of the procedure and the content of any decision taken |
| | (g) Reference (restricted) to Convention on Data Protection; no reference to European Convention on Human Rights | No reference to any data protection Conventions but reference to European Convention on Human Rights |

*Comment by The Dutch Standing Committee of Experts in International Immigration, Refugee and Criminal Law*

1. There is a growing trend whereby countries are endeavouring to establish repatriation treaties with countries of origin. These treaties govern the repatriation of asylum-seekers who are nationals of those countries and whose application for asylum has been refused. As far as the Netherlands is concerned, the treaty between the Netherlands and Vietnam[339] is a precedent in this regard. Countries have the autonomous power to deport rejected asylum-seekers to their country of origin and do not, in fact, require a treaty to do so. Nonetheless, countries are trying to conclude treaties, not least because they want to assure themselves of the cooperation of the country of origin. The Standing Committee also regards such treaties as important in guaranteeing the safety of rejected asylum-seekers. After all, the possibility of returning rejected asylum-seekers to their countries of origin is grounded on assumptions about the actual and legal human rights situation in the countries concerned. If there are absolutely no doubts about the safety and human rights situation in a country, an asylum-seeker whose application has been refused can be returned to that country without more ado – assuming that there are no humanitarian grounds, or grounds relating to the personal circumstances of the asylum-seeker concerned, for not expelling him or her. If there are reasonable grounds for doubt about the safety and human rights situation, the Standing Committee is of the opinion that the forced repatriation of rejected asylum-seekers must be covered by additional safeguards. In such a situation, deportation should only take place on the basis of a treaty that provides these additional safeguards, including safeguards against abuses of human rights.

2. The Standing Committee sees repatriation treaties as the counterpart and reflection of the concept of "safe countries of origin". Asylum-seekers who come from an "unsafe country of origin" cannot automatically be classified as entitled to asylum, but the unsafe situation does mean that their repatriation after the final rejection of their request for asylum must be hedged around by the obligations arising from the European Conven-

339 Tractatenblad van het Koninkrijk der Nederlanden 1994, 121.

tion on Human Rights (ECHR) which ban any form of collective expulsion.

- An asylum-seeker should not be deported to the country of origin if he or she wishes to go to a third country. He or she will be allowed a reasonable length of time and all the necessary conditions will be created to lead to the fulfilment of this wish, provided that the asylum-seeker can make out a case showing that he or she has a realistic chance of being admitted to a third country.

- The repatriate is protected in the country of origin against prosecution for actions undertaken prior to his or her repatriation. Otherwise, there could be a question of extradition without a specific extradition treaty as required by Article 2 of the Dutch Constitution, which permits extradition only in the event of the offence constituting a crime in both countries; he or she is protected against torture, or cruel, inhuman or degrading treatment or punishment, as referred to in Article 7 of the International Covenant on Civil and Political Rights and Article 3 of the ECHR.

- In the country of origin the repatriate will be treated in accordance with fundamental human rights and will live there in conditions that cannot be described as abnormal in terms of the local circumstances.

- Any repatriation incentives, financial or otherwise, will be granted to the repatriate with no distinction as to whether he or she is being repatriated voluntarily or involuntarily. A person's willingness or unwillingness to be repatriated after the final rejection of the request for asylum is an apparent distinction which is so dubious that it must not be allowed to have any effect on whether or not a person qualifies for financial or other support. The distinction is moreover a dangerous one. Repatriation with the explicit label "non-voluntary" can easily lead to serious repercussions in the country of origin.

- The right of every repatriate to apply to the competent international organizations and to representation of the Netherlands, and to request that those provisions which protect his position be observed by the Netherlands.

5. Finally, the consequences of the country of origin's failure to comply with the terms of the treaty must be spelled out - not only in the treaty itself but in the ratification legislation concerned. To this end there must be a provision in the ratification legislation providing for the right of readmission to the Netherlands in the event of a violation of the provisions of the repatriation treaty. In the context of the request for readmission by means of an application for a visa, the Dutch Court can then investigate whether the provisions of the treaty really have been breached.

# 19 RESOLUTION on minimum guarantees for Asylum Procedures[340]

THE COUNCIL at its meeting in Brussels on 20 June 1995

HAVING REGARD to Article K.1 of the Treaty on European Union, which includes asylum policy as a matter of common interest,

DETERMINED in keeping with the common humanitarian tradition of the Member States, to guarantee adequate protection to refugees in need of such protection in accordance with the Geneva Convention of 28 July 1951 relating to the Status of Refugees, as amended by the New York Protocol of 31 January 1967,

RECALLING the Member States' commitments under the European Convention for the Protection of Human Rights and Fundamental Freedoms of 4 November 1950,

NOTING that, under national legislation, Member States may exceptionally allow aliens to stay for other compelling reasons not covered by the 1951 Geneva Convention,

AFFIRMING the intention of Member States to apply the Dublin Convention of 15 June 1990 determining the State Responsible for Examining Applications for Asylum Lodged in one of the Member States of the European Communities,

CONVINCED that this requires decisions on asylum applications to be taken on the basis of equivalent procedures in all Member States and common

---

340 5585/95 adopted 20 June 1995, Brussels.

procedural guarantees to be adopted for asylum-seekers to that end, taking into account the conclusions of the Executive Committee of the United Nations High Commissioner for Refugees and Recommendation R(81) 16 of the Committee of Ministers of the Council of Europe,

HEREBY ADOPTS THIS RESOLUTION:

*I.* The guarantees provided for in this Resolution will apply to the examination of asylum applications within the meaning of Article 3 of the Dublin Convention, with the exception of procedures to determine the Member State responsible under the said Convention. The specific guarantees applicable to those procedures will be determined by the Executive Committee set up by the Dublin Convention.

*II. Universal principles concerning fair and effective asylum procedure*

1. Asylum procedures will be applied in full compliance with the 1951 Geneva Convention and the 1967 New York Protocol relating to the Status of Refugees and other obligations under international law in respect of refugees and human rights. In particular, the procedures will comply fully with Article 1 of the 1951 Convention concerning the definition of a refugee, Article 33 relating to the principle of *non-refoulement* and Article 35 concerning cooperation with the Office of the United Nations High Commissioner for Refugees, including the facilitation of its duty of supervising the application of the Convention.

2. In order to ensure effectively the principle of *non-refoulement*, no expulsion measure will be carried out as long as no decision has been taken on the asylum application.

*III. Guarantees concerning the examination of asylum applications*

3. The regulations on access to the asylum procedure, the basic features of the asylum procedure itself and the designation of the authorities responsible for examination of asylum applications are to be laid down in the individual Member States' legislation.

4. Asylum applications shall be examined by any authority, fully qualified in the field of asylum and refugee matters. Decisions shall be taken independently in the sense that all asylum applications will be examined and decided upon individually, objectively and impartially.

5. When examining an application for asylum the competent authority must, of its own initiative, take into consideration and seek to establish all the relevant facts and give the applicant the opportunity to present a substantial description of the circumstances of the case and to prove them. For his part the applicant must present all the facts and circumstances known to him and give access to all the available evidence.

   Recognition of refugee status is not dependent on the production of any particular formal evidence.

6. The authorities responsible for the examination of the asylum application must be fully qualified in the field of asylum and refugee matters. To this effect, they must:

   - have at their disposal specialized personnel with the necessary knowledge and experience in the field of asylum and refugee matters, who have an understanding of an applicant's particular situation;

   - have access to precise and up-to-date information from various sources, including information from the UNHCR concerning the situation prevailing in the countries of origin of asylum-seekers and in transit countries;

   - have the right to ask advice, whenever necessary, from experts on particular issues eg a medical issue or an issue of a cultural nature.

7. The authorities responsible for border controls and the local authorities with which asylum applications are lodged must receive clear and detailed instructions so that the applications, together with all other information available, can be forwarded without delay to the competent authority for examination.

8. In the case of a negative decision, provision shall be made for an appeal to a court or a review authority which gives an independent ruling on individual cases under the conditions laid down in paragraph 4.

9. Member States must ensure that the competent authorities are adequately provided with staff and equipment so that they can discharge their duties promptly and under the best possible conditions.

*IV. Rights of asylum-seekers during examination, appeal and review procedures*

10. An asylum-seeker must have an effective opportunity to lodge his asylum application as early as possible.

11. Declarations made by the asylum-seeker and other details of his application are very sensitive data requiring protection. National law must therefore provide adequate data protection guarantees, particularly as against the authorities of the asylum-seeker's country of origin.

12. As long as the asylum application has not been decided on, the general principle applies that the applicant is allowed to remain in the territory of the State in which his application has been lodged or is being examined.

13. Asylum-seekers must be informed of the procedure to be followed and of their rights and obligations during the procedure, in a language which they can understand. In particular:

- they must be given the services of an interpreter, whenever necessary for submitting their case to the authorities concerned. These services shall be paid for out of public funds, if the interpreter is appointed by the competent authorities;

- in accordance with the rules of the Member State concerned, they may call in a legal adviser or other counsellor to assist them during the procedure;

- they must be given the opportunity, at all stages of the procedure, to communicate with the Office of the United Nations High Commissioner for Refugees (UNHCR) or with other refugee organizations which may be working on behalf of the UNHCR in the Member State concerned, and vice versa.

In addition, asylum-seekers may enter into contact with other refugee organizations under procedures laid down by the Member States.

The opportunity for an asylum-seeker to communicate with the UNHCR and other refugee organizations need not necessarily prevent implementation of a decision.

- The representative of the Office of the UNHCR must be given the opportunity to be informed of the course of the procedure, to learn about the decisions of the competent authorities and to submit his observations.

14. Before a final decision is taken on the asylum application, the asylum-seeker must be given the opportunity of a personal interview with an official qualified under national law.

15. The decision on the asylum application must be communicated to the asylum-seeker in writing. If the application is rejected, the asylum-seeker must be informed of the reasons and of any possibility of having the decision reviewed. The asylum-seeker must have the opportunity, inasmuch as national law so provides, to acquaint himself with or be informed of the main purport of the decision and any possibility of appeal, in a language which he understands.

16. The asylum-seeker must be given an adequate period of time within which to appeal and to prepare his case when requesting review of the decision. These time-limits must be communicated to the asylum-seeker in good time.

17. Until a decision has been taken on the appeal, the general principle will apply that the asylum-seeker may remain in the territory of the Member State concerned. Where the national law of a Member State

permits a derogation from this principle in certain cases, the asylum-seeker should at least be able to apply to the bodies referred to in paragraph 8 (court or independent review authority) for leave to remain in the territory of the Member State temporarily during procedures before those bodies, on the grounds of the particular circumstances of his case; no expulsion may take place until a decision has been taken on this application.

*Manifestly unfounded asylum applications*

18. Manifestly unfounded asylum applications within the meaning of the Resolution adopted by the Immigration Ministers at their meeting on 30 November and 1 December 1992 will be dealt with in accordance with that Resolution. Subject to the principles laid down therein, the guarantees laid down in the present Resolution will apply.

19. By way of derogation from paragraph 8, Member States may exclude the possibility of lodging an appeal against a decision to reject an application if, instead, an independent body which is distinct from the examining authority has already confirmed the decision.

20. The Member States observe that, with due regard for the 1951 Geneva Refugee Convention, there should be no de facto or de jure grounds for granting refugee status to an asylum applicant who is a national of another Member State.

    On this basis, a particularly rapid or simplified procedure will be applied to the application for asylum lodged by a national of another Member State, in accordance with each Member State's rules and practice, it being specified that the Member States continue to be obliged to examine individually every application for asylum, as provided by the Geneva Convention to which the Treaty on European Union refers.

21. Member States may provide for exceptions to the principle in paragraph 17 in limited cases, under national law, when, in consideration of objective criteria extraneous to the application itself, an application is manifestly unfounded in accordance with points 9 and 10 of the

Resolution adopted by the Immigration Ministers on 30 November and 1 December 1992. However, in such cases it should at least be guaranteed that the decision on the application is taken at a high level and that additional sufficient safeguards (e.g. the same assessment, before the execution of the decision, by another authority which must be of a central nature and have the necessary knowledge and experience in the field of asylum and refugee law) ensure the correctness of the decision.

22. Member States may provide for exceptions to the principle in paragraph 17 with respect to asylum applications where, under national law, the host third country concept is applicable in accordance with the Resolution adopted by the Immigration Ministers at their meeting on 30 November and 1 December 1992. In such cases Member States may also provide, by way of derogation from paragraph 15, that the decision rejecting the application, its underlying reasons and the asylum-seeker's rights may be communicated to him orally instead of in writing. Upon request, the decision will be confirmed in writing. The third country authorities must, where necessary, be informed that the asylum application was not examined as to substance.

*Asylum applications at the border*

23. Member States will adopt administrative measures ensuring that any asylum-seeker arriving at their frontiers is afforded an opportunity to lodge an asylum application.

24. Member States may, in as much as national law so provides, apply special procedures to establish, prior to the decision on admission, whether or not the application for asylum is manifestly unfounded. No expulsion measure will be carried out during this procedure.

Where an application for asylum is manifestly unfounded, the asylum-seeker may be refused admission. In such cases, the national law of a Member State may permit an exception to the general principle of the suspensive effect of the appeal (paragraph 17). However it must at least be ensured that the decision on the refusal of admission is taken by a ministry or comparable central authority and that additional sufficient safeguards (for example, prior examination by another central authority) ensure the correctness of the decision. Such authorities must be fully qualified in asylum and refugee matters.

25. In addition, where, under national law, the host third country concept is applicable in accordance with the Resolution adopted by the Immigration Ministers at their meeting on 30 November and 1 December 1992, Member States may provide for exceptions to the principles in paragraphs 7 and 17. Member States may also provide, by way of derogation from paragraph 15, that the decision rejecting the application, its underlying reasons and any possibility of appeal may be communicated to the asylum-seeker orally instead of in writing. Upon request, the decision will be confirmed in writing.

    The procedure in the cases referred to in the first sentence of the preceding subparagraph may be carried out before the decision on admission has been taken. In such cases, admission may be refused.

*V. Additional safeguards for unaccompanied minors and women*

*Unaccompanied minors*

26. Provision must be made for unaccompanied minors seeking asylum to be represented by a specifically appointed adult or institution if they do not have capacity under national law. During the interview, unaccompanied minors may be accompanied by that adult or representatives of that institution. These persons are to protect the child's interests.

27. When examining an application for asylum from an unaccompanied minor, his mental development and maturity will be taken into account.

*Women*

28. Member States must endeavour to involve skilled female employees and female interpreters in the asylum procedure where necessary, particularly where female asylum-seekers find it difficult to present the grounds for their application in a comprehensive manner owing to the experiences they have undergone or to their cultural origin.

*VI. Residence where the criteria for classification as a refugee are met*

29. A Member State which, notwithstanding national provisions on application of the host third country concept, has examined an asylum application must grant refugee status to an asylum-seeker fulfilling the criteria of Article 1 of the Geneva Convention. Member States may provide, in accordance with their national law, that they will not make full use of the exclusion clauses contained in the Geneva Convention.

    The refugee should in principle be granted the right of residence in the Member State concerned.

*VII. Other cases*

30. This Resolution does not affect the laws and regulations of the various Member States regarding the cases covered in point 11 of the Resolution on manifestly unfounded asylum applications adopted by the Immigration Ministers at their meeting on 30 November and 1 December 1992.

*VII. Further action*

31. Member States will take account of these principles in the case of all proposals for changes to their national legislation. In addition, Member States will strive to bring their national legislation into line with these principles by 1 January 1996. In conjunction with the Commission and in consultation with the UNHCR, they will periodically review the operation of these principles and consider whether any additional measures are necessary.

*IX. More favourable provisions*

32. Member States have the right to enact national provisions on guarantees provided by procedures applicable to asylum-seekers which are more favourable than those contained in the common minimum guarantees.

*Statement by the Austrian delegation for the Council minutes*

"On the occasion of the adoption of the Council Resolution on minimum guarantees for asylum procedures, it is the Austrian representative's understanding that:

1. this Resolution will be without prejudice to the Resolution on manifestly unfounded asylum applications, adopted by the Immigration Ministers at their meeting on 30 November and 1 December 1992, and that

2. for application of paragraph 8, the appeal provided for in Austrian law, which is referral to the Federal Ministry of the Interior, meets the requirements of individual, objective and impartial examination."

*Statement by the Belgian delegation for the Council minutes*

"The Belgian delegation interprets the reference to the European Convention on Human Rights as implying that compliance therewith will not be affected:

– either by the use of the possibility offered by Article 15 of that Convention to derogate significantly therefrom;

– or by departures from the case law of the European Court in the interpretation of Article 13 of that Convention on the right to 'an effective remedy'."

*Statement by the Irish delegation for the Council minutes*

"In relation to the appeal against a decision referred to in paragraphs 8 and 17, in the Irish context the appeal is against the recommendation of the examining authority to the Ministry of Justice".

*Statement by the United Kingdom and Danish delegations for the Council minutes*

The United Kingdom and Denmark state that they will apply the procedure provided for in the second sentence of paragraph 20 insofar as the legislation of their countries so permits.

*Statements by the Swedish delegation for the Council minutes*

*Re paragraph 8*

"In relation to the appeal against a decision referred to in paragraph 8, in the Swedish context the appeal is against the recommendation of the examining authority to the Government".

*Re paragraph 17*

"In relation to the authorization to apply for leave to remain in the territory of the Member State temporarily during procedures before the review authority, in the Swedish context this application will be decided on by the Swedish Immigration Board."

*Commentary:*

*Status:* Resolution of the Member States as adopted by the European Council on 20 June 1995 in accordance with Article K.1(3) of the Treaty on European Union.

*Entry into force:* The Member States undertake to take account of the principles of the Resolution in the case of all proposals for changes to their national legislation. They will also strive to bring their national legislation into line with the principles of the Resolution by 1 January 1996.

*International obligations engaged:*

(1) UN Convention relating to the Status of Refugees 1951 and Protocol 1967
(2) UN Convention against Torture and other Cruel, Inhuman or Degrading Treatment or Punishment 1984
(3) European Convention on Human Rights 1950
(4) Dublin Convention 1990.

*Summary:*

The Resolution is divided into nine sections containing a total of 31 articles referred to as paragraphs in the document itself. The Member States acknowledge their obligations under the UN Convention relating to the Status of Refugees and recall their commitments under the ECHR. The guarantees contained in the Resolution apply to asylum applications as defined in the Dublin Convention excluding the determination of the Member State responsible for considering an asylum application. In respect of these determinations the provisions of the Dublin Convention itself apply.

The procedures must comply with the the requirements of articles 1 and 33 of the UN Convention[341] and article 35 as regards cooperation with UNHCR. The Resolution does not seek to regulate or harmonise national procedures on access to the asylum procedure itself. However, once an application enters the asylum procedure the Resolution applies. The main guarantees of the Resolution are:

- applications must be examined by a fully qualified authority (III (3)); these authorities must have specialized personnel, access to precise and

341 Article 1A of the UN Convention contains the definition of a refugee and article 33 prohibits the return of a refugee to a place where he or she fears persecution.

up-to-date information from various sources including UNHCR on countries of origin and transit, the power to seek advice from experts where appropriate (III(6));

- authorities must take into consideration and seek to establish all relevant facts (III(5));

- in the event of a negative decision there shall be a right of appeal to a court or a review authority which gives an independent ruling (III(8)); it is unclear whether this applies if the asylum applicant is a national of another Member State (IV(20)); where the host third country concept is applicable.[342] Member States may derogate from the principle of a right of appeal (IV(22));

- details of asylum applications are recognised to be sensitive data and must be the subject of adequate data protection guarantees (IV(11));

- the asylum applicant must be allowed to remain on the territory of the Member State for the duration of the procedure (IV(12) and (17)); this suspensive effect must continue until a decision has been taken on any appeal against a negative decision or at least until a court or independent review authority has an opportunity to determine whether expulsion pending a full consideration by the court or independent review authority of the appeal is to be permitted (IV(17)); Member States may derogate from the principle of suspensive effect where the application is determined to be manifestly unfounded within the meaning of that Resolution[343] but in such circumstances the decision must be taken at a high level and with additional safeguards (IV(21)); Member States may also derogate from the principle of suspensive effect where they apply the host third country concept in accordance with that Resolution[344] (IV(22)); where the asylum application is made at the border suspensive effect only necessarily applies for the duration of the

342 See Document 3 supra.
343 See Document 2 supra.
344 See Document 3 supra.

determination whether the application is manifestly unfounded within the meaning of that Resolution (IV(24));

- the applicant is entitled to the services of an interpreter if needed, at public expense if engaged by the authorities, a legal adviser or other counsellor during the procedure and at all stages access to UNHCR or organisations which may be working on behalf of UNHCR though such contact need not prevent implementation of a decision (IV(13));

- the applicant is entitled to a personal interview with a qualified official before a final decision is taken on the application (IV(14));

- the decision, reasons and information about review procedures must be communicated in writing (IV(15)) but Member States may derogate from the requirement of written decisions and information where they determine that the host third country concept applies (IV(22) and (25)); in such cases the decision and information must be given orally and on request confirmed in writing;

- applications which are determined to be manifestly unfounded within the meaning of that Resolution shall be dealt with in accordance with the provisions of that Resolution (IV(18)); those procedures permit the absence of an appeal right so long as an independent body has confirmed the decision (IV19));

- a rapid and simplified procedure may apply to asylum applications by nationals of other Member States;

- Member States shall ensure an opportunity to apply for asylum at the border, though such applications may be dealt with summarily.

*Comments: Guarantees only for Some*

The harmonisation of asylum policy in the European Union has been a high priority, first of the inter-governmental cooperation, and, following entry into force of the Treaty on European Union under the Third Pillar. The first fruit of the inter-governmental process was the Dublin Convention[345] itself, in 1990 which was followed two years later by the Resolution on manifestly unfounded applications for asylum, the Resolution on harmonised approach to questions concerning host third countries and the Conclusions on countries in which there is generally no serious risk of persecution all adopted on 30 November and 1 December 1992.

The Dublin Convention itself sets out a system whereby asylum applicants can expect to have their application for asylum determined in one of the Member States according to the rules set out in the Convention relating to where the applicant is deemed either to have sufficient links through residence or family members or the first state in which the asylum applicant arrived. The element of choice as to where he or she will seek asylum, usually an illusory concept for an asylum applicant who is fleeing persecution in his or her own country, is limited by the Convention. However for such a system to be fair to the asylum applicant, the determination procedure in all of the Member States must be equivalent. While all of the Member States are parties to the UN Convention relating to Status of Refugees 1951 and the 1967 Protocol it is apparent from a survey of national asylum procedures that they are not necessarily equivalent among the Member States.[346]

The adoption of the Resolution on manifestly unfounded applications for asylum highlighted this problem. In establishing criteria whereby certain types of application, in particular those where the asylum applicant has passed through a country considered safe during his or her flight from the country of origin to the Member State, are to be dealt with quickly and with minimal procedural guarantees the Member States presuppose that there are certain common standards applicable throughout the territory of the Union. However, at the time that the Resolution was adopted, for instance in Ireland, no legal provisions at all existed providing for an asylum determination procedure.

345 See Document 1 supra.
346 European Council on Refugees and Exiles, Asylum in Europe, October 1994.

Notwithstanding the extensive work which was undertaken on coordination of various aspects of asylum policy after 1990 the problem of procedural guarantees was not addressed until this Resolution was adopted in 1995. However, the issue of minimum procedural guarantees for asylum applicants has been addressed in other fora in which the Member States participate.

The Executive Committee of UNHCR adopted Conclusion No 8 (xxviii), determination of refugee status, in 1977. A number of the Member States were represented on the Executive Committee. Further, the Member States within the context of the Council of Europe adopted Recommendation R(1981) 16 on harmonisation of national procedures relating to asylum through the Committee of Ministers. Accordingly, the Member States have been active in other venues concerning the question of procedural guarantees for asylum applicants.

It is clear that the Resolution has taken into account the work which has been done both in the context of the Executive Committee of the UNHCR and the Council of Europe in this field. In general, assuming the proper implementation of this Resolution, any application for asylum which is considered substantively on its merit in any Member State should be protected by sufficient procedural guarantees to satisfy the requirements of the rule of law and the Member States obligations undertaken in other fora. The same cannot be said, however, for the guarantees which apply in respect of asylum applications which are characterised as manifestly unfounded, in particular, on the basis that there is a safe host country to which the asylum applicant may be returned, where the application is made at the border or where the application is made by a national of another Member State.

The most dramatic change of asylum policy in Europe lies here - the attempt to define out of admission to the full asylum determination procedure as many applicants as possible. This process has become increasingly sophisticated and coordinated throughout the Member States. The main tools used in this defining out process are:

(i) the principle that the first country through which an asylum applicant travels should be responsible for him or her contained in the Dublin

Convention[347] as regards the Member States and in the Resolution on a harmonised approach to questions concerning host third countries.[348]

(ii) the principle that some countries may be determined to be "safe" *per se* and therefore asylum applications from nationals of those countries should be subject to a negative presumption contained in the Conclusions on countries in which there is generally no serious risk of persecution.[349]

(iii) the implementation of limited procedural guarantees for all asylum applicants categorised as coming within (i) or (ii) as contained in the Resolution on manifestly unfounded asylum applications.[350]

(iv) perhaps most controversially, the abolition of suspensive effect of review or appeal procedures for applicants categorised as coming within (i) or (ii).

The consequence of this policy is to seek to move to third countries, normally on the borders of the Member States, the burden of asylum determination and care of asylum applicants pending determination.[351] The concern which this policy is provoking on the Union's Eastern borders has been eloquently put by Professor Nagy regarding the Hungarian situation "Hungary cannot become the target country and destination of all those forced and voluntary migrants who are excluded from Western Europe. With a GDP five to eight times less than that of the EC Member States, Hungary cannot assume the burdens Western Europe claims incapable to carry".[352]

347 See Document 1 infra.
348 See Document 3 infra.
349 See Document 4 infra.
350 See Document 2 infra.
351 See comments on Documents 2 and 3.
352 Asylum Seekers and Refugees: Hungarian Dilemmas, B Nagy, Acta Juridica Hungarica, 1992 34 No 1-2 pp 27-47.

*Determination of substantive applications*

A comparison of the guarantees contained in the Resolution with Conclusion No 8 of the UNHCR Executive Committee and Recommendation R (1981) 16 of the Council of Europe Committee of Ministers is warranted.

Both the UNHCR Conclusion and the Council of Europe Recommendation require that:

(i) clear instructions for dealing with asylum applications be provided to the authorities responsible for frontier control.[353]

This requirement is reflected in Section III article 7 of the Resolution.

(ii) Decisions on a asylum applications shall only be taken by a higher authority (UNHCR Conclusion No 8) or by a central authority (Council of Europe Recommendation).

This requirement is not clearly reflected in the Resolution. In Section III article 4 the Member States undertake that asylum applications shall be examined by any authority, fully qualified in the field of asylum and refugee matters. There is no requirement, however, that this be a "higher authority"[354] or a "central authority".[355]

(iii) According to both the UNHCR Conclusion and the Council of Europe Recommendation the consideration of the asylum application must respect the principle of non-refoulement[356] that is to say the obligation not to return a refugee to the state where he or she fears persecution.

353 Paragraph (e)(i) UNHCR Conclusion No 8 and paragraph 3 Council of Europe Recommendation R 1981(16).

354 UNHCR Conclusion No 8.

355 Council of Europe Recommendation paragraph 2.

356 UNHCR Conclusion No 8 paragraph (e)(i) and Council of Europe Recommendation paragraph 3(i).

The principle, contained in article 33 of the UN Convention, is stated specifically to apply to the Resolution. Two questions arise:

First, does the obligation of non-refoulement apply only up until the point at which a decision is taken on an asylum application or must it necessarily extend until a final decision by a court or tribunal? This is fundamentally the question whether refugee status is a fact precedent, that is to say a person is a refugee because he or she fulfils the conditions of Article 1 of the UN Convention and is recognised by a state because he or she is a refugee. Alternatively, a person is not a refugee unless recognised as such by a state and if recognition is refused then from the date of refusal it is clear the person is not a refugee unless of course the decision is reversed by a court or tribunal. The position of UNHCR is clear: recognition as a refugee is only declaratory of a status which the person already has by virtue of fulfilling the definition of article 1A of the UN Convention.[357]

The basic issue in any appeal against refusal of recognition of as a refugee is whether the person will be subject to persecution or returned on to a country where he or she fears persecution if the applicant is expelled from the state. For a right of appeal or review of a decision that a person is not a refugee to have meaning, the person must not be returned to another state pending the outcome as otherwise the outcome of the appeal becomes irrelevant. If the person was correctly afraid of persecution the likelihood is high that he or she will have suffered such treatment before the appeal hearing is complete. If the decision to refuse recognition was correct, then the person may be returned safely. If the person is expelled pending the appeal or review procedure the chances of him or her being able to pursue the appeal or review effectively are substantially diminished. The person's oral evidence and the court or review body's ability to assess credibility on the basis of oral evidence is no longer possible. Further, the person's incentive to pursue an appeal or to give effective instructions

357 Handbook on Procedures and Criteria for Determining Refugee Status, Geneva 1988.

to lawyers or counsellors acting on his or her behalf is greatly diminished.

In view of what is at stake, it would seem inconsistent to suggest that the fact precedent presumption exists only before an initial negative decision but not during the appeal procedure. Further, it is difficult to understand how the structure of international refugee protection can operate in the absence of a fact precedent presumption.

The second problem is whether or to what extent a state which is seized of an asylum application can be relieved of its obligations as regards non-refoulement by returning the asylum applicant to a third country. To what extent, if at all, is the sending state under an obligation to ensure that the purported safe third country will not send the asylum applicant back to the country where he or she fears persecution without a substantive consideration of the asylum application? This raises another question, insofar as the Member States have agreed a set of minimum procedural guarantees which apply to the determination of any asylum application, must they then ensure, when seeking to return an asylum applicant to a third country, that equivalent procedural guarantees apply? The answer must be affirmative.

If the Member States have agreed a minimum set of standards which are necessary for the consideration of an asylum application to be fair, then these same standards must apply wherever the application is to be determined. The asylum applicant's right to a fair consideration of his or her application would be impugned if the state where he or she applied for asylum were permitted to return the person to a state with few or no guarantees as to the fairness of the asylum determination process.

In the context of article 3 ECHR, the prohibition on torture, inhuman or degrading treatment, the European Court of Human Rights has held that a state seeking to return a person to a country where he or she is likely to suffer such treatment would be acting in contravention of the obligation.[358] Whether this jurisprudence can be applied to the UN Convention directly has not been established. However in most cases an asylum applicant will be a person who fears torture, inhuman or degrading treatment in his or her country of origin and therefore return to a third country which may not protect the person from return to a country where he or she may be subject to treatment contrary to article 3 ECHR would also constitute a breach of that obligation. The non-refoulement obligation is inextricably connected to the suspensive effect of any appeal or review against a negative decision.

(iv) An asylum applicant should be given the necessary facilities, including services of a competent interpreter for submitting his or her case to the authorities concerned.[359] This obligation is reflected in the Resolution at Section IV article 13.

(v) The intervention of a lawyer should be permitted at an appropriate stage of the procedure.[360] Again this is contained in the resolution at Section IV article 13.

(vi) Applicants should be given the opportunity, of which they should be duly informed, to contact a representative of UNHCR.[361] This obligation is also contained in the Resolution with the clear indication that an asylum applicant must be given the opportunity at all stages of the procedure to communicate with UNHCR or other refugee organisations which may be working on behalf of UNHCR. The Resolution also makes it clear that UNHCR representatives have a right to contact the asylum applicant.

(vii) Where a negative decision is reached it shall be notified to the applicant and he or she shall be informed in an appropriate manner of the reasons on which the decision is based and the possibilities of

---

358 *Soering v. UK* [1989] Ser. A No 161.

359 UNHCR Conclusion No 8 paragraph (e)(iv) and Council of Europe Recommendation paragraph 6.

360 Council of Europe Recommendation paragraph 6.

361 UNHCR Conclusion No 8 paragraph (e) (iv).

appeal or review.[362] This obligation is reflected in the Resolution at Section IV articles 15 and 16. The Resolution provides helpful clarification of this obligation in that it specifies that the asylum applicant must be informed of the main purport of the decision and the possibility of appeal in a language which he or she understands. Further, an adequate period of time within which to appeal and to prepare his or her case when requesting a review together with early information on time limits is included in the Resolution.

(viii) There shall be provision for appeal to a higher administrative authority or to a court of law against a negative decision on an asylum request. Failing that there shall at least be an effective possibility of having the decision reviewed.[363] If the applicant is not recognised he should be given a reasonable period of time to seek a formal reconsideration of the decision, either to the same or to a different authority, whether administrative or judicial according to the prevailing system.[364] The obligation to provide a right of appeal or independent review is contained in the Resolution at Section III article 8. Specifically, provision shall be made for an appeal to a court or a review authority which gives an independent ruling on individual cases. This requirement in the Resolution is usefully augmented by the obligation to give decisions in writing in most circumstances or at least to confirm the decision in writing and to provide adequate time within which to appeal (Resolution Section IV articles 15 and 16).

(ix) The Resolution provides that an asylum applicant shall in all circumstances be given the opportunity of a personal interview with an official qualified under national law before a final decision is taken on the asylum application (Section IV article 14). This requirement does not appear either in the Council of Europe Recommendation or the UNHCR Conclusion. Nonetheless, it is an important safeguard to the asylum determination procedure.

---

362 Council of Europe Recommendation paragraph 8.
363 Council of Europe Recommendation paragraph 5.
364 UNHCR Conclusion paragraph (e)(iv).

*Suspensive effect*

The most problematic aspect of the Resolution is that relating to the suspensive effect of a right of appeal to a court or a review authority which gives an independent ruling. This is reflected in the development of policy on asylum among the Member States whereby the objective of the Member States to determine asylum applications quickly and to remove those applicants refused recognition as quickly as possible from the territory has created a most unfortunate tension with the principles of rule of law.

For an asylum applicant who fears that either he or she will be returned to the country of origin directly and suffer persecution there or removed to a third country which will not respect the non-refoulement obligation of article 33 of the UN Convention, a right of appeal without suspensive effect is valueless. Where the person has been expelled to some other country pending the appeal procedure, the whole basis of the appeal itself is compromised as the issue at stake is whether the person can safely be returned to some other country. Therefore, insofar as appeal procedures which guarantee the rule of law are seen as an obstacle to a rapid determination procedure, the removal of suspensive effect of the appeal procedure itself may be seen as an effective way to discourage the exercise of appeal rights and indeed their effective exercise.

Both the UNHCR Conclusion and the Council of Europe Recommendation permit the disapplication of suspensive effect of appeal procedures in certain limited circumstances. In the UNHCR Conclusion "the applicant should be permitted to remain in the country pending a decision on initial request by the competent authority...unless it has been established by that authority that its request is clearly abusive. He should be permitted to remain in the country while an appeal to a higher administrative authority or to the courts is pending".[365] According to the Council of Europe Recommendation "the applicant shall be allowed to remain in the territory while an appeal or review is pending unless facts come to light in the course of the appeal or review procedure which, if they had been known at the time of the initial examination of the request by the central authority, would have lead the

365 UNHCR Conclusion paragraph (e)(vii).

latter to decide that the request was manifestly based on grounds having no connection with asylum."[366]

On the wording of both provisions, it is clear that suspensive effect of any appeal procedures is the norm and it should be respected. The UNHCR Conclusion is somewhat unclear what should prevail where the request is "clearly abusive". The threshold for a determination of clearly abusive must, nonetheless, be very high. The categorisation of an asylum application as manifestly unfounded or susceptible to be treated as if manifestly unfounded on the grounds that the person passed through a third country as provided for in the Resolution on manifestly unfounded asylum applications[367] when read in conjunction with the Resolution on a harmonised approach to questions concerning host third countries[368] is unlikely to meet this high threshold. This is particularly so where there is no guarantee that the asylum applicant will have access to the asylum determination procedure in the host third country or that the determination procedure is characterised by the same minimum level of guarantees as contained in this Resolution.

In respect of the Council of Europe Recommendation it is clear that suspensive effect should apply at least until the appeal or review procedure is fairly advanced. The removal of suspensive effect and the consequent expulsion of the individual is only consistent where "facts come to light in the course of the appeal or review procedure". This therefore presupposes that the person should be permitted to remain on the territory pending the review procedure at least until the appeal or review procedure is substantially developed. It would also indicate that the justification of the discontinuance of an appeal procedure on the basis of such facts requires that the circumstances which have come to light are very weighty indeed.

Accordingly, the Resolution does not appear to comply with the obligations undertaken by the Member States elsewhere. Specifically, Section IV permits a derogation from the principle of a suspensive effect if the host third country concept as contained in the Resolution of that name[369] Applies.

---

366 Council of Europe Recommendation paragraph 6.
367 See Document 2, article 1(b).
368 See Document 3, article 1.
369 See Document 3.

Further, in a special section on asylum applications at the border Member States are permitted to apply an exception to the general principle of suspensive effect provided that the decision on refusal of admission is taken by a ministry or comparable central authority. Reference is also made to additional sufficient safeguards to ensure the correctness of the decision however no reference is made to an appeal to ensure this correctness. Surely it is accepted in all Member States that it is ultimately the role of a court or independent tribunal to ensure the correctness of administrative decisions not the role of the administration itself.

Even in respect of applications which are considered substantively, Member States are permitted to derogate from the principal of suspensive effect provided that the applicant has the possibility of applying to a court or independent review authority for permission to remain on the territory temporarily during the appeal procedure.[370] From a practical perspective this must be a rather expensive way of establishing an appeal procedure as it will entail a further, interim appeal to a court and a hearing on the question of suspensive effect in addition to the main appeal hearing. As a matter of principle, such a procedure is a further impediment to the asylum applicant securing a full and fair review of the refusal of his or her application.

A separate regime applies, according to the Resolution, to manifestly unfounded asylum applications. In particular, the Member States are entitled to exclude the possibility of lodging an appeal against a decision on this ground so long as an independent body which is distinct from the examining authority has confirmed the decision.

The Resolution is without prejudice to the procedural measures contained in the Resolution on manifestly unfounded asylum applications, which as pointed out above, may include asylum applicants who are to be returned to host third countries without a substantive consideration of their applications in the Member State. The accelerated procedure contained in the Resolution on manifestly unfounded asylum applications does not include any obligation for an appeal or review procedure against a negative decision. Further, there is no guarantee that where such appeal or review procedure

370 See Resolution article 17.

does exist it should have suspensive effect. By specifically excluding from the scope of the Resolution on minimum guarantees decisions based on manifestly unfounded grounds the Member States are excluding a substantial number of asylum applicants from the basic guarantees of the Resolution.

Under the manifestly unfounded Resolution there are two grounds on which an application may be so determined:

(i) There is clearly no substance to the applicant's fear of persecution in his/her own country. This category includes: anyone whose fear of persecution is not based on a Convention ground; there is no indication that the person will be exposed to a fear of persecution; the applicant's story is inconsistent, contradictory or fundamentally improbable and therefore lacks creditability; the applicant could seek effective protection in another part of his or her own country and it would be reasonable to expect the applicant to go there. If the asylum applicant has passed through a country which fulfils the criteria of the Conclusions on countries in which there is generally no serious risk of persecution the application for asylum may not be subject to determination by a Member State of refugee status.

(ii) The claim is based on deliberate deception or is an abuse of asylum procedures. An application comes within this category where the applicant: maintains that false documents or a false identity are genuine and bases the claim upon them; deliberately makes false representations about the claim after applying; in bad faith destroys, damages, or disposes of any passport, other document or ticket either to establish a false identity for the asylum application or to hinder the consideration of the application; deliberately conceals that an asylum application has been made in another country; makes an application to forestall an impending expulsion measure when there were earlier opportunities to make the application; flagrantly fails to comply with substantive obligations relating to the asylum procedure; where an application made in another country has been rejected after an examination comprising adequate procedural guarantees and in accordance with the UN Convention.

As can be seen a refusal on the basis that an application is manifestly unfounded includes a rag bag of different grounds, some of which may well come within the scope of "clearly abusive" of the UNHCR Conclusion, for instance where the fear of persecution is not based on a Convention ground, but others, such as the destruction of a travel document or concealment of a previous asylum application, do not necessarily come within the scope of "clearly abusive".

Further, the protection which the Council of Europe Recommendation seeks to provide to ensure that any decision to remove suspensive effect is subject to adequate guarantees in that it cannot be taken except in the course of the appeal or review procedure, is completely lacking. To this extent, the Resolution on minimum guarantees resiles from the protection agreed in other international fora for the fair determination of asylum applications.

# Annex

# The Palma Document

Free Movement of Persons. A Report to the European Council by the Coordinators' Group

NOTE ON THE FREE MOVEMENT OF PERSONS

I

1. The Single European Act sets as an objective for the Community the establishment by 31 December 1992 of "an area without internal frontiers in which the free movement of goods, persons, services and capital is ensured in accordance with the provisions of this Treaty".

   The Rhodes European Council, reviewing the establishment of the Internal Market, called on the Council to step up its efforts in all areas where progress was slow, such as the free movement of persons. "The achievement of the Community's objectives, especially the area without internal frontiers, is linked to progress in inter-governmental cooperation to combat terrorism, international crime, drug trafficking and trafficking of all kinds. This cooperation will be stepped up in order to achieve rapid and concrete results which will enable the Community, for its part, to take the necessary measures to turn Europe into a tangible reality for its citizens. To this end each Member State will appoint a person responsible for the necessary coordination."

2. The Group of persons responsible for coordination (Coordinators' Group-Free movement of persons) met on 22 February, 17 March, 5 April, 26 April and 17 May in Brussels and from 4 to 6 June in Palma de Mallorca. Member States' representatives were Mr Pastor (Presidency), Mrs Delvaux (Belgium), Mr Vesterdorf (Danish), Mr Neusel (FRG), Mr Georgiou (Greece), Mr Blanc (France), Mr Crowley (Ireland), Mr De Michelis (Italy), Mr Elsen (Luxembourg), Mr Grosheide (Nether-

lands), Mr Sousa Vicente (Portugal), Mr Hyde and Mr Langdon (United Kingdom). The Commission of the European Communities was represented by Mr Bangemann, Vice-President.

3. In the course of the Group's discussions it was recognised that differing views were held on their legal and political framework, in particular on the interpretation and scope of the relevant Treaty provisions inter alia Article 8a of the EEC Treaty, and the obligations flowing therefrom, the extent to which political decisions in this field had already been taken and where the competence for taking decisions and action lay. It was agreed to set those differences on one side for the purposes of the Coordinators' discussions, and this is reflected in this report. Accordingly, the report in general, and the recommendations for measures to be taken, represent practical steps upon which all could agree and do not prejudice the legal and political questions. In many instances the measures proposed, for example those regarding provisions on immigration, mutual legal assistance and greater cooperation between law enforcement agencies, are ones which are desirable in their own right, though equally their implementation assumes greater urgency and importance in the light of the objective of free movement.

4. The Co-ordinators' meetings are not an extra forum for discussions; the Co-ordinators are responsible for:

   - coordinating, giving an impetus to and unblocking the whole of intergovernmental and Community work in the field of the free movement of persons; and

   - submitting to the Madrid European Council a report on the free movement of persons and the establishment of an area without frontiers, including the measures to be adopted by the responsible bodies and a timetable for their implementation.

5. Issues connected with the free movement of persons pose a problem as to methods to be pursued, owing to the multiplicity of fora in which they are discussed – the Community, Political Cooperation, Ministers for Immigration, Trevi Group, Council of Europe – and which will have to be coordinated.

II The Co-ordinators' Group initially:

(a) drew up a catalogue of the measures which must be adopted, making a distinction between essential and desirable measures:

(b) defined, with due regard for their respective fields of competence, the main fora within which the measures could be examined with a view to taking a decision:

* the ad hoc Working Group on Immigration for the conditions governing the crossing of barriers;
* the Trevi Group and in particular the Trevi 1992 Group with regard to cooperation on law enforcement and, if necessary, related legal problems;
* the Working Group on Judicial Cooperation as part of European Political Co-operation (international treaties, national and Community legislation);
* Community bodies for matters within the Communities' jurisdiction.

These Groups would keep the Coordinator's Group regularly informed of their activities;

(c) proposed the priorities for adopting these measures and suggested target dates for adopting all the measures.

The data which emerged from the discussions are given in Annex 1.

2. The Co-ordinators' Group, with the authority conferred on it by the mandate from the Rhodes European Council, seeks confirmation from the Madrid European Council that its tasks should be the following:

(a) to ensure that the various bodies mentioned in the Annex carry out the tasks assigned to them in accordance with the agreed target dates,

(b) to give an impetus to the progress or conclusion of the proceedings in the various bodies. In this context, each coordinator should give the proceedings the impetus necessary to eliminate the obstacles which prevent delegations from supporting a possible consensus.

To carry out its task more efficiently in the short term, the Coordinators' Group concluded that it should concentrate on fora within Community competence and covered by inter-governmental cooperation among the Twelve.

III. The achievement of an area without internal frontiers could involve, as necessary, the approximation of national laws and their rules of application and scope, collaboration between national administration and a prior strengthening of checks at external frontiers. It is a task with two facets: "ad intra" and "ad extra".

A. In its "ad intra" facet the abolition of internal borders affects a whole range of matters, in particular:

(a) Combating terrorism, drug trafficking, and other illicit trafficking

The creation of an area without internal frontiers, in accordance with the Treaty, will require checks at external frontiers to be tightened up, which will involve increased inter-governmental cooperation.

(b) Improved cooperation on law enforcement: This improvement will in particular involve closer co-operation between the Member States' law enforcement agencies, and an improved system for exchanging information.

(c) Judicial co-operation: Judicial cooperation should be intensified, particularly in criminal matters, in order to combat terrorism, drug trafficking, crime and other illicit trafficking. In this context, the possibility of harmonising certain provisions should be studied.

(d) Control of articles accompanying travellers:
1. Veterinary checks
2. Plant health checks
3. Protection of endangered species of flora and fauna

4. Weapons
5. Drugs
6. Checks on illicit trafficking in works of art
7. Exchange controls
8. Tax checks

(e) Matters such as those deriving from family problems ("legal" abduction of children and trafficking in minors, for example) should also be mentioned.

B. In its "ad extra" facet, the creation of an area without internal frontiers would necessitate tighter controls at external frontiers.Controls carried out at those frontiers are in fact valid for all the Member States. Those controls must be highly effective and all the Member States must be able to rely on them. If necessary, consideration should be given to the conditions and the manner in which the Community might contribute to financing certain types of infrastructure, bearing in mind that controls at its external frontiers are being strengthened.

To this end, a set of legal, administrative and technical instruments should be established, as criteria will need to be harmonised on treatment of non-Community citizens. Amongst the legal measures, attention should be drawn to the following:

– the conditions governing entry into the Community of nationals of third countries. This point relates particularly to visa policy, especially:

* establishment of a common list of countries whose citizens are subject to a visa requirement;
* establishment of a common list of persons to be refused entry;
* harmonisation of the criteria for granting visas, while allowing for the specific circumstances of certain applicants to be taken into account;
* a European visa;

– grant of asylum and refugee status; a common policy will be based on Member States' obligations pursuant to their accession to the Geneva Convention and the New York Protocol. This policy will initially focus on the following aspects:

* acceptance of identical international commitments with regard to asylum;
* determining the State responsible for examining the application for asylum;
* simplified or priority procedure for the examination of clearly unfounded requests;
* conditions governing the movement of the applicant between Member States;
* study of the need for a financing system to fund the economic consequences of implementing the common policy.

In keeping with the traditional values of the Member States of the Community, the Coordinators insist that the stepping-up of controls at external frontiers should not go beyond what is strictly necessary for safeguarding security and law and order in the Member States. They also draw attention to the Declaration against Racism and Xenophobia adopted in 1986 by the European Parliament, the Council, the Representatives of the Member States and the Commission.

# REPORT from the Ministers responsible for immigration to the European Council meeting in Maastricht on immigration and asylum policy [371]

## A. SUMMARY, WORK PROGRAMMES AND CONCLUSIONS

### I. INTRODUCTION

The Luxembourg European Council, having received proposals from the German delegation, requested the Ministers responsible for immigration to submit proposals on the harmonisation of immigration and asylum policies at its meeting in Maastricht.

This report is in response to those instructions.

The report addresses the various issues without stating an opinion on the institutional framework within which they should be dealt with in the future, as these problems will be examined at the Intergovernmental Conference on Political Union.

This issue was nevertheless the subject of an exchange of views during the ministerial meeting. Minster attached great importance to a decision on this matter being taken at the European Council in Maastricht.

371 Brussels, 3 December 1991 (05. 12) (OR.f) SN 4038/91 (WGI 930).

In accordance with these instructions, the attention of the Ministers responsible for immigration focused on the work to be carried out immediately by way of transitional measures and preparation of the policy which will be set in place progressively as from the entry into force of the Treaty on Political Union.

This report contains a brief outline of the various problems examined and a priority work programme for migration policy and asylum policy respectively, followed by a more detailed and more comprehensive analytical document (see B, p.11).

## II TOWARDS THE HARMONISATION OF MIGRATION AND ASYLUM POLICIES

Over recent years Member States have increasingly felt the need to harmonise their migration and asylum policies with regard to third-country nationals.

The prospect of attaining the objective of Article 8a, in particular in respect of freedom of movement for persons, will have consequences for the way in which Member States implement their national policies and will make co-operation between them even more necessary.

The initial results of co-operation between Member States – the Dublin Convention determining the State responsible for examining applications for asylum and the draft Convention between the Member States on the crossing of their external frontiers – in themselves call for more thorough harmonisation.

Other phenomena indicate the same path, in particular the substantial intensification of migratory pressure now exerted on almost all Member States, which they obviously cannot contemplate resolving individually to the detriment of their Community partners, and the massive increase in the number of unjustified applications for asylum, a method which is used – in most cases in vain – as a means of immigration by persons who do not meet conditions of the Geneva Convention.

The work programmes annexed to this report have been drawn up pragmatically: harmonisation has not been regarded as an end in itself but as a means of re-orienting policies where such action makes for efficiency and speed of intervention.

As regards immigration, the main topics which would appear to require priority treatment are harmonisation of admission policies, the development of a common approach to the problem of illegal immigration, labour migration policies and the situation of third-country nationals residing legally in the Community.

As regards asylum, in the first place the protection of persons who are victims of persecution should be reaffirmed and the Geneva Convention applied. As for the tasks to be performed, priority would appear to go to preparing implementation of the Dublin Convention and harmonising the substantive rules of asylum law in order to ensure uniform interpretation of the Geneva Convention. Harmonisation of procedural aspects, on the other hand, seemed less urgent, apart from the fact that every effort must be made to shorten asylum application procedures, particularly in the case of clearly unjustified applications. Harmonisation of expulsion policy would also appear to be necessary, as would examination of reception conditions for asylum seekers and a permanent updating of knowledge regarding the various aspects of this question.

## III. WORK PROGRAMME CONCERNING MIGRATION POLICY

On the basis of the above considerations, it is possible to establish a concrete work programme, the broad lines of which are set out below. In general, the Ministers responsible for immigration could perform a sort of management and monitoring function in respect of the implementation of this entire programme, on the understanding that preparation of certain measures may fall within the competence of other Ministers.

It is important that existing structures should assist Ministers in co-ordinating programme implementation.

Between now and entry into force of the Treaty on Political Union, the following subjects should be dealt with. They are listed in order of priority under each heading. If necessary, this work must be continued after that date.

*A. Harmonisation of admission policies*

- harmonisation of policies on admission for purposes such as family reunion and formation and admission of students;

- harmonisation of policies on admission for other purposes such as humanitarian aims and work as an employed or self-employed person;

- harmonisation of legal provisions governing persons authorised to reside.

*B. Common approach to the question of illegal immigration*

- co-operation on border controls within the framework of the Convention on the crossing of external frontiers;

- harmonisation of conditions for combatting unlawful immigration and illegal employment and checks for that purpose both within the territory and at borders;

- harmonisation of principles on expulsion, including the rights to be guaranteed to expelled persons;

- definition of guiding principles on the question of policy regarding third-country nationals residing unlawfully in Member States;

- co-operation with countries of departure and transit in combatting unlawful immigration, in particular as regards re-admission.

*C. Policy on the migration of labour*

- harmonisation of national policies on admission to employment for third country nationals taking account of possible labour requirements in Member States over the years to come;

- increased mobility of Community nationals, in particular by improving the functioning of the SEDOC system.

*D. Situation of third country nationals*

- examination, within the appropriate fora, of the possibility of granting third country nationals who are long-term residents in a Member State certain rights or possibilities, for example concerning access to the labour market, held by Member State nationals once nationals of the twelve Member States enjoy the same conditions of freedom of movement and access to the labour market.

*E. Migration policy in the broad meaning of the term*

- preparation of agreements on re-admission with countries of origin and transit of unlawful immigration;

- establishment of an information programme and preparation of training and apprenticeship contracts for East European and North African countries in particular;

- strengthening of the rapid consultation centre.

The subjects under A, B and D could be dealt with by the Ministers responsible for immigration.

Suitable co-ordination with other Ministers, such as the Social Affairs, Employment and Foreign Affairs Ministers, will be necessary in the case of points C and E.

In addition to the priority subjects referred to earlier, a number of more general measures need to be taken, for which action by the Ministers with responsibility for immigration would depend on the proceedings of other bodies, including European Political Co-operation and Community action properly speaking:

- analysis of the causes of immigration pressure;
- removal of the causes of migratory movements by an adjusted policy in the field of development aid, trade policy, human rights, food, environment and demographics;
- strengthening of support for accommodating refugees in their countries of origin;
- incorporation of the migration aspect into economic, financial and social co-operation.

## IV. WORK PROGRAMME CONCERNING ASYLUM POLICY

This work programme for harmonisation of asylum policies has been drawn up on the basis of the objectives laid down by the Luxembourg European Council. The subjects mentioned below should be dealt with between now and the entry into force of the Treaty on Political Union. If necessary this work must be continued after that date. Moreover, the work programme may be supplemented subsequently in the light of discussion, with the result that the list is not exhaustive.

### A. *Application and implementation of the Dublin Convention*

1. Determining a common interpretation of the concepts used in the Convention;
2. Exchanges of information;
3. Implementing mechanisms;
4. Drawing up a practical manual for application of the criteria in the Convention;

5. Combating asylum applications submitted under a false identity.

*B. Harmonisation of substantive asylum law*

1. Unambiguous conditions for determining that applications for asylum are clearly unjustified;

2. Definition and harmonised application of the principle of first host country;

3. Common assessment of the situation in countries of origin with a view both to admission and expulsion;

4. Harmonised application of the definition of a refugee as given in Article 1A of the Geneva Convention.

*C. Harmonisation of expulsion policy*

1. Common assessment of the situation in the country of origin;

2. Determination of various aspects of an expulsion policy.

*D. Setting up a clearing house*

Setting up such a centre at the General Secretariat of the Council:

1. Written exchanges of information on legislation, policy, case law and information concerning countries of origin, together with statistical information;

2. Oral exchanges of information through informal meetings of officials responsible for implementing asylum policy.

*E. Legal examination*

Examination of the problem of guaranteeing harmonised applications of asylum policy.

*F. Conditions for receiving applicants for asylum*

1. Collection of data on current conditions for receiving applicants;

2. On the basis of that collection of data, study of possible ways of approximating these points.

V. CONCLUSION

The Ministers responsible for immigration invite the European Council to signify its agreement to the above work programmes. If implemented, they could considerably increase the effectiveness of Member States' policies in these fields in the new and gradually developing context and will constitute a stage – an ambitious but realistic stage – along the path to harmonisation.

## B. DETAILED NOTE

I. GENERAL INTRODUCTION

The European Council in Luxembourg asked Ministers responsible for immigration to submit proposals on immigration and asylum.

This note defines a general framework for immigration and asylum policies, as set out in sections II and III respectively. The two sections provide a concrete work programme and establish priorities.

1. *Why Harmonisation*

It is specifically when setting priorities regarding the topics to be harmonised in the frame work of immigration and asylum policy that it is important to formulate a number of basic principles for the harmonisation process. Harmonisation is not an end in itself, but stems from a need felt by Member States for a common policy in this area.

The need for harmonisation of immigration policy has grown increasingly in recent years. Until the mid-'80s, European co-operation in this field had been very limited: admittedly, Member States have been co-operating for many years with regard to freedom of movement for EC nationals and a coherent system of European law had been established. However, policy regarding third country nationals was still essentially the subject of national measures.

Co-operation in other areas became more intensive only after discussions had started in an intergovernmental framework (ad hoc Group on Immigration, Ministers responsible for immigration) spurred on by the determination to achieve the Internal Market by 1 January 1993. In this regard, considerable attention was paid to drafting Conventions on the responsibility for examining applications for asylum (Dublin Convention) and on the crossing of the Community's external frontiers.

Although apparently of only limited scope, the ultimate effect of these Conventions is much greater than was perhaps originally expected. For example, the establishment of responsibility for examining applications for asylum implicitly presupposes that Member States have confidence in each other's asylum policies, as one Member State consents to an application for asylum lodged with it being processed by another Member State in accordance with the latter's national legislation. Harmonisation of basic asylum policy is therefore merely a logical step towards giving this confidence more substance.

The Convention on the crossing of external frontiers is also an inducement, in many respects, to carrying harmonisation further. Firstly, it stipulates that foreigners in possession of a residence permit for one of the Member States are exempt from visa obligations for movement through other Member States. This makes it easier for this category of foreigners to stay in other Member States for short periods. By the same token there is an increased danger of such foreigners taking up residence in another Member State as employees or self-employed persons. This process may result in a certain tension and pressure on national immigration policies.

In addition, the Convention provides for co-operation on expulsion policy: the Member States generally assume responsibility for escorting illegal foreigners to EC frontiers. However, if one of the Member States subsequently re-admitted the foreigner in question on the grounds that it was permissible under its national immigration policy, the expulsion would immediately lose its effect and co-operation between Member States would be impaired.

A similar phenomenon occurs when a foreigner is entered on the common list of inadmissible persons: if the foreigner is already entitled to reside legally in one of the Member States but poses a threat to public order or national security for one or more other Member States, he can be entered on the common list only if the Member State concerned is prepared to withdraw his residence permit. Thus, here again there is a certain discrepancy which can be solved only through harmonisation.

The reverse may also occur: if national immigration policy results in the admission of a foreigner notified as an undesirable person, he must consequently be removed from the common list.

The above example show that the Convention on the crossing of external frontiers starts from a situation in which immigration policies have not yet been harmonised, but that its effect would be considerably improved if these policies were in fact harmonised. The two Conventions are therefore an inducement to harmonise policy.

Beyond that, deeper causes calling for a harmonised immigration policy may be instanced. The pressure of immigration on most Member States has increased significantly in recent years. The conviction that, confronted with these developments, a strictly national policy could not provide an adequate response has been consistently gaining ground: although differences still exist between Member States with regard to the nature and size of migratory movements, major similarities may also be observed.

On that basis, it would appear advisable to define a common answer to the question of how this immigration pressure can be accommodated. It is neither judicious nor politically desirable to shift migratory movements from one Member State to another: the aim is to make the problems manageable for the entire Community. This will require instruments which are based on an extended form of co-operation among Member States while ensuring that the policy of one Member State does not have negative effects on other Member States' policies.

## 2. *A pragmatic approach to the harmonisation process*

In general, the harmonisation process will need to be pragmatic in character: re-orienting policies where such action improves efficiency and speed of intervention.

In some areas, this may lead to the conclusion that harmonisation should be rapid and deep-going. This is true in the case of material asylum law, for example. In recent years, submitting an application for asylum has increasingly become the alternative route for migrants who do not meet the requirement of (restrictive) immigration policies. The immigration pressure referred to above applies by definition to policy aspects that are still flexible to some degree. If admission to the status of employee or equivalent becomes in practice extremely limited, foreigners will look for other ways. Since submitting an application for asylum indicates that a foreigner considers that he has a well founded fear of persecution in his country of origin within the meaning of Article 1A of the Geneva Convention, Member States must consider such a request carefully. This justified meticulousness in turn results in lengthy processing periods and, in conjunction with the growth in the number of asylum seekers, increasingly strong pressure on asylum policy as such.

The asylum problem has become a matter of urgency for virtually all Member States and is a perfect area in which common answers can be found to common challenges. While recognising the need for a procedure based on essential guarantees, Member States will have to attempt to reduce procedural abuses in this area. A first requirement would be that in all cases the same interpretation is given to the Geneva Convention, so that the conditions for recognition of refugee status are the same in all Member States. In addition, expulsion policies for rejected asylum seekers will have to be implemented in accordance with the same procedures in all Member States. Only with regard to the procedural aspect of asylum policy may it be held that harmonisation is of a less urgent nature due in particular to the situation of the administrative and legal system in the Member States.

Immigration policies are a more complicated issue as not all areas lend themselves to immediate harmonisation. Section B will return to this point in greater detail, but it will be seen that, even in this area, some policy elements lend themselves very readily to harmonisation and that this too is a necessity for a dynamic policy.

In the area of family reunion and formation, for example, Member States' policies can and will have to be harmonised within a relatively short period. The same also holds true for policies to combat illegal immigration: by definition, immigration has little concern for national borders and will have even less once checks are relaxed and/or abolished. A common response to these problems is therefore considered generally desirable.

3. *Basic principles for the level of harmonisation*

If the harmonisation process were initiated without defining basic principles, harmonisation might be carried out at the lowest level. Assuming that immigration into Member States must remain limited, it is above all the restrictive opinions which could dominate. It is clearly true that a European immigration policy is of necessity restrictive, with the exception of refugee policy and family reunion and formation policies, as well as policies providing for admission on humanitarian grounds. It must, however, be borne in mind that the European tradition is based on principles of social justice and respect for human rights, as defined in the European Convention on Human Rights.

The social justice aspect is particularly evident in the ways Member States deal with foreigners entitled to lawful residence. The basis for this policy is that these persons integrate into the society of the particular Member State. This integration process can be promoted by a policy regarding legal status which is strongly based on form and substance.

This issue is all the more topical as a number of Member States are experiencing growing tensions between foreign and native populations. Recent xenophobic developments call for vigorous counteraction. On the one had, this means that anti-discrimination policies in Member States must be expanded and consolidated. On the other hand, this will intensify the need for thorough integration policies and legal status policies which would remove legal obstacles to integration as far as possible where the nationality of Member State is not required for the pursuit of certain activities.

Once nationals of the twelve Member States enjoy the same conditions of movement and access to employment, the question will arise as to whether the difference made between EC nationals and non-EC nationals takes sufficient account of the position of this group of foreigners who, at national level, have often acquired a legal status comparable to that of a Member State's own nationals. As endeavours are made to give greater substance to a Citizen's Europe for EC nationals, these foreigners will also have to be able to associate with this process: they too will have to be able to identify themselves increasingly with Europe. Section II will therefore specifically examine the position of foreigners legally resident in Member States of the Community.

The European Convention on Human Rights has for many years provided a legal framework which also sets guidelines for certain components of immigration policy. This is particularly true of Article 8 thereof, which deals with the protection of family life and which the European Commission on Human Rights and the European Court of Human Rights interpret as also being decisive for policies on admission for purposes of family reunion.

Article 3 of the Convention sets limits on the possibilities for expelling foreigners. If they can expect inhumane or humiliating treatment in their country of origin, according to the case law of the institutions in Strasbourg they cannot be expelled.

Other Articles of the Convention (5, 13) can also influence immigration policy in that they establish in particular guarantees for the procedures and administrative measures to be applied. Finally, Article 14 (non-discrimination) could play an important role here, at any rate in relation with other rights listed in the Convention.

The harmonisation process must therefore of necessity fulfil two criteria: first, it must promote a dynamic migration policy and, second, it must be strictly in keeping with the European traditions of social justice and human rights. This implies the definition of a just and balanced immigration policy. That will be no mean task and will certainly require much more time and energy. Section B of this memorandum attempts to indicate how this process can be started in practice.

### 4. *Presentation of the harmonisation policy*

The discussions by the Twelve on the free movement of persons attract considerable public attention, sometimes of a critical nature. Such criticism is particularly aimed at the fact that deliberations are not public. Despite informal contacts made by different Presidencies with the European Parliament's contacts with its national parliament, the impression remains that there is insufficient transparency in this area. That view ignores the fact that, while at international level negotiations are exclusively between governments, the results of negotiations are submitted to national parliaments so that there can be public and parliamentary discussion. Furthermore, contacts with the press are invariably organised whenever a ministerial meeting is held.

It may be advisable to step up the briefing of the European Parliament, the Twelve's national parliaments and those of non-member countries insofar as the measures adopted concern them. Consideration should also be given to the manner in which contacts with external organisations could be formed in the framework of discussions on a uniform European immigration policy and how the results could be presented.

It is impossible to over-rate the importance which political circles must attach to the question of immigration policy in a period of great tension; the more the activities undertaken in the harmonisation process are favourably perceived by society and the political world, the greater will be the chances of success.

## II. MIGRATION POLICY

### 1. *Introduction*

The title of this Section contains the concept of "migration policy". The term "immigration policy" is often used in this context, but it may be misleading in that no EC Member State currently conducts a policy focused on immigration. It is on the contrary the control of immigration that is involved. If the term "migration policy" is used, the focus is also widened in two respects: on the one hand, emigration and return of foreigners to their countries of origin or third countries can also be taken into account and, on the other hand, the legal or illegal movements of foreigners already residing in a Member State may be considered as an element of migration policy.

A European migration policy must cover not only migratory movements from third countries to the Twelve and vice versa, but also migratory movements of non-EC nationals within the Twelve. However, migration of EC nationals is not taken into consideration here, as policy on this matter has already crystallised to a large extent and is administered by Community legislation.

In addition, this memorandum covers a wide area which partly goes beyond the competence of Ministers responsible for immigration. However, for a proper approach to the migration problem, it is very important to consider the various aspects in relation to each other. Areas such as labour market policies, human rights policies, development aid and integration policies are all of direct importance for supporting a European migration policy. A measure of co-ordination between these areas and more traditional policies on foreigners will be necessary, both at national and at European level. EC Ministers responsible for immigration must in particular pinpoint those aspects which are related to migration policy in the strict sense of the term.

2. *Developments in migratory movements*

Although none of the Member States conducts a policy to promote immigration as such, it must nonetheless be noted that they have all become de facto immigration countries, with the exception of Ireland.

The most important migratory movements to the EC are based on:

- asylum;
- family reunion;
- temporary migration for education, training periods and similar activities;
- illegal immigration.

In addition, foreigners are admitted for imperative humanitarian reasons and for reasons of national interest. In the latter case, admission for employment is the main category. After this type of immigration flourished in the '60s and '70s, labour market conditions in subsequent years were such that immigration for reasons of employment virtually disappeared.

Insofar as admission for reasons of national interest was possible, migratory pressure could be channelled by that means. When that door was closed in most Member States in the late '70s, increasing recourse was had to the asylum procedure because, apart from family reunion, it became the only remaining path of admission. If the Member States succeed in conducting an asylum policy which guarantees solely the protection of refugees and which, at the same time, results in more rapid rejection of applications for asylum that are clearly unjustified, other channels may well be used once again. In that event, possibilities for illegal immigration would probably be used increasingly. The first signs are already there: some rejected asylum seekers are residing illegally in Member States, and illegal migration is also on the rise.

Although the formal analysis given here is logical from the standpoint of the immigration countries themselves, the picture becomes quite different if the immigration phenomenon is considered from a geographical angle. Thus, the Twelve are facing migratory pressure from three directions:

- North Africa;
- Eastern Europe;
- other countries of origin of asylum seekers, as well as countries with which Member States have very long standing ties.

The preceding distinction then loses some of its explanatory value: it is a case of an immigration pressure selecting the path of least resistance at that time. Beyond that, it should be noted that due to their geographical location and certain historical considerations, some Member States experience pressure from these regions to greater or lesser degrees. For example, pressure from North Africa is highest in the Mediterranean countries, whereas the United Kingdom, for historical reasons, has many immigrants from Asia.

It is therefore important for the Twelve to work along two tracks. On the one hand, harmonisation of elements of migration policies is conceivable and desirable. This memorandum provides a number of specific proposals in this regard. However, even if agreement were reached on this matter soon, results will be limited unless the causes of migratory pressure are also addressed. For this reason, European migration policy will have to have a broader scope than harmonisation of admission policy alone.

Finally, a distinction should be drawn between migration to EC Member States and migration among EC Member States. Detailed Community legislation already provides for the free movement of EC nationals. For non-EC nationals, this principle is applicable only as a derived right, ie, if they are members of EC nationals' families. In parallel with the development of a European migration policy, attention must also be paid to the position of such persons.

3. *Migration policies in the broad sense*

Migratory pressure on Europe is coming from three sources, each of which requires its own approach, ie, from North Africa, Eastern Europe, and other countries in Africa, Asia and other parts of the world that are home to many asylum seekers, or with which Member States have long standing relations.

(a) *Countries neighbouring on Europe*

The migratory pressure coming from North Africa and Eastern Europe is due to a number of factors. In general, there are factors relating to the economic and social situation, and ethnic tensions. In addition, in certain regions demographic growth is posing further problems for economic development and also gives rise to migratory pressure.

It is not possible in a general sense to put forward solutions which would eliminate causes of immigration from those countries without taking into account the specific situation in each country. In some countries the main reason behind migration would be the socio-economic situation, whereas in other countries ethnic tensions or demographic factors might be predominant.

Nevertheless, the following approach might be taken. Whenever the socio-economic situation could be regarded as the dominant factor explaining the migration pressure, attempts could be made to expand economic, social and financial co-operation. If the required economic reforms are carried out and job opportunities in the region could be increased as a result, such co-operation could indeed be successful. In this respect, co-operation presupposes the full responsibility of the countries concerned to do their utmost to bring about the necessary economic reforms.

Economic developments could possibly be increased by offering work placement programmes for training and work experience to citizens of the countries concerned. With the experience obtained in Member States, those citizens might have better opportunities to strengthen the economic structure of their home countries. These kinds of facilities might be incorporated into special agreements with these countries. Participation in these programmes should be possible especially for those who, after completing the programme, would have adequate opportunities in their country of origin so that not only their formal return is guaranteed, but also their material well being. If these exchanges are left to private initiative and migration polices are secondary in this regard, the chances that these foreigners will return are less likely. Thus, the temptation to prolong the stay in EC Member States on the part of business as well as on the part of participating people themselves might turn out to be relatively strong.

Where ethnic tensions are the basic factor causing migratory pressure, every effort should be made to try to reduce such tensions, primarily by political co-operation and an adequate human rights policy. Whenever economic factors exacerbate ethnic tensions, for example because of high unemployment or general social unrest, the economic co-operation measures as outlined above might also help to alleviate them.

Demographic factors are by their very nature the most difficult to influence. Very often traditions and religious factors are behind a certain demographic development. Insofar as population growth is connected to a bad socio-economic situation, one might expect the demographic factor to decline over the years, once the general socio-economic situation improves. On the other hand a high population growth might also undermine economic policies where economic growth does not keep pace with population growth.

Apart from the factors mentioned above, there is a general tendency for immigration to increase whenever a certain number of people from a specific country are already present in the host country. The Member States of the

EC have long established ties with their neighbours. This implies that from those countries there are already a considerable number of migrants residing in the EC. Within overall migration policy, specific attention should therefore be paid to these very countries.

The traditional ties with the countries concerned, however, also provide many opportunities for close co-operation. Apart from the general economic, social and financial co-operation, as referred to above, specific agreements could be made with these countries in order to combat illegal migration and to further the repatriation of the citizens of those countries who have entered or stayed illegally within the Community.

In addition, policies might be conducted to provide information to the population in the countries concerned. The objective of such information policies would have to be that honest and clear information be given with regard to the possibilities and impossibilities for long term stays in EC Member States. At the moment, many foreigners have difficulty understanding the relevant regulations. On the one hand, arrangements have been made to further contacts between the various populations. For example with regard to Eastern Europe, the CSCE process contains specific measures concerning "contacts between people" as part of the "human dimension". On the other hand, these arrangements do not allow for unlimited possibilities for immigration.

In addition to this structural approach, policies for dealing with incidents are required as well. These could be a sudden deterioration in living standards, such as food scarcity or the lack of basic medical facilities. Emergency aid policies might alleviate these problems.

(b) *Other countries of origin*

North Africa and Eastern Europe have in common that they border on EC Member States. From a physical viewpoint at least, this makes migration fairly simple. In most cases, the situation is quite different for the other countries of origin. Foreigners from these countries often have to travel long distances by boat or aeroplane before they can reach Member States. Often, agents are used to arrange their trip.

There are various causes for immigration from these countries. Sometimes, traditional colonial ties are a pulling factor. Also, the presence of compatriots may be an important factor for migration. In that case, no specific pushing factors need to exist in the country of origin. On the other hand, there are often circumstances in the country of origin which cause migration, such as human rights violations, civil war, poverty, famine, natural disasters, etc. These may be reasons for people to make big financial sacrifices in order to travel all the way to EC Member States.

In this regard as well, European migration policies will have to deal with the pushing factors that are present in those countries. This means: relevant human rights policies, substantial development aid, global food and environmental policies, and controlling regional conflicts. Even if these structural problems could be tackled through such a set of measures, no short term reduction of migratory pressure could be expected. On the contrary, the opposite might be true in some cases: due to improved living standards, increased numbers of people in those countries would be able to overcome the geographical barrier of long distances. A "brain drain" from these countries should not be excluded, but it should be prevented as far as possible.

For this reason, such policies will not result in short term miracles to reduce migratory pressure. However, these measures are essential for situations where conditions in the countries of origin are so hopeless that, for some people, migration appears the only way out of their misery.

In addition, relevant policies could be conducted in order to curb or prevent sudden migration. In this regard, an early warning system could first be developed, either within the framework of the system for monitoring migration flows, established by the European Commission in co-operation with the ad hoc Group on Immigration, or within the activities of a "clearing house" managed by the Council Secretariat. Such a system would register, in good time, any sudden increase in migration from specific countries of origin, so that relevant measures could be taken in order to find and overcome the causes for this sudden migration. The system would have to operate on a global level, ie, also control sudden migration flows from Eastern Europe and North Africa.

Thirdly, contacts with the main countries of origin should not only be focused on limiting migratory pressure, but also on supporting the UNHCR in the Organisation's quest for possibilities for providing refuge to asylum seekers in the region itself. UNHCR has consistently indicated that refugees should be given refuge in their own region rather than be relocated elsewhere.

In the fourth place, the travel route of these foreigners could be taken into consideration. A common policy for airlines which transport large numbers of undocumented foreigners without good reason might increase the effectiveness of current national policies. The same applies with regard to policies on mala fide agents.

4. *Migration policy in the strict sense*

The development of a European migration policy, in the strict sense, involves on the one hand harmonisation of admission policies and expulsion policies and, on the other hand, finding a common response to illegal migration. European migration policy must comprise a restrictive admission policy in order to enable immigrants resident in Member States to be satisfactorily integrated. Obviously these considerations do not hold as regards family reunion and admission on humanitarian grounds.

Beyond that it is important to check regularly whether the justification for a restrictive admission policy is still valid. For example, demographic developments in the shorter or longer term might lead to the authorisation of limited or temporary forms of migration. However, current developments are not such that they could cast doubt on the case for a restrictive policy.

*(a) Harmonisation of admission policy*

The conditions of access for third country nationals to the labour market of the Twelve are an important aspect of the harmonisation of admission policy.

Full harmonisation of admission policy linked to employment presupposes that this policy will cease to be defined exclusively at national level, as it will no longer be possible unilaterally to extend or tighten the national labour market when conditions for admission are determined at European level. It therefore seems necessary to intensify talks in this regard while endeavouring to achieve harmonisation, in order to achieve a European labour migration policy.

It is very important to react in time to changes on the labour market in order to introduce a European migration policy in practice. If a sudden labour shortage occurred in one specific market segment of one of the Member States, the proposed improvements to the existing SEDOC system would be capable of producing greater mobility on the part of nationals of the Twelve in order to cope with the shortage, in accordance with the system of Community preference.

In addition, once full equality of rights has been secured between nationals of the Twelve, it would perhaps be possible to make use of the potential of foreigners residing legally in the Member States. For that purpose, consideration could be given to the possibility of creating a SEDOC type system for such foreigners or integrating them into the system itself, with employers first being obliged to consult the system before being able to recruit outside the Twelve.

Identical problems occur with the harmonisation of the admission of self-employed persons. In this regard, however, a move should be made to approximate Member States' policies restrictively to take account of their economic and social situation.

Special attention must be paid to harmonisation of policy on admission of students and trainees, some of whom are inclined to stay beyond their study or training period. Harmonisation of the policy on admission of artists is a very complicated matter given the differences currently observed in this field.

As for harmonisation of family reunion policies, the interpretation of Article 8 given by the European Commission on Human Rights and the European Court of Human Rights has already provided a measure of uniformity. Within that legal framework, however, national rules still contain a fair number of differences, particularly as regards the waiting period and majority threshold. Nonetheless, harmonisation of these features is, in itself, conceivable.

The possibility of harmonising humanitarian policy is much less certain. By definition, this policy is determined by the person's specific individual circumstances; these are persons who do not meet the other conditions for admission but who cannot be reasonably required to return to their country of origin given their individual situation. Even at national level, few or no written rules exist for humanitarian policy: at most, rules of thumb are given to the official handling the case. Only objective factors such as the actual period of stay would be open to greater harmonisation between Member States.

Harmonisation in this area therefore seems an uphill battle. More can be expected from setting up a clearing house, as has been proposed in the case of asylum. A system of this nature, together with personal contacts between the officials responsible, should promote the emergence of common implementation practices among the Twelve.

In addition to the harmonisation of the above aspects of admission policies, policies regarding the legal situation of foreigners already admitted, and in particular conditions for renewal of residence documents, also call for specific attention. The rules governing the loss of this legal situation should also come under close scrutiny. These matters are largely related to issues of public order and national security. Given that questions of public order fall within the competence of Member States, full harmonisation in the short term will not be possible in this case either. However, it is conceivable that certain agreements would be concluded, particularly as regards the proportions to be respected between the duration of the residence permit, the punishment incurred and the consequences drawn as regards the person's legal situation.

(b) *Position of third country nationals*

As from 1 January 1993, the nationals of the twelve Member States will enjoy equal rights as regards freedom of movement and access to the employment market. In the context of a future European migration policy, attention must also be given to inter-European migratory movements by foreigners already residing in one of the Member States. These types of migration vary considerably in their legal nature:

- migration which is at present legally possible;
- migration which is legally impossible at present for foreigners residing in an EC Member State;
- Illegal immigration.

An example of migration which is at present already legal would be admission to another Member State for the purposes of family reunion. An example of migration which is not yet possible legally for third country nationals would be freedom of movement for employees and self-employed persons. Instances of illegal migration would be illegal migration by third country nationals and illegal residence by foreigners. These could be foreigners who have entered the Community illegally, foreigners who were admitted for short stays an then stayed on afterwards, or ex-nationals of third countries who no longer fulfil the conditions for a long stay.

Possibilities for legal migration covered at present may be left aside in the remainder of this text. They already form part of the admission policy referred to earlier and will be implemented in that framework. Only illegal migratory movements will be dealt with below: these call for a global approach,whether in the case of intra-European migration or illegal migration from outside the EC.

From the viewpoint of social justice, the general approach here should be to examine which rights third country nationals should be able to enjoy among those enjoyed by Member State nationals. However, this aspiration may not be seen independently from the process of harmonisation of admission policy and from the development of a Community approach to illegal migration.

This approach may be illustrated by dint of the following example. The volume of third country nationals is at present still completely determined by national admission policies. Whereas the group is currently estimated at approximately 8,3 million persons, that number could increase considerably following a sudden regularisation measure. If the Twelve wished to grant further rights to third country nationals it would be necessary to have at least a probable estimate of the size of the group. In other words, Member States will have to have such confidence in each others' policies that the consequences of a gradual extension of rights may be readily evaluated and that an effective integration policy is not constantly undermined by the addition of further groups of third country nationals.

This does not mean that admission policy has to be fully harmonised before the situation of third country nationals is improved. The process of European integration is by its nature fragmentary: the rights of EC nationals were not created overnight. What is involved here is the progressive strengthening of their legal position.

It must be known here exactly which rights are involved and a differentiated approach must then be applied according to the topic. The ERASMUS programme, for instance, is already open to third country nationals without that being considered a problem by Member States. Other similar programmes could also be established for third country nationals and consideration could be given to according priority to third country nationals when filling job vacancies that could not be filled by EC nationals. It seems very important to draw up such an inventory of rights in the short term and to set out the conditions for equal rights in an action programme. That action programme could be accompanied by a timetable in line with the progress achieved in harmonising admission policy and the development of a common approach on illegal immigration. Finally, within that action programme, a distinction could be drawn between various groups of third country nationals. For example, the legal position of foreigners established within Member States for a very long period could be more favourable than for those who had only been resident for a short period.

*Illegal migration*

Harmonisation of admission policies must be combined with a common approach to the problem of illegal immigration.

To the extent that policy on acceptance of new immigrants is inevitably restrictive, with the exception of the acceptance of refugee and family reunion, allowance will have to be made for an increase in illegal immigration as long as migration policy in the broad sense has not been able to eliminate migratory pressure. The question will then arise as to the extent to which it is possible effectively to curb illegal immigration without infringing the democratic principles of the Member States of the EC.

Strict surveillance would be required both at borders and within Member States for an approach to be efficient. The first consideration in controlling borders is the long sea borders of the Member States. It seems practically impossible to introduce border controls there which would entirely eliminate clandestine immigration.

The points set out above do not call into question the principle that border controls can play a certain role in practice. Collaboration between EC Member States on the basis of the Convention on the crossing of external frontiers may fulfil an important function in this respect. In addition, the Convention provides for the adoption of measures to combat illegal immigration.

Checks within the territory of Member States on persons who have entered illegally are also an important feature in the fight against clandestine immigration, although such checks must be carried out without infringing individual freedoms.

The following features appear when specifying and refining that policy of public authorities. Firstly, it must be ensured that social measures do not offer an invitation to illegal residence given that, for humanitarian or emergency reasons, illegally resident persons could qualify for such measures. Secondly, policies for reducing illegal employment will have to be intensified. Here the role of the employer as guilty party who takes advantage of the precarious position of the foreigner in a situation of illegal residence must take centre stage.

Thirdly, an extremely reserved position will have to be adopted regarding the large scale regularisation of illegal residence. Apart from the (by definition) rather arbitrary nature of such regularisation measures, this bolsters the hope that in the long term illegal residence is rewarded, which merely serves to encourage further waves of illegal immigration. Such measures also undermine the situation of foreigners in legal residence: by abruptly extending this group, the margin of manoeuvre for effective political integration is in many instances reduced.

Finally, a flexible, humane but effective expulsion policy will have to be implemented. The expulsion policy will have to reckon with the hopeless existence of numerous foreigners in illegal residence and put forward solutions in the country of origin or in a third country of emigration. It is desirable that the Member States of the European Community develop a common return policy for this purpose.

Harmonisation of this policy will be possible only little by little given that an entirely new area of co-operation is at present being opened up for co-operation between the Twelve. Many areas of national policy are involved. However, it would be possible to give shape to a common European approach by setting down the basic principles for such a policy along the broad lines set out above.

5. *Work programme concerning migration policy*

See A, III, pp. 4 to 7.

### III. ASYLUM POLICY

A. *Outline of a harmonised European asylum policy*

In line with their common humanitarian tradition, the Member States, all of which are signatories to the Geneva Convention, have offered and continue to offer a refuge and protection to those who have reason to fear persecution for the reasons cited in that Convention.

It is on those humanitarian principles that any action to harmonise asylum law, as regards both form and substance, must be based.

Harmonisation of asylum policy is a logical component of the increasing co-operation amongst the Twelve on immigration.

The Member States' signing of the Dublin Convention means that a common asylum policy must be defined.

At the same time, almost all the Member States are confronted with sharp increases in applications for asylum.

By way of illustration: 1988, 1989 and 1990 the number of applications for asylum lodged in the twelve Member States of the European Community was respectively 156,000, 214,000 and 321,500.

International co-operation, and, in particular harmonisation of asylum law, are increasingly being regarded as a means of dealing concertedly and effectively with the asylum issue.

1. *Harmonisation of formal asylum law -v- harmonisation of substantive asylum law*

Harmonisation of asylum law can be split up into harmonisation of the procedures involved in examining applications and harmonisation of fundamental policy rules. Certain matters, such as the principle of "first host country" and the treatment of "clearly" unjustified "applications", involve both procedural and substantive aspects.

Asylum procedures are strongly influenced by national tradition. It may be noted that, beyond the differences in these procedures, there exists an overall equivalence. In most Member States the initial decision on an application for asylum is taken by an administrative authority. After that stage, however, procedures differ strongly, depending on both the type of application for asylum and the system opted for by the Member State concerned. In some cases, an initial rejection can be appealed against in court, while in others the administrative authority itself can be requested to review the earlier decision, a number of Member States rely on independent bodies for part of the decision making process.

If, in harmonising asylum law, too much emphasis were put on uniform procedures in the Twelve, the harmonisation process could become bogged down quite simply through the complexity of the issue. This is because the status of administrative bodies of varying degrees of independence and the role of national courts in asylum procedures are matters which concern fundamental aspects of a State's organisation.

Yet this by no means implies that no attempt should be made to harmonise formal asylum law. Agreements would certainly be desirable on a time limit for examining applications, on the introduction of a uniform priority procedure for clearly unjustified applications, etc.

In the short term, priority should, however, be given to harmonising substantive rules. Tangible results in this area will in any event guarantee that, irrespective of how the procedure is organised in each Member State, the outcome will be the same everywhere.

2. *Harmonisation of substantive asylum law: the context*

Harmonisation of substantive asylum law in Twelve centres on a uniform interpretation of the Geneva Convention and the New York Protocol. Here Member States' replies to the questionnaire issued by the ad hoc Group on Immigration are highly relevant.

However, before discussing major principles in this area, the Twelve should consider what direction to take and what is feasible and what is not.

On the one hand, substantive asylum law is the subject of many textbooks, which deal with it on the basis of theoretical principles. Most States also have substantial national case law on the matter. On the other hand, asylum law is a daily reality for officials facing a host of individual applications for asylum. Each application is different and has to be judged carefully on its own merits. Special considerations intervene in each case. The officials concerned build up personal experience, judging cases on the basis not only of textbook instructions but also and especially of their knowledge of many individual cases.

Against this background the concept of the harmonisation of substantive asylum law becomes much more complicated. It is wrong to assume that a set of legal rules can be introduced at European level alone so as to form a system capable of guiding the whole process of examining applications for asylum. A more or less abstract legal framework for assessing applications for asylum is quite conceivable, but dealing with them in practice requires more than that.

It must be realised that the abstract legal concepts present in asylum law usually become practicable only after having been amplified by data on the countries of origin. If one wishes, in general, to introduce the idea of indicators, ie, data showing whether an application for asylum is justified, it should be possible for general indicators to be provided by the general legal framework; however, these indicators would still leave the responsible official with too little to go on. In order to be relevant in examining applications for asylum, such indicators need to be supplemented with information on countries of origin.

It must therefore be realised that harmonising substantive asylum law is not to be equated with reaching agreement on a legal structure. Much more important in practice appears to be the existence of a consensus on appraisal of the situation in the country of origin wherever it is relevant to consideration of the asylum application. Over the next few months an inventory could be drawn up on precise information requirements in this area. After that, the means best suited to meeting these information requirements could be considered.

However, the fact that uniform rules have been drawn up does not mean they will be applied in the same way. In each individual case, further factors are important for the actual assessment. Examples of such factors are the manner in which an application for asylum is lodged, how particulars of the escape are recorded and the extent to which the asylum seeker is given an opportunity to supply new or adjust previous data. Consequently, uniformity is not effectively achieved even where both the legal framework and the country data are streamlined.

More is needed to attain this goal. In that connection the Ministers of the Member States of the European Community responsible for immigration have decided to set up a clearing house, whereby in addition to a written form of information exchange, provision is made for periodic informal meetings of representatives from the executive authorities responsible for dealing with individual asylum applications.

Where certain parts of asylum law have been harmonised, the guarantee that asylum policy will be uniformly applied must be examined. In that context the question of judicial control will be taken into consideration during the discussions.

The adoption of a harmonised asylum policy should influence the flow of asylum seekers in that the chances of being granted refugee status or admission will be the same everywhere. In that situation, other factors will influence foreigners to a greater extent than at present in choosing a particular country in which to apply for asylum. One such factor is the treatment given to asylum seekers during the asylum procedure. If the allowances granted in the twelve Member States differ widely, certain countries will be more attractive than others. Should there be large differences between the Twelve in the treatment of asylum seekers, in the context of a uniform asylum law asylum flows could easily shift towards those countries where the arrangements are relatively more favourable, ie, not only in terms of material conditions but also as regards the degree of freedom of movement accorded, for example.

Accordingly, it will be necessary in the longer term to consider aligning reception policies as well. As a first step, a questionnaire could be issued in order to collect information on current policy; subsequently, more precise decisions could be taken on what the reception arrangements should be.

Asylum seekers will also let themselves be guided by many other factors: the possibility of being admitted other than as refugees or at any rate of not being expelled – ie, of being able to remain in the country de facto – is an important factor. Consequently, these aspects too will need to be inventoried and discussed in greater detail if a harmonised European asylum policy is to be brought about.

A questionnaire has been drawn up on expulsion policy even though in the main this concerns matters that can be addressed only in the longer term. An inventory should also be made of the information on the country of origin needed for the actual expulsion of an asylum seeker who has exhausted all remedies, and proposals should be formulated for closer co-operation at European level in collecting such information. A clear analogy exists with the above-mentioned country data.

### 3. *Harmonisation of substantive asylum law: determining priorities*

The first step to be taken in discussing the harmonisation of substantive asylum law is to draw up an inventory of specific topics. The replies to the questionnaire provide a sound basis for such an inventory. The UNHCR Handbook and the use made of it, as well as the reservations expressed by the States involved, could also be taken into account.

A survey of the most striking similarities and differences in the substantive asylum law of the Twelve has been established. This survey has led to a concrete work programme being prepared (see A). On the basis of the replies to the questionnaire and earlier discussions in the ad hoc Group, the Presidency has already given priority to two topics, viz. the principle of first host country and interpretation of the concept of "clearly unjustified applications for asylum". These two subjects are set out below.

Special attention must also be given to maintaining the exchange of information. The replies to the questionnaire are in fact a mere snapshot. Examining individual applications for asylum is a continuous process that constantly poses new questions. Developments in national case law are of major importance in this connection. From time to time, courts deliver judgments that affect policy in this area. In that connection use could also be made of a clearing house, to be set up as indicated above.

### 4. *Clearly unjustified applications for asylum*

A distinctive feature of the current asylum issue is the fact that applications for asylum are submitted by many foreigners who are not refugees as defined by the Geneva Convention. Their real aim is to migrate for other (mostly economic) reasons. Because of the necessarily restrictive nature of the immigration policy pursued by the Twelve, other legal immigration possibilities are thwarted, forcing those concerned to fall back on submission of an application for asylum. In this connection ,being able to stay on during the examination of the application for asylum and the hope of not being expelled in any case, even if refugee status or admission on humanitarian grounds is not granted, are strong incentives for lodging an application for asylum. In practice, many asylum seekers also achieve their aim: although few seem to qualify for admission, most have a chance of remaining in the country concerned nevertheless, either lawfully as "tolerated" persons or unlawfully. Expulsion difficulties that arise are greater the longer the foreigner has stayed in the country.

These and other considerations have prompted a number of States to make a distinction between clearly justified applications for asylum, clearly unjustified applications and those requiring further examination. The first two categories should be dealt with as quickly as possible. Clearly unjustified applications for asylum reflect the above trend on the part of many to consider the asylum procedure as a last resort for what amounts to deliberate migration for what are in fact economic reasons. However, these applications encumber the procedures for other categories of applications. Particularly sad is the case of clearly justified applications for asylum made by refugees who sometimes have to wait for a long time before being granted that status. It is equally important for this category that a decision on the application should be taken as quickly as possible.

Definition of the concept of a "clearly unjustified application for asylum" should result in rules on the minimum conditions to be fulfilled by any simplified or priority examination of such applications in the Twelve. The Ministers of the Twelve responsible for immigration concluded at their meeting in Brussels on 28 April 1987 that in certain cases applications for asylum could be examined using a simplified or priority procedure (in accordance with national legislation). In this context those Member States which have such a simplified or priority procedure, or are planning to introduce one, could envisage agreements on the duration of the procedure and on the rights to be accorded such applicants for asylum, while ensuring that the desire for more efficient processing of this category of application does not stand in the way of proper legal protection and legal assistance.

The UNHCR Executive Committee also recognises in Conclusions Nos 28 and 30 that it is important to introduce a special accelerated procedure for clearly unjustified applications for asylum, provided that a number of minimum conditions are satisfied regarding procedure and legal protection. Conclusion No 30 refers in this connection to applications for asylum which are clearly unjustified because they involve misuse or improper use of the asylum procedure. These Conclusions were further confirmed by the UNHCR's 42nd EXCOM of October 1991. Recommendation No R(81) 16 of the Committee of Ministers of the Council of Europe is based more or less on similar principles and guarantees.

The first thing to be done now is to define better this concept of clearly unjustified applications for asylum. Various criteria are important in deciding whether an application for asylum can be accepted. They are of a formal/procedural, or a substantive nature in that the credibility and relevance of the account of the flight may be decisive. The following survey includes criteria of both sorts. Moreover, assessment of the justification for an application for asylum is indissolubly linked to an (as) clear (as possible) interpretation of the Geneva Convention and the New York Protocol.

An application may be regarded as clearly unjustified if:

(a) the applicant for asylum comes for a "safe" country, ie, a country which can be clearly shown, in an objective and verifiable way, not to generate refugees or where it can be clearly shown, in an objective and verifiable way, that circumstances which might in the past have justified recourse to the 1951 Geneva Convention have ceased to exist.

An application for asylum by a foreigner who comes from a "safe" country is deemed clearly unjustified out of hand unless sufficiently convincing evidence shows that there might be a justified claim under Article 1A of the Geneva Convention. It is for the foreigner to prove that he has good grounds for fearing persecution even though he comes from a country regarded as "safe". This means that individual examination of applications for asylum which may, be of varying intensity, should also be the basic approach in cases involving the safe country principle. Application of the safe country principle as outlined here can speed up the procedure. Applying the principle that certain countries generally do not produce refugees may be a major deterrent to potential applicants for asylum.

The safe country principle also appeared on the agenda for the UNHCR's 42nd EXCOM. It is important to note in this connection that there was also discussion of use of the cessation clause and that in her intervention at the EXCOM meeting the High Commissioner explicitly stated that consideration could be given to whether it was possible to apply the cessation clause to the countries of Eastern Europe. The EXCOM decided that it would continue discussion of the concept of a safe country with a view to reaching a conclusion. The draft conclusion is therefore in abeyance. However, many delegations subscribe to the tenor of a conclusion containing the concept set out here.

The simultaneous application of the aforementioned principle to a number of countries will have to be clarified by the Twelve as soon as possible. If the safe country principle can be applied in co-operation with the UNHCR, it will enhance the authoritativeness of such a policy.

(b) certain grounds adduced are clearly in no way related to the principles set out in Article 1A of the Geneva Convention. An example could be where the asylum seeker himself adduces economic reasons;

(c) the asylum seeker has voluntarily re-availed himself of the protection of the country of his nationality;

(d) having lost his nationality, the asylum seeker has voluntarily regained it;

(e) the asylum seeker has acquired a new nationality and enjoys the protection of the country of his new nationality;

(f) the asylum seeker has voluntarily established himself in the country which he left or outside which he remained owing to fear of persecution.

(g) the asylum seeker receives protection or assistance from United Nations bodies or agencies other than the UNHCR;

(h) the asylum seeker is recognised by the competent authorities of the country in which he has taken up residence as having the rights and obligations attaching to the possession of the nationality of that country.

Grounds (c) to (h) have been taken directly from Articles 1C to E of the Geneva Convention. They are cited in it as grounds for cessation and exclusion in respect of recognised refugees. However, the situation referred to is where one of these aspects obtains in the actual course of the procedure concerning persons whose application for asylum has not yet been the subject of a definitive decision.

There are also a number of criteria which may establish clear lack of justification for the application for asylum although not necessarily in each individual case. This occurs where:

(a) the application for asylum is based on false identity, where the foreigner concerned has also submitted an application for asylum under his correct identity.

In this case it will have to be established which identity is the correct one. Applications for asylum submitted under a false identity can therefore be regarded as clearly unjustified. An application submitted under the correct identity recognised as such will be examined, although stricter conditions may be imposed on the foreigner with regard to the acceptability of his application for asylum as his credibility will have been damaged as a result of the submissions of false information on his identity.

(b) the applicant has attempted wilfully to deceive the authorities of the country in which he submitted his application for asylum by:

(i) submitting false or forged documents or information which he knowingly presents as authentic;

(ii) knowingly submitting travel or identity papers or information which bear no relation to him;

(iii) systematically submitting inconsistent and/or inaccurate information on essential parts of the asylum file (as compared with available information), unless the applicant for asylum can make an acceptable case that this cannot reasonably be held against him .

These criteria presuppose that the applicant for asylum has already left the country in which he considers that there is justification for fearing persecution, and that there is no longer any reason for knowingly continuing to maintain the authenticity of false or forged identity papers, documents or information. The possession of false or forged documents of any kind may but need not by definition mean that the applicant for asylum is acting in bad faith, but in such cases it is for the applicant for asylum to provide evidence in support of the credibility of his motives for fleeing the country.

It is possible to apply one or more of these criteria in order to establish that an application for asylum is clearly unjustified, irrespective of the stage reached in the asylum application procedure at that time (examination as to admissibility, substantive decision, review or appeal). If a simplified or priority procedure already exists in certain Member States, that procedure may be applied on the basis of the above criteria to requests for asylum which can be regarded as clearly unjustified.

*5. "First host country"*

The twelve generally apply the "first host country" rule. This rule provides that where a foreigner can obtain adequate protection against expulsion in the State where he had been staying before his arrival in the State where he lodged an application for asylum, the latter State may send him back to the "first host country". The Twelve have already developed the first host country principle in their mutual relations and given it partial substance by adopting the Dublin Convention. The logical consequence would be to work out a common attitude to third countries. This would enable the Twelve to project a uniform image to the outside world, whilst creating possibilities for exerting joint pressure on first host countries reluctant to assume their responsibilities. This presupposes, however, uniform application of the first host country principle.

For practical application of this rule there are three options (which occur in practice within the Twelve):

*(a) Application to refugees*

Return to a first host country is carried out where the procedure concerning the application for asylum is under way and the justification for the application has been investigated. If the application is refused, it is then in principle possible to remove the applicant either to the first host country or to the country of origin. If the person concerned proves to be a genuine refugee, then he can in principle be removed only to the first host country and in any case not to his country of origin.

The advantage of this practice is that the person concerned is granted refugee status as quickly as possible and as such will be able to enjoy rights under the Geneva Convention. From the point of view of efficiency, however, there are also clear disadvantages. This practice entails higher costs and a longer procedure.

*(b) Application to all applicants for asylum, irrespective of whether they can be regarded as refugees*

Examination of an application for asylum is excluded in any event where a first host country exists. Under this practice it is assumed that the first host country, if it is a party to the Geneva Convention, assumes responsibility for examining the application for asylum.

In any case, the first host country must protect the applicant for asylum sufficiently against expulsion. The advantage of this practice is that it places a small a burden as possible on the asylum procedure. The disadvantage is that a refugee is not at first recognised as such and is not therefore guaranteed in advance the rights arising from the Geneva Convention.

*(c) Mixed practices*

In certain Member States there exists between these two extremes a mixed practice whereby a distinction is made between applicants for asylum who are already in the territory of the Member State and those who are still at the border of the State and submit an application for asylum at the border post. In the first case, all applications for asylum are examined and the justification for them investigated (a) before determining whether a first host country exists. In the second case, the justification for the application for asylum is not investigated if a first host country exists (b).

The Twelve generally apply the "first host country" principle as described in (a) and (b), although a number of Member States use both options in parallel as described in (c).

There are, moreover, two opposite tendencies. All Member States of the European Community recognise that from the point of view of expediency option (b) is preferable. At the same time a number of Member States are building up case law which on the contrary favours option (a). As part of harmonisation of asylum policy, efforts should be made to achieve a uniform approach in this area. The ad hoc Group on Immigration should be invited to examine this question.

In order to determine whether a first host country exists, it is important to decide on the criteria which a country must fulfil.

It is proposed taking as a general principle that the foreigner must in any case have had the opportunity of contacting the authorities of the third country designated as the first host country in order to inform them that he is applying for acceptance as a refugee.

Certain Member States require other guarantees. The ad hoc Group on Immigration is invited to consider this question.

Another general assumption is that the first host country must in practice comply with the principle of non-expulsion.

In the case of an applicant for asylum not yet demonstrated to be a refugee (option (b)), the Member States consider that the question of his recognition as a refugee is in the first instance a matter for the sovereign responsibility of the third country, with the UNHCR monitoring compliance with the Geneva Convention in accordance with Article 35 thereof. As for foreigners whose applications for asylum have not yet been refused by the State concerned, and foreigners who have been recognised as refugees by that State, it must be ensured that they will not be sent back by the State to the country in which they claim they have justification for fearing persecution (non-expulsion).

In the case of a refugee who has already been recognised as such by a Member State of the European Communities (option (a)), it must also be ensured that the third country to which the foreigner is being removed complies with the principle of non-expulsion.

In general, the Twelve will require more specific (minimum) guarantees regarding treatment of refugees where the country involved has not ratified the Geneva Convention or has ratified it subject to a reservation, eg, with reference to the way in which the country in question complies with obligations resulting from international agreements on human rights.

In certain Member States additional guarantees are required regarding the processing of asylum applications and the existence of minimum living conditions. This matter must be studied in greater depth by the ad hoc Group on Immigration.

The principle of first host country as described above is in any case not applied where the foreigner has been able to prove that he rightly feared persecution by the State in question or that he would face inhuman or humiliating treatment in that country.

The principle of first host country may also not be applied where the foreigner has been able to prove that he has clear ties with the Member State of the European Communities to which he has submitted his application for asylum and where that Member State takes account of such ties for humanitarian reasons.

B. *Implementation of the Dublin Convention*

The Dublin Convention may be regarded as a first major step in co-operation on asylum policy between the Twelve.

The Convention provides that every application for asylum lodged in the territory of the Twelve is in every case to be examined by one of them. Moreover, the Convention regulates the allocation of responsibilities amongst Member States. Each Member State remains free, however, to consider an application even if it is not bound to do so by the criteria of the Convention.

For the Dublin Convention to be effectively implemented following ratification by the Twelve, a number of implementing measures will still have to be adopted.

As a general rule for implementation of the Convention, Member States have agreed that action should be pragmatic and taken on the basis of the principle of good will. For the purpose of determining responsibility, information will be provided by all Member States which are assumed in the best position to do so. Any Member State which requests another Member State to take back or take charge of a refugee must attach to its request the information on which it is based. A standard document is planned for this purpose, the content of which will largely be based on the standardised application form already approved by the Member States (WGI 262), with the difference that it will now gather data authorised by the Member State involved. The Member State to which the request is addressed will co-operate to the best of its ability in order to assume responsibility as quickly as possible. In general, a Member State which claims an exception will make known the facts and circumstances justifying derogation from the principal rule regarding the attribution of responsibility.

In addition, a network of contacts needs to be built up. These can speed up the allocation of responsibility. Once responsibility for examining an application has been established, such contacts will make it possible to continue practical co-operation, should the Member State responsible ask for data on the asylum dossier of the foreigner concerned, and the latter agrees to such data being given. The asylum seeker himself will have to be handed over to the competent authorities of the State responsible. Questions arising in this connection are: for example, is the asylum seeker allowed to travel to that State by himself or is he literally handed over? Does such hand over take place at the border and do any special arrangements have to be made, given that border controls at internal borders are to be abolished?

Finally, it will have to be determined how the whole system could be implemented as effectively as possible. A practice already very common among asylum seekers is to lodge several applications in a single State under different names. Once it is known that the Dublin Convention provides for a single responsible State and the system works, asylum seekers will be very tempted to submit another application for asylum in another State under (slightly) different name. Account should be taken here of the fact that, in the case of certain nationalities, the names of asylum seekers are very similar and sometimes do not constitute a criterion for identification. As such, finger printing should prove an effective means of combatting such a practice.

The Twelve have now agreed to examine this matter in greater detail and to consider in particular the advisability of carrying out a feasibility study on a common system for exchanging and comparing the fingerprints of applicants for asylum.

The Dublin Convention incorporates a system of responsibility criteria. It is necessary to ensure that the determination of the State responsible, the furnishing of evidence and the actual transfer of the examination do not take longer than, for instance, the rejection of an application for asylum as clearly unjustified. Consultations could be held on the drawing up of clear and uniform instructions concerning this point.

C. *External contacts and presentation of the asylum policy*

General points on the presentation of immigration and asylum policies have already been made in the general introduction to this memorandum (see page 17).

As regards asylum policy proper, the importance of contacts with the United Nations High Commissioner for Refugees should be underlined.

UNHCR representatives have already signalled their organisation's desire to express its view in one way or another in the course of the Twelve's harmonisation process. Contacts with the UNHCR have in the meantime been cemented by regular discussions between the Troika of the ad hoc Group on Immigration and representatives of the UNHCR.

D. *Work programme concerning asylum policy*

See A, IV, pp. 8 and 9.

# DRAFT CONCLUSIONS on the implementation of controls on persons under the Convention on the crossing of external frontiers

*1. Article 2(5): Controls on persons – maritime traffic*

Text of Article 2(5):

*"The Committee provided for in Article 26 shall adopt the exceptions and specific rules applicable to particular categories of maritime traffic for the crossing of external frontiers, and the arrangements for local frontier traffic."*

*Conclusion 1: Place where the control is carried out*

The control of passengers crossing the external frontiers of Community Member States by sea will normally take place in the port areas designated for that purpose. The control may also be carried out at any other appropriate place.

The control of passengers will take place either on board ship or the port area and passengers may not leave that ship or that area until control has been carried out.

Controls will be carried out subject to the entry arrangements applicable to crew members.

After passengers have been through departure control, they will no longer be allowed to disembark without special authorization.

*Conclusion 2: Use of passenger lists and crew lists*

Member States must make the use of crew lists compulsory.

Member States will encourage shipping companies to draw up passenger lists in cases which do not involve regular sea links running to set timetables.

Member States may take into account the recommendations in the IMO Facilitation Convention regarding the way in which such lists are to be drawn up.

*Conclusion 3: Duties of the captain*

Member States must ensure that the captain is obliged to:

- alert the authorities responsible for controls on persons to the arrival of his vessel;
- alert the authorities responsible for controls on persons when a vessel arrives in port to the presence of stowaways, and provide any available information on their identity;
- keep a copy of the crew list referred to in Conclusion 2 for the duration of the stay in the territory of a Member State and to notify any changes to the control authorities when the departure control is carried out;
- keep a copy of the passenger list, if there is one, for the duration of the stay in the territory of a Member State and to notify any changes to the control authorities when the departure control is carried out.

*Conclusion 4: Exceptions to the entry arrangements in the case of crew members*

1. A crew member is considered to fulfil the requirement set out in Article 7(2)(a) if:

- he is in possession of a travel document recognized under bilateral or multilateral international Conventions and designed for use by crew members;

- he seeks entry to the territory of the Member States in order to sign on with or transfer to a vessel berthed, or about to berth, at a port within the territory of the Member States, and is in possession of documents proving this, or because he wishes to transit via the territory of the Member States.

2. Once the list of crew on board has been checked a crew member need not pass through a frontier crossing point to reach the quay if he is going ashore for only a short period.

*Conclusion 5: Exception for regular ferry connections between Member States*

The obligations arising from the Convention do not apply to controls on persons travelling on a vessel providing a regular ferry service on the basis of a set timetable between ports in two or more Member States, provided the vessel does not put in at a port in a third country and does not pick up or disembark passengers between those ports.

*Conclusion 6: Exception for cruise ships*

*A cruise ship* is a vessel making a voyage to a set timetable whose passengers are taking part in a group programme involving temporary tourist stops in various ports, with no passenger embarking or disembarking during the voyage.

In the case of cruise-ship passengers, controls on persons are generally carried out only at the first port within the territory of the Member States and at the last port within the territory of the Member States, if the vessel has not put in to an intermediate port outside the territory of the Member State.

*Conclusion 7: Exception for coastal fishing*

Controls on persons are not normally carried out on crew members aboard vessels which have home ports or which put into a port within the territory of the Member States and which return practically every day to that port or to any other port within the territory of the Member States without anchoring at a port within the territory of a third country. If, however, the coast of a third country is very close to that of a Member State, it is desirable that spot checks be carried out as a means of combatting illegal immigration.

Controls on persons will normally be carried out by means of spot checks on persons aboard vessels which have home ports or which put into any other port within the territory of the Member States and which return there after putting into a port within the territory of a third country.

Persons aboard vessels other than crew members will be subject to normal controls.

Controls on persons and crew members aboard vessels with home ports within the territory of a third country are not covered by the exceptions to the normal control arrangements.

The captain is obliged, should the case arise, to notify the competent authorities of any change in the crew list and in the number of persons aboard the vessel.

*Conclusion 8: Exception for pleasure boating*

(i) Pleasure boating means the private use of sail and/or motor-powered boats for sport or tourism.

(ii) As a general rule, controls on persons aboard pleasure craft coming from a third country will be carried out, on entry and on departure, at a port serving as an authorized crossing point in the territory of the Member States.

However, if a pleasure boat wishes, exceptionally, to enter a port which is not an authorized crossing point, the control authorities will, if possible, be informed before entry or in any case on arrival. The presence of passengers will be notified to the local authorities by means of a list of persons on board the vessel, which will be submitted to them and available to the control authorities.

(iii) Any Member State may decide that pleasure craft coming from a third country may put in only to an authorized port of entry in which controls on the persons on board are carried out.

At the time of the control a document will be submitted setting out all the technical characteristics of the vessel and the names of the persons on board.

A copy of this document, called the "Community log", will be handed to the authorities at the first authorized port of entry, another copy will be given to the authorities at the last authorized port before departure for a third country and a copy must be kept with the ships' papers as long as the vessel remains within the territorial waters of one of the Community Member States.

If, for reasons of force majeure, the vessel is obliged to put in to another port, the authorities of the nearest authorized port of entry must be contacted.

2. *Article 3: Co-operation in the surveillance of external frontiers*

Text of Article 3:

*"External frontier stretches other than authorized crossing points shall be kept under effective surveillance by mobile units or by other appropriate means. Member States shall undertake to provide surveillance yielding similarly effective results along all their external frontiers; their surveillance services shall consult and co-operate to that end."*

*Conclusion 9: Legal basis for co-operation between frontier surveillance services*

The Committee provided for in Article 26 may, on the basis of Article 5(3), lay down more detailed arrangements governing co-operation between Member States' frontier surveillance services, so that similarly effective results may be obtained with regard to the surveillance of external frontiers and controls at frontier crossing points.

*Conclusion 10: Joint handbook*

This co-operation between frontier surveillance services is linked to the production of a joint handbook on the implementation of the obligations arising from the Convention, including those in connection with particular categories of traffic. The handbook must contain practical guidance for the officials responsible for frontier surveillance.

*Conclusion 11: Exchange of information*

There are three levels of information exchange:

- between Member States;

- between central departments responsible for frontier controls;

- where necessary, between frontier crossing points.

The information to be exchanged in the context of co-operation between Member States covers the following subjects:

- legal immigration flows;

- illegal immigration flows (country of origin, routes, means of transport);

- applications for asylum;

- illegal immigration networks (with a view to preventing and halting attempts at illegal immigration);

- genuine, forged or falsified travel documents;
- the organizational problems of frontier surveillance services.

*Conclusion 12: Specific data for the purposes of information exchange*

1. All Member States shall ensure that a journal is kept at all frontier crossing points. This journal shall serve to register any specific incidents so that relevant information can be provided to other Member States.
2. Each frontier crossing point that carries out checks on persons in transfrontier traffic shall register the following:
   - name of the officer in charge and the officers on duty in the respective shift;
   - derogations from controls on persons in accordance with conclusions 23 to 25;
   - the issue of documents substituting for passports and of visas or authorizations at the frontier;
   - apprehension of persons and complaints (criminal and administrative offenses);
   - cases of refusal of entry or prohibition to leave, by number and nationality;
   - other police or prosecution measures of major importance;
   - specific events.
3. Frontier crossing points in ports shall in addition keep a register of shipping movements.

*Conclusion 13: Secondment of officials to services in other Member States*

The arrangements for the exchange of officials could be as follows:

- seconded officials would not take an active part in the work of the service to which they were seconded, acting simply as observers in order to improve their knowledge of how frontier controls are carried out by the Member State concerned;

- liaison officers would be seconded with the power to collect and impart information in the service to which they were seconded; they would thus have a more active role;

- in both cases liaison officers would have only consultative and informative responsibilities in the host country; they would have no operational responsibilities in respect of the nationals and officials of that country.

*Conclusion 14: Co-operation with third countries*

1. Member States may second experts to specific "problematic" airports whose task, in co-operation with their diplomatic and consular missions, would be to support and counsel airlines and possibly frontier control authorities with a view to combatting illegal immigration.

2. The experts posted at such airports shall assist one another and, to the extent possible, also represent the interests of Member States which have not seconded experts.

3. Member States shall, if possible, make efforts to achieve these objectives in co-operation with IATA.

4. For the same reasons and under the same conditions as referred to in paragraphs 1 and 2, Member States may also second exports to maritime frontier posts.

*Conclusion 15: Joint training*

The training of officials responsible for frontier surveillance should be as harmonized as possible. Arrangements for joint training should also be looked into. The training of officials in national services should also deal with co-operation between Member States' services.

*3. Article 5(3)*

Text of Article 5(3):

*"The Committee provided for in Article 26 shall lay down the detailed rules for applying the controls."*

*Conclusion 16: Subsections of the control upon entry of EC nationals and their families.*

Upon entering the territory of EC Member States, EC nationals are subject to control on persons involving:

- a visual control under circumstances which permit their identity to be established by examination of their travel documents;
- a check on whether they represent a threat to public policy, national security or public health in the Member States, in accordance with Community legislation (in particular, Directive 64/221/EEC). This check may therefore include consultation of national lists of wanted persons and may result in a decision to refuse entry.

Nationals of third countries who are subject to Community law, and are members of the family of a Community national who has exercised his right to freedom of movement, are subjected to the single additional control of an entry visa issued in accordance with Community law where they are nationals of a third country the citizens of which are subject to such an obligation.

*Conclusion 17: Stamps to be applied to travel documents*

1. Member States shall develop a uniform procedure for the application of stamps to travel documents.

2. At the control upon entry into a Member State an entry stamp shall be applied to:

   (a) travel documents with a valid visa or transit visa:

(b) travel documents of third country nationals who are issued with an entry or transit visa or authorization for Member States at the frontier;

(c) travel documents of certain third-country nationals who are not under a visa requirement.

3. An exit stamp shall be applied to travel documents in which there are visas for several entries with a limited total duration of stay.

4. If possible, the stamps shall be applied so as to cover the edge of the visa. The endorsements in the visa shall be legible and not affect the security measures.

5. In order to certify entry or departure, a uniform stamp for all Member States shall be applied. Its characteristics shall be defined at a later date.

6. No entry stamp shall be applied in the case of:

(a) persons who on principle are not subject to controls on persons;

(b) passports or documents taking the place of a passport of third country nationals who are exempted from the passport requirement;

(c) travel documents of seamen and ship passengers who stay in the territory of a Contracting Party only during the stopover of the ship in the area of the port of call.

7. In exceptional cases, where the third-country national so requests, the control authorities may waive the application of an entry or exit stamp if the stamp would result in a serious prejudice to the third country national. In such cases, the entry or departure of the third country national shall be certified on a separate sheet by indicating his name and passport number.

*Conclusion 18: Identification*

When the requirement set out in Article 7(1)(a) is being checked, special attention should be paid to examination of those parts of the document which make it possible to identify a person.

Where he considers it necessary, the frontier-surveillance official may investigate a person's identity in greater detail.

*Conclusion 19: Checks on whether a person represents a threat to public policy or national security*

Controls on persons who are not Community nationals who may represent a threat to public policy or national security, on the basis of Article 7(1)(c), must be carried out by consulting the common information system and possibly national lists of wanted persons.

Controls may also take into account certain specific circumstances likely to constitute a threat to public policy or national security within the meaning of Article 7(1)(c). The information supplied by other States may provide a valuable basis for carrying out this type of control.

*Conclusion 20: Check on the availability of sufficient means of subsistence both for the period of the intended stay or transit and for return to the country of origin or a third country*

(In due course, the conditions for the application of Article 7(1) will have to be included in this conclusion following their approval by the Ministers.)

*Conclusion 21: Check on the purpose of the journey and the circumstances of the intended stay*

The check on the purpose of the journey is designed to establish the reasons for the visit and the intended period of stay within the territory of the Member States. All non-Community nationals must be able to prove that they fulfil the requirements for entry to the territory of the Member States.

Any non-Community national seeking entry to the territory of the Member States for a long stay without being in possession of documents proving that he fulfils the entry requirements must in principle be refused entry. If a non-Community national expresses the wish to work in a Member State, he must be able to produce the requisite documents for that purpose.

If a non-Community national first of all expresses the wish to enter the territory for a long stay without being in possession of the requisite permit and then subsequently requests entry to the territory of the Member States for a short stay, permission for the latter must in principle be refused.

The following documents may be regarded, inter alia, as indicating the purpose of a journey, without however providing systematic access to the territory:

(b) for official meetings or business meetings:
- invitations;
- documents from which an official or business link can be deduced in some other way;

(b) for training purposes:
- documents indicating enrolment at an educational establishment for the purpose of attending courses, invitations, enrolment for courses or course programmes;

(c) for other purposes:
- invitations from individuals;
- travel bookings.

*Conclusion 22: Requirements relating to the detection and prevention of threats to public policy or national security and measures to combat illegal immigration*

Controls on persons entering or leaving, as provided for in Article 5(1), will take into account requirements relating to the detection and prevention of threats to national security or public policy and the objective of combatting crime, particularly in the area of illegal immigration networks. These controls may also relate to such persons' vehicles and baggage.

[CONCLUSION 23]

*Conclusion 24: Meaning of the term "relaxation"*

The following order of priority will apply in relaxation:

1. Relaxation of departure controls, priority being given to entry controls;

2. Abandonment of entry controls on nationals of certain third countries with which the Member States have concluded agreements to facilitate access to their territory;

3. Relaxation of the requirements laid down in Article 7 of the draft Convention, in accordance with the following arrangements:

   - the requirements of Article 7(1) will have priority over the requirements of Article 7(2);

   - within Article 7(1), subparagraphs (a), (b) and (c) will have priority over subparagraphs (d) and (e);

   - where a person is a national of a third country not subject to a visa requirement, subparagraph (c) of Article 7 will have less priority than subparagraph (a).

4. In exceptional circumstances, the taking of other appropriate measures, in particular the reduction of spot checks to a minimum. This situation should be avoided as far as possible;

5. The measures to be taken to cope with sudden, sizeable immigration flows are a matter for the political authorities.

   Where an official responsible for controls on persons decides to check a traveller, he must take account of objective and specific considerations which are consistent with the principles universally accepted and applied by the Member States, such as the principle that there must be no discrimination based on a person's race.

*Conclusion 25: Conditions under which relaxation is possible*

A period of relaxation must be as short as possible and therefore may never extend beyond what is required by the situation at the frontier crossing point.

# CONCLUSIONS
## on conditions for the readmission of persons who are illegally resident in a Member State but who hold a residence permit for another Member State [373]

*Crossing external frontiers*

The Council adopted the following conclusions on conditions for the readmission of persons who are illegally resident in a Member State but who hold a residence permit for another Member State (Article 8(3) of the draft External Frontiers Convention);

*Conclusion 1: Scope*

The provisions on taking back pursuant to Article 8(3) are applicable to persons who are not nationals of a Member State, who hold a valid residence permit or valid provisional residence permit within the meaning of Article 8(1) and (2) and who are illegally resident in the territory of another Member State.

The provisions do not affect Member States' obligations under the Dublin Asylum Convention to take back applicants for asylum who are illegally resident in another Member State.

---

373 General Affairs Council - 31.10.94

*Conclusion 2: Voluntary departure or return to the Member State which issued a valid residence permit or valid provisional residence permit*

Where a person covered by conclusion 1 entered a Member State from another Member State without a visa for the purposes of a short stay or transit, under Article 8(1) or (2), and is illegally resident there, that person must go without delay to the Member State for which he holds a residence permit unless he is authorised to go to another country to which he is certain to be admitted, in accordance with Article 15(1).

If a foreign national wishes to go to another country, he must provide documentary evidence that he may be admitted to that country, e.g. in the form of an entry permit or valid visa, and that he is in possession of the necessary resources, e.g. in the form of a ticket or other documentation that allows him to travel, and cash or a bank deposit in order to secure his transportation and his residence in the country to which he may be admitted.

If the person has provided documentary evidence that he may be admitted to another country and that he is in possession of the necessary resources to travel to and take up residence in that country, his wishes should normally be accepted.

*Conclusion 3: Member State which is required to take back the person if he does not leave voluntarily*

If a person who is not a national of a Member State and who is illegally resident in the territory of a Member State refuses to leave voluntarily, Member States are required to take him back in accordance with the guidelines set out below.

a. *Persons holding a valid residence permit or valid provisional residence permit for another Member State*

   If the person holds a valid residence permit or valid provisional residence permit for another Member State, the Member State which issued the valid residence permit or valid provisional residence permit is required to take him back.

If the person holds more than one valid residence permit or provisional residence permit issued by different Member States, the Member State required to take him back is:

(a) the State which issued the residence permit or provisional residence permit allowing the longest period of residence; or

(b) where the residence permits allow the same period of residence, the State which issued the residence permit or provisional residence permit with the latest expiry date.

*b. Persons holding an expired residence permit for another Member State*

In case the person concerned holds a residence permit or a provisional residence permit the validity of which has expired by no more than two months, the Member State which has issued the residence permit will take back the person, provided that the requesting State:

- has discovered the illegal presence of that person in its territory within this period; and

- has lodged the request for taking him back within a period of an additional month at the latest.

If the person holds more than one residence permit, the validity of which has been expired by no more than a period of 2 months, the Member State required to take him back is:

(a) the State which issued the residence permit which had allowed the longest period of residence; or

(b) where the residence permits allowed the same period of residence, the State which issued the residence permit with the latest expiry date.

*Conclusion 4: Taking back*

The person is to be taken back after a request has been made by the competent authorities in the requesting State establishing that the person in question holds a valid residence permit or provisional residence permit for the taking back Member State.

The request must be accompanied by a copy of the administrative act establishing the person's unlawful presence in the Member State in question and stating, inter alia, when and where he was found to be unlawfully present.

A Member State receiving a request in accordance with conclusion 3 must reply to the request within 8 days. If the Member State does not respond within that time, it will be deemed to have agreed to taking back, unless it has expressly requested a one-week extension of that time limit.

The Member State to which the request was addressed is required to take in, within a month at most, the person it has agreed to take back. That time limit may be extended by agreement between the two Member States concerned, upon submission by the requesting Member State of an explicit and justified application.

Member States are to exchange lists of competent authorities to consider requests for taking back and of points at borders where the taking back can take place.

*Conclusion 5: Costs for taking back*

The financial costs entailed by the taking back are to be met by the person concerned. Where the person is unable to meet the expenses, the expenses up to the point of taking back are as a rule to be met by the State requesting the taking back.

# INDEX